CHRISTIANITY AND BLACK OPPRESSION:
DUPPY KNOW WHO FE FRIGHTEN

ZAY DILETTE GREEN

KINGS-SVG PUBLISHERS
ST. VINCENT AND THE GRENADINES

PUBLISHED BY

KINGS-SVG PUBLISHERS
BOX 2713, ST VINCENT AND THE GRENADINES
AND
BOX 702, MADISON, NJ 07940, USA
www.kingsinn-svg.com
kingba@aol.com

**CHRISTIANITY AND BLACK OPPRESSION:
DUPPY KNOW WHO FE FRIGHTEN**
BY
ZAY DILETTE GREEN

ISBN: 978-1479191451

PUBLICATION DATE: AUGUST 2012

PRINTED IN THE USA

COVER PHOTO: A COLLAGE OF IMAGES OF JAMAICA, WEST
INDIES

CONTENTS

DEDICATION

This book is dedicated to
My spouse, Dr. Junior Everet Green,
My children
Tamaro, Ayodele and Jaylen,
My grandchildren
and
to the memory of
Egbert Joseph Ricketts, my father
Lena Claire Ricketts, my mother
The Honorable Marcus Mosiah Garvey
Dr. Walter Rodney
And to all those who have struggled
For
The liberation of the oppressed.

PREFACE:

Several books have been written, primarily by individuals of European descent, which question the Christian religion and the belief in God. Many of these books use philosophical and scientific reasoning to support an atheistic viewpoint. This work, *Christianity and Black Oppression: Duppy know who fe frighten* sets out to address the tenets of Christianity and belief in God from the cultural standpoint of an African Caribbean female. How is it, I often wonder, that within the Christian religion which promulgates God as being omnipotent and perfect, and the sovereign ruler who intervenes in history, the oppression of African people in the Americas still prevails in spite of four hundred and in some cases five hundred years of being Christianized? How is it that within the Christian religion that postulates egalitarianism, blacks are perceived as carrying a stigma that is genetic and can be transmitted and so blacks are subjected to ostracism and segregation in spite of being Christians for centuries? Based on writings of blacks, and my own experience, I argue that in terms of the status of blacks, that is, the deplorable and inhumane conditions of blacks and the fact that God is the sovereign ruler of the universe or universes, and who intervenes in history then blacks are subjected to divine racism.[1] God is the sum total of his acts.

Christianity and Black Oppression: Duppy Know Who fe Frighten evolved out of years of discussions I had with primarily black Christians who often overtly or covertly assert that as a black female I *must* believe in Jesus Christ. It is as a black female atheist that I see how much Christianity pervades the thinking and world view of blacks, and particularly the assertion that Christianity is unquestionably the moral agent in the lives of blacks. You cannot be moral, if you do not believe in God. Yet, as I argue in this work, in spite of the fact that blacks are for the most part Christians, they are perceived as morally inferior. I point out that from Africans' first encounter with Christians, Africans were perceived as pagan, savage, primitive, and uncivilized. It was postulated that the world view that would transform the lives of Africans is Christianity. Christianity has failed to transform the lives of blacks; blacks are still perceived as morally inferior.

The Christian religion, I contend, plays a significant role in the social ostracism of blacks. Segregated churches exist in the United States as a result, to a large extent, of whites' unwillingness to worship and socialize with blacks. In spite of the existence of black churches and white churches in

---

[1]See William R. Jones, *Is God a White Racist? : A Preamble to Black Theology,* (Boston, MA: Beacon Press, 1998, c1973).

5

the United States, Christianity is led and dominated by whites, and so in reality, black Christians are dependent on whites. Christianity is a very costly and expensive religion which impoverishes black communities and enriches whites economically, politically, socially, and psychologically. In this work, I make a comparison between the ostracism of Dalits, formerly Untouchables, in India, as a result of the Dalits' outcast status within the Hindu religion and the ostracism of blacks as a result of the outcast status of blacks in Christianity.

I make a link between the condition of poor blacks in Jamaica and blacks in the United States in the light of poverty, unemployment, injustice, black on black crime, and the number of blacks in prison. Poverty and crime are associated with blacks.

I conclude that blacks can find moral values within black struggles in the West, that is, within black history and culture. Values, such as, dignity, pride, discipline, courage, intelligence, creativity, community spirit, cooperation, responsibility, humor which blacks have demonstrated throughout their four hundred to five hundred years encounter with whites are not generally associated with blacks. Blacks are rich in resources in terms of their history and culture to transform their lives.

No published work is ever based solely on the thoughts, and ideas of any one person and *Christianity and Black Oppression: Duppy Know who fe Frighten* is certainly no exception particularly in the light of the fact that this book has been in the making for many, many years. A lot of this work is based on the thoughts, ideas, research and experience of others. I am in the debt of many. There are the numerous men and women—family, friends, associates, passing strangers—who have spent hours with me discussing Christianity, and who have in many ways clarified my thinking and contributed to my intellectual growth. I want to particularly thank my friend, Mrs. Eileen Austin, for her sustained friendship for many years in spite of our religious ideological differences. Not only has she been a source of encouragement and support with regard to this endeavor, but her willingness to discuss questions and issues from her Christian perspective has been invaluable. Mr. William Comer has been truly remarkable. His sense of humor, his display of tremendous tolerance and encouragement to express my atheistic viewpoints without the fear of being shunned or ostracized by him as a Christian are greatly appreciated. His constant inquiries about the progress of the book were very encouraging.

I want to thank Dr. John McClendon III for his encouragement and for allowing me to present a paper based on this work at a Philosophy Born of Struggle Conference at Michigan State University. I want to express profound thanks also to Dr. Silvia Federici who was very supportive particularly at low moments during the writing of this text.

For being an integral part of my life and hence my story—for this in some sense is what *Christianity and Black Oppression: Duppy Know Who Fe Frighten* is, my story—I want to thank my siblings. They have in many ways contributed to my personal and intellectual growth. Special thanks to Shannon Ricketts for her willingness to read the entire manuscript—it was Shannon's response to each chapter that caused me to lose a lot of my diffidence regarding submitting the work for publication. Shannon also recommended and gave me books that contributed to the development of my research and reflections. Thanks particularly to Audrey Green and other members of my extended family for their support and for sharing their thoughts and views on the issues addressed in this work.

My profound gratitude to my spouse, Junior Everet, for his devotion and commitment which were often displayed in concrete terms, such as, helping with technology, and doing a lot of the chores around the house. Most of all I want to thank him for his encouragement of my intellectual growth. Mainly due to his influence, I have certainly developed from a timid, naïve, "born again" fundamentalist Christian to a courageous free thinker. It was Everet who first revealed to me that I was living a life of inauthenticity and bad faith in pretending to believe something that I did not. He encouraged my critical thinking by sharing books from his seminarian and doctoral studies in philosophy. Everet was the first person to give me books to read on atheism. My children's constant cry of "When is that book going to be finished?", their technological expertise, their recommendation of books, and their willingness to be engaged in lengthy discussions about Christianity were of extreme importance.

Last but not least I want to express profound gratitude to Dr. Baldwin King, and his lovely wife Cheryl, both of whom I have known for many years, for their willingness, time, and commitment to undertake the editing and publishing of this book.

I would like to state that in relating some of my experiences, some relatives, friends, and associates appear in this work. To preserve their anonymity, I have used pseudonyms and in some cases initials.

INTRODUCTION

How could someone who was born and confirmed in the Episcopalian Church, who in her teenage years became an ardent Fundamentalist Christian, someone who taught Sunday school, someone who played the organ and piano for Church services, someone who attended prayer meetings and Bible Study regularly, and someone who married a Baptist minister now declare she is no longer a Christian? This work is in part a response to these questions which I am frequently asked during the almost daily confrontations I have with Christians, mainly of African descent, as to why I am no longer a Christian. The implication from the numerous probes, questions, and discussions I have about the Christian religion is that I, as a female of African descent, *must* believe in Jesus Christ. Some are fascinated by my story and have encouraged me to write. This, however, is not an autobiography, although some of my personal experiences are included in this work. It is a critical analysis of the Christian religion written from my standpoint as a female of African descent.

Several books have been written that question the existence of God based on scientific and philosophical reasoning.[2] I felt confident that my Christian friends and family would be convinced by rationality and logic regarding my atheistic viewpoint whenever I countered their beliefs with arguments that I culled from books that postulated atheism based on philosophical and scientific reasoning. Forgetting how angry, hostile, and implacable I often was when, as a fundamentalist Christian, I was confronted with rational arguments by atheists whom I was trying to convert, I am often

---

[2]See, for example, Dan Barker, *Godless : How an Evangelical Preacher Became One of America's Leading Atheists,* (Berkeley, CA: Ulysses Press, 2008); Richard Dawkins, *The God Delusion* (New York: Houghton Mifflin, 2006); Ludwig Feuerbach, *The Essence of Christianity,* translated by the German by George Eliot (New York, NY: Harper, 1957); Sigmund Freud, *The Future of an Illusion* ; translated and edited by James Strachey with a biographical introduction by Peter Gay (New York, NY: W. W. Norton, 1961); Joachim Kahl, *The Misery of Christianity : A Plea for Humanity Without God,* (Harmondsworth, England: Penguin, 1971); John W. Loftus, *Why I Became an Atheist: A Former Preacher Rejects Christianity,* (New York, NY: Prometheus Books, 2008; Michael Martin & Ricki Monnier, *The Impossibility of God* (New York, NY: Prometheus Books, 2003); Bertrand Russell, *Why I am not a Christian and other Essays on Religion and Related Subjects,* (New York, NY: Simon and Schuster, 1957).

dismayed at Christians' anger, hostility and refusal to see reason whenever I try to liberate them from the shackles of Christianity. It does not matter whether the Christian is a holder of a Ph.D. or is barely literate. At some point, the red flag will go up; the responses are usually the same. (i) I know all the reasons for not believing in God. I believe in the Bible. You have to have faith. (ii) I believe in God because of my own personal experience of God working in my life. (iii) You cannot be a moral person if you do not believe in God. Although the subsequent alienation and social isolation which usually follow these responses are painful, the responses led to further exploration of my reasons for becoming an apostate.

Consequently, the discussions that I have with Christians, particularly black Christians, are not exactly futile. I realize that "cerebral" reasons, that is, philosophical and scientific arguments, seldom counter experience. I began to focus on the responses of black Christians particularly in terms of (i) their experience as Christians and (ii) Christianity as a moral agent. This led me to a number of observations.

The scientific and philosophical arguments, postulated by individuals of European descent, some of which though they verified the reasons for my doubt, did not really speak from my experience as an African descended female. It gradually dawned on me that the main reason for my loss of belief was my *experience* as an outcast within the Christian religion. The discussions also led to the observation that the Christian religion is very pervasive amongst blacks. Black atheists are extremely rare. I found myself asking the questions: Since Christianity is the moral agent for blacks, how is it that blacks are for the most part Christians and yet blacks are stereotyped as criminals, lazy, promiscuous? How is that crime and poverty are associated with blacks? In spite of the strides some blacks have made since the Civil Rights Movement, many blacks still see whites as a privileged group and blacks as an oppressed group.[3]

The main objective of this study is to address the issue of the Christian religion and the status of blacks. Based on my own experience and the writings of a number of blacks, I contend that in spite of four hundred and in

---

[3]Dorothy Roberts, *Killing the Black Body: Race, Reproduction, and the Meaning of Liberty,* (New York, NY: Pantheon Books, 1997); Angela Davis, *Women, Race and Class,* (The Woman's Press, 1982); Shannon Sullivan and Nancy Tuana, editors, *Race and Epistemologies of Ignorance,* (Albany, NY: State University of New York, 2007); Charles W. Mills, *Blackness Visible : Essays on Philosophy and Race,* (Ithaca, NY: Cornell University Press, 1998); -----, *The Racial Contract,* (Ithaca, NY: Cornell University Press, 1997).

some cases, in the Caribbean, five hundred years of Christianity, blacks are stereotyped as morally inferior and, for the most part, are identified with poverty and crime. If God is the sovereign ruler of all and he is a benevolent God, then one cannot help but conclude that blacks are subjected to divine racism[4] in the light of the status and conditions of poverty, suffering, and oppression of many blacks and the Christianization of blacks for more than four to five centuries.   Related to the primary objective of this study, then, is to demonstrate the interlocking forces of Christian religious ideology, morality, and power.   There is a need, I claim, to search for norms, ethics, and mores within the black experience in the Americas.   This work also seeks to make the case for greater dialog between blacks in the United States of America and blacks in the Caribbean.

2012 marks the fiftieth anniversary of Jamaica's Independence. It is also the one hundred and twenty-fifth anniversary of Marcus Garvey's birth. There has been a lot of cross fertilization of ideas between blacks in the United States and blacks in Jamaica. While Marcus Garvey contributed to the Black struggle in the Americas, Jamaicans have been beneficiaries of the long struggle of blacks through slavery, the Jim Crow era, and the Civil Rights Movement in the United States.

How many African Americans and Jamaicans know that the first Baptist Church in Jamaica was established in the Eighteenth Century by two African Americans, George Liele and Moses Baker, and that African Americans played a major role in the proliferation of Baptist Churches in Jamaica?[5] How many African Americans and Jamaicans know that after slaves were emancipated in Jamaica in 1834, while African Americans were still enslaved, many Jamaican blacks would rescue African American slaves from ships and help them to escape to the great annoyance of the American Consulate stationed in Jamaica?[6]

This work evolved out of a lot of my personal struggles, discussions, and observations about the Christian religion in Jamaica, Canada and the United States of America, as well as works I have read in terms of my personal search for answers, courses I have taken, or just simply as a result of serendipity.

I could not help but note as a librarian at one stage of my life, and a

---

[4]Jones, *Is God a White Racist?*

[5]Philip D. Curtin, *Two Jamaicas : The Role of Ideas in a Tropical Colony, 1830-1865,* (Cambridge, Harvard University Press, 1955); Shirley C. Gordon, *Our Cause For His Glory : Christianisation and Emancipation in Jamaica,* (Jamaica: The Press of the West Indies, 1998).

[6]Gordon, *Our Cause For His Glory.*

history and mathematics teacher at another, the disparity in the field of information between people of European descent and people of African descent. It grieved me as a librarian to see the number of black books weeded, and sometimes they were, without any agony expressed, the first to be removed from over crowded shelves. I began to note in my discussions with a number of black Christians that the more I read of black history and culture the more acrimonious would be the debates and the more entrenched blacks are in the Christian religion, the more unlikely they are to read analysis of black culture and history.

Many Black Christians are intimately acquainted with the writings or exploits of Isaiah, Job, Moses, Daniel, Paul, Luke, John, Mathew, Mark, Peter, James but have very limited knowledge of the contents of the works of writers and scholars, such as W. E. B. DuBois, Frederick Douglass, James Baldwin, C. L. R. James, Marcus Garvey, Angela Davis, Carter Woodson, Patricia Williams, Malcolm X, Cheik Anta Diop, Amos Wilson, Mae Jemison, Neil DeGrasse Tyson, Walter Rodney, Richard Wright and Claude McKay. I began to see a relationship between the weeding of black books from libraries, the performance of black children in school and churchgoing Bible touting black Christians. As I will argue below, there is a wide gulf between black academia and black Christians within my social sphere.

In 1991, John Ogbu, as a result of a study of minorities in California, pointed out how the academic performance of black middle class students is not only lower than their white peers, but also lower than other minorities.[7] Ogbu did receive a lot of flack from blacks who were upset by the study. However when I hear black students, and these include Jamaican children, some twenty years later state that learning is white, when black students make fun of other black students who apply themselves, and I see minimum effort being made by a number of black students, I often think of Ogbu's study and how relevant it is today. The moment a student of Asian descent walks into a classroom, he is considered "bright", and that perception is maintained not only by teachers but by peers even if, during classes, he is wrong four out of five times, as I have witnessed. Instead of doing the assignment, the black student will, if allowed, sit at the back of the room and recite a lengthy rap song maintaining an intricate rhythm with his hands while he emphatically declares that he cannot do the math because it is too hard. A number of studies have been done promoting ideas, such as African American children are more "kinetic" and teachers need to "make it more

---

[7]John U. Ogbu, "Low School Performance as an Adaptation : The case of Blacks in Stockton, California" in Margaret A. Gibson and John U. Ogbu, eds., *Minority Status and Schooling,* (New York: Garland Publishing, 1991).

fun for them" to deal with the disparity in academic performance between blacks, on the one hand, and whites and other minorities, on the other.[8] The reality of rigorous tests of assessment that demand adequate preparation and curricula in colleges that focus on traditional methods of learning, are often overlooked.

There are other factors, besides academic performance, why there is a disproportionate number of blacks in prison. It is very disconcerting, however, when one considers the number of brilliant black people in prison simply wasting away while jobs go overseas to Asian countries.

Religion is not included in the several valid factors, such as the low caste status of blacks, or peer pressure from other blacks not to perform, that are generally proffered for the lack of synchronization between parents' aspirations for college and their children's low academic performance. The Christian religion is excluded in many studies and is not seen as an important aspect of the culture that contributes to the empowering of whites and the subordination of blacks. A number of black professionals will counter this assertion. Blacks cannot, however, effectively compete if they are made to feel that knowledge is a threat to being good, that is, there is a positive correlation between being good and not using one's intelligence, and that the main purpose of education is to better the social status of their parents.

I know that there will be many who will counter my argument that the role of the Christian religion is a negative factor in the intellectual development of blacks, and thus fosters the oppression of blacks, by pointing to several black college graduates who attribute their success to the support of a church community. I can also cite several cases including that of the writer where ministers and other Christians have actively discouraged the pursuit of studies in fields or areas that conflict with the Christian faith. Blacks can boast of a number of majors in the fields of business, communications, marketing, law, and the social sciences: what about the fields, however, of biology, chemistry, mathematics, medicine, physics? Christianity was used and is still being used as an effective tool in the intellectual stranglehold of blacks.

Indeed in a seminal study on the Black Church, E. Franklyn Frazier postulated how the Black Church plays a significant role in the lowly status of Blacks. The social segregation of blacks is an important contributory factor to the intellectual inferiority of the black church. This inferior status

---

[8]For arguments regarding learning styles of African American children see, for example, Jawanza Kunjufu, *Critical Issues in Educating African American Youth (A Talk With Jawanza)*, 1st ed., (Chicago, IL: African American Images, 1989).

is transferred to other areas of the lives of blacks. The "Negro Church and Negro religion", asserts Frazier, "have cast a shadow over the entire intellectual life of Negroes and have been responsible for the so-called backwardness of American Negroes."[9] Taking Frazier's study as a point of departure, I intend to focus not on the Black church and Black religion but on the Christian religion and how the religion fosters the oppression of blacks.

If we are to be honest, I think we can apply what Patricia Williams, depicts as "castration from blackness" and "intellectual castration" in order to be accepted by whites[10] not just to the Black Church and Black religion but to the Christian religion. Herein, lies the root cause of Black oppression.

It is significant to note that with regard to the mental and the intellectual, it seems to me that there is a wide gulf between black academia whether in the United States or in the Caribbean and the black community as a result, to a large extent, of the failure of black scholars to critically analyze the issue of religion, particularly Christianity. Race, class, and gender are key factors which are often addressed in black scholarship. The role of the Christian religion is seldom seriously questioned. As a result, quite a number of blacks, that is, members of my family, my friends, co-workers, people I meet in my neighborhood, at social gatherings, at functions, as members of organizations, at school and college affairs and activities, in planes, in trains, on the buses, and from views expressed in the media, are absent from the pages of black academia.

I have been subjected to alienation, ostracism, and social isolation, for besides age, gender, marital status, and profession, belonging to a church or denomination is a very important or in some cases the most important index of social status amongst blacks. What I have also learnt, as a result of becoming an apostate or non-believer is how (i) Christianity pervades black consciousness and (ii) there is a wide gulf between the analysis of black academia and most black Christians, at least in my social circle, about racism. This may seem astonishing, but for most black Christians, whom I encounter, Christianity trumps race. That is not to say that these blacks will not be vociferous in their complaints and condemnation regarding racism for after all, most of them attend all black churches. They are also equally vociferous regarding their concern about blacks who by their behavior and

---

[9]See E. Franklin Frazier, *The Negro Church in America,* bound with C. Eric Lincoln, *The Black Church since Frazier,* (New York, NY: Schocken Books, c.1974, c. 1963), p. 90

[10]Patricia J. Williams, *The Alchemy of Race and Rights,* (Boston, MA: Harvard University Press, 1991), p. 198.

conduct perpetuate stereotypical images of blacks which they view as the major contributory factor to whites holding stereotypical beliefs of blacks. They do believe that attending church, praying, reading the Bible, are the necessary steps to alleviate the black condition.

In sermons, while Biblical figures, such as, Jesus, Job, Daniel, David, Abraham, Moses, Paul are sources of inspiration, with the exception of reference to Martin Luther King, Jr. once a year, the lives of Black leaders, such as, Frederick Douglass, Harriet Tubman, Marcus Garvey, W. E. B. DuBois, Malcolm X, Fanny Lou Hamer, Paul Robeson, Nat Turner, Sojourner Truth, Angela Davis, Richard Allen, George Liele, in spite of their struggles and the contributions they made to black survival, are not considered worthy to be emulated by Christians much less to be characterized as holy.

Consequently, books written by or about black freedom fighters and leaders are weeded from book shelves, tossed in the garbage heap or can be obtained for pennies on Amazon.com. It is not only a matter that these works are regarded as secular, but how can the painful lives of black leaders and activists compete with God's delivery of Daniel from the lion's den, David overcoming Goliath, the saving of Noah and his family from the flood, Joshua's successful march around the walls of Jericho, and Jesus' resurrection?

In the light of the marginalization and total eclipse of black history and culture in black churches - the foremost agent of social control[11] amongst blacks - I am at a loss as to why I am often dismayed about the fact that black Christians, at least those in my social circle, do not attribute any kind of success to their hard work, intelligence, discipline or the sacrifices and struggles that were made by the ancestors of blacks as well as other freedom fighters. God has led them thus far, and in his own good time, he will liberate black people. We need to address how the ethos of the Christian religion based on an alien culture and the dismissal and sometimes disparagement of skills and accomplishments of blacks are major factors in the perpetuation of the oppression of blacks. There is a link between on the one hand, "castration from blackness" and "intellectual castration" and on the other, oppression.

For where should blacks learn their history? It is not taught in schools

---

[11]Frazier, *The Negro Church in America*. The Black Church has lost some of its influence since Frazier's study but it is still the most dominant institution in the lives of blacks; See also C. Eric Lincoln and Lawrence H. Mamiya, *The Black Church in the African American Experience*, (Durham, NC: Duke University Press, 1990).

and it is certainly not taught in the churches. As I have pointed out, one may discuss the history or culture of the Jews in the sanctuary of the church. That history, a number of blacks have told me, is holy. The history and struggles of blacks may be discussed in the basement of the church, but almost never in the sanctuary. There is just a slither between knowledge of black history and culture as secular or of the world, and knowledge of black history and culture as sinful.

Often absent also from black academia, is an in-depth analysis of the critique of black people who view the Christian religion as a major factor in their oppression. Even those who study the Rastafarians, one of the few groups in the West, who have forthrightly delineated some kind of alternative world view to Christianity, generally subsume the Rastafarians' critique of the Christian religion as an oppressive social structure under the Rastafarians' cultural and political resistance to oppressive domination. Although Barry Chevannes and Joseph Owens do address aspects of the Rastafarians' critique of the Christian religion, their works, however, are written from the perspective of Christianity as normative.[12]

Owens's major position is that the Rastafarians have been criminalized to a large extent but if one listens and talks with the Rastafarian, one will find that a number of their fundamental beliefs are in keeping with Christian values and norms. The Rastafarians therefore are for the most part reacting to the pernicious discrimination against black and poor people in the Jamaican society.[13] Chevannes' work focuses on the evolution of the Rastafari religion out of the Revivalist tradition as part of the reaction and resistance to colonialism and slavery.[14] While the economic and political oppressiveness of the society is highlighted, no attempt is made to question in depth whether there is some justification regarding the Rastafarians' allegation, as often stated to me in confrontations about Christianity, that Christianity is "white man's religion".

As Rex Nettleford points out, critique of the Christian religion played a major role in the development of Rastafarian thought.[15] Indeed a number of scholars have asserted that the Rastafarians were influenced by Marcus Garvey's belief that the inability of blacks to identify with the God of the

---

[12]Barry Chevannes, *Rastafari : Roots and Ideology,* (New York, NY: Syracuse University Press, 1994); Joseph Owens, *Dread : the Rastafarians of Jamaica* (Kingston, Ja.: Sangster, 1976).

[13]Joseph Owens, *Dread.*

[14]Chevannes, *Rastafari.*

[15] Rex M. Nettleford, *Mirror Mirror : Identity, Race and Protest in Jamaica,* (Great Britain: William Collins and Sangster (Jamaica), 1970).

Europeans in terms of skin color is a pivotal factor in the subordinate status of African peoples.[16] Garvey claimed:

> If the white man has the idea of a white God, let him worship his God as he desires. If the yellow man's God is of his race, let him worship his God as he sees fit. We as Negroes have found a new ideal. Whilst our God has no color, yet it is human to see everything through one's spectacles, and since the white people have seen their God through their spectacles, we have only started out (late though it be) to see our God through our own spectacles[17]

Christianity played a pivotal role in the colonization of blacks. Christianity developed in some sense what W. E. B. DuBois termed the "ethical paradox" of being black[18] and for us as Jamaicans, as well as being colonized. Such was the oppressiveness of the religion that it was impossible to attain any kind of mainstream status or respectability unless one became a member of a church.[19]

My problem with the Rastafarians is that although they did play an important role in questioning the imagery and whiteness of the Christian God, their beliefs are locked in metaphysics based on the Old Testament.

I see much of their belief system as a result of the Bible being the only book or set of books to which most Jamaicans were exposed for it was the belief of Europeans that Christianity was the moralizing agent for Africans.[20] The British government insisted that Bible reading, hymns, and prayers, as a moralizing agent, be an integral part of the curriculum in schools. In the

---

[16] See for example, Horace Campbell, *Rasta and Resistance : from Marcus Garvey to Walter Rodney* (Trenton, NJ: Africa Press, 1990, c.1987); Chevannes, *Rastafar*; Rex M. Nettleford, *Caribbean Cultural Identity : the Case of Jamaica; an Essay in Cultural Dynamics,* (Kingston: Institute of Jamaica, 1978).

[17] Marcus Garvey, *The Philosophies and Opinions of Marcus Garvey or Africa for the Africans,* vols. I & II, compiled by Amy Jacques Garvey, new preface by Tony Martin. *The New Marcus Garvey Library,* no. 9 (Dover, Mass: The Majority Press, 1986, c. 1923). pp. 33-34.

[18] W. E. B. DuBois, *The Soul of Black Folk,* with introduction by Dr. Nathan Hare and Alvin F. Poussaint, revised and updated Bibliography, (New York, NY: Penguin Books, 1979). p. 222.

[19] Gordon, *Our Cause for His Glory.*

[20] Curtin, *Two Jamaicas*; Gordon, *Our Cause for His Glory.*

primary schools, prayers were said morning and evening and Scripture was imperative for First Year Jamaica Local Examination.

The voices of the black people who see the Christian religion as inextricably linked to the ideologies which oppress them, are also muted by liberation theologians and black theologians who claim to be in solidarity with black oppression but who postulate that the Christian religion is the ideology to liberate black people. James Cone, one of the chief proponents of black theology[21] fails to address the fundamental moral issue which is the disparagement and the "untouchability" status of black history and culture within the Christian religion. Besides, William R. Jones postulates that Cone fails to address the theodicy which he, Cone, raises in terms of Christianity as a liberating ideology in the light of the persistent, disproportionate and enormous suffering of blacks compared to whites. This therefore leads to the issue of divine racism and the question: *Is God a White Racist?*[22]

On the other hand, some black scholars dismiss religion as belonging to the metaphysical and therefore totally outside the purview of secular scholarship. Why deal with issues that Camus, Copernicus, Darwin, Feuerbach, Freud, Galileo, Marx, Nietzsche, Russell, Sartre, have combated? From my standpoint, however, any social, economic, and political critique of racism, if it is to do justice to blacks, must include a critique of the Christian religion because the Christian religion is pervasive in the black culture. As much as we would like to think otherwise, it is also dominant in the white culture. Many white doctors, judges, librarians, policemen, politicians, professors, teachers are Anglicans, Baptists, Brethren, Catholics, Methodists, Pentecostals, Seventh Day Adventists, Mormons, etc. It is naïve to think that attending an all white divinely sanctioned segregated church on Sunday will not have an impact on attitudes, beliefs, and behavior from Monday to Saturday.

The church is the foremost institution in terms of socialization of peoples. It is not only the primary institution where families and other individuals meet and mingle but it is also the institution where this socialization is divinely sanctioned particularly in terms of the rites from birth to death, that is, infant baptism, christening, confirmation, communion, marriage, and burial. "White Americans", observes Everett C. Hughes, "who became white because they had black slaves, having made Christians of their field hands, did not want to commune with them from the same cup".

---

[21]James Cone has written several books on the subject of Black Theology. See, for example, James H. Cone, *God of the Oppressed,* rev. ed. (Maryknoll: Orbis Books, 1997, c. 1975.)
[22]Jones, *Is God a White Racist?*

Consequently "at birth, confirmation, communion marriage, death, and all the great turning points and festivals, Negro and white were alien to each other".[23] Whites' exclusion of blacks from white churches, and consequently from important social rites sanctified by God, is not only pivotal to the social ostracism of blacks within the society but also transfers to the economic and political spheres. Segregated churches then play a salient role in blacks' marginalization socially, politically, and economically.

Other black intellectuals are either cautious or fearful of being ostracized as arrogant if they critically analyze Christianity. To be black and poor, and critical of Christianity is one thing, but to be black, middle class and critical of Christianity is considered a blatant disregard of black sensibilities. Christianity, as Shirley Gordon points out, is equated with respectability.[24]

There are, however, some black scholars who are very wary of humanistic or scientific world views for these world views have been, in a number of instances, even less charitable to blacks than Christians. Alexander Thomas and Samuel Sillen, for example, recount how science was used to buttress racism.[25] Sometimes in forums whenever the issue of Christianity is raised, there are a number of black scholars who are genuinely concerned about the psychological damage that may result from challenging an oppressed people about the one factor that gives them hope. But can we continue to pay the price of lost lives and wasted intellectual resources and the fostering of our own oppression? Then of course there are black scholars who openly declare that they are Christians such as Cornel West, and the late Derrick Bell.[26]

We cannot, however, as Freud reminds us, continue to support an illusion[27], the Christian religion, in which blacks are stigmatized and ostracized as mentally and morally inferior, and thus are subjected to perpetual oppression. It was as a child in Sunday School in Jamaica that I first heard about the Dalits, formerly Untouchables. As the Sunday School

---

[23] Everett C. Hughes, "E. Franklin Frazer: A Memoir" in Frazier *The Negro Church in America*, p [5].

[24] Gordon, *Our Cause His Glory*.

[25] Alexander Thomas and Samuel Sillen, *Racism and Psychiatry* (New York, NY: Carol Publishing Group, 1991, c. 1972).

[26] Derrick Bell, *And We Are Not Saved : The Elusive Quest for Racial Justice* (New York, NY: Basic Books, 1987);-------, *Faces at the Bottom of the Well: The Permanence of Racism* (New York: Basic Books, 1992); Cornel West, *Race Matters* (Boston, MA: Beacon Press, 1993)

[27] Freud, *The Future of an Illusion*.

teacher spoke about how fortunate we were as Christians I found myself, as a springy hair, cinnamon complexioned, round tipped nose African-descended female, identifying with the Dalits in what was then the white dominated Anglican Church. In my search for acceptance and approval in the Christian Church, the feeling of being a Dalit has never really left me as I wandered from denomination to denomination whether in Jamaica, Canada, or the United States. I am not singular in my experience, and the works of black theologians, and a number of literary writers, such as Richard Wright[28] and James Baldwin[29] attest to the fact that Black Christians are really outcasts within the Christian religion. Many white Christians would sooner accept a Buddhist, a Muslim, a Jew and even a Communist or atheist as brother or sister (as long as they are not predominantly of African descent) rather than a Black Christian.

The Dalits pollute by touch. Hence the individual is an "untouchable" and has to be socially isolated. The African American passes on mental and moral inferiority through the individual's offspring. Although many Hindus are critical of the treatment of the Dalits which they regard as inhumane, the orthodox Hindu will postulate that untouchability is rooted in the Hindu religion.[30] Although some white Christians like the Mormons have used Scripture to justify black as stigma,[31] many Christians deny that the system of stratification that exists in the Americas has anything at all to do with the precepts of the Christian religion.[32] The question we need to ask is: How is it that two cultures that have such diametrically opposed views in the principle of their religious ideology in terms of the status of human beings in relationship to each other could be so similar in their methods and practice of the inhumane treatment of a sector of their society?

Since this study seeks to look at blacks in the United States of America

---

[28]See Richard Wright, *Black Boy (American Hunger) : A Record of Childhood and Youth)*, (New York, NY: HarperPerennial, 1993, c. 1944).

[29]James Baldwin, *Go Tell it on The Mountain*, (New York, NY: Dell, 1953, c.1952).

[30]K. M. Sen, *Hinduism*, (New York: Penguin, 1967); J. Michael Mahar, ed., *The Untouchables in Contemporary India*, (Tuscan, Arizona: The University of Arizona Press, 1972); V. T. Rajshekar, *Dalit: The Black Untouchables of India*, 3rd ed., (Atlanta, GA: Clarity Press, 1995, c. 1987).

[31] John J. Stewart, *Mormonism and the Negro*, (Utah: Bookmark, 1960).

[32]See for example Cone, *God of the Oppressed*; Martin Luther King, *Strength to Love* in *The Essential Writings and Speeches of Martin Luther King,Jr.* ed. by James M. Washington, (New York, NY: Harper, SanFrancisco, c. 1986).

as well as blacks in Jamaica, it is important to point out that whereas blacks in the United States may define themselves as a caste, it is not as clear cut in the Caribbean where the issue of race is more complex. In Jamaica, what developed, since the time of slavery, are essentially three groups—whites, browns, and blacks or as Curtin asserts, "three racial castes...white, colored, and black"[33] Added to these groups are Chinese and Indians who were "imported" into Jamaica after slavery and Jews and Syrians, and progenitors of these groups with whites, browns and blacks.

What is of extreme significance is that the issue of skin color based, to a large extent, on anti-African sentiment pervades the Jamaican society. Walter Rodney claims that there are "some West Indians who still refuse to see the society as racist" although the "West Indian society is a veritable laboratory of racialism."[34] In Jamaica, according to Curtin, the race question was often hidden behind other issues, while in the American South other issues tended to hide behind the racial conflict".[35] This makes liberation of blacks more complicated in Jamaica.

However, what Rex Nettleford observed in 1970 is still applicable today. "One thing is certain", claims Nettleford, "there must be the liberation of the Jamaican black, whether he be peasant, proletarian or struggling middle class, from the chains of self-contempt, self-doubt and cynicism". It is significant to note that Nettleford also postulates that "there will" also "have to be liberation of Jamaican whites, real and functional, from the bondage of a lop-sided creole culture which tends to maintain for them an untenable position of privilege". It is only then that "the harmony which so many well-intentioned Jamaicans claim to exist will begin to transform itself from fiction into fact...no John Crow living will feel a need to 'tink him pickney white". [36]

In North America, at present a number of Africana American philosophers are addressing the issue of whiteness and white supremacy which often translates into white privilege and white entitlement. However, from the 1980's, Roy Morrison raised the question of theodicy and the Black Enlightenment by exhorting Blacks to use the critical philosophical method

---

[33]Curtin, *Two Jamaicas*. 18.

[34]Walter Rodney, *The Groundings With My Brothers*, (Chicago, IL: School Times Publication, 1990, c. 1969), p. 60.

[35]Ibid., p. 173.

[36]Nettleford, *Mirror, Mirror*, p. 211.

in addressing their oppression and marginalization in the society. [37]

In terms of the sovereignty of God, what accounts for white privilege and white supremacy? This is a question that black Christians need to address.

John McClendon asserts that we need to "focus on reconstituting the social relations, institutions and practices that give rise to white supremacy"[38]. If we are to pursue McClendon's directive, then it is imperative that we critique and analyze the institution, that is, the Church and its concomitant world view - the Christian religion - that dominates the thinking of many whites and blacks.

To summarize: in many analyses of race and racism by black scholars, the issue of the role of the Christian religion is seldom or only marginally addressed although the Churches are some of the most segregated, if not the most segregated institutions in America, and in spite of the fact that Christian religious beliefs are embedded in Black culture and White culture. Nearly every denomination is represented in Jamaica and churches are prevalent in the society and yet what Jamaica needs, exclaim white missionaries and black missionaries in the light of the statistics regarding the poverty and the crime, are Bibles, Christian doctrines, and churches. A little known fact is that many Jamaicans have been Christianized by Jamaicans.[39] For over five hundred years it has been claimed that the Christian religion is the moralizing agent for blacks including African Americans, and Jamaicans particularly African Jamaicans who are for the most part poor. What accounts for the appalling conditions of blacks in the light of four hundred to five hundred years of the investment of time, energy, and money in the Christian religion? This work seeks to address this question.

While a number of works have critiqued the black church, not many works by black authors have systematically subjected the Christian religion to rigorous and critical analysis. Although my arguments are culled from a wide variety of sources, Jones', *Is God a White Racist?* and Frazier's, *The Negro Church in America* did play a pivotal role in the development of my thinking regarding the Christian religion and blacks. However works, such

---

[37]Roy D. Morrison II, "Black Enlightenment: The Issues of Pluralism Priorities and Empirical Correlation," in *Journal of the American Academy of Religion,* Vol. XLVI, Issue 2, p 217-240.

[38]John H. McClendon III, "On the Nature of Whiteness and the Ontology of Race: Toward a Dialectical Materialist Analysis" in *What White Looks Like: African American Philosophers on the Whiteness Question,* (New York, NY: Routledge, 2004), p. 224.

[39]See, for example, Gordon, *Our Cause for His Glory.*

as, W. E. B DuBois' *The Souls of Black Folk*, Patricia Williams' *The Alchemy of Race and Rights*, Charles Mills, *The Racial Contract*, and several volumes on the Dalits, formerly Untouchables, were also critical in my analysis of the outcast status of blacks within the Christian religion and culture. The general layout of my argument is as follows:

Chapter One—A Caste System: Dalitization of African peoples addresses the issue of blacks as outcasts of the society. This is highlighted by a comparison with the Dalits, formerly Untouchables of India. This chapter lays the foundation for the argument that blacks are outcast within the Christian religion.

Chapter Two—A Question of Morality—raises the issue of morality in the light of the oft-repeated assertion that Christianity is the moralizing agent for blacks and the outcast status of blacks based, to a large extent, on the perception of blacks having little or no morality. This chapter addresses the stereotypical beliefs of whites that blacks have little or no morality.

Chapter Three—A Question of Morality: Whose Morality is It?—pursues the question of morality. This chapter highlights the Christianization of blacks for more than four hundred years, and in some parts of the Caribbean, more than five hundred years. The chapter endeavors to show how blacks share the same belief system and hence the same moral principles of whites.

In Chapter Four—Christianity: Gulf Between Practice and Precept?—based primarily on the writings of blacks from the Nineteenth Century to the Twentieth Century, I point out how white Christians in their treatment of blacks diverge from what is postulated as Christian beliefs and practices. The treatment of blacks by whites is integral and central to the issue of morality. Indeed I contend that Christianity is fundamental to a racial contract[40] where racism is seen as good behavior.

Chapter Five—The Racial Contract: The Whiteness of God—begins a critical analysis of the Christian religion in terms of the reality of blacks. In this Chapter, I begin an exploration of my own experience from my African Jamaican experience as a child growing up in the Caribbean where anti-Black and anti-African sentiments were often the norm.

Chapter Six—Confirmation, Chapter Seven—Becoming a Fundamentalist I: Wolmer's High School for Girls, Chapter Eight—Becoming a Fundamentalist II: Atomization, Chapter Nine—The Four Legs of the Chair—continue the exploration of the Christian tradition within the Jamaican culture related mainly from my own experience. In these chapters, I raise issues of the social and psychological disruption of traditional mores

---

[40]Mills, *The Racial Contract.*

and norms as a result of the impact of an influx of fundamentalist Christians during the mid-twentieth century.

Chapter Ten—"The Wretched of the Earth"—I discuss how in spite of the Christianization of Jamaicans for more than five hundred years, poverty and crime are associated with blacks. I address the role Christianity plays in the oppression, and in perpetuation of negative stereotypical beliefs.

Chapter Eleven—Divine Racism: Turning Back—demonstrates, based to a large extent, on my own experience, how fundamentalist Christians are generally unable to overcome cultural, particularly anti-Black and anti-African, biases.

Chapter Twelve—Jesus is Black Theology: Castration From Blackness probes the Jesus is Black theology as a response to the charge of Christianity as a white religion, a religion that is anti-Black and anti-African.

Chapter Thirteen: Conclusion: Does God Exist?: A Cultural Perspective raises the issue of God's existence in terms of God's relationship with Blacks as a group, as a collective. God's existence has to be questioned in the light of God's goodness, perfection, love, and omnipotence, and the status of blacks in spite of blacks four to five hundred years of investment in Christianity. I conclude with the postulation that blacks need, as an alternative, as a number of writers and activists have postulated, moral principles and ethics which blacks can find in their four hundred to five hundred years of history, culture, and struggle against oppression, an oppression in which Christianity played and does play an integral role.

Chapter Fourteen—Postscript: Humanitas: Towards a Black Narrative for Black Liberation—uses a vignette based on allegory—two groups of ministers debate the issues—to highlight the points I raised in this work. This chapter also emphasizes the need of a humanistic alternative that fosters growth and knowledge, and not marginalization of black history and culture.

CHAPTER ONE

A CASTE SYSTEM:
DALITIZATION OF AFRICAN PEOPLES

Whiteness is originally coextensive with full humanity, so that the nonwhite Other is grasped through a historic array of concepts whose common denominator is their subjects' location on a lower ontological and moral rung.[41]

Writers and scholars particularly in the middle of the Twentieth Century in their observation of the American system of stratification and the Indian caste system agree that the word caste is as applicable to the American system of stratification as it is to the Hindu.[42] The main thrust of the argument of scholars, writers, and activists in their comparison of the two social systems is not just that these two groups are ostracized, that is, the Dalits are outside the four main castes of India—the Brahmins, the Kshatriyas, the Vaishyas, and the Sudras[43]—and the African Americans are

---

[41]Mills, "White Ignorance" in R*ace and Epistemologies of Ignorance,* p. 26.

[42]See, for example, B. R. Ambedkar, *What Congress and Gandhi Have Done to the Untouchables,* (Bombay, India: Thacker, 1946, c. 1945); Gerald D. Berreman, "Caste in India and the United States" in *American Journal of Sociology,* vol. 66, 1960; S. Chandrasekhar, "Foreword—Personal Perspectives on Untouchability in *The Untouchables in Contemporary India,* J. Michael Mahar, editor, (Tuscan, Arizona: The University of Arizona Press, 1972); John Dollard, *Caste and Class in a Southern Town,* (Madison, WI: University of Wisconsin Press, 1988, c. 1937); Martin Luther King, Jr. *The Autobiography of Martin Luther King,* (New York: Time Warner, 1998), -----, *Why We Can't Wait* (New York, NY: Mentor, 1964); Lajpat Rai, *Unhappy India,* (Calcutta, India: Banna Publishing, 1928); V. T. Rajshekar, *Dalit: The Black Untouchables of India,* 3rd ed. (Atlanta, GA: Clarity Press, 1995, c. 1987).

[43]See, for example, B.R. Ambedkar, *What Congress and Gandhi Have Done to the Untouchables;----------, Who Were the Shudras? How They Came to be the Fourth Varna in the Indo-Aryan Society,* (Bombay, India: Thacker, 1947); --------, *Why Go For Conversion?* (Bangalore, India: Dalit Sahitya

outside the three main classes of the United States of America—the upper, the middle, and the lower class, [44] but it is the nature of the ostracism to which these two groups are subjected. The ostracism has certain peculiarities and features which are common to both societies.

The justification for the ostracism in both cultures is based on inherent characteristics of the ostracized which cause him/her to be inferior. These inherent characteristics which are a stigma and a curse are genetic. Therefore the stigma or curse cannot be removed during the lifetime of the Dalit or the person of African descent. The stigma or curse is passed onto the offspring so that the unborn is stigmatized. Thus, the stigma is determined.

The inherent characteristic that is stigmatizing for black people is skin color while for the Dalit, skin color is not the definitive feature although there is a lot of controversy surrounding this.

For V. T. Rajshekar, for example, skin color is a factor in the stigmatization of Dalits. Rajshekar claims that untouchability evolved as a result of the conquest of the darker skinned peoples, who according to him are of African ancestry, by the lighter skinned Aryans.[45] According to K.M. Sen, the "Hindu society is a product of many races and many cultures."[46] Therefore Sen claims that there would be some "racial element" regarding the caste system in a "society as multi-racial as ancient India."[47] The "Aryans who conquered most of India do [sic] not seem to have had much

---

Academy, 1981); --------, *The Untouchables, Who Were They? And Why They Became Untouchables,* (New Delhi, India: Amrit Book, 1948); Deepak Kumar Behera, *Ethnicity and Christianity : Christians Divided by Caste and Tribe in Western Orissa,* (Delhi, India: I.S. P. C. K., 1989); Hazari, *Untouchable: The Autobiography of an Indian Outcaste,* (New York, NY: Praeger, c. 1951); Lajpat Rai, *Unhappy India*; V. T. Rajshekar, *Dalit: The Black Untouchables of India.*

[44]See, for example, Derrick Bell, *And We Are Not Saved: The Elusive Quest for Racial Justice* (New York, NY: Basic Books, 1987); ---, *Faces at the Bottom of the Well: The Permanence of Racism in America,* (New York, NY: Basic Books-Division of HarperCollins, 1992); *The Autobiography of Martin Luther King, Jr.,* edited by Clayborne Carson, (New York, NY: Intellectual Properties Management in Association with Warner Books, 1998); Patricia J. Williams, *The Alchemy of Race and Rights,* (Cambridge, MA: Harvard University Press, 1991); Bruce Wright, *Black Robes, White Justice,* (Secaucus, NJ: Lyle Stuart, 1987)

[45]Rajshekar, *Dalit;* Ambedkar: *The Untouchables, Who Were They?*

[46]Sen, *Hinduism.* p. 17.

[47]Ibid., p. 28.

respect, at least initially, for the dark-skinned natives."[48] Thus, Sen to some extent concurs with Rajshekar. He, however, concludes that the "economic element" was more pervasive than skin color because even in the earliest times "mixed complexions seem to have been represented in every caste."[49] For B. R. Ambedkar, untouchability is not based on race but on the defeat of certain tribes who became "broken men" and eventually untouchables.[50] One distinguishes the Dalit by such factors as clothing, family name, birthplace, etc.

Besides the congenital factor of the stigmatized, the other very significant feature regarding the nature of the ostracism to which blacks are subjected in America and Dalits in India is the fact that those who are stigmatized are able to transmit their stigmatization to others. The very touch or presence of the Dalit is polluting. One drop of black blood is polluting.[51] Since the stigmatized are able to transmit their stigmatization, we find therefore that in these two cultures, contact with the stigmatized has to be avoided. Ellison's poignant portrayal of a black man who is so ostracized that he is rendered totally invisible vividly underscores the nature of the social isolation of African Americans.[52] According to Ambedkar, what is actually established is a "social boycott" of the stigmatized which in many ways is worse than violence.[53] However, contact cannot always be avoided and in both societies, enforced deference is demanded from Blacks and Dalits whenever there is interaction between Blacks and Whites, and Dalits and caste Hindus.[54]

Prior to the 1970's, the laws instituted to enforce social isolation and deference in both cultures were remarkably similar. In many parts of India, Dalits were prohibited from a)voting as a separate electorate (as the Muslims, for example, had the right to do) so that the Dalits were effectively depoliticized b)worshipping in the same temples as caste Hindus c)marrying caste Hindus d)attending the same schools and universities as caste Hindus e)being employed except in the most menial tasks f)using many of the same public facilities including bathing places and wells as caste Hindu g)living in the same neighborhood as caste Hindus h)using the same eating vessels as

---

[48]Ibid., p. 27

[49] Ibid., p. 28-29.

[50]Ambedkar, *The Untouchables, Who Were They?*

[51]See, for example, Wright, *Black Robes, White Justice.*

[52]Ralph Ellison, *The Invisible Man,* (New York, NY: Vintage Books, 1972, c. 1947).

[53]Ambedkar, *What Congress and Gandhi Have Done*, p. 44-45.

[54]Berreman, "Caste in India and The United States."

caste Hindus i)using the same hospitals as caste Hindus j)having the same burial rites as caste Hindus.[55]

In many parts of the United States, African Americans were forbidden a)to vote so that they were effectively depoliticized b)to worship in the same churches as whites c)to inter-marry with whites d) to attend the same schools and universities as whites; e)job opportunities for African Americans were limited in fields other than the most menial; f)it was illegal for African Americans to use the same public facilities such as restrooms, swimming pools, etc as whites; g)African Americans could not live in the same neighborhood as whites; African Americans were forbidden h)to eat in the same restaurants and use the same utensils as whites i)to use the same hospitals as whites j)to bury their dead in the same cemeteries as whites.[56]

In spite of the current prevailing view that there have been tremendous changes in America since the Civil Rights Movement and indeed some attest that we live in a post racial society, a number of scholars currently claim that negative stereotypical beliefs about blacks continue to circumscribe attitudes to blacks. As Williams asserts, the "blackness of black people in this society has always represented the blemish, the unclenanliness, the barrier separating the individual and society."[57]

Where there is major divergence, however, amongst writers regarding the comparison of the stratification of the American society with that of India is the role that religion plays in these two cultures. Whereas the hierarchical caste system is rooted in the Hindu religion, Christianity, it is claimed, is an egalitarian religion.[58] There is also the implication that the

---

[55]Ambedkar, *The Untouchables, Who Were They?*; --------, *What Congress and Gandhi have Done*; Hazari, *Untouchable;* Mahar, *The Untouchables of India.*

[56]See, for example, Melba Patillo Beals, *White is a State of Mind: a Memoir* (New York, NY: Putnam, 1999); Dollard, *Caste and Class*; DuBois, *Souls*; John Hope Franklin & Alfred A. Moss, Jr., *From Slavery to Freedom: A History of African Americans,* 8th ed. (New York, NY: Alfred A. Knopf, 2001, c.1947); James Foreman, *The Making of Black Revolutionaries: A Personal Account,* (New York, NY: MacMillan, c. 1972); King, Jr., *The Autobiography of Martin Luther King Jr.;*-----, *Why we Can't Wait*; John A. Williams, *The King God Didn't Save : Reflections on the Life and Death of Martin Luther King,* (New York, NY: Coward-McCann, 1970).

[57]Williams, *Alchemy,* p. 198.

[58]See, for example, Ambedkar, *What Congress and Gandhi Have Done*; Berreman, "Caste in India and The United States"; Behera, *Ethnicity and Christianity.*

Hindu religion encourages passivity while the Christian religion fosters agency. What difference is there between the treatment of the Dalits of India who for many Christians are irrationally and unjustly stigmatized even before birth and the treatment of blacks in the Americas who are perceived as inherently evil?

It is significant to note, however, that whereas the Hindu religion has been subjected to rigorous analysis by Christians, and Hindus, there is the view somehow that the Christian religion is normative and pristine and needs not therefore be subjected to the same critical analysis as other religions. Besides Christianity is a proselytizing religion and it seems as though this feature of Christianity gives it the mandate to critique other religions in order to fulfill its mission of the conversion of non-Christians. Christians then tend to subject other religions to rigorous analysis using Christianity as the norm.

Usually the tendency is to conclude that the behavior of the followers of non-Christian religions is, to a large extent, determined by their beliefs. This is not the criterion used for judging Christianity. When inhumane and unjust behavior of Christians is pointed out, Christian apologetics are quick to assert (i) that the person or persons is or are not a Christian or Christians (ii) The behavior may be as a result of the world view of a particular era (iii) The behavior may be due to the devil. Underlying all this is the belief that the Christian God is good, just, benevolent, and perfect. We therefore find that there is one set of criteria for judging Christianity and another for judging the behavior of other religious beliefs. Rigorous intellectual scrutiny of Christianity may reveal why there is a great gap between the practice of segregation and the precept of egalitarianism.

We need to address the issue of how is it that Dalits are ostracized within a religion, the Hindu religion, that some claim purports a hierarchical structure and blacks in the Americas suffer from a similar type of ostracism within a religion, Christianity, which promulgates egalitarianism?

Over the past two centuries, a number of writers have published works about the outcast status of blacks in American society. Generally these works include the following arguments: Blacks are subjected to a peculiar set of discriminatory practices termed racism or racist behavior. Racism or racist behavior is, to a large extent, the major contributory factor regarding the deplorable social and economic conditions of the majority of blacks. Racism is due to the beliefs that Europeans and their descendants or whites hold about blacks. Whites generally believe that blacks are inferior, and the appalling conditions under which the majority of blacks live are empirical evidence of their inferiority. Many whites believe that blacks need to change their behavior in order to move up the social ladder. However, the persistent or systemic racism, these scholars argue, which excludes blacks from white controlled economic, social, and political resources fosters a sense of hopelessness and despair amongst blacks. Hopelessness and despair are exacerbated by the fact that even those few blacks who attain outstanding success are subjected to the painful stigmatization and social ostracism based on skin color discrimination in spite of the efforts of these blacks to overcome the many hurdles imposed by whites as barriers to black accomplishment and achievement. Many blacks are skeptical about the mores and values of the white institutions because of the wide gulf between precept and practice and the fact that very often whites while condemning and harshly punishing blacks exonerate the behavior of whites. Indeed the evils of the society are often projected unto blacks.[59]

Patricia Williams, a law university professor, is a scholar who asserts that racism still exists in the post Civil Rights era. For Williams, historical factors affect the conditions of blacks. It will be difficult to address in one lifetime the legacy of the past. Blacks are often the scapegoats for the evils of white society. In her "own lifetime segregation and antimiscegnation laws were still on the books in many states. During the lifetime of" her "parents and grandparents and for several hundred years before them, laws were used to prevent blacks from learning to read, write, and own property, or vote". Thus, "blacks were by constitutional mandate, outlawed from the hopeful, loving expectations that come from being treated as a whole, rather than three-fifths of a person". It is significant to note Williams' conclusion. "When every resource of a wealthy nation is put to such destructive ends, it will take more than a generation to mop up the mess".[60]

Like Williams, Wright argues that a lot of problems blacks face in the latter part of the Twentieth Century, are rooted in slavery and like Williams, Wright feels that it will take several generations to undo the damage done. "It is astonishing in a nation with so many colleges and universities that few

---

[59]See, for example, Bell, *And We Are Not Yet Saved;* --------, *Faces at the Bottom of the Well;* Ellis Cose, *The Rage of a Privileged Class: Why are Middle Class Blacks Angry?: Why Should America Care?*, (New York, NY: HarperPerennial, 1995); Frederick Douglass, *Narrative of the Life of Frederick Douglass an American Slave* (New York: Signet Books, 1968 [1854]); DuBois, *The Souls of Black Folk*; Bruce A. Jacobs, *Race Manners : Navigating the Minefield Between Black and White Americans* (New York: Arcade Publishing, 1999); King, *Why We Can't Wait* ; Cornel West, *Race Matters* (Boston: Beacon Press, 1993); Williams, *The Alchemy of Race and Rights;* Bruce Wright, *Black Robes, White Justice.*
[60]Williams, *The Alchemy of Race and Rights,* pp. 60-61.

people realized", postulates Wright, "the abrasive debt that slavery and its consequences would inflict on future generations, with financial, emotional, and moral burdens that will be borne by many generations to come."[61]

It is significant to note that in the field of education, Wright argues that there should be changes in the curriculum of colleges to reflect the aspects of American history with regard to slavery particularly how slavery was legalized for such a long period of time and how it has influenced the perspective of blacks. The curriculum should also include focus on the "sociology of inner city and urban existence" plus studies of "black heroes...black American patriots, black inventors and black family life..."[62]

Bruce Wright's assertions are similar to Williams' in terms of the privileging of whiteness. "Whites seem to follow a 'rules-of-the-game' code of acceptance of other whites," claims Wright. "It is as though life in America is an exclusive white club, and the members can do no wrong."[63] Citing incidents in his own experience growing up as a son of a black father and an Irish mother, Wright points out how racism and not inherent black inferiority retards the aspiration and the development of black people. For Wright, the biased discriminatory practices in the legal system are destructive of a lot of lives particularly those of poor blacks and Hispanics. Many poor blacks and Hispanics "lack advisory services available to whites...through religious organizations and other social groups."[64] For many poor black and Hispanics a day in court may mean not only the loss of a day's pay, but also loss of a job. Many cannot afford the cost of bail and having an attorney.[65]

Incidentally, Ambedkar a lawyer and the outstanding Dalit (formerly Untouchable) leader made similar observations about the Dalits in India. "One must have courage" according to Ambedkar, to go to the courts, money to employ legal knowledge, and meet legal expenses, and means to live during the case and appeals.[66]

Wright asserts that the "disparity in sentencing and the harshness of sentencing imposed on blacks and Hispanics, as opposed to those imposed on whites" have resulted in "the change of population in the states' prisons from white to black and Spanish."[67] Indeed Wright claims that it seems that

---

[61]Wright, *Black Robes,* p. 106.
[62]Ibid., p. 195.
[63]Wright, *Black Robes, White Justice,* p. 110.
[64]Ibid., p. 150.
[65]Ibid, p. 124 ff.
[66]Ambedkar, *What Congress and Gandhi,* p. 50.
[67]Wright, *Black Robes.,* p. 129-130 & p. 79.

there is a "fostered belief that blacks have a higher tolerance for pain than whites and are more peacefully stoical about deprivation."[68]

It would seem that the aim of these black scholars is to convince whites of the need to change their behavior in terms of the laws. It would seem also that these black scholars are appealing to whites for a more equitable distribution of resources, equal opportunity in the education system, and a change in attitude which is a tendency to negatively stereotype all blacks. In order to "rule out racist abominations," asserts Wright, there needs to be "legislative atonement." [69]

Tokenism is not the answer to discriminatory practices. "Once again," declares Wright, "I had the old token defense, the quota limitation thrown at me. *One* was the quota. *One* was white society's favor, its generous boom, its grudging intellectual handout from the intellectual welfare rolls."[70]

Martin Luther King also addressed the issue of tokenism. For King, many whites, particularly moderate whites "could countenance token changes and they always believed that this would make the Negro content...They were ready to build a new brand ghetto for him with a small exit door for a few." King goes on to state, however, that what blacks want is a more equitable distribution of "jobs, housing, education and social mobility."[71] For Bell, tokenism is one of the barriers to black academic unemployment. "While the lack of an adequate pool of blacks with traditional qualifications serves as the major excuse for little or no progress", Bell asserts, "the drop in interest in minority recruitment after one or two blacks are hired demonstrates that there is an unconscious but no less real ceiling on the number of blacks who will be hired in a given department—regardless of their qualification."[72]

In his work, *Race Manners*, Bruce Jacobs' stated objective is to foster dialog between blacks and whites which he hopes will engender more racial harmony. Jacobs is concerned about the great chasm that exists between blacks and whites. "In America you will witness skin hate everywhere, even in places you would least expect it." One will be "shocked. Hatred is expressed among all skin colors but appears to be keenest", asserts Jacobs, "between the very light-skinned descendants of enslavers... and the very dark skinned descendants of...African slaves"[73]

---

[68]Ibid., p. 90.
[69]Ibid., p. 133.
[70]Ibid., p. 156. Italics his
[71]King, *Why we Can't Wait*, p. 119.
[72]Bell, *Faces at the Bottom of the Well*, p. 141.
[73]Jacobs, *Race Manners*, p. 60-61.

Indeed DuBois' line of reasoning postulated in *The Souls of Black Folk* published at the turn of the twentieth century can be found in many works on the black conditions in the latter part of the twentieth century. In this seminal study, DuBois claims that whites' argue that "if they had nothing to change but the color and physical characteristics of blacks, there would not be a problem." What can whites say, however, about blacks' "ignorance, shiftlessness, poverty, and crime? Can a self-respecting group hold anything but the least possible fellowship with such persons and survive? "[74]

For DuBois, "thinking" Blacks' response is that "the condition of our masses is bad: there is certainly, on the one hand adequate historical cause for this," but there is also "unmistakable evidence that no small number have, in spite of tremendous disadvantages risen to the level of American civilization." However, "when by proscription and prejudice, these same" Blacks "are classed with and treated like the lowest of their people, simply *because* they are" Blacks, "such a policy", blacks claim, "not only discourages thrift and intelligence among black men, but puts a direct premium on the very things you complain of—inefficiency and crime".[75]

DuBois concludes that both blacks and whites "must change or neither can improve to any great extent."[76]

It is not that there have not been some changes as the credentials of some of the writers of the late twentieth century attest. W. E. B. DuBois was barred from pursuing undergraduate studies at Harvard. After finally being admitted to Harvard where he pursued graduate studies, DuBois was unable to teach there or at any white institution. Today, there are a number of black undergraduates and black professors at Harvard and other prestigious universities. However, some of the graduates and professors at these elite institutions maintain that their achievements do not preclude them from being subjected to harassment from the police or being subjected to humiliating experiences in encounters with white workers, such as, store clerks, secretaries, security guards, and strangers on trains or in elevators or on the streets.

A number of black writers claim that no matter how hard they try or no matter what they accomplish, they will be perceived as criminals, drug addicts, lazy and promiscuous. What is even more disconcerting for middle and upper class blacks is that their presence as blacks at prestigious universities, and colleges, indeed their high status position, is perceived by whites as tantamount to lowering the academic, productive, or moral

---

[74]DuBois, *Souls,* p. 208.
[75]Ibid., p. 208, italics, his.
[76]Ibid,, p. 209.

standards. Amongst their white peers, black intellectuals are often subjected to social isolation. In other words, members of the privileged class are subjected to the same stereotypical treatment as poor blacks. "Most contemporary black students, though spared the overt hostility that barred DuBois from every social activity except the Philosophy Club," claims Bell, "do encounter color based discrimination in many subtle and debilitating forms and suffer slights and disparaging assumptions about their abilities no less harmful than those DuBois endured".[77]

Wright who was barred from entering Princeton University because of the color of his skin asserts similar sentiments regarding daily insults which blacks have to endure. "Blacks with a well-expressed intelligence quotient are thought of as freaks, and in a manner of speaking, it may be supposed that they are," asserts Wright, "because they have survived intact those mental defects that warrant confinement. Insults to the black persona, official and unofficial" Wright continues, "are daily accumulations, as though to serve as reminders of history-as-a-threat."[78]

This should not be the case. Achievement in the field of education with its implied concomitant values of hard work and discipline were supposed to be the criteria to gain acceptance into the white world. What these writers document is that any white person from the lowest rung of the white world can in a second topple any black person from the highest rung to the very bottom of the society—"defeated as easily as the turn of the head," as Williams puts it.[79] "It has to do with being totally and capriciously stripped of status at a moment's notice," writes Cose.[80] Cose collected a lot of data regarding the anger of middle class blacks who are subjected to humiliation based on their skin color.

There is repetition of similarity in experiences that transcends over a century. DuBois wrote of his being "surprised" when one of his young school mates refused his visiting card.[81] Growing up in Great Barrington, Massachusetts, he did not often feel that he was the subject of racial discrimination. It was only later in reflecting about his life that he realized that "puzzling distinctions" were "social and racial".[82] He would attribute

---

[77]Bell, *Faces At the Bottom of the Well*, p. 129.

[78]Wright, *Black Robes*, p. 90.

[79]Williams, *Alchemy*, p. 44.

[80]Cose, *Rage of a Privileged Class*, p. 34.

[81]DuBois, *The Autobiography of W. E. B. Dubois: A Soliloquy on Viewing My Life from the Last Decade of Its First Century*, ([n.d.]: International Publishers, c. 1968), p. 94.

[82]Ibid., p. 94.

lack of awareness to be due in part to his own "keen sensitiveness." He did not initiate social contact. His "companions" had "to seek" him "out and urge" him "to come as indeed they often did. When my presence was not wanted they had only to refrain from asking."[83] Mainly from his experience and observation in the South, DuBois would speak of the "veil" and the oft referenced "double consciousness…measuring one's soul through the tape of a world that looks on in amused contempt and pity. One ever feels" DuBois postulates, "his twoness,—an American, a Negro; two souls, two thoughts, two unreconciled strivings; two warring ideals in one dark body, whose dogged strength alone keeps it from being torn asunder."[84]

Almost one hundred years later, Williams writes of blacks as being "othered" and "outsiders". Like DuBois, Williams' sister experienced social exclusion at an early age. In the Fourth Grade, Williams' sister was the only black child in that grade. Her white classmates "ripped up the Valentine cards she had sent them and dumped them on her desk" when the teacher was out of the room. Her mother's response to her daughter's performance which plummeted as a consequence of that traumatic experience was that she should "show them by outperforming them." But according to Williams, this would have an impact on their education. For Williams, "their roles repeatedly defined as 'outsiders' in both cruel and unintentional ways caused them to be faced with a curious dilemma." They "could continually try to be insiders, which could have been quite frustrating" for "'insider' is not an act of will but a cooperative relation, defeated as easily as the turn of a head; or we could resign ourselves to being outsiders." Williams goes on to point out that a "few exceptionally strong people, usually reinforced by an alternative sense of community, can just ignore it and carry on" although it does have an impact on the "relational" aspect of education. "The outsider status either motivates individuals to become overachievers or it drives them to become underachievers."[85]

Indeed, some of the authors of works on the status of blacks claim that there is a pattern to the behavior of whites. At certain points in history, whites give blacks the hope that there will be equality in America. As soon as blacks believe, however, that their aspirations for equal status can be attained, whites enact laws and display attitudes to frustrate these aspirations, and as a consequence, disillusionment takes place amongst blacks.

There seems to be a cyclical pattern, for blacks, hope followed by despair. For just before emancipation of the slaves, blacks had hopes that

---

[83]Ibid., p. 94
[84]Dubois, *Souls*, p. 45.
[85]Williams, *Alchemy*, p. 89.

they would have equal access to opportunities as whites. *The Souls of Black Folk* is a testament to the squashing of these hopes. DuBois underscored in that work the despair evident among Blacks after Emancipation. The Civil Rights movement brought with it the hope that at last white America would correct many of the wrongs and injustices to which blacks were subjected. *Alchemy of Race and Rights, And We Are Not Saved, Black Robes, White Justice, Faces at the Bottom of the Well, Race Matters. Rage of a Privileged Class* are all testaments of the disillusionment of the inheritors of that movement which engendered the hope that one day in America, race would not be a determining factor in shattering dreams.

Bell speaks of the "continuing faith of a people who have never truly gained their rights in a nation committed to the rights of all." Asked to write the 1985 foreword to the "most prestigious periodical, the *Harvard Law Review,* Bell "sought a method of expression adequate to the phenomenon of rights gained, then lost, then gained again." He argues that is a "phenomenon that continues to surprise even though the *cyclical* experience of blacks in this country predates the Constitution by more than one hundred years."[86] According to Wright, "it is the déjà vu quality of the struggle which has discouraged so many blacks. Opposition to repression has hit highs and lows."[87] Cornel West argues that currently despair and hopelessness are the dominant moods amongst many young black people. West terms the despair and hopelessness, nihilism. For West, *"nihilism"* is not *"a philosophical doctrine that there are no rational grounds for legitimate standards of authority."* Nihilism West claims *"is the lived experience of coping with a life of horrifying meaninglessness and (most important) lovelessness".*[88]

One could also deduce from the presentation and arguments of many of these writers that there is a strong belief that clarity, logic, and reason can be effective in convincing whites that they need to be more actively engaged in redressing the injustices in the society regarding blacks. Indeed, these writers seem to share DuBois' sentiments in terms of how to deal with racism which DuBois expressed in *The Souls of Black Folk* regarding confronting color prejudice in the South. Reason must be used to confront racism. We may "decry the color-prejudice in the South, but it must be reckoned with *soberly".*[89] It cannot be countered by laws and being "stormed at". Only "one way" racism can be dealt with and that is, *"by the*

---

[86]Bell, *And We Are Not Saved,* p. xi
[87]Wright, Black Robes, p. 22.
[88]West, *Race Matters,* p. 14, italics his.
[89]DuBois, *Souls,* p. 123, italics, mine.

breadth and broadening of human reason, by catholicity of taste and culture."[90]

Alvin Poussaint in the Introduction to *The Souls of Black Folk* claims that "*The Souls of Black Folk* symbolizes an ever-recurring stage which most Black intellectuals reach at some point in their cultural development." Many black intellectuals, according to Poussaint, do believe in the power of reason. For the young black intellectual, there is often the "temptation to indulge himself...in the thought that" maybe "the problem has never been presented to the white man in a way he could truly understand"...maybe "*this* time *he* would find a way...for transmitting the urgency of black America to the white man."[91]

The last two decades of the twentieth century confirmed Poussaint's observation as a plethora of writers, many of them graduates of the most prestigious universities of the United States of America, have published works which evidently seek to use reason to convince whites that the social conditions of blacks are not due to inherent inferiority of blacks but to the appalling conditions to which blacks are subjected as a result of racism.

The repetition of the same arguments by black intellectuals is very significant. Usually radical or revolutionary ideas develop as a result of successive generations building and critiquing thoughts, ideas, and theory of previous generations. Rarely are the same ideas repeated beyond a generation. This is not so with the black intellectual ideas regarding racism. As pointed out, DuBois' arguments and analysis may be found in many of the black scholars' critique of the status of blacks in the latter part of the twentieth century. "Most of what can be said about racial issues in this country, "states Derrick Bell, "has been said, and likely more than once. Over and over again, we have considered all the problems, tried many solutions....Library shelves creak under the weight of serious studies on racial issues."[92]

We need to ask ourselves: how effective are the arguments postulated by black intellectuals that (a) the conditions of blacks, to a large extent, are due to the racist policies of whites and not to inherent black inferiority, and (b) that whites, and not only blacks ought to change their behavior? How effective are these arguments in the light of the ever widening gulf between the perception of blacks and whites regarding the behavior of blacks and the behavior of whites? How effective are these arguments, we need to objectively ask, in spite of the arguments being reiterated for nearly two

---

[90]Ibid, p. 123, Italics, mine.
[91]Ibid, p. xxxii-xxxv, italics, his.
[92]Bell, *And We Are Not Saved,* p. 4.

centuries? As Bell cogently states, "scholars have not been silent."[93]

Very little reference is made to the reasoning of the black elite when pronouncements are made by politicians, journalists, and judges on criminal and other negative behavior of blacks. The members of the black elite are quite invisible in terms of main stream presses, television, and other sources of information. Indeed, Dr. Bledsoe's comment to the Invisible Man seems to be applicable to the highly educated black man and woman in America.

> You are a black educated fool son. These white folk have newspapers, magazines, radios, spokesmen to get their ideas across. If they want to tell the world a lie, they can tell it so well that it becomes the truth..."You're nobody, son. You don't exist—can't you see that?"[94]

Williams, a Harvard Law graduate speaks of her own feelings of invisibility. White people, "look through me, as if I were transparent. By itself, seeing me would see" her "substance" her "anger", her "vulnerability" and her "raging despair". What is "deeply humiliating" is "to uncover it and have it devalued by ignore-ance, to hold it up bravely in the organ of my eyes and to have it greeted by an impassive stare...." Williams claims that she was taught by her parents to "look at people, particularly white people."[95] This, however, makes her feel like a "thin sheet of glass" and that "white people see all the worlds beyond me but not me." For Williams, "there are days of the week when I feel so invisible that I cannot remember what day of the week it is..."[96] *Rage of a Privileged Class* is something of a shock in its revelation that there are a number of Blacks in administrative and managerial positions in the United States.

The very fact that there is a proliferation of works on race in the latter part of the twentieth century is evidence that whites are not convinced regarding the arguments postulated by blacks that the social conditions of blacks are, to a large extent, due to the racist policies and attitudes of whites and that both blacks and whites need to change their behavior. In other words, in spite of black appeals to logic, clarity, and reason, whites have not radically changed their behavior regarding their relationship with blacks. From time to time, studies do appear in the media regarding the disparity between blacks and whites in terms of the justice system, education, health,

---

[93] Ibid, p. 4
[94] Ellison, *Invisible Man,* p. 143.
[95] Williams, *Alchemy of Race and Rights,* p. 222.
[96] Ibid., p. 228.

and access to financial institutions that would validate a lot of the arguments of the black elite. Since studies by blacks show that there are disparities between blacks and whites in many areas such as health, education, the criminal justice system, and since there are charges of police brutality and racial profiling, it is evident that whites have not heeded the arguments of the black elite. We have to confront this issue.

It would seem that the focus of the arguments on the historical, economic, political, and legal issues by the black elite do not fully address the basic charge of whites which is that blacks have little or no morality. The fundamental issue, then, to a large extent, is a moral one. One wonders whether black scholars really believe that a defense cannot be built in terms of a denial of this charge and therefore black behavior has to be explained in terms of the legal, political, economic, and social ramifications of slavery and the segregation laws after emancipation.

Undoubtedly, slavery and segregation laws have had devastating consequences on black lives and apparently it is the intention of black writers to highlight this fact. However, the arguments of the black elite which focus on why blacks have little or no morality do not address the fundamental allegation of whites that blacks have little or no morality. Indeed blacks are inherently immoral. One should be able to rise above any economic, political, and social injustice. Blacks are therefore viewed in United States of America, the same way that Dalits (formerly Untouchables) are perceived in the Indian society.

It is not political, social, or economic conditions that posit the Dalits as outcastes, but the fact that the Dalits are inherently morally inferior because of their violation in a previous life of the moral laws, conduct, dharma, of the universe. The Dalit is not only inherently inferior but he or she can transmit his or her inferiority to others. The Dalit pollutes and hence the Dalit has to be ostracized.[97] There is a commonality between the perception of the Dalits in India and the perception of Blacks in the Americas. Dalits are inherently inferior; they pollute. Blacks are inherently inferior; they pollute.

As irrational and painful as it may be, we need to address the allegation of whites that blacks have little or no morality, not simply in terms of why blacks have little or no morality, but whether it is indeed a fact that blacks have little or no morality, that is, that blacks are inherently inferior.

---

[97]Mahar, *The Untouchables in Contemporary India*; T. N. Madden, ed., *Religion in India,* (New Delhi, India: Oxford University Press, 1991; Arun Shourie, *Hinduism: Essence and Consequence: A Study of the Upanishads, the Gita and the Brahma-Sutras,* (Ghaziabad, U.P. India: Vikas Publishing House PVT Ltd, 1979); Sen, *Hinduism.*

It may appear that the arguments postulated by some black elites are adequate disclaimers to the arguments of whites that black behavior is evidence of blacks' lack of morality and consequently whites have to isolate themselves from blacks. Although, in many respects the black elite has put up a strong defense for the behavior of blacks, if one carefully examines the arguments of the black elite, one cannot but conclude that essentially, very often, the black elite concurs with the allegations of whites that blacks, particularly poor blacks have little or no morality. The major difference between the arguments of the black elite and the arguments of whites is that whereas whites believe that black behavior stems from a lack of morals, principles, and values, the black elite believes that black behavior stems primarily from the social conditions of blacks. In other words, blacks and whites differ only in the *reasons* for black behavior.

Cornel West, for example, as already pointed out, argues that what exists in the black community is a state of nihilism. Indeed, Chapter One of his work, *Race Matters* is entitled, "Nihilism in Black America." According to West, there are generally two perspectives regarding the analysis of black behavior. There are those who focus on social structures who West categorizes as liberal structuralists and there are those who focus on behavior who West categorizes as conservative behaviorists. The conservative behaviorists believe that black behavior is due to the "wanting of the Protestant ethic—hard work, deferred gratification, frugality, and responsibility—in much of black America" whereas the liberal structuralists believe that structural constraints such as "slavery, Jim Crowism, job and residential discrimination, skewed unemployment rates, inadequate health care, and poor education" are "constraints on the life chances of black people."[98]

Incidentally, we find a striking similarity of what Ambedkar claims are the two "methods" postulated for "uplifting" the "Depressed Classes" (Dalits) to West's analysis of the two perspectives regarding Black behavior. According to Ambedkar, one method "proceeds on the assumption that the fact of the individual belonging to the Depressed Classes is bound up with his personal conduct." His suffering "from want and misery" must be due to the fact that he is "vicious and sinful." Consequently, "this School of social workers concentrates all its efforts and its resources on fostering personal virtue" in order to make the individual "a better and virtuous individual". For Ambedkar, the method that views the "fate of the individual" as "governed by his environment and the circumstances he is obliged to live under" is "the more correct." If "an individual is suffering from want and

---

[98]West, *Race Matters,* p. 11.

misery it is because his environment is not propitious"[99].

West contends that in the analysis regarding black behavior, three issues are overlooked. The first is that structures and behavior are intricately linked. "How people act and live are shaped—though in no way dictated or determined—by the larger circumstances by which they find themselves."[100] The second issue is that structure is not just economics and politics. "Culture", argues West, "is as much a structure as the economy or politics; it is rooted in institutions such as families, schools, churches, synagogues, mosques and communication industries (television, radio, video music)."[101] Besides, asserts West, the economy also plays a role in developing "particular cultural ideals of the good life and the good society." West claims that the third issue which both "liberals" and "conservatives" need to address is "the murky waters of despair and dread that now flood the streets of black America. To discuss factors, such as unemployment, infant mortality, incarceration, teenage pregnancy, and violent crime is one thing." However, "to face up to the monumental eclipse of hope, the unprecedented collapse of meaning, the incredible disregard for human (especially black) life and property in much of black America is something else."[102]

There is the implication, quite often from the writings of the black elite that the black middle class has a different set of values from poor blacks and therefore should not be judged by the same criteria. The black middle class are good blacks who should receive the same respect and regard as the good middle class whites.[103]

West, however, does not spare the black middle class a piercing analysis with regards to the behavior of its members. There is a greater amount of black politicians and black intellectuals than any other time in American history. This class, however, is more "deficient" and more "decadent" than their "predecessors".[104] There is a general decline of intellectual and political leadership in America, but amongst blacks, it is more acute. Few black political leaders are "race transcending political leaders" which for West is the ideal. Most political leaders are either "race-effacing managerial leaders" or "race-identifying political leaders."[105] The black middle class like their white peers are driven by consumerism and status symbols which

---

[99]Ambedkar, *What Congress and Gandhi Have Done,* p. 134-135.
[100]West, *Race,* p. 12.
[101]Ibid., p. 12.
[102]Ibid, p. 12.
[103]See, for example, Cose, *Rage.*
[104]West, *Race Matters,* p. 36.
[105]Ibid., p. 39.

have contributed to class divisions in the black society. Yet, West derides black intellectuals for not donning the "Victorian three piece suit" in the style of W. E. B. DuBois which signify "intellectual vocation" and for wearing "shabby clothing" which display their "utter marginality".[106] Amongst blacks, there is also the decline of "personal, family, and communal relations". The problem is that blacks have few resources to combat the "hedonism" and the "mass culture" that pervade American culture as a result of the "economic boom" after 1960. Personal, family and communal relationships amongst blacks although often "fragile and difficult to sustain" have proved necessary for the "moral commitment to and courageous engagement with causes beyond that of one's self and family."[107]

"Presently", claims West," black communities are in shambles, black families are in decline, and black men and women are in conflict (and sometimes combat)". It is significant to note that West concludes by stating that there are "few, if any, communal resources to help black people cope with this situation."[108] This is very significant when churches abound in the black community.

I contend that we have to focus on the allegation that moral principles are lacking in the black community. Who am I, some may ask, to critique some of the most brilliant minds in America? My major qualification is my experience as a woman of African descent, as a librarian and a teacher.

There are three factors that influenced my perspective regarding the analysis of a number of black scholars and writers on the status of blacks in America. One factor is, as I have pointed out in the Introduction, the almost daily discussions and debates I have with black people particularly black women about religion. Irrespective of the initial topic, at some point, a religious perspective will be introduced as an integral factor in the analysis. Most issues, in my encounter with blacks, are seen through the prism of religion. The religiosity of blacks is not addressed in the critique regarding race. The second factor that influenced my thinking regarding a number of black scholars' analysis is the outcast status of blacks, borne out by scholars and writers for over two centuries. The third factor is the stereotypical belief that blacks, particularly poor blacks, have little or no morality. It is important that we see how these three factors (i) the pervasiveness of religion in the American culture (ii) the outcast status of blacks and (iii) blacks having little or no morality are intricately linked.

---

[106]Ibid., p. 40.
[107]Ibid., p.36-37.
[108]Ibid., p. 37

CHAPTER TWO

A QUESTION OF MORALITY?

The oppressed offspring of Ham will rise at the life-giving call of Christianity, and meekly array themselves in beauty and power[109]
James M. Phillippo—Baptist Missionary

We need to ask whether by focusing on the social and economic conditions regarding the plight of the majority of blacks, blacks do not in a sense fail to address the fundamental issue underlying the charges of whites, which is, that blacks have little or no morality. In the final analysis, it would appear that the arguments of black scholars support whites' contention that blacks are morally inferior. For if the behavior of blacks is to a large extent, determined by legal, economic, and social factors, it would seem that blacks are lacking in a fundamental moral characteristic, that is, having some kind of agency.

For many whites, the will to overcome tremendous odds and obstacles is very important. Indeed, it is not unusual to hear a white individual claim that he or she has risen by his or her hard work, and diligence. Very few whites will admit that their success stems from their control of resources and that more money is spent on whites than on blacks. In response to cries of blacks being poor, many whites and some black immigrants too, will state how they came to this country with only a suitcase and how hard they worked to be successful. Oprah Winfrey, Michael Jordan, Bill Cosby and President Obama will be cited as examples of the possibility of black achievement. Nothing is more impressive than stories of individuals overcoming difficulties and adverse circumstances. The costs in terms of pain and suffering are often discounted and dismissed.[110]

Besides, most whites believe that racism in America is something of the past.[111] "No one sits at the back anymore", is a statement that is often repeated to blacks whenever blacks allege that whites are being racist.

---

[109]James M. Phillippo, *Jamaica its Past and Present State*, (Westport, CT: Negro Universities Press, 1970, c. 1945), p. 191

[110]These arguments can often be heard on television Talk Shows. Often they appear in Letters to the Editor or in newspaper and magazine articles. See also Cose, *Rage of a Privileged Class.*

[111]Kevin Sack and Janet Elder, "Poll Finds Optimistic Outlook but Enduring Racial Division", *New York Times,* Tuesday, July 11, 2000. From the poll, whites have a far more optimistic outlook than blacks.

Indeed the plethora of books on how racism is still persistent in the society and how racism blights the hopes and aspirations of blacks is, to a large extent, a response to this denial of racism on the part of whites. "Whenever I have raised the subject of the bar association discrimination against blacks," Wright claims, "my white colleagues profess never to have noticed any such thing."[112] Many whites do not perceive themselves as racists. For a number of whites, racists are those who are usually members of groups such as the Klu Klux Klan who carry out willful overt crimes against blacks. In their day to day existence, many whites do not even have to address the issue of racism. Often blacks have to point out to whites that their actions and attitudes unfairly discriminate against blacks.

What, however, is even of greater significance is that what is regarded as racism by many blacks, is good appropriate behavior for whites. A judge who sentences a black man to prison for a long jail term may be viewed as harsh by blacks but for many whites the judge is an outstanding citizen who is saving the community from crime. According to Wright, those who "preside" over criminal cases are usually "middle class" and they are "ambitious, yearning for positions of power, advertised respectability and that prestige they believe themselves entitled to by reason of their self appraised worth."[113] We cannot help but note a parallel with the Dalits. Ambedkar, claims that "most cases depend upon the decision of the first court ; and these courts are presided over by officials who are sometimes corrupt and who generally, for other reasons, sympathize with the wealthy and landed classes to which they belong".[114]

For many whites, to associate with blacks means lowering one's standards. Even black professors who have graduated from the most prestigious law school are not immune to be "Dalitized" by whites. "When some first-year law students walk in and see that I am their contracts teacher", states Williams, "I have been told, their whole perception of law school changes." The students in the "margins of their notebooks, or unconsciously perhaps, they deface me." To the students, she "looks like a stereotypical black person...not an academic". They see" her "brown face and they draw lines enlarging the lips and coloring in 'black frizzy hair.' They add 'red eyes, to give...a demonic look.' In the margin of their notebooks" she is "obliterated".[115]

An all white staff or an all white neighborhood are indices of

---

[112]Wright, *Black Robes,* p. 87

[113]Ibid., p. 72.

[114]Ambedkar, *What Congress and Gandhi,* p. 50.

[115]Williams, The Alchemy of Race and Rights, p. 115.

competency, efficiency, and impeccable behavior. Even those who carry out willful overt acts against blacks may be regarded as loving dutiful sons, daughters, husbands, fathers, mothers, community workers. The member of the Klu Klux Klan or the slumlord may be a kind and devoted father who works hard to provide for his family and is generous to family, church, and community.

Indeed Charles Mills poignantly argues that white behavior which is normative is really based on a Racial Contract which is not, as is commonly felt, peripheral to the norms, beliefs, and philosophy of the society but is the very moral fabric of the society. In other words, racism is not some mere deviation from what is normative in American culture, but what is normative in American culture is actually racism. According to Mills, it is not that "all people have tried to live up to the norm but, given inevitable human frailty, have sometimes fallen short." Racism is the norm, "not merely in the sense of de facto statistical distribution patterns, but...in the sense of being formally codified, written down and proclaimed *as such.* Accordingly then "duties, rights, and liberties" are assigned on the basis of race. Therefore in order to "understand the actual moral practice of past and present" we need to be fully aware of "how the Racial Contract creates a *racialized* moral psychology."[116]

Much of what Mills highlights has been said or implied by a number of black writers. For example, Bell, Williams, and Wright have pointed out how racist practices of whites towards blacks are codified in the constitution, the slave laws, and segregation laws of the United States. "Built into the society," claims Wright, "is a natural kind of racist animus."[117] For Wright, "whites, even liberal whites are weaned on racism. They live and breathe the superiority of options, choices, opportunities that are available to those who wear the white skin."[118]

Mills' significant departure, however, is his emphasis that racism is not just an aberrant factor that is built into society but racism is actually the moral code or norm of the society. For whites, then, there is nothing morally dissonant about racist behavior. Mills goes on to make the very salient point that racism as normative affects the thinking process of whites so that they are not even able to know or detect that acting racist is immoral. "Whites will then act in racist ways while thinking of themselves as acting morally. In other words, they will experience genuine cognitive difficulties in recognizing certain behavior *as* racist." Thus, "apart from questions of

---

[116]Mills, *The Racial Contract,* p. 93, italics his.
[117]Wright, *Black Robes,* p. 29.
[118] Ibid., p. 53.

motivation and bad faith they will be morally handicapped simply from the conceptual point of view in seeing and doing the right thing". Mills adds the very significant point that the "Racial Contract prescribes as a condition for membership in the polity, an epistemology of ignorance."[119]

Good behavior, then, for whites often demands discriminatory policies regarding blacks. This may seem objectionable and indeed irrational. We see racism as a moral lapse which is a more rational and less appalling perspective. We think that by repeatedly pointing out to whites, behavior which we perceive as discriminatory, changes will be brought about in keeping with what is supposed to be the norms of the society in theory, that is, liberty and equal justice for all. We do not see that for many white people discriminatory practices as it pertains to black is normative. And it is because we do not see discriminatory practices with regards to blacks as normative, why blacks, particularly middle class blacks, as expressed by a number of black intellectuals, are often shocked by racist practices.

Charles Mills' assertion that racism is not a deviation of the norm within the society, but that racism is actually normative in the American culture is part of a shift in emphasis by a number of black scholars. Whereas, as pointed out in Chapter One, black scholars focused on the devastating impact of racism on blacks, a number of African American philosophers are now turning the spotlight on the power, privileges and normativeness of being white.

The focus then will be looking at the power and privilege of whiteness. This is very important for although in 2008 after the election of President Obama, there was a lot of euphoria that we are now living in a post racial society, many blacks now shake their heads in disbelief at deeply entrenched racist attitudes and comments in offices, talk shows, via e-mail, etc.

It is true that blacks do not have to ride on the back of the bus anymore nor drink from separate water fountains etc. but in many ways the status of blacks in America is similar to the status of Dalits in India, that is, being ascribed with certain inherent inferior characteristics that cannot be eradicated.

The late Justice Bruce Wright once told the story of how after having a mild heart attack, he was taken directly, dressed in his suit, from his office to the hospital. As he lay on the bed awaiting the doctor, he observed in the room with him a disheveled homeless looking white man. After a few minutes a doctor briskly entered the ward asking: "Where is the Judge? He looked at Judge Wright lying on the bed in his suit and walked past him to the disheveled homeless white man. "Now Judge, he said to the white man,

---

[119]Mills, *The Racial Contract,* p. 93, italics, his.

what happened"?

Alas we also have to look at how as blacks we have internalized stereotypical views and therefore subject each other to the kind of indignities that whites often inflict on blacks. Some years ago, in a discussion, a female cocoa brown complexion doctor commented that as she walked the wards in Jamaica, no matter how many times the patients were told that she is a doctor she would be addressed as nurse. "Nurse, Nurse, come here, Nurse". A few years ago, a relative, a cinnamon complexion springy hair doctor, related to me that as she was about to examine a black male patient in a hospital in Philadelphia, he loudly exclaimed that he wants to be seen by a "real doctor", that is, a white doctor. A professor at the University of the West Indies was distressed about the fact that often in his daily activities in Jamaica, he is jostled, pushed, shoved and addressed in derogatory manner for it is assumed from his dark cocoa brown complexion that he cannot be "smaddy"; he cannot be from the upper or middle class, he must be from the lower class.

We need a shift in focus in terms of a critical analysis of racism but I cannot help but ask Africana philosophers: Will this shift of emphasis be mainly addressed to whites, as it has been done in the past, based on an underlying belief, as Poussaint points in the Introduction to *The Souls of Black Folk*,[120] that somehow whites are going to listen to reason? It is not only that I am not optimistic that the attitude of whites will change based on reason alone, but it is crucial that black academicians also address blacks. The exclusion of the majority of blacks from the discussion demonstrates the marginalization and indeed invisibility of blacks in the academic world. If critical studies of whiteness from Africana philosophers are primarily aimed at whites, are not African American philosophers participating in the world view that they are addressing and that is the normativeness and superiority of whiteness?

I maintain that there is a wide gulf between black academia and the black "common folk" which could include doctors, lawyers, teachers, librarians, policemen, firefighters, businessmen. Is there as wide a gulf between white academia and "white common folk"? This may seem simplistic but how many white people can graduate in the fields of teaching, medicine, philosophy, psychology without some knowledge of their history and culture? A black person can graduate as a doctor, teacher, librarian, and even a philosopher without having to read one book written by or about a black person. There are a number of black people who are professionals who have never read books by or about W. E. B. Dubois, Martin Luther

---

[120]Dubois, *Souls,* p. xxviii ff.

King, Jr., Frederick Douglass, Marcus Garvey, Malcolm X, Paul Robeson, Claude McKay, Angela Davis, Harriet Tubman, Sojourner Truth, Franz Fanon, C.L.R. James, etc. Indeed, sometimes in my confrontation with blacks and whites, it is more likely for whites to suggest books written by black authors (although mostly literary) to counter and (sometimes to corroborate) my views than blacks. A black man once told me that he lives racism so he does not have to read books about racism.

He is not unique in his feelings. Indeed reading about Malcolm X, Marcus Garvey, Fannie Lou Hamer, Cater G. Woodson, Amos Wilson, Stokely Carmichael, Franz Fanon, Walter Rodney or even W. E. B. DuBois is somewhat of a source of embarrassment for many blacks. One cannot discuss these books with one's co-workers unless one is working in a predominantly black environment. Black culture and history are stigmatized. Some blacks in my social circle express ennui with what they consider my "militant", "irreligious" and not too "respectable" stance which is seen as an impediment to getting ahead.

I think that it is important to include blacks in the outreach of a focus on whiteness so that we can address our own internalization of whiteness as normative. Besides more and more young people are graduating from schools and colleges totally unaware of their history and culture including the Civil Rights Movement. When I try to remind students about the struggles of blacks regarding education—they tell me that it is not important—they do not need education—they can become wealthy by being rap artists or football players or basketball players. They laugh as they ask me: how many degrees do you have? Then in reference to my cheap non-designer shoes, they disdainfully comment, "Look at the shoes you are wearing".

Many black adults are disheartened when they read of young men being gunned down because of a gold chain, or designer shoe or jacket or a disrespectful look or a passing stray bullet. Black adults express concern that young people are totally unaware of the struggles of the Civil Rights Movement. Did the many blacks, and whites too, who marched, were arrested, fire hosed, murdered, to bring about more equitable changes in the field of education do so in vain? At the same time, in many of these communities stand several churches. As I already pointed out the Christian religion pervades the black community. How can we critically analyze issues that deal with the black community without including a critique of Christianity?

If the present conditions of black youth are due to an unjust, inequitable racist system, then this must include an analysis of religion. One question I keep asking myself in the light of Charles Mills' postulation that a Racial

Contract undergirds racism as morally right: what accounts for the metamorphoses and yet persistence of racism? We must admit that there have been some changes during the period between slavery and the election of President Obama, and yet as a number of scholars point out the poorest white often feels that he or she is superior to the wealthiest black. Is there some worldview or ideology that undergirds the Racial Contract?

I have a very heavy book of 1,483 pages which I rescued from being weeded from a library and thrown into the dump heap. It is entitled, *A Moral Dilemma: the Negro Problem and Modern Democracy.*[121] The research and publication of this work are examples of white power, resources, and privilege. Under the direction and leadership of Gunnar Myrdal, this work had the input of many scholars and experts to study as seen from the title, "the Negro problem".

It is significant to note, however, that Myrdal in the Introduction states that "[a]lthough the Negro problem is a moral issue both to Negroes and to whites in America, we shall in this book have to give *primary* attention to what goes on in the minds of white Americans."[122] This in a sense corroborates African American philosophers' current focus on whiteness. Myrdal sees the "negro problem" as "a moral dilemma". Myrdal makes the important point of the significance of the role of morality in research. "It is sometimes assumed", claims Myrdal that "good "research" is "to disregard the fact that people are moral beings and that they are struggling for their conscience". For Myrdal, "this is bias and a blindness, dangerous to the possibility of enabling scientific study to arrive at true knowledge". He concludes that every "social study must have its center in an investigation of people's conflicting valuations and their opportune beliefs."[123] With this I whole heartedly agree particularly when we take into consideration the fact that Christianity is the dominant religion amongst blacks and whites and yet blacks are stereotyped as mentally and morally inferior.

According to Mrydal, racism is a moral dilemma for many whites not only in terms of conflict with other whites but within the individual for it is a violation of the American Creed. A "poor and uneducated white person in some isolated and backward rural region in the Deep South, who is violently prejudiced against the Negro," states Myrdal" and who "is intent upon depriving him of civic and human independence" will also have "a whole compartment in his valuation sphere housing the entire American Creed of

---

[121]Gunnar Myrdal, *An American Dilemma : The Negro Problem and Modern Democracy*, (New York, NY: Harper & Brothers, 1944).
[122]Ibid., p. li., italics his.
[123]Ibid., p.l

liberty, equality, and justice, and fair opportunity for everybody". This person *"is actually also a good Christian and honestly devoted to the ideals of human brotherhood and the Golden Rule."*[124]

It is significant to note that Myrdal claims that there are three major contributors to the American Creed: The Philosophy of Enlightenment, Christianity, and English law. I think that we can all agree that Black scholars have addressed racism and philosophy and racism and law. What has not been critically and rigorously addressed by black scholars is racism and Christianity. As I have pointed out, Christianity is pervasive in the black community. It is also dominant in the white community. We need to critically analyze how is it that a white person who is "violently prejudiced against" blacks "is actually also a good Christian and honestly devoted to the Golden Rule."[125]

There is one other issue in terms of Mrydal's analysis that to me is a cogent argument for analyzing racism and Christianity and that is that whites have been and are influenced by black behavior. Although as Myrdal points out, it is the "white majority group that naturally determines the Negro's "place" yet "[n]ew impulses from the Negro people are constantly affecting the American way of life, bending in some degree all American institutions and bringing changes in every aspect of the American's complex world view."[126] Blacks are not entirely lacking a sense of agency.

There is nothing new about the allegation that blacks have little or no morality. This in spite of West's assertion that "though always fragile and difficult to sustain" blacks had personal, family and communal values in the past.[127] In every generation, since the arrival of blacks in America, blacks have been perceived as having no morals, that is, as being criminals, promiscuous, and lazy. Unquestionably, for the nearly three hundred years duration of slavery, blacks were regarded as lacking in morality. Indeed the immorality of Africans was one of the chief arguments used to justify slavery. Africans are cursed; they are children of Ham.

Frederick Douglass, who was born into slavery and lived many years as a slave, hoped that a "very different class of people from those originally brought to this country from Africa...will do away with the force of the argument that God cursed Ham and therefore American slavery is right."[128]

---

[124]Ibid., p.xlviii, italics mine.

[125]Ibid.

[126]Ibid., p. li, liii

[127]West, *Race Matters*, p. 35-37.

[128]Frederick Douglass, *Narratives of the Life of Frederick Douglass an American Slave*, (New York, NY: Signet, 1968), p 24.

Since so many, adds Douglass, like himself "owe their existence to white fathers, then "[i]f the lineal descendents of Ham are alone to be scripturally enslaved, it is certain that slavery at the South must soon be unscriptural."[129] Blacks were treated as beasts. "By far the larger part of the slaves", claims Douglass, "know as little of their ages as the horses of theirs and it is the wish of most masters to keep them ignorant."[130]

At the evaluation of Captain Anthony's property, Douglass recounts how "horses and men, cattle and women, pigs and children" had "the same rank in the scale of being and were all subjected to the same narrow examination."[131] At times, the slaves were treated worse than animals. Colonel Lloyd was more concerned about the care of his horses than the treatment of the slaves. "The slightest inattention" to the horses "was unpardonable and was visited upon those under whose care they were placed, with the severest punishment."[132] Indeed Douglass often wished that he was a "beast". He "preferred the condition of the meanest reptile...Anything, no matter what, to get rid of thinking. It was the everlasting thinking of my condition that tormented me. There was no getting rid of it."[133]

In 1905, DuBois published his seminal work, *The Souls of Black Folk* to counter the dominant attitude of whites that blacks had no souls.[134] It is not that blacks are a problem, asserts DuBois, but blacks are a "seventh son, born within a veil." Blacks can only see themselves through the "revelation of the other world." This results in a "peculiar sensation", a "double consciousness" which is a "sense of always looking at one's self through the eyes of others, of measuring one's soul by the tape of a world that looks on in amused contempt and pity."[135]

DuBois' defense of blacks' promiscuity and blacks having no family values are echoed in many works in the latter part of the twentieth century. While "sociologists gleefully count his bastards and his prostitutes, the very soul of the toiling, sweating black man is darkened by the shadow of a vast despair."[136] DuBois is at pains to show how blacks, to a large extent, have

---

[129]Ibid., p. 24.
[130]Ibid., p. 21.
[131]Ibid., p. 59.
[132]Ibid., p. 34
[133]Ibid., p. 55
[134]See for example, Chas. Carroll, *The Negro a Beast or In the Image of God"* ([n. s.], 1900).
[135]DuBois, *Souls*, p. 45.
[136]Ibid., p. 50.

been handicapped by slavery and how the policies and attitudes of whites exclude blacks from political, economic, and social spheres. DuBois asks whether it is "possible, and probable, that nine millions of men can make effective progress in economic lines if they are deprived of political rights, made a servile caste, and allowed only the most meager chance for developing their exceptional men."[137]

It is significant to note that in whites' first encounter with Africans, the Africans were regarded as savages, primitive beings, evil and uncivilized.[138] The European, however, possessed the ideological tool that would civilize the African.

The ideological tool the Europeans possessed was religion—the Christian religion. There were of course some Europeans who claimed that the Africans had no souls and were irredeemable. However, those who felt that the Africans could be civilized postulated the view that Christianity would transform the African from the wild, savage, beast to a cultivated human being, somewhat akin to the European. Thus Phillippo, a Baptist minister to Jamaica, declared that Christianity did transform the Africans. According to Phillippo, the "crafty Eboes," the Coromantes who were "violent and revengeful", the "debased and semi-human Moco and Angolan and all the tribes" who Phillippo claims, "historians described as 'more brutal and savage than the wild beasts of the forest and utterly incapable of understanding the first rudiments of the Christian religion' were all transformed". And what kind of transformation took place? According to Phillippo, they were now "subdued" and "converted." He also points out that "they were now raised to the dignity and intelligence of men, of sons and daughters of the Lord Almighty that they bring "forth the fruits of holiness, happiness and heaven."[139] Christianity transformed "wild beasts" into "civilized" people.

For Phillippo, then, as for many whites, Christianity would provide Africans with the morals which Africans lacked. Although a number of planters opposed the Christianization of the slaves, many missionaries worked hard to rid the Africans of their world view. How is it then, that

---

[137]Ibid., p. 88.

[138]One will find these disparaging terms in almost every European work up to the early twentieth century regarding Africans and their culture whether in the fields of history, anthropology, sociology or literature. See for example, Winthrop D. Jordan, *White over Black: American Attitudes Towards the Negro, 1550-1812,* (London: W. W. Norton & Co., 1977, c. 1968) for documentation on this issue.

[139]Phillippo, *Jamaica: Its Past and Present State,* p. 386-387.

after the elimination completely of the African world view and exposure to Christianity for more than four hundred years, and in parts of the Caribbean more than five hundred years, African descended peoples are still regarded as lacking in morality as their ancestors? We can only say then that like the Dalit of India, the African is perceived as inherent and innately evil and like the Dalit the perception of the African as stigmatized is based on religious ideology: the Hindu religion in the case of the Dalits, and the Christian religion in case of the Africans.

It is significant to note, at this point, that many Africans throughout their encounter with Europeans were not only converted to Christianity but participated in the spreading of the gospel. At the risk of loss of lives and arrests, blacks were involved in preaching, building churches, evangelistic and missionary work, even during the time of slavery.[140]

During the period of the Revolutionary War, Richard Allen, after buying his freedom, worked as a Methodist preacher. Allen traveled mostly on foot from Delaware to New Jersey to Maryland and to Philadelphia preaching the gospel. He was reputed to have converted many blacks and whites to Christianity. In Philadelphia, Allen attracted many blacks to the St. George Methodist Episcopal Church. The whites were concerned about the number of blacks in the church and decided to segregate the blacks. They implemented this by evicting three blacks including Richard Allen while they were on their knees praying. The blacks then, en masse, withdrew from the church. Allen then formed his own church. Other independent churches met in Philadelphia on April 9, 1816 and formed the African Methodist Episcopalian Church under the leadership of Richard Allen.[141]

Blacks were very instrumental in spreading the gospel amongst Blacks, that is, in missionary and evangelical activity. DuBois recounts how Alexander Crummell established a chapel in New York where he worked very hard "in poverty and starvation scorned by his fellow priests" who were white. Crummell then traveled to Queens College, England where he gained his degree in 1853. From England, Crummell went to Africa and worked as

---

[140]Andrew Billingsley, *Like a Mighty River: The Black Church and Social Reform,* (New York, NY: Oxford University Press, 1999); Lincoln and Mamiya, *The Black Church in the African American Experience*; Marcia M. Mathews, *Richard Allen,* (Baltimore-Dublin: Helicon, 1963); Carter G. Woodson, *The History of the Negro Church* 2nd ed. (Washington, D.C.: The Associated Press, 1945, c. 1921).

[141]Lincoln and Mamiya, *The Black Church in the African American Experience,* p. 50-52; Mathews, *Richard Allen*; Woodson, *The History of the Negro Church.*

a missionary for twenty years.[142]

The existence of the Baptist denomination in Jamaica is primarily due to the work of two African American Baptists. As already mentioned, George Liele and Moses Baker were amongst slaves brought to Jamaica by many Loyalists who migrated to the island after the Revolutionary War. Liele and Baker preached to the African Jamaicans and built Baptist churches. It was, to a large extent, the response to the appeal of Moses Baker that Baptist missionaries from England went to Jamaica to assist in building Baptist churches there. While the memory of white Baptist missionaries, such as Phillippo and Knibb, are kept alive by churches and schools being named after them, except for brief sentences in textbooks, Baker and Liele are almost forgotten. The issue of the perpetuation of the memory of whites as good and as "saviors" of blacks is a major contributory factor to the Racial Contract that a critical analysis will reveal.

The Baptist churches built by African American slaves formed the nucleus of what would be known as the native Baptist Churches. These churches would play an important role in the social, economic, and political lives of African Jamaicans.[143]

Having lost their religion and culture, during slavery, which were the sources of African morality, many blacks turned to the Christian religion. The Christian religion is an integral part of black culture.[144] Dr. Martin Luther King, Jr. rued the lack of support of many white churches in the struggle of blacks for justice. But then he asserts that he cannot but love the church for he is a descendant of preachers. His father, his grandfather, and his great grandfather were preachers.[145] Today in almost every black community, the church is the dominant institution.

Proportionately, blacks have higher church membership than whites. According to the *Princeton Religion Research Center,* 78% of blacks claim church membership whereas 68% of whites do.[146] On a weekly basis, 44% of blacks attend church services whereas 40% of whites do. Blacks have a higher rate, 37% of being super churched, that is, attending church on other days besides Sunday, than whites, 31%. Blacks give more money and time

---

[142]DuBois, *Souls,* p. 241.

[143]Curtin, *Two Jamaicas*; Gordon, *Our Cause,* Lincoln & Mamiya, *The Black Church.*

[144]Billingsley, *Like a Mighty River*; DuBois, *Souls*; Frazier, *The Negro Church*; Lincoln & Mamiya, *The Black Church*; Woodson, *The History of the Negro Church.*

[145]King, *Why We Can't Wait,* p. 91

[146]*Princeton Religion Research Center,* 1996, p. 41.

to the Churches than any other organization. Black denominations have not shown a loss of membership as some white denominations, such as, the Episcopalian, the United Presbyterian, and the Disciples of Christ.[147]

Given the above observations, it is quite remarkable that the vast majority of blacks are perceived as morally and mentally inferior. Given the above observations, it is quite remarkable how any study could undertake an analysis of the conditions of blacks in the society without discussing in detail the issue of religion, particularly the Christian religion and the role of the Christian religion in black culture. To exclude the Christian religion from studies pertaining to blacks is tantamount to excluding many blacks and indeed many whites from the analysis.

---

[147]*Yearbook of American & Canadian Churches,* 1993, Kenneth Bedell, editor (Nashville: Abingdon Press, 1994) p. 1. See also *Princeton Religion Research Center, 1996 Report,* p. 41.

Christianity and Black Oppression: Duppy Know Who Fe Frighten

CHAPTER THREE

A QUESTION OF MORALITY: WHOSE MORALITY IS IT?

What people think about God, Jesus Christ and the Church cannot be separated from their own social and political reality.[148]
James Cone - *God of the Oppressed.*
The goal of black agitation should be in the cause of not permitting the Christian morality of America to sink, once again into holding blacks in bondage, and to work to heal America of its racism.[149]

In the Introduction, I stated that a factor that influenced this study are the insights and knowledge I gained as a result of the frequent discussions, discourses, and debates I had (and do have) with members of the black community regarding Christianity. From my experience, most people, especially black women view the world through the prism of religion. And the religion through which a number of black women view the world is, for the most part, the Christian religion. Some black scholars might be flabbergasted to know that for a number of black people, at least in my social circle, religion is far more salient a factor than race.

For some black Christians, any kind of race consciousness, that is, militancy or radicalism is regarded as sinful or wrong. For many of my Black Christian friends and family, racism is a sin. However, the "true" Christian must not harbor anger towards whites; the "true" Christian needs to pray for whites; the "true" Christian cannot at any time display to Whites, the same type of discriminatory practices to which Blacks are subjected by Whites. Besides, some of the racist attitude of whites is also the fault of blacks who are irresponsible. To be conscious of race, to join race conscious organizations (except perhaps a Black organization of one's profession, that is, a counterpart to the White's) is not being a "true" Christian.

By not joining race conscious organizations, many blacks may appear as if they are not "race conscious". However, the fact that they drive past several white churches to worship at a black church is evidence of the awareness that they are black. As a matter of fact,

---

[148]James H. Cone, *God of the Oppressed,* (Maryknoll, NY: Orbis Books, 1997, c. 1975), p. 41.
[149]Wright, *Black Robes,* p. 97.

attendance at an all black church is better than being outside of the church, some of my Black Christian middle class friends tell me reproachfully, for membership of the black church demonstrates an appreciation for black culture and heritage. These black Christians are aware sometimes that they have to deal with a lot of "nonsense", but they are not too "hoity toity" to worship with the "masses".

At the same time, however, if some of my black middle class friends perceive a conflict between issues that have to do with race and their religious beliefs, then the religious beliefs will take priority. For example, I know black Christians who will not participate in organizations that deal exclusively with race, do not celebrate Kwanzaa, regard a black painting of Jesus as sacrilegious, will not read certain black books, and view wearing one's hair natural or in dreads, if not exactly sinful, as not meeting God's approval. For the most part, black Christians do not see that the basic issue then becomes the question of skin color, and not the intellectual ideas that are fostered in the churches. Indeed the difference between the white churches and the black churches is more style than substance.

Generally there are three schools of thought regarding the Christian religion within my social sphere. I define this social sphere as an inner social sphere which would include family, friends, and those I interact with in my neighborhood, at work, social gatherings, etc. The outer social sphere is comprised of people I may never meet but who influence my thoughts or thinking through books, writing, films, etc. This outer social sphere then transcends geographical location. One school of thought, a very tiny minority, mostly men, views the Christian religion as oppressive; they may for one reason or another be disillusioned with the church. Those who find the Christian religion oppressive generally tend to offer some alternative world view, such as, the Rastafari or some African traditional spiritual belief. The second school regarding Christianity is comprised mainly of scholars, some Marxists or socialists, who maybe as a result of their focus on class, race, and gender, have a somewhat epiphenomenal view of Christianity and its role in social issues. Although these scholars may include a critique of Christianity, the critique is peripheral and generally no alternative to Christianity is suggested.

The third group of blacks is overwhelmingly Christian. These blacks, particularly women, are implacable in their view that not only is life totally meaningless without the precepts of the Christian religion, but one needs to be a believer and a follower of Christ to live a moral life. You *must* be a Christian—you *must* belong to some Church and if you have left a church as a result of some bad experience, you cannot blame God. What you need to do is *find another church.* Whereas poor black men, to some extent, may be forgiven for being "unchurched", middle class black women must belong to a church.[150]

It is this belief which is dominant amongst blacks that blacks cannot have principles, blacks cannot be moral unless blacks belong to a church, that is, a black person must be a Christian to have principles and be moral that I think needs to be addressed. There are a number of issues that I would like to highlight with regard to this belief: (i) whether there is any validity to the assertion that a black person cannot live a principled or moral life unless the black person is a Christian (ii) what is the morality that the black person as a Christian is supposed to display or possess in concrete terms and (iii) whose morality is it?

A number of black Christians have little tolerance for adherents of world views, including those of other major world religions and denominations which are outside of their specific denomination and dogma. Some black Christians (and this includes holders of graduate degrees) really do believe that non-Christians and many who are outside of their particular denomination are doomed for hell, damnation, and destruction. This not only has an impact on intellectual growth, but it also has an impact on relating to others. This is ironical because black Christians do not see how, in many ways, they support non-Christian families—they buy goods made in China, they see doctors, dentists, therapists who do not belong to their faith, they attend non-denominational colleges and universities, they spend money in shops and stores that are not owned by adherents of their denomination. Yet, they will socially isolate and alienate a family member because he or she is not Baptist, Brethren, Jehovah Witness, Pentecostal, Seventh Day Adventist, etc.

Slights, being held at arm's length, ensuring that their children do not have contact with you less you pollute them with your atheistic ideas is often the lot of the unbeliever. Yet these Christians will raise very little or no objection if they or their children have to mingle or interact, and indeed will gracefully and cheerfully do so if needs be, with whites, Jews, Indians, Chinese, who believe that there is no God and if Jesus did exist, he is not the son of God. I have come to the conclusion that the Christian God is very, very fragile and needs to be constantly protected from intellectual rigor. We need to stop and ask: What kind of morality is it that states that it is right for you to socially isolate and indeed ostracize

---

[150]See, for example, Lincoln, *The Black Church in America,* Chap. 6.

a family member, friend, or co-worker who does not share your Christian belief?

Besides the intolerance of a number of black Christians regarding divergent views, is the lack of critical analysis, mainly as a result of Christian beliefs, of the status of and history of blacks that are fundamental to the question of black morality.

Many black scholars would be greatly surprised to know that their analysis widely differs from the analysis of the black "masses" regarding the status and conditions of blacks in the society. A number of members of my inner social circle, that is, members of my extended family, friends, acquaintances, many of them, college graduates, have never even heard of some of the most popular black scholars, much less to have read their works. For many black Christians of my inner social circle, the roots of black moral depravity lie not in the legacies of slavery but in the turning away from God. Slavery was abolished a long, long, long time ago, my black Christian family members, friends, associates, say. The present racist policies, they will acquiesce, may contribute to the conditions of blacks. At the same time, however, it is very important that one does not lose one's faith.

For quite a number of Black Christians, their lives are shining examples of what belief can do for one particularly when they see the misery of many poor blacks. Then they know that they are blessed! When the godly sons of godly women are routinely stopped on their way to church, and patted down in a most humiliating manner, these Christian mothers tell their sons that this kind of action or racial profiling is the work of the devil and that they should not permit the devil to stop them from going to church or cause them to lose their faith.

Many middle class blacks or striving middle class blacks take pride in their Christian righteousness. Nevertheless, they all see themselves, although unwilling to admit it, as somewhat under a "cloud", the "cloud" of racism. Whenever, however, you ask: What role does God play in the daily indignities you face? the response is: "you cannot blame God", "it is of the devil" or "it is man's doing and in time human beings will pay. God will punish them."

Black Christians do not see how this "cloud" often affects their Christian righteousness. Hypertension, diabetes, stroke, heart attack plague blacks, aggravated by food, often used as an antidote for stress, worry, and anxiety. Because dancing is held to be a sin by a number of black Baptist and fundamentalist Christians, black Christians deprive themselves of a very good source of exercise, enjoyment, relaxation, and pleasure—factors which studies show often attenuate the onset of life threatening diseases, hypertension, diabetes, stroke, etc., that are prevalent amongst blacks.

It is ironic that while many black Christians are forbidden to dance because dancing is sinful, whites not only participate in this activity, but have incorporated black dancing style, although this will not formally be admitted, in forms of exercise, and dance classes from which they make huge profits. Although dancing is a sin, Black Christians will sign up for exercise classes because "they have to lose weight" or dance classes as an activity for their children. It is interesting that many Baptist Churches, now institute what is termed Praise Dance in which, as I have observed at Black events, the dancers will carry out the same motions, and gyrations of the dancers of what must be, if we are to pursue the logic, "Devil Dancing" or "dancing of the world". I guess the sanitized praise dance is to attract and garner young people for the church but I am baffled as I have been for a long time as to the difference between dancing in a building called a church and dancing elsewhere.

No matter what black Christians tell me, they worry. They worry above and beyond the normal everyday concerns of existence as a human being. They worry about the cloud, the "veil" as Dubois puts it of racism. They worry when their sons do not return at an expected time; they worry about being given only night and week-end shifts whereas whites work in the day; they worry when young whites are given seniority over them when they have been an employee of the company for many more years. They worry about whether they will be turned down for a job solely based on their skin color. They worry that they will be the first to go when the company downsizes. They worry whether the white teacher will be fair in the assessment of their children's performance at school.

Just as how "Sankritization" efforts of the Dalits, that is, carrying out high class rituals, and living moral lives failed to change the attitude of caste Hindus towards the Dalits[151] so no matter how much Blacks attend church and read their Bibles, they are not perceived as Christians by whites. In spite of the fact that black Christians are in Church every Sunday and often during the week, whites do not see blacks as pious. Whites, however, see themselves as good. Blacks do not see how their social conditions in relationships to whites affect the moral landscape.

Whites' sense of their goodness will be enhanced, for example, as teachers on a staff where whites are the majority in a school and the majority of children are black. Here as white teachers, they can make the

---

[151]Eleanor Zelliot, " Gandhi and Ambedkar—A Study in Leadership" in *The Untouchables in Contemporary India.*

claim of doing a superhuman job to educate black children who are from broken homes, inner city, the ghetto, and who do not want to be educated. Whereas a majority of teachers on a staff of an all black school may be white, the reverse will never happen, that is, the majority of teachers being black in an all white school. Indeed blacks are sometimes excluded by white administrators, superintendents, principals from teaching in a majority black school and if they are hired they often have to conform to the views of the majority white staff even if these views counter their knowledge and experience of effectively educating black children. Opportunities are often denied black teachers of doing a superhuman job, and frequently their efforts are not recognized. A number of black Christian teachers express frustration at being unable to relate to black students because of bureaucratic strictures and rulings by white experts who have little or no experience with regard to actual teaching in the classroom. These black Christians, however, will display some discomfort and agitation, when I ask them: What is God's role and function in the structure of the school system? Black Christians tell me that it has nothing to do with God; it is "human beings". "We are given trials to test our faith". I do not press my point by commenting on the dominant role of whites in the education system and how black Christian teachers have to acquiesce to a large extent to rules, regulations, and norms of whites.

Goodness is associated with whites. When one thinks of the word missionary, one thinks of a white person although blacks have been and are missionaries. A white missionary from the United States, England, or Canada can with very little hindrance gain access to almost any Third World country. White people will also undertake missionary activities in black neighborhoods in the United States. On the other hand, black people from Third World Countries and black neighborhoods would face major obstacles if they attempt to carry out missionary work in white neighborhoods. Black men, in particular, in white neighborhoods would arouse suspicion. The cops would be called! Cops, however, would not be called for white men working as missionaries in black neighborhoods.

In other words, since God is sovereign ruler, and holds sway over all resources, and since God intervenes in history then it would seem that whites are given far more resources to do good than blacks. It would seem that God gives whites, since he has the power to intervene in history, far more opportunities to do "good" than blacks.

Furthermore, whites' goodness is often tangibly measured by their achievement and their success—good jobs, spouses who have well paying jobs, appointments to boards and important committees, children doing well in school, a house in the suburbs, two or three cars, being able to afford to travel abroad for vacations, to dine well, to entertain, to belong to clubs, to visit museums and to be involved in some form of recreation. How many blacks can attest to that?

It is significant to note, however, that some Christian blacks who are well off in conversations with whites are careful not to highlight any success. A few years ago a friend told me how appalled she was to hear a young black colleague of hers disclose to her white co-workers the renovations she was making to an already opulent home. My friend thought this was very naïve; experience, said my friend who lived in a very comfortable home in the suburbs, taught her to reveal as little as possible to her white co-workers about her assets, resources, achievement or success. Just like the Dalits in India, she feared discriminatory retaliation from whites for daring to step out of the mode as a black person having little or no rights, resources, or privileges.

According to Ambedkar, Dalits will be subjected to a "stringent boycott simply because" they wear "the sacred thread" or "have bought a piece of land" or "put on good clothes or ornaments" or "carried a marriage procession with the bridegroom on the horse through the public street."[152] Ambedkar terms the discriminatory treatment of Dalits in India, a social boycott[153], a term which can be aptly applied to the discriminatory practices of white Christians vis-à-vis black Christians.

When I point out the anomalies with regard to white Christian behavior, my black Christian friends cheerfully tell me that the only thing that matters is their relationship to God. James Cone, to some extent, echoes the view of my Christian friends with the claim that God is on the side of the oppressed.[154] I wonder though if the economic and political as well as the social and psychological ramifications of oppression are fully analyzed.

Oppression has very painful social and psychological consequences. What does it do to one's psyche, one's ego, one's self, to be constantly on your guard, to have to conceal your thoughts and your feelings, to avoid spontaneity, to perpetually feel that you are slighted because of your skin color? These feelings, these thoughts, this being "behind a veil" prevent honest relationships not only with whites but often with blacks. I contend moreover that if there is a Supreme Being, God, these feelings which become so much part of the personality of blacks are

---

[152]Ambedkar, *What Congress Have Done*, p. 44.
[153]Ibid.
[154]Cone, *God of the Oppressed*.

bound to affect blacks' perception and relationship with the Supreme Being, God.

The feelings of being behind a "veil", a "cloud" are not something that can be easily shed; they become a part of you. It is my belief that black Christians project these inauthentic feelings unto God. God is the father, the great provider, who cares for them, and, very significant to note, who intervenes in history. Black Christians believe that God is in complete control of their lives and the universe, and *who will intervene on their behalf.* Yet when you point to black Christians the comparative wealth, and well being of whites, they tell you that wealth does not matter. Black Christians are very thankful to God for their achievements, for their accomplishments—the attainment of the certification as a teacher, doctor, lawyer, nurse and when you try to raise the issue as to God's role in the establishment of the requirements for certification you are told that does not matter with a lot of repressed anger. It is often pointless in these discussions to show how (i) requirements often exclude blacks that (ii) requirements have changed over the years and (iii) attainments of blacks today are as a result of the work of activists over centuries particularly in the Civil Rights Movement and colonial struggles.

What I am often baffled about, however, is how God who is very supportive of accomplishments which require intellectual rigor can at the same time be totally contemptuous, intolerant, and hostile to intellectual critical analysis when it pertains to him. Black Christian friends and members of my family will discuss issues in a logical, rational manner and then the red flag goes up as soon as religion is introduced, which it often is, generally, to demonstrate God's goodness. Whenever the demonstration of goodness is followed by any kind of exploration of who or what accounts for evil, suffering, oppression, then it is: "let us not go there", "we have to agree to disagree", "evil has to do with human beings or the devil", "sometimes God tests our faith." I have to desist from any kind of analysis regarding "God as the sum of his acts"[155] particularly with regard to God's relationship with Blacks as a collective.

If this rationality, irrationality, suspension of intellectual critical analysis, repressions of emotions is not evidence of inauthentic feelings in terms of relationship with God, I do not know what else is. This is expressed in behavior that is erratic, for the same God that is very strict about certain rules, mores, and laws can be very lax about others. On Sundays, at services during the week, at individual devotional times, the

---

[155]Jones, *Is God a White Racist?* p. 114

black Christian can be almost an entirely different human being from the one who works from Monday to Friday in often a very hostile environment.

If Black Christians have to conceal their thoughts and feelings, if they have to conform to rules and regulations that counter their beliefs, and if they respond to slights and indignities with feelings of anger, rage, hurt and vindictiveness, will not God be aware of all of these feelings, behavior, attitude, and will not these feelings, behavior, attitude, affect black Christians' interaction with God? Indeed, blacks are often faced with what DuBois terms an "ethical paradox."[156] Blacks must not only think about their "inner life" but they also have to deal with the problems of being Black.[157] After a century, this is still the situation for blacks. Indeed for Dubois', the conflicts that blacks have to constantly face must "mean a time of intense ethical ferment of religious heart searching and intellectual unrest."[158] Blacks have to "live a double life" as "an American" and a Black person as he lives in two eras, "the fifteenth century" and the "nineteenth".[159] DuBois concludes that from this having to live a double life "must arise a painful self consciousness, an almost morbid sense of personality and a moral hesitancy which is fatal to self confidence".[160] I contend that this "painful self consciousness, an almost morbid sense of personality and a moral hesitancy which is fatal to self confidence"[161] must have an impact on blacks' perception of God and blacks' relationship with God.

Sometimes black Christians in response to indignities do stoically decide to turn the other cheek usually with the caveat that God will judge the misdeeds and injustices of whites in the end. Sometimes, however, turning the other cheek is just too much and the pent up feelings erupt to the "shock" and "amazement" of white co-workers. Then, "Oh dear, I am so sorry you took offence to that statement. I did not mean anything by it". Then there will be talk about playing the "race card", the "victim" game, being too "sensitive" or relating slights that their particular ethnic group, Irish, Italians, Jews, had to endure. Do not the feelings of mortification and humiliation sap the energy of the black Christian often impeding him or her from focusing on the job at hand or relating with co-

---

[156]DuBois, *Souls,* p. 222.
[157]Ibid., p. 221
[158]Ibid., p. 221
[159]Ibid., p. 221
[160]Ibid., p. 221.
[161]Ibid., p. 221

workers in a healthy way?

When the black Christian is bombarded by negative reporting of blacks in the media, how does that affect his or her relationship with God? For when whites commit a crime, the reaction is not to hunt every white person down as potential criminals. When a white person commits a crime, it is the individual white who commits the crime. However, when a black person commits a crime, although you may be a black person who lives a thousand miles away from the scene of the crime, you are as culpable of the crime as the black person who commits it. Similarly if one black person is successful, then all black people have the potential to be successful. After hiring one black person, whites need not hire any more because one black person on the staff represents all black people.

Black people are viewed as a collective—not as individuals. One would think being viewed as a collective does affect the relationship with God. I may say that I have an individual relationship with God but I contend that perpetual underlying feelings of being part of a group that is stereotyped as lazy, promiscuous, lacking in morality and mentality inferior must affect my relationship with God. My expectations in terms of my prayers being answered are restricted to my status. I have no rights and privileges. Thus, I accept, as God's will, being overlooked for the umpteenth time for the promotion in spite of my experience and qualifications.

Something that struck me forcibly in my research on the Dalits is how the children of Dalits and caste Hindus learn from early childhood their status in the society. The children of Dalits and the children of Caste Hindus observe how their parents socially interact with others and how the interaction depends on their status. J. Michael Mahar asserts that the "inculcation of attitudes of inferiority may be seen in the everyday experience of the very young." It does not take very long for "the Sweeper child accompanying his mother on her daily rounds to realize his position in society." Indeed the "nature of the tasks performed by an Untouchable's (Dalit's) parents, the mode of address and the tone of voice used by upper castes in issuing instructions, are readily apparent to children." Similarly children of the upper caste "learn their superior station by observing how their parents issue orders" to those of lower status. Besides, and this is very significant, the "inculcation of upper caste attitudes and manners are furthered by a variety of means including the telling of religious stories praising the heroic exploits of their Rajput ancestors in struggles for temporal power" What about the "achievements of the Untouchables' mythical ancestors"? They are in "the other worldly realm of religion".[162]

Black children and white children learn from very young their status in the society. Black children learn from the time they are very young, their inferior status from sitting in segregated black churches. [163] Just as how the celebration of the exploits and deeds of the ancestors of caste Hindus foster feelings of superiority in the children of caste Hindus, so the celebration of the achievements of whites foster feelings of superiority in the children of whites. White Christians experience no cultural dissonance in celebrating and to a large degree apotheosizing their ancestors—Thomas Jefferson, George Washington, Christopher Columbus, Martin Luther, John and Charles Wesley, Immanuel Kant just to name a few. Catholic children have an entire slew of saints about whom they have to spend months learning, sometimes years, before they can be confirmed in the church. Whites are immortalized by having schools, universities, states and even countries named after them or in their honor. As Wright postulates "America prefers to remember the cherry tree mythology and I-Cannot-Tell-a-Lie apocrypha of George Washington rather than his Christian devotion to slave holding."[164]

Many black Christians would shudder in horror were you even to suggest that black freedom fighters be elevated to sainthood and accounts of their heroic deeds and achievements be an integral part of their Church services, and their lives. At what point in the lives of black children do the inauthentic feelings that are inculcated in them from very young, particularly in the Church become transformed to an individual relationship with God that transforms the stigma of being black?

It is not that white Christians do not have cares, concerns, pain but on top of the suffering that is the lot of human beings, the black Christian is faced with added and often needless suffering of pain, loss, indignity as a member of a collective group termed a race based on skin color. Whites will more openly talk about their son's drug addiction, a family member being arrested, an alcoholic spouse, being diagnosed with cancer, their teenage daughter being pregnant, being a single parent without the fear of yet further proof of stereotypical behavior of a collective group or being deservedly punished by God because of the behavior of the collective group.

In terms of their relationship with God, whites do not have to think

---

[162]Mahar, "Agents of Dharma" in *The Untouchables in Contemporary India,* p. 23-24.
[163]Frazier, *The Negro Church.*
[164]Wright, *Black Robes,* p. 63.

about issues having to do with skin color; black Christians do whether they want to admit it or not. For whites then, there is not the cultural dissonance, the feelings of being behind "a veil" or under a "cloud" which I purport affect the relationship of black Christians vis-à-vis God, and the relationship of God vis-à-vis black Christians so that in spite of blacks' commitment of time, money, and energy to the Christian religion, the output is nowhere tantamount to the input.

In the light of their religion, blacks work very hard spending many hours on Sunday in Church, sometimes attending church services during the week, reading their Bibles and praying daily, and tithing. Blacks are grateful to God for whatever they perceive as being positive, which are usually material benefits, in their life without taking into account the inordinate amount of time and effort they put into their relationship with God. They are very grateful for what I consider to be mere pittance when compared to the lifestyle and resources of white Christians who in many instances make far less effort.

There is often the implication of course of an eschatological world view which is really a "pie in the sky" perspective. This world cannot be it. There is too much injustice here. The tables will turn in heaven. I often futilely try to point out that if there is really a heaven, there will be very little difference in terms of relationships between blacks and whites in heaven. If there is a heaven, it will undoubtedly be affected by factors on earth.

I flatter myself if I think God is going to send the white planter to hell for enslaving my black ancestor when the white planter as a slave master was able to accrue a lot of wealth that enabled him to aid in the spread of the gospel by generously giving money for the building and maintenance of churches, to buy Bibles, etc. The white slave master was also able to leave a legacy of wealth to his progenitors so that they can not only live comfortably but carry on charitable works. Besides, even if the white planter is sent to hell, how would that erase the tragedy of the life of my black ancestors— nameless, three-fifths human beings who could not leave any type of legacy for their progeny except the brutal, inhumane, social alienating badge of slavery?

The eschatological view built on hope and promises that in the end pain and suffering will be appeased, undermines the psychological and social consequences of suffering and human behavior. Besides, there is cause and effect; behavior has consequences. There are decisions that my grandparents made and events that occurred in their lives that presently have an impact on my life, and no amount of tears, washing away of sin, eternity can eradicate the consequences of those decisions and events. The decisions that I have made, am making, and will make and events that occurred and are occurring in my life will have consequences for my grandchildren, great grandchildren, and so on.

We cannot dismiss slavery as having no impact on our lives today. It is not an event that can be simply wished or willed away. We are bounded by history, time, and events that no amount of plea for divine intervention can change. The belief that the past has nothing to do with our current lives is living in a state of delusion.

A number of Christians tell me that as a Christian they are guided by God with regards to making the right decision. A whole book could be written in response to that for in many cases what happens is that decisions are made based on a number of exigencies over which sometimes black Christians have little control. The black Christian faced with a choice of course (a) or course (b) is likely to choose course (a) because course (a) offers more opportunities or benefits over course (b). However, the Christian will unabashedly let you know that God led him or her to course (a).   If course (a) does not work out, the Christian forgets that God led him or her to course (a).   You dare not ask the Christian about unhappy marriages some ending in divorce, or dead end frustrating jobs that were at some point perceived as a result of divine intervention, an answer to prayer, God's will.

The dominant role of whites in the lives of blacks in terms of jobs, health care, schooling, justice, the laws, etc. is not often an issue that is raised amongst black Christians. This, I feel, is as a result of the need for blacks to feel some kind of agency. It does not matter whether the laws, the structure and organization of the society are dominated by whites, black Christians can plea to God for divine intervention. This is indeed a painful question to ask: why is it that in the light of the great amount of time and effort blacks invest into the Christian religion, God often works through whites to respond to their requests?   Black Christians particularly black theologians often cite Emancipation and the Civil Rights movement as two events where God demonstrates his support for Black liberation. Besides the fact that many generations were born and died in slavery, and there were many martyrs as a result of the Civil War and during the Civil Rights Movement, in the final analysis blacks had to rely on predominantly white institutions of government: the Senate, the House, the President, Federal troops, white justices, to achieve any kind of "liberation".

James Cone's *God of the Oppressed* is a classic example of DuBois' "religious heart searching and intellectual unrest" in terms of blacks' perception and relationship with God. It would seem from Cone's work that God, when engaging with white people, is rational in the light of a theology of hope, existential theology, systematic theology, etc. When interacting with black Christians, however, God is totally irrational subjecting black people to centuries of oppression while still claiming that he is on the side of blacks. The view that Blacks do not need to use their intellect or engage in rigorous critical analysis is laced throughout *God of the Oppressed*. For example Cone writes that "White theologians built logical systems" while "black folks told tales. While "Whites debated such issues as "the validity of infant baptism" or "predestination" or "free will", blacks "recited biblical stories about God leading the Israelites from Egyptian bondage, Joshua and the battle of Jericho, and the Hebrew children in the fiery furnace" While "White theologians" discussed scientific matters and "Darwin's *Origin of the Species*" blacks were "more concerned about their status in America and its relation to the biblical claim that Jesus came to set the captives free". I find Cone's conclusions puzzling. "White thought on Christian view of salvation" claims Cone, "was largely 'spiritual' and sometimes 'rational,' but usually" not linked to the "concrete struggle of freedom in this world. Black thought was largely eschatological and never abstract, but usually related to blacks' struggle against earthly oppression".[165]

It is interesting to note that in this polemical work, Cone presents the arguments of the white theologians in a structured, reasoned, cogent style. Indeed regarding Niebuhr's theology, from which Cone acknowledges much of his black theology is deduced, Cone states: "The complexity of this theological problem is brilliantly analyzed in H. Richard Niebuhr's *Christ and Culture.*[166] On the other hand, black views and thoughts, in spite of the tremendous body of research by scholars, are based on spirituals, the Bible, and oral tradition. The reasoning in terms of the oppression of blacks and God being on the side of blacks is illogical, irrational and circular, particularly in the light of the more than three hundred years of oppression of blacks. The style of writing seems to be in two modes, "the double consciousness" of DuBois: on the one hand, rational, cogent, articulate in terms of white theology and on the other hand, irrational, illogical, and circular in terms of black theology."

I want to point out that Black Christians do not deviate from the majority Christian population in terms of erratic behavior as a result of a belief in a God who is purported to have the attributes of omnipotence, omniscience, being perfect, loving, just, and yet, who at the same time

---

[165]Cone, *God of the Oppressed,* p. 49-50.
[166]Ibid., p. 78.

supports or allows, in the light of these attributes, inhumane conditions such as slavery, colonization, brutal extermination of native peoples, wars, unjust prison system, repressive racist laws, norms, mores. Black morality, however, is to a large extent shaped by the "veil" and "double consciousness" as a result of racism. To repeat, God must be the sum of his acts.

In the final analysis, black Christians share the same doctrinal beliefs, norms, and mores as white Christians. This is so in spite of the existence of segregated churches in America. There is really very little difference between black churches and white churches in terms of substance; the main difference is one of style. In spite of Cone's assertion that black churches are vanguards of liberation struggle,[167] and indeed a number of black Christians will be upset at glaring racial discrimination, yet far more time is spent in and outside of the churches including Bible Study meetings, discussing issues, such as, being born again, whether infants should be baptized, the Second Coming, the Rapture, sin, salvation, redemption, women keeping silent in the churches, the attainment of the Holy Spirit, whether women wearing their hair natural is sinful than on social, political, and economic issues regarding the welfare of the black community.[168] The underlying belief of most Christians, I encounter, is that of individual salvation. For them, the most appalling social conditions are no excuse for moral decadence. Yet many Christian blacks are perceived by whites, and some blacks, as having little or no morality.

If, as some black scholars assert, the behavior of blacks is, to a large extent, determined by historical and socio-economic conditions, then we must ask: What determines the behavior of whites? If racist policies and racist attitudes affect black behavior so that many blacks do end up as criminals, low achievers, irresponsible parents, we need to ask: what are the factors that foster white behavior in terms of their discriminatory attitudes and their discriminatory policies towards blacks? It is often asserted that white attitudes are rooted in a belief in white supremacy. "White people are conditioned from the time of their birth to their preferred status of their skin color," states Wright. "Their views of the world at large and their own environment become solidified by circumstances, presuppositions, myths, and clichés.[169] We need to

---

[167]See for example, James H. Cone, *A Black Theology of Liberation,* (New York, NY: J. B. Lippincott, 1970).
[168]Lincoln, *The Black Church,* p. 150-157.
[169]Wright, *Black Robes,* p. 19.

rigorously explore the circumstances, presuppositions, myths and clichés. If not, it would appear that whites are inherently racists and this could validate the argument that blacks are inherently inferior.

For a number of black scholars, the roots of white supremacy or racism can be traced to slavery. The adverse effect of the slave laws, they argue, is still having disastrous effect on African Americans. Slavery lasted for a long time—for more than two hundred and fifty years in America.[170] Indeed in some parts of the Caribbean and Latin America, slavery lasted for more than three hundred years. Many people were born in slavery and died in slavery.

I contend that there must have been some moral underpinnings for the institution of slavery to have survived for at least over two centuries and a fundamental moral underpinning was the Christian religion. According to Mark Twain, "Sir John's work [John Hawkins] was the invention of Christians."[171] It "was to remain a bloody and awful monopoly in the hands of Christians for a quarter of a millennium…"[172] Slavery was not an aberration in the Americas. It was the norm. This is not to say that there were not a few Europeans who voiced their opposition to slavery. They were in the minority. It was not until the latter part of the eighteenth century, that there was a serious movement to end slavery. According to Eric Williams the chief motivating factor behind the movement was economic. West Indian and American sugar manufacturing was in decline.[173]

The second factor that should be noted with regard to slavery is that many good, outstanding citizens who were leaders of churches and government participated in the slave trade. Indeed, many Christian leaders played a pivotal role in the slave trade. Mark Twain makes some very cogent observations about Christian participation in slavery and the slave trade. "Christian England supported slavery and encouraged it for two hundred and fifty years, while the "Church's consecrated ministers looked on, sometimes taking an active hand, the rest of the time indifferent. England's interest in the business may be called a Christian interest, a Christian industry." Homes and families were destroyed "to

---

[170]Mark Twain, "Bible Reading and Religious Practice" in *The Complete Essays of Mark Twain,* edited with an introduction by Charles Neider (Garden City, NY: Doubleday, 1963), p. 570.

[171]Ibid., p. 570

[172]Ibid., p. 570.

[173]Eric Williams, *Capitalism and Slavery*; introduction by D. W. Brogan (London, England: Andre Deutsch, 1964).

the end that Christian nations might be prosperous and comfortable, Christian churches be built, and the gospel of the meek and merciful Redeemer be spread abroad in the earth." Those involved in slavery were, in many respects, very noble citizens of the highest rank. Respectability was attached to slave-trading. "English parliaments aided the slave trade and protected it; two English kings held stock in slave-catching companies." John Hawkins was rewarded with a knighthood after he was successful "in the matter of surprising and burning villages, and maiming, slaughtering, capturing, and selling their unoffending inhabitants..." Twain asserts that there was "hidden prophecy" that Hawkins should name his ship *The Jesus.*[174]

Many Christians, then, were involved in the slave trade. Some Europeans saw the slave trade and slavery as means of Christianizing and saving the souls of Africans.[175] The business of slavery was not conducted by men and women who were simply motivated by sheer greed, but was actually led by individuals many of whom were very pious religious people.[176]

Matthew Gregory Lewis' *Journal* is a classic study in terms of how the white planter perceives himself as a good moral person.[177] The *Journal* also shows how planters had other motivations besides economic greed in terms of slavery such as wanting to be loved, worshipped, adored, and being held in high esteem by others. The behavior of whites was not only economically determined but was sanctioned by their belief system, that is, their religion. Christianity was fundamental to the racial contract during slavery.

In answer to the question, the subheading of this chapter: Whose morality? It is unequivocally white morality, that is, Christian morality.

I want to point out that the view that racism is to a large extent the result of slavery and slavery not the outcome of racism overlooks one very important issue, that is, the treatment of, and the attitude towards the African slaves. African slavery in the Americas is unique in the annals of human history. A number of black scholars have alluded to the physical and psychological brutality of slavery in terms of the capture

---

[174]Twain, "Bible Reading and Religious Practice, p. 570.
[175]Jordan, *White Over Black.*
[176]See, for example, Matthew Gregory Lewis, *Journal of a West India Proprietor, Kept During a Residence in the Island of Jamaica,* (New York, NY: Negro Universities Press, 1969); Originally published (London: John Murray, 1834).
[177]Lewis, *Journal.*

and shackling of slaves in Africa, the long sea voyages in shackles and cramped holds, the auctioning and separation of African families in the Americas to slave holders, the use of the whip and other brutal physical forms of punishment on the old, the young, women, pregnant women, men, the sick, and the treatment of the Africans as beasts and in some instances worse than beasts.[178] References have also been made to the fact that the Africans were not permitted to learn to read and write (and this was particularly cruel in the light of the fact that Africans were living in a very advanced literate society) and were coerced into giving up their language, religion, and their culture and indeed their African identity.

There are, however, a few black scholars who, while noting that slavery was harsh and brutal, argue that brutality was the ethos of the age and that indeed many whites were subjected to harsh and brutal punishment.[179] This outlook, however, is myopic in the light of its focus on physical cruelty of slavery. It does not take into account all the other psychological factors (and we are not even going to include at this point economic factors) alluded to, such as, the break up of families, slaves being regarded as three fifths of a human being, slaves not being permitted to read and write, and the important fact that the badge of color, for the African, was always present. But even in the light of these dehumanizing traumatic psychological experiences, to which whites were not subjected, we would not have addressed the most brutal aspect of slavery which is the coercion of the slave to surrender the African worldview. Our epistemology has been influenced by the dominant European view so that even when we highlight the trauma of slavery in the Americas, we do not really analyze the institution from the perspective of the slaves as human beings. No doubt influenced by European culture, DuBois used disparaging terms, such as "savage"[180] regarding the African. In my reading, however, he comes closest to asking some pertinent questions from the standpoint of the African as human being.

I can almost categorically state that books on slavery do not raise the issue, as DuBois did, regarding philosophical questions with which the slaves must have wrestled regarding slavery and life: "What did slavery

---

[178]See for example, Bell, *And We Are Not Saved*; Bell, *Faces*; Douglass, *Narratives*; DuBois, *Souls*; King, *Why We Can't Wait*; Frazier, *The Black Church*; Williams, *Alchemy*; Wright, *Black Robes*.

[179]A proponent of this view is Eric Williams. See Williams, *Capitalism and Slavery*.

[180]DuBois, *Souls,* p. 212

mean?...What was the attitude to the World and Life? What seemed to him good and evil—God and the Devil?"[181] Rarely do we ponder or reflect as DuBois did, about the "longings and strivings" and the "heart burnings and disappointments"[182] of the slave. It is very significant to note that DuBois asserts that "[a]nswers to such questions can only come from a study of Negro religion as a development, through its gradual changes from the heathenism of the Gold Coast to the institutional Negro Church of Chicago".[183] The "religion" of the Africans from the Gold Coast is "heathenism".[184]

Very few black scholars have attempted to systematically refute the allegation that Africans are inherently morally inferior, and that the African belief system is identified with that which is evil. Some black scholars have responded to the charge that Africans are primitive savages by pointing to the barbarity of the Europeans in the light of their colonialism, their treatment of indigenous peoples, and their involvement in slavery and the slave trade.[185] Some scholars have asserted that Africa had a glorious civilization of the past which included the building of the pyramids of Egypt.[186]

Walter Rodney warned, however, that although black people have to counter "historical myths" postulated by Europeans, the goal should be to motivate black people for revolutionary action and not to "impress" whites. According to Rodney, scholars have tended to focus their studies on highly developed African states, such as "Egypt, Kush, Ethiopia, Ghana, Benin." As a result, the focus has been on the "elite groups and dynasties" and thus the "culture" and the "everyday lives" of millions of Africans are excluded from African history and these include not only those who live outside these kingdoms, but those ordinary men and

---

[181]Ibid., p. 212-213.

[182]Ibid., p. 213

[183]Ibid. p. 213

[184]Ibid., p. 214

[185]Aime Cesaire, *Discourse on Colonialism,* translated by Joan Pinkham (New York, NY: Monthly Review Press, 1972, c. 1955); Cheik Anta Diop, *Civilization or Barbarism: An Authentic Anthropology,* translated from the French by Yaa-Lengi Meena Ngemi, edited by Harold J. Salemson and Marjolijn de Jager (Chicago, IL: Lawrence Hill Books, 1991, c. 1981).

[186]See for example, Molefi Keti Asante, *The Afrocentric Idea,* (Philadelphia: Temple University Press, 1987);-------, *Kemet, Afrocentricity and Knowledge,* (Trenton, NJ: Africa World Press, 1992, c. 1990); Diop, *Civilization or Barbarism.*

women who live within these politically developed kingdoms. For Rodney, we can be very proud of African mores and values. "In reconstructing African civilizations," Rodney claims, "the concern is to indicate that African social life had meaning and value, and the African past is one with which the black man in the Americas can identify with pride." Rodney then lists some of the important values in African society, such as "hospitality, the role and treatment of the aged, law and public order, and social tolerance."[187]

It needs to be emphasized that the African psyche had to undergo a radical transformation not only in the light of the often cited brutality of slavery in terms of floggings, break up of families, rape of women, inaccessibility to literacy and learning but in terms of the African having to adopt an entirely different worldview. "It was a terrible social revolution," as DuBois asserts, even though he adds the caveat that "some traces were retained of the former life..."[188] It is significant to note that Frazier is not all in agreement with DuBois about the retention of African culture. Frazier feels that African culture was almost entirely eliminated. Slavery "not only destroyed the traditional African system of kinship and other forms of organized social life but it made insecure and precarious the most elementary form of social life which tended to sprout anew, so to speak, on American soil—the family.[189]

Therefore when my black Christian family and friends tell me that "nothing matters but the individual relationship with God", I cannot help but think that individual relationship with God reduces the individual to the state of "atomization"[190] and thus perpetuates the individual's oppression. Atomization—separation from family, kin, and community—was the chief psychological weapon whites used to enforce slavery. Not only does atomization lead to social isolation and hence social death[191]—an important dimension of slavery—but it totally obfuscates the reality and the ugliness of social, political, and economic injustices from the purview of the individual. The individual can bend

---

[187] Walter Rodney, *The Groundings With My Brothers*, (London, UK: Bogle-L'Ouverture, c1975, c. 1969);-------, *How Europe Underdeveloped Africa*, rev. ed., (Washington, DC: Howard University Press, 1981, c. 1972), p. 50-58.

[188]DuBois, *Souls*, p. 216.

[189]Frazier, *The Negro Church in America*, p. 13.

[190]Ibid., p. 12.

[191]Orlando Patterson, *Slavery and Social Death: A Comparative Study*, (Cambridge, MA: Harvard University Press, 1982).

the mind of God according to his or her need.   Thus oppression is perpetuated. "The slave trade", as Frazier points out, "was one of the important factors that tended toward the atomization and the dehumanization of the slaves."[192]

What is of extreme significance and needs to be addressed is that the world view that the African was forced to adopt, demanded that the African learn concepts, such as sin, redemption, incarnation, heaven, hell, faith, eternity, hope, salvation, resurrection, communion, divine forgiveness, etc. Communication with the spirit world or "supreme being" would be radically different. The African now had to deal with a metaphysical world view that, as p'Bitek argues, is alien to the African.[193] Not only did the African have to accept a metaphysical world view in terms of religion, but he or she had to accept the European terms, concepts, ideas, and a frame of reference regarding people who are not Christians including Africans. They could be Moors, heathens, pagans, or idol worshippers.

The Christian worldview of Africans as pagans or heathens has several implications. As far as some Europeans were concerned, there was not one good element within the African culture; there was not one redeeming feature.[194] According to Albert J. Raboteau, "European travelers frequently identified African gods with demons or devils and often accused Africans of devil worship."[195]

Every aspect of African culture had to be totally uprooted. This is of extreme significance, and a very important aspect of what Charles Mills terms, the Racial Contract, that is not addressed. The complexion and physiognomy of the Africans compounded the view that the African culture is evil.[196]

To attribute this disparaging European perspective of the African world view which would have devastating consequences for the Africans, solely to the desire of the planters to make a profit, although this aspect is important and very significant, renders a somewhat shallow and superficial analysis of slavery. Viewing the African culture as barbaric, savage, pagan, heathen and uprooting the African culture were integral

---

[192] Frazier, *The Negro Church,* p. 12

[193] Okot p'Bitek, *African Religions in European Scholarship,* (Kampala, Uganda: Uganda Literature Bureau, 1980).

[194] See, for example, Phillippo, *Jamaica.*

[195] Albert J. Raboteau, *Slave Religion:" The Invisible Institution in the AnteBellum South"* (New York, NY: Oxford University Press, 1978), p. 9

[196] Jordan, *White over Black.*

parts of European morality, based on Christianity, and hence salient factors of the Racial Contract. Many Europeans believed, and some blacks and some whites do currently share that belief, that slavery redeemed Africans from total depravity and immorality. Not only were sermons preached to the African based on the Word of God, the Bible, about Africans' worship of the devil, the evil ways of the Africans, and the need for Africans to become Christians, but Africans who resisted being converted to Christianity and those who insisted in pursuing the culture of their ancestors were subjected to persecution which included death.[197] Many Africans, then, were coerced into giving up their African beliefs and way of life. Some willingly became Christians finding Christianity a superior religion particularly in the light of Christianity having a written text and the perception of Christianity as more powerful than African traditional religions since Christianity was the religion of the powerful slave holders.[198]

The Christian religion, then, was not used simply to justify slavery. It is not as though the Christian religion played a passive role in slavery. The Christian religion gave divine sanction and hence moral sanction to the establishment and the perpetuation of the slave trade and slavery. The slave trade, as Mark Twain pointed out, was "indeed a Christian invention"[199]. Not only did European Christians actively engage in slavery and the slave trade, but the Christian religion was used to strip the Africans of their culture.

Christianity was supposed to provide the regenerative values that would transform the lives of the Africans.

In terms of transforming human lives, no other religion promises its adherents the moral redemptive power as Christianity. Christian ministers preach sermons which claim that baptism, christening, speaking in tongues, being born again, confirmation are means of radically changing one's life. Ministers and preachers point to passages of Scripture where Jesus stated that those who follow him "shall not walk in darkness but shall have the light of life." Most other religions require of their followers rigorous sacrifices, rituals, or discipline to meet the criteria of morality. Many Christian adherents claim, and even non-Christians too, that the very demand of other religions that their followers adhere to sometimes a very strict code of discipline, demonstrates the

---

[197]See, for example, Curtin, *Two Jamaicas*; Phillippo, *Jamaica*.

[198]See for example, Curtin, *Two Jamaicas*; Gordon, *Our Cause His Glory*; Phillippo, *Jamaica*.

[199]Twain, "Bible Reading and Religious Practice", p. 570.

inferiority of the other religions to the Christian religion. Compared to other religions, Christianity also makes some moral claims that support the perspective that it is a superior religion. The Christian religion is open to everyone. One does not have to be born into the religion. Christianity preaches love for all and forgiveness. Above all, Christianity preaches egalitarianism.

It is apparent, however, that Christianity has not been the transformative ideology in terms of the redemption of Africans. After almost four hundred years, and five hundred for parts of the Caribbean, of exposure and conversion to Christianity, blacks are still perceived as they ever were, as morally degenerate.

Indeed Williams' observation that the "blackness of black people in this society has always represented the blemish, the uncleanliness, the barrier separating the individual and society"[200] indicates that there has not been any change over the centuries in the perception of blacks as "hardened in idolatry, wallowers in human blood, cannibals, drunkards...cursed...with all the vices.....brutal and savage... and utterly incapable of understanding the first rudiments of the Christian religion."[201]

The perception of blacks in spite of three centuries and in some cases four centuries of being Christianized has not really changed. We find a striking similarity with regard to the perception of blacks and the perception of the Dalits of India. According to Ambedkar, "there is nothing that can make" the Dalits "pure. They "are born impure, they are impure while they live, they die...impure, and they give birth to children who are born with the stigma of Untouchability affixed to them. It is" concludes Ambedkar, "a case of permanent, hereditary stain which nothing can cleanse."[202] It would seem to me in the light of appalling economic and social conditions of blacks—disproportionate number of black men and women in prison, failing schools, unemployment, black on black crime—the fact that blacks have been Christianized for more than three centuries, and the regenerative power of Christianity, then blacks must carry a "permanent, hereditary stain which nothing can cleanse." This is even more incredible in view of the fact that not only are blacks Christians; blacks devote an inordinate amount of time, money, effort and energy to Christianity, in many instances, far more than whites.

---

[200]Williams, *The Alchemy,* p. 198.

[201]Phillippo, *Jamaica,* p. 386-387.

[202]Ambedkar, *The Untouchables,* p. 21.

The Christian will adamantly claim that while the orthodox Hindu will find justification for the social ostracism of the Dalit based on passages of Hindu Scripture, no such justification for the ostracism of blacks will be found in the Bible. Indeed Christians will point to passages of Scripture that emphasize equality, love, and unity. A passage that is often quoted is "There is neither Jew nor Greek, there is neither bond or free, there is neither male nor female, for ye are all one in Jesus Christ. (Galatians 3: 28 KJV).

The problem with this approach is that one can always find Scripture passages to counter verses that purport integration and unity. Let us not forget that Christian religious leaders found Scripture passages to support slavery[203] for centuries. Although undoubtedly the Bible contributes to the perpetuation of oppression of blacks, you will not find the answer for the reasons with regard to the wide gulf that exists between the practice of Christianity in terms of the stigmatization and oppression of blacks on the one hand and the postulation of Christianity as egalitarian on the other in the Bible alone. One has to look at Christianity to a large extent as a whole in terms of its history, doctrines, and precepts.

---

[203]Kahl, *The Misery of Christianity.*

CHAPTER FOUR

CHRISTIANITY:
GULF BETWEEN PRECEPT AND PRACTICE?

> *One of the shameful tragedies of history is that the very institution which should remove man from the midnight of racial segregation participates in creating and perpetuating the midnight.*[204]

Martin Luther King, Jr.

It is not that some black scholars and some black writers have not, in their analysis of the black condition, raised the issue of the Christian religion. Frederick Douglass in his *Narratives* cites many instances to support his claim that the more religious the slave holders are, the crueler they are likely to be. Douglass argues "most unhesitatingly that the religion of the south is a mere covering of the most horrid crimes—a justifier of the most appalling barbarity,—a sanctifier of the most hateful frauds,—and a dark shelter under which the darkest, foulest, grossest, and most infernal deeds of slave holders find their strongest protection."[205] Douglass recounts in graphic detail the cruelty of Thomas Auld, and Mr. Covey who are very religious. "Prior to his [Thomas Auld] conversion, he relied upon his own depravity to shield and sustain him in his savage barbarity; but after his conversion, he found religious sanction and support for his slaveholding cruelty."[206]

There is a very wide gulf between the precepts of Christianity and the practices of its followers. The issue of Christians acting in a most barbarous and inhumane manner struck Douglass forcibly for it was not only religious slave masters "who were the meanest and basest, the most cruel and cowardly" but also ministers of religion and religious leaders. Rev. Weeden owed a female slave whose "back, for weeks, was kept literally raw, made so by the lash of this merciless *religious* wretch."[207] Rev. Hopkins "was even worse than" Rev. Weeden for the former's "peculiar feature of his government was that of whipping slaves in advance of deserving it."[208] There were also the religious leaders who would rather see the slaves

---

[204]King, *Strength to Love,* p. 500.
[205]Douglass, *Narrative,* p. 86.
[206]Ibid., p. 67, See also Chap IX, X, and Appendix.
[207]Ibid., p. 87, italics his.
[208]Ibid., p. 87.

"wrestling, boxing, and drinking whiskey" than "learn how to read..."[209]

According to Douglass, "between the Christianity of this land, and the Christianity of Christ, I recognize the widest possible difference...."[210] To call the "religion of this land, Christianity" is "the climax of all misnomers...."[211] Douglass lists a litany of "inconsistencies" between the Christian religion and what is actually practiced. "We have," asserts Douglass, "men stealers for ministers, women-whippers for missionaries, and cradle-plunderers for church members."[212] The same person who "wields the blood-clotted cowskin during the week fulls the pulpit on Sunday...men" are "sold to build churches, women sold to support the gospel, and babes sold to purchase the Bibles for the *poor heathen!*"[213] He points out how "the slave prison and the church stand near each other." One may hear simultaneously the "clanking of fetters and the rattling of chains in prison, and the pious psalm and solemn prayer in the church." The "pulpit" is supported by "blood stained gold" and the "pulpit, in return, covers his infernal business with Christianity."[214]

It is very significant that Douglass highlights not only the discrepancies between religious beliefs and actual practice in the light of the inhumane and barbaric treatment of slave masters towards their slaves but he actually underscores the fact that the more religious the slave master is, the crueler he is likely to be. "Were I to be again reduced to the chains of slavery," writes Douglass, "next to that enslavement, I should regard being the slave of a religious master, the greatest calamity that could befall me. For of all slaveholders with whom I have ever met, religious slave holders are the worst."[215]

I am trying to think how it would help his cause, that is, appealing to abolitionists by highlighting the fact that religious slave masters are the worst. This view is supported by the fact that in an Appendix to the *Narratives,* Douglass states that as he re-read what he had written, he feared that he may have conveyed the impression based on his "tone" and "manner respecting religion" that he is "an opponent of all religion."[216] He is against "*slaveholding religion* of this land, and with no possible reference to

---

[209]Ibid., p. 89
[210]Ibid., p. 120.
[211]Ibid., p. 120
[212]Ibid., p.120-121.
[213]Ibid., p.121.
[214]Ibid., p. 121.
[215]Douglass, *Narrative,* p. 86-87.
[216]Ibid., p. 120.

Christianity proper....”[217]

I guess it would be too much to ask of Douglass, a former slave, in the Nineteenth Century to delve into reasons: 1) why the more religious slave masters are, the crueler they are likely to be 2) why there is a great discrepancy between Christian precept and practice. Douglass speaks of the “Christians of America” as “they who are represented as professing to love God whom they have not seen, whilst they hate their brother whom they have seen.”[218]

About a hundred years prior to Douglass’ observations that the more religious a slave master is, the crueler he is likely to be, a number of blacks formed their own churches because of indignities to which they were subjected in white churches. These indignities included sitting in the rear of the church or sitting in the galleries, being dragged off their knees while praying because they were sitting in the front of the gallery and not at the rear, and not being allowed to preach or minister to white congregations.[219] In the mid-twentieth century, a hundred years after Douglass wrote, white missionaries would flock Jamaica ostensibly to convert Jamaicans in an effort to stem the tide of communism. While every attempt was made to convert Jamaicans, white American missionaries were absolutely silent about their segregated churches in the United States of America and the fact that blacks have very rarely been accepted by white Christians as brothers and sisters in Christ.

I have already alluded to the fact that in *The Souls of Black Folk,* DuBois made some very cogent observations about religion and blacks. In *The Souls of Black Folk,* Dubois makes a significant departure from Douglass, however, in that whereas Douglass points to the failings of white Christianity, DuBois’ main focus is on the black church and how the religion poses for blacks an “ethical paradox” in the light of the stigmatization of blacks. It is only in a brief biography of Alexander Crummell that some issues regarding the behavior of white Christians are raised.

Crummell, a committed African American Christian, is thwarted at every step by the prejudice of white Christians. He is unable to attend a school in New Hampshire because the “godly farmers hitched ninety yoke of oxen to the abolition schoolhouse and dragged it to the middle of a swamp”.[220]   Crummell is barred from entering General Theological

---

[217]Ibid., p. 120.

[218]Ibid., p. 123.

[219]Frazier, *The Negro Church*; Lincoln and Mamiya, *The Black Church*; Mathews, *Richard Allen.*

[220]Ibid., p. 235.

Seminary of the Episcopalian Church because he is black. Maybe some time in the future, blacks will be admitted, he was told, but not now. According to DuBois, when Crummell tried to reason with them, he was firmly turned down, was actually physically removed, and told he was rebelling against "God's law".[221] DuBois makes the same observation that Douglass made some fifty years before and King would make a hundred years later. Often the main perpetrators of the oppression of blacks are good Christian individuals. The men who barred Crummell from entering the seminary were not "wicked men,—the problem of life is not the problem of the wicked, —they were calm good men, Bishops of the Apostolic Church of God, and strove towards righteousness."[222]

Crummell was eventually ordained an Episcopalian priest. It is significant to note that according to DuBois, Crummell was concerned about the "great shortcoming", the "fatal weakness" of blacks, "the dearth of strong moral character, of unbending righteousness."[223] It is the same theme repeated over the centuries: blacks are immoral. Crummell sees their immorality as a result of "long years of mistreatment" under "slavery and servitude."[224] The panacea would be the same as the panacea for their heathen, pagan, devil worshipping forbears: they should be Christianized.

In 1842, Crummell succeeded in having his own church in Providence. In spite of his hard work, preparing his sermons, visiting the sick, talking often to people on the streets, the membership of his church dwindled. Crummell, claims DuBois, was not only plagued by self doubt but also doubt about blacks' willingness to rise from their "squalor". When dealing with blacks, what could he *expect*?[225] We need to ask what was the "squalor" of the blacks and what did Crummell hope to accomplish in a denomination that saw him as an inferior being based on his ancestry?

Admitting failure to his Bishop, based to some extent on the fact that there were not many blacks in his parish, Crummell was sent with a letter to the Bishop of Philadelphia where there was a larger black population. He was told by the Bishop of Philadelphia that his application would be accepted only under the conditions that no Black priest or any Black church could be represented at the convention. Crummell refused to accept the church on those terms.[226] He then built a church in New York where

---

[221]Ibid., p. 236-237.
[222]Ibid., p. 236-237.
[223]Ibid., p. 238.
[224]Ibid., p. 238.
[225]Ibid., p. 238, italics, his.
[226]Ibid., p. 240.

according to DuBois, "he labored in poverty and starvation scorned by his fellow priests."[227] In spite of DuBois' salient analysis regarding religion, for DuBois, Christianity is the norm. African religion is superstitious, barbarous, and heathenish.[228]

Martin Luther King's *Why We Can't Wait* is to a large extent his response to criticisms from Christians and other religious groups regarding his leadership in the Civil Rights struggle. In *Why We Can't Wait*, King is at pains to outline the decadent conditions of Blacks as a result of inhumane segregation laws and attitudes. He also points out why Christians must be involved to bring about changes. In King's famous *Letter from the Birmingham Jail* written specifically to white Christian and Jewish clergymen who had publicly admonished him, King echoed the sentiments expressed by DuBois and Douglass regarding the repressive behavior of people of good will. "I have sometimes reached the regrettable conclusion", claims King, "that the Negro's greatest stumbling block in the stride towards freedom is not the White Citizens Councilor or the Klu Klux Klanner, but the white moderate...who paternalistically feels that he can set the timetable for another man's freedom."[229] King asserts that he finds that at times he has "wept over the laxity of the church"[230]. "The contemporary church", states King, is a weak ineffectual voice with an uncertain sound. It is so often the arch-supporter of the status quo."[231] The "power structure" is "not disturbed by the presence of the church," rather it is "consoled by the church's silent and often even vocal sanction of things as they are."[232]

Most of the scholars of the latter part of the twentieth century do not include religion in their critique and analysis of the status of blacks although the Christian religion, as DuBois points out, plays a very important role in the lives of blacks and is an important aspect of American history.[233] Indeed some of the scholars who have critically analyzed the status of blacks are Christians.

For Cornel West, the Christian religion is an important aspect of his philosophy. What is needed to counter the nihilistic threat that exists in the Black community is a "politics of conversion". The center of this "politics

---

[227]Ibid., p. 241

[228]Ibid., p. 218.

[229]Martin Luther King, Jr., "Letter from Birmingham Jail" in *The Essential Writings and Speeches of Martin Luther King, Jr.*, p. 295.

[230]Ibid., p. 299.

[231]Ibid., p. 300.

[232]Ibid., p. 300.

[233]DuBois, *Souls,* p. 213.

of conversion" is a "love ethic". The "love ethic has nothing to do with sentimental feelings or tribal connections. Rather it is a last attempt of generating a sense of agency among a downtrodden people".[234]

According to West, blacks have only a "few, if any communal resources" to help them "cope with the onslaught of a market driven economy and consumerism". If blacks do not have "vital communities to hold up previous ethical and religious ideals, there can be no coming to a moral commitment—only personal accomplishment is applauded."[235] The only "beacons of hope" within the black community "are the Christian churches, the Muslim mosques, and character-building schools".[236]

We have then a repetition of the theme: blacks are immoral—what blacks need is Christianity. Should it not be the case then that since most blacks are Christians and since Christianity is the source of morality that most blacks should be regarded as upright moral citizens? This, however, is not what we find. The "moral, upright" black is the exception rather than the rule. Most blacks are regarded as lazy, criminals, promiscuous, drug addicts. Blacks are far more likely to be frisked by policemen than whites.

In Bell's allegorical work, *And We Are Not Saved*, the Curia Sisters claim that even though the Bible was given to the slaves by white men to be a "pacifier", the slaves used the Bible as a source of inspiration. It inspired the slaves to "survive" and it created the "spirituals", a theology in song.[237] I can't help but ask: How did the slaves "survive"? Slavery lasted almost three hundred years. A number of generations, then, were born and died in slavery. It is interesting to note that for Douglass, slave songs were poignantly painful. Douglass "is astonished since" he "came to the North to find persons who would speak of the singing among slaves as evidence of their contentment and happiness". For Douglass, it "is impossible to conceive of a greater mistake. Slaves sing most when they are unhappy".[238]

Bell's intimation that the slaves found in Christianity a source of inspiration for their survival is somewhat diametrically opposed to Franklin Frazier's view on the matter. Frazier agrees that the "Negro spirituals" is evidence that the "Negro slave found in Christianity a theology and a new orientation toward the world at large and in doing so he adapted the Christian religion to his psychological and social needs."[239] Frazier,

---

[234]West, *Race Matters,* p. 18-19.
[235]Ibid., p. 37.
[236]Ibid., p. 58.
[237]Bell, *And We Are Not Saved,* p. 252.
[238]Douglass, *Narrative,* p. 32.
[239]Frazier, *The Negro Church,* p. 19.

however, warns about interpreting the "Spirituals with a revolutionary meaning or to claim that they represented disguised plans for escape from slavery" as a number of "Negro intellectuals encouraged by white radicals" assert.[240] Most of the spirituals actually reflect the slaves "concern with death" which was always uppermost in the slave's thoughts. This constant thinking about death then led to the dominance of an "other worldly outlook in the Negro's religion."[241]

If Bell's postulation is that the Bible helped the slave to "survive" slavery by providing solace and comfort in the belief that the next life will be better than this, then from a number of spirituals, the Bible did provide such comfort. I can think of some spirituals however which clearly demonstrate the anguish, pain, humiliation, debasement, barbarity, and dehumanization and indeed atomization of slavery. Not all the spirituals demonstrate hope, joy, or certainty of a future life. For example think of:

> Not by brother or my sister
> But it is me, O Lord
> Standing in the need of prayer
> Not the preacher or the teacher
> But it is me, O Lord
> Standing in the need of prayer...

What could be more heart wrenching than:

> Sometimes I feel like a motherless child
> Sometimes I feel like a motherless child
> Sometimes I feel like a motherless child
> A long way from home, A long way from home

Brought up as many of us were in white institutions of learning where we were often told that the Christianization of the Africans brought civilization to Africa, and the cruel slave master was the deviant rather than the norm, we have developed an epistemology of not seeing, our ancestors, Africans, as human beings and we have actually minimized the pain, suffering, and anguish of slavery. In actual fact we really do believe that Africans were far better off under slavery where they were exposed to

---

[240]Ibid., p. 19
[241]Ibid, p. 20-21.

Christianity than in Africa where they were pagans, devil worshippers, and evil doers.

Bruce Wright is somewhat singular in his critique of the Christian religion. Like Douglass, Wright feels that the Christian religion is intricately linked to discriminatory practices. Unlike Douglass, however, Wright is not apologetic regarding his scathing assessment of the Christian religion and indeed Christian morality. According to Wright, the "Criminal Courts buildings...reflect the ethos not only of New York City but of the Christian prejudices of the nation."[242]

Wright cites several instances where white Christians systematically barred him, based on his skin color, from attending certain colleges or from participating in certain activities. Thus his hopes, like the hopes of many blacks were blighted from attending certain schools and institutions or participating in certain activities. Unlike Douglass, however Wright makes no apologies about his view regarding religion. Wright openly declares his apostasy. It was the exclusion from Princeton "that famous citadel of learning that refuge for Einstein and Thomas Mann and other persecuted intellectuals" that caused Wright to "turn my back on Christianity and ridicule its pretensions, its pomp and its rituals, especially as exhibited in the half royal, half-pagan trappings of Roman Catholicism, the branch of Christianity into which I was born"[243]

Incidentally, on June 4, 2001, sixty-five years after Bruce Wright was barred from Princeton University because "university officials noticed the color of his skin...in an effort to address the university's past...Princeton graduating seniors made Justice Wright...83 years old an honorary member of their class". [244]

Wright's rejection from Notre Dame "the most famous of the Catholic universities" was to be another critical blow. Eventually, Wright had no other recourse but to attend Lincoln University the college opened for blacks in 1854. Wright points out how blacks were barred from other white Christian organizations. Blacks were excluded "totally and without exception" from the white Y.M.C.A.".[245]

I think we can unequivocally state that from a review of the literature regarding blacks and their experience of racism in America that in terms of the more than two hundred years of black experience within the Christian

---

[242]Ibid., p. 95.

[243]Ibid., p. 32.

[244]Karen W. Arenson, "Princeton Honors Ex-Judge Once Turned Away For Race", *The New York Times,* Thursday June 05, 2001.

[245]Ibid., p. 30-38.

religion there is a wide gulf between precept and practice regarding the Christian religion.

Unfortunately, in my view there has been a lack of an in-depth and rigorous analysis of the Christian religion by most black scholars in their critique of American society when that religion permeates so profoundly the lives of black people. The lack of in-depth analysis by black scholars is very significant. There is very little scholarly work to counter a prevailing view that Christianity was a major contributing factor with regard to the survival of blacks through slavery and the Jim Crow era. I must say, however, the failure to rigorously critique and analyze the Christian religion in the light of black experience in America may not be entirely due to a reluctance to do so.

I should point out that Mills in his postulation of the Racial Contract does make the claim which I will address later that the Christian religion is built into the Racial Contract.[246]

Some of the possible reasons for the lack of analysis of the Christian religion by black authors may be due to the way the Christian religion is packaged and promulgated in the wider society. This is very important because inherent factors in the attitude and perception of the Christian religion by the wider society serve to obfuscate the weaknesses of the Christian religion and thus is a salient factor in the oppression of blacks.

When judging other religions and other world views, every act, and every deed of the adherents of the non-Christian religion is usually examined and itemized with microscopic detail. Conclusions are generally drawn about the religion from the data gathered, that is, the acts and the deeds of the adherents of the religion irrespective of the values, mores, and norms of the religion.

If the adherents of a particular religion fall short of the stated doctrines and creeds of the religion, the failure is attributed to the weakness and inferiority of the gods or the god of that particular religion. Where there are no stated doctrines and creed, such as, the African traditional religions or the Native American religions, values and norms cannot possibly be extrapolated from the beliefs and customs of its adherents. The reasoning is as follows: The gods of the Africans are evil; therefore the Africans commit evil deeds or the Africans commit evil deeds; therefore the gods of the Africans are evil. Thus Naylor asserts that it is the religious beliefs of the pagan Africans that cause them to commit the most barbaric and savage deeds.[247] It is the religious beliefs of the Hindus that cause them to carry out

---

[246]Mills, *The Racial Contract.*

[247]Wilson S. Naylor, *Daybreak in the Dark Continent,* (New York, NY: Young People's Missionary Movement, 1904).

the most repressive acts.[248]   African scholars, such as, Kamuyu-wa-Kang'ethe, V. E. Akubueze Okwuosa, and Okot p'Bitek have pointed out how European missionaries, and scholars have vilified African traditional religion while upholding Christianity as the norm.[249]

The criterion of the Divine, that is the God, or Gods or Goddesses, is the sum of his or their acts is not what is applied to the Christian religion. If Christians fail to live up to the precepts of their religion (which for the most part they do) several reasons are given for the wide gulf between practice and precept. (i) The person is not a true Christian (ii) the behavior is due to the period or time they lived in. (iii) the person or denomination is being unfairly persecuted by the media. A number of Christians have used this argument with regard to the accusation of abuse and other violations by powerful magnates in the Church. (iv) It does not matter what anybody including the minister does, the important thing is my relationship with God.

I do not think there is any other group that is more likely to give these reasons in terms of Christian apologetics than black Christians, particularly black Christian women.   They do not see how their perception of Christianity particularly the "individual relationship" with God leads to atomization of their personhood, and that the "atomization" is a major factor of their oppression. I know quite a number of black Christians who tithe. I ask them: Where does that money go? They tell me, it does not matter what the minister does with the money (that is, one-tenth of every paycheck—and some ministers or pastors demand one-tenth from the gross income!). They are giving that money to God.

My sister told me a couple years ago that West Indians in a church in Toronto were given graphic details in the newspaper of the wealth that their white pastor and his son had accrued from the donations of the congregation. One would think, my sister felt, that the West Indians had enough ammunition to question the minister and sever ties from the church. Instead, the West Indians were very offended by the article and declared their support of the minister.   They would continue to pour money into his wealthy coffers.

A number of Christians really do believe that if they cease to tithe, they

---

[248]J. A. DuBois, *Hindu Manners, Customs, and Ceremonies,*   (Oxford, England: Clarendon Press, 1899).

[249]Kang'ethe, "The Death of God: an African Viewpoint" in *Caribbean Journal of Religious Studies,* Vol. 6, No. 2,   p. 1-23;   V. E. Akubueze Okwuosa, *In the Name of Christianity:: the Missionaries in Africa,* (Philadelphia, PA: Dorrance and Co., 1977); p'Bitek, *African Religions in European Scholarship.*

will lose whatever they have, their health, etc. It was from several discussions with black Christians that I learnt how ingrained the Christian religion is in blacks. The issue of tithing was often a source of debates. No amount of argument or reasoning could dissuade one particular black Christian woman from her belief that she *has* to give one-tenth of her salary to keep her job and to maintain good health. Discussions with her pained me very much, particularly because I knew she worked very hard. To tithe was a tremendous sacrifice for her. Her untimely death was shocking. Her husband and her eleven year old daughter, who was very attached to her mother, were heart broken.

I can relate several stories of people who believe in tithing but who nevertheless have lost their jobs or who live almost in penury after several years of generously giving to churches. The ministers in urging members to tithe do not relate such stories. I have yet to meet one person, except ministers, who have amassed a fortune as a result of tithing. If you really do believe that you have to give one-tenth of your salary to God, why don't you put it in a bank somewhere as God's? That money should grow exponentially, according to your belief. When you give money to the church it will end up in a bank anyway, usually as someone's, generally the minister's, account.

I talk about tithing because it is indicative of how blacks view their religion, money, and economics which play an integral role in black oppression. Blacks do not trace where the money goes and how the money that they say they give to God is spent. If they do, they will find that most of that money finally ends up in the bank account of whites whether in terms of payments for cars, mortgages, electricity, water, expensive organs and other equipment, Bibles, hymn books, church robes, furniture, etc.

Some black Christians are at pains to let me know that their churches contribute to Black colleges and some point out that their churches carry out programs to aid the community. This is not enough. The vast amount of wealth that is poured into black churches should be reflected in black communities. In the light of the poverty, and unemployment of a number of black communities and the display of wealth and opulence by black ministers, based to a large extent on the sacrifices of struggling blacks, it is time for blacks to urge accountability of the ministers and the churches regarding finances.

For many black Christians, the pastor can do no wrong. As a result a number of black ministers are, as Frazier points out "authoritarian" and "petty tyrants" and this attitude is transferred to "other" Black organizations". Because the Church plays a dominant role in the lives of blacks, blacks have had "little education in democratic processes."[250]

It is no longer sophisticated to speak of non-Christian religions as the devil (although some Christian denominations still do) as it was in the past. The point, however, is if other religions have to withstand scathing criticism of their doctrines and creeds particularly when there is a large gap between norms and behavior, then Christianity should not be spared rigorous analysis in the light of the wide gulf between practice and precept. If in other religions, the Gods and Goddesses are the sum of their acts, then in the Christian religion, the Christian God should be the sum of his acts.

Another major reason for the deflection of Christianity from critical analysis is unlike other religions, particularly major religions, the term Christianity is rarely applied as a descriptor. No one in political, economic, or social analysis speaks of Christian Jamaica or Christian Haiti or Christian United States or Christian Rwanda or Christian Latin America or Christian Britain. No one talks about the Christian judge, or the Christian policeman or the Christian teacher or the Christian governor or the Christian congressman or the Christian president.

The label Christian is only applied to the Christian Right generally regarded as fundamentalists or evangelicals. However, in my interaction with a number of Christians, I have found that there are many Catholics, Episcopalians, and Methodists who are as orthodox about their Christian religious beliefs as the fundamentalists. When atrocities were committed in Rwanda, the fact that Rwanda is a Christian country was not included in the analysis. The fact that Haiti, Jamaica, Latin America are Christian countries is not included in the economic and social analyses of these countries. In spite of the postulation that there is separation between Church and State in the United States of America, Christianity plays a critical role in the American society. This fact is highlighted during elections, particularly presidential elections. Yet the fact that most Americans are Christians lies dormant in political, economic, and social analyses.

Consequently, although Christianity plays an integral role in political, economic and social oppression, Christianity's role is obscured by a lack of inclusion in analyses. Why is it that many Latin American and Caribbean countries in which at least ninety-nine percent of the population are Christians are encumbered by poverty, vast inequities in wealth, and crime? Why is it that black Christians who are living in the wealthiest country in the world should almost be living in the same conditions as many of their fellow Christians from Latin America? Should not Christianity as an egalitarian religion, transcend social caste, race, and national boundaries? The identity

---

[250]Frazier, *The Negro Church*, p. 90.

of other religions is regarded as significant with regards to the behavior of their adherents. Not so Christianity. Christianity is compartmentalized and isolated from world view. Black Christians and Latin American Christians do not perceive that they subscribe to a religion that is dominated by medieval thinking; they do not see how this contributes to their oppression.

Christian adherents have not only attacked and in some cases vilified other religions, but secular world views particularly Marxism, and communism, have also been subjected to scathing critical analysis. Marxism and communism are condemned as inherently evil based primarily on the criteria Christians use for other belief systems or world views except their own, the weaknesses, failures and flaws of its adherents. Fingers point to the deeds and acts of socialists and Marxists. The failure of communism in many parts of the globe demonstrates that the communist or Marxist worldview is inherently evil. In the 1960's particularly, Third World students were warned about reading Marx and often had to surreptitiously do so.

A number of writers, however, assert that capitalism and market values are the great progenitors of evil as though the society is basically comprised of two groups: those who are totally driven by profit and greed and those who passively accept their role as major contributors to the wealth of greedy capitalists.[251] One cannot condemn capitalism without looking at the role of Christianity in the rise of capitalism.[252] Maybe black secular scholars feel that Max Weber has exhausted the topic. A black and Third World perspective regarding the role of Christianity in the perpetuation of capitalism and black oppression could be added to Max Weber's thesis.

As I have somewhat intimated, the oversight of a critical analysis of Christianity in the black experience could possibly be due to a distinction between the secular and the sacred in white scholarship. From the dawn of Christianity, but particularly from the Middle Ages, white scholarship has attacked many of the beliefs of Christianity. Works by philosophers and thinkers such as Charles Darwin, Sigmund Freud, Karl Marx, Friedrich Nietzsche, Thomas Paine, Bertrand Russell have systematically critiqued the Christian religion. Indeed J. Everet Green argues that the Afrocentric movement is not really a threat to western scholarship as some have propounded. Western philosophers have been chipping away at the

---

[251]See, for example, West, *Race Matters.*

[252]Max Weber, *The Protestant Ethic and the Spirit of Capitalism,* translated by Talcott Parsons, introduction by Anthony Giddens, (New York: Charles Scribner's Sons, c. 1958).

European thought prior to the Afrocentric movement.[253]

However, like the chameleon, the Christian religion has the remarkable capacity to change and adjust to pervading thoughts, ideas and critique, perceived or otherwise. I can distinctly remember the animosity and hostility of a number of Catholic priests and fundamentalist Christian friends when the personal computers bombarded the market. Some of my fundamentalist Christian friends including a number of Catholic priests declared that "computers were of the world". They would resist buying computers. There were jokes about God being more interested in knee-mail than e-mail. And then to my utter amazement, God found the Internet. In a matter of months, as Christian web pages increased at a phenomenal rate, gone was the view that "computers were of the world". My Christian friends had no qualms about adding the latest computers, and all the technological artifacts—e-mail, web pages etc., to their collection of goods.

There was a time when my fundamentalist Christian friends expressed great skepticism about psychotherapy. A number of denominations shared similar views. Psychology undermined the Christian religion particularly in terms of the concept of original sin, and salvation. Freud not only attacked religion,[254] but proffered solutions to the human condition based on radicalized perception of human beings as controlled by the id, ego, and superego[255] and not a Divine or Holy Spirit. Currently (thirty to forty years ago this was not the case) it is a requirement for a number of denominations that seminarians undergo a battery of psychological testing before they can enter the priesthood. A number of Christians are trained as "Christian counselors" and see no dissonance between being a Christian and giving psychological counseling.

When I was growing up, who would have thought that Praise Dance would ever be performed in Church? Dancing, up to a few years ago, was considered a sin in the Baptist Church. Now dancing is sanitized and presented as Praise Dance.

---

[253]J. Everet Green, "Is the Afrocentric Movement a Threat to Western Civilization?" in *Philosophy Born of Struggle,* ed., Leonard Harris, (Iowa: Kendall/Hunt Publishing, 2000), p.354-367.

[254]Freud, *The Future of an Illusion.*

[255]Sigmund Freud, *The Ego and the Id,* translated by Joan Riviere, revised and edited by James Strachey with a biographical introduction by Peter Gay, (New York, NY: W. W. Norton, c. 1960);-----, *Civilization and Its Discontents,* translated and edited by James Strachey with a biographical introduction by Peter Gay, (New York, NY: W. W. Norton, c. 1961).

James Cone's Black Theology[256] was a response to the cries of Black leaders who had begun to critique the Christian religion as a contributory factor to black oppression.[257] In many ways James Cone and other black theologians silenced the voices that undertook a radical critique of Christianity and black oppression by stating that Jesus identifies with Blacks and therefore Jesus is black.

The World Wars in Europe particularly the Second World War shattered the worldview chiefly of the upper class that life is stable, harmonious, and predictable. Existentialism's preoccupation with dread, despair, death, and meaninglessness filled a cultural vacuum and the existence of an omnipotent God was called into question. White European theologians, such as Jurgen Moltmann, Rudolf Karl Bultmann, Paul Tillich, Karl Barth, the Niebuhr brothers[258] were not amiss in developing theologies that would respond to the assertion of some existentialist philosophers that the universe is meaningless.

Indeed some theologians declared that God is dead. The Death of God theology was a culmination of Nietzsche's pronouncement which called into question the traditional interpretation of Scripture and the notion of a moral order in the universe. Famous among these Death of God theologians were Bultmann, Bonheoffer, and Tillich. Bultmann completely accepted the scientific worldview and pronounced that the majority of New Testament text represents a mythical view of the world.[259] Bonhoeffer engaged in a

---

[256]Cone, *A Black Theology of Liberation*; ----, *God of the Oppressed*.

[257]Foreman, *The Making of Black Revolutionaries*; Malcolm X, *Malcolm X Speaks:* Selected Speeches and Statements edited with prefatory notes by George Breitman, (New York, NY: Grove Press, 1965).

[258]M. Douglass Meeks, *Origins of the Theology of Hope,* (Philadelphia, PA: Fortress Press, 1974); Jurgen Moltman, *Theology of Hope,* (London, England: SCM Press, 1967); Rudolf Karl Bultmann, *Keryma and Myth,* (New York, NY: Harper Collins, 2000); Paul Tillich, *The Courage to Be,* (New Haven, CT: Yale University Press, 1952); -------, *The Shaking of the Foundations,* (New York, NY: Charles Scribner's Sons, 1948);---------, *Biblical Religions and the Search for the Ultimate,* (Chicago, IL: University of Chicago Press, 1955); Reinhold Neibuhr, *Moral Man and Immoral Society: A Study of Ethics and Politics,* (New York, NY: Charles Scribner's Sons, 1932);-------, *Christianity and Power Politics,* (New York, NY: Charles Scribner's Sons, 1940); Karl Barth, *The Humanity of God,* (Louisville, KY: John Knox Press, 1960); H. Richard Niebuhr, *The Kingdom of God in America,* (New York, NY: Harper and Row, 1959).

[259]Bultman, *Keryma and Myth*

sustained critique of the Christian religion in his internationally famous text, *The Cost of Discipleship.*[260] Paul Tillich emphatically claimed that you can only speak of God symbolically.[261] This cultural critique of Western theological construction is the culmination of Frederick Schleiermacher's announcement in 1799 that religion is based primarily on feeling.[262]

Blacks are yet to carry out any serious intellectual critique of their received religion.

Liberation theology squelched Marxist critique in Latin America. Feminist theology sought to respond to the analysis of women that the Church is patriarchal and sexist. The Church has always had the apologists to defend its oppression of peoples.

We must not forget also the barbarous and inhumane practices including burning at the stake, whipping, shooting, imprisonment, harassment, ostracism Christianity has used to silence criticism.[263] Many black Christians are totally unaware of how they support inhumane practices against those who are critical of the religion.

While there is, at present, in the United States of America the statutory understanding of the separation between church and state, it is significant to note that the church played a significant role in the establishment of universities and colleges. Harvard is actually named in honor of a young minister, Rev. John Harvard, who bequeathed his library and half his estate to the institution. Yale was founded by a group of clergymen. Gradually universities became increasingly secular and in some cases completely severed academic ties with religious bodies. Consequently for black scholars to raise questions regarding issues which permeate the lives and thoughts of many black Christians, such as the existence of God, the inerrancy of the Bible, the incarnation, redemption, the Second Coming would seriously raise the question as to whether black scholarship is returning to the Middle Ages.

The important issue we need to address, however, is the wide gulf between precept and practice with regard to the Christian religion. It is significant to note that there have been several movements usually by the poor that seek to address the non-egalitarian practice of the Christian religion

---

[260]Dietrich Bonhoeffer, *The Cost of Discipleship,* (Beaverton, OR: Touchstone Press, 1948).
[261]Tillich, *The Courage to Be*; --------, *The Shaking of the Foundations*; --------, *Biblical Religions.*
[262]Friedrich Schleiermacher, *On Religion: Speeches to its Cultural Despisers,* (Cambridge, MA: Cambridge University Press, 1996, c. 1799)
[263]See, for example, Kahl, *The Misery of Christianity.*

particularly in the light of the black experience as stigmatized peoples. The Rastafarian religion largely arose out of the outcast status of blacks within the Jamaican culture. Jamaica has been a Christian country ever since the European occupation of the island in 1494. In 1655, the British captured the island. Under Christian monarchs, Jamaica suffered a most brutal form of slavery, first under the Spanish and then under the British for more than three hundred years.

It always surprises me when African Americans and whites express astonishment that there was slavery in Jamaica. One cannot measure pain and suffering, but slavery in Jamaica was very cruel,[264] and I would say in some instances slavery was more cruel and brutal than it was in the United States. It was on the Jamaican plantations that slaves were prepared for their lives of slavery in the United States and elsewhere. The cruelty of Jamaican slavery was, to some extent, exacerbated by a practice known as "absenteeism". It was not unusual for planters to own plantations in Jamaica while living, except for an occasional visit, in England.[265]

This kind of arrangement, as one can imagine, entailed numerous problems. It was not that planters were particularly humane but managers termed overseers were for the most part not well educated and ill-bred. The fact, too, that these overseers did not have financial investment in the plantation they were now administering undoubtedly often contributed to an indifference to the counter productivity of mal-treatment, inhumane, and cruel treatment of slaves. Indeed, a number of overseers who were from the poor oppressed classes in Britain saw slavery as the opportunity to assume the behavior and attitude of the upper class in Britain. They would mete out to the slaves the treatment, although in many cases far worse, to which they were subjected in Britain.[266]

One very sad thing about slavery in the Caribbean is that there is very little first hand documentation by blacks, as in the case of Frederick Douglass and other slaves in the United States, of an account of slavery. Although some white missionaries kept records about the lives of the slaves, yet the missionaries generally wrote from the European perspective. Indeed it was not unusual for a number of missionaries to identify with whites and to view any kind of resistance by blacks as a threat to them also. At times therefore the Church then worked with the status quo to keep black people in

---

[264]Phillippo, *Jamaica: its Past and Present State*; Lewis, *Journal*.
[265]Phillippo, *Jamaica: its Past and Present State*; Lewis, *Journal*.
[266]Lewis, *Journal*.

oppression.[267] It is out of this oppression that we have the rise of the Rastafari movement.[268]

Unlike the United States, there is very little critical analysis of the Christian religion in terms of oppression written from the experience of the author in Jamaica. The studies on the Rastafarians, like most studies on blacks and oppression in Jamaica, are written from socio-economic perspective and not so much from a critique that includes personal experience. I am going to veer somewhat and share with you in the next few chapters my own personal struggles with the Christian religion and the role the Christian religion played in the stratification and oppression of Blacks in Jamaica.

Before we move to the next chapter, it is very important that we keep in mind Mill's assertion about the Racial Contract, particularly in the light of the fact that many Jamaicans believe that we do not have a "race problem" in Jamaica. The Racial Contract is not limited to the United States. The Racial Contract impacts many areas of the world. "Both globally and within particular nations" claims Mills, "white people, Europeans and their descendants, continue to benefit from the Racial Contract which creates a world in their cultural image."[269] The "interests of whites are "differentially" favor[ed]" by "political states."[270] The "economy" is "structured around the racial exploitation of others" and very significant "a moral psychology (not just in whites but sometimes in nonwhites also) skewed consciously or unconsciously toward privileging them…"[271] For whites, "the status quo of differential racial entitlement" is "normatively legitimate, and not to be investigated further."[272] The Christian religion, I contend is the main worldview that fosters the "differential racial entitlement."

---

[267]Gordon, *Our Cause for His Glory;* Phillippo, *Jamaica: its Past and Present State.*

[268]Leonard E. Barrett, Sr., *The Rastafarians: Sounds of Cultural Dissonance,* revised and updated edition (Boston, MA: Beacon Press, 1988, c. 1977); Campbell, *Rasta and Resistance*; Chevannes, *Rastafari.*

[269]Mills, *The Racial Contract,* p. 40.

[270]Ibid., p. 40.

[271]Ibid., p. 40

[272]Ibid., p. 40.

CHAPTER FIVE

THE RACIAL CONTRACT AND THE WHITENESS OF GOD

Christianity and Black Oppression: Duppy Know Who Fe Frighten

CHAPTER FIVE

THE RACIAL CONTRACT
AND
THE WHITENESS OF GOD

All things bright and beautiful
All creatures great and small
All things wise and wonderful
The Lord God made them all

Each little flower that opens
Each little bird that sings
He made their glowing colors
He made their tiny wings

All things bright....

The rich man in his castle
The poor man at his gate
God made them high and lowly
And ordered their estate

All things bright...

Anglican Hymn

What would land me into serious trouble was my critical analysis of the personality, lifestyle and role of Jesus in terms of our moral development. Every Sunday, and often during the week, it was instilled in us how we should make Jesus Christ the model for our lives. But somehow, trying to fit Jesus in the Jamaican culture was, for me, a clear case of cultural dissonance; he was of a different time, a different place, a different skin color and facial features. In my mind's eye I saw him, as portrayed by the glass stained windows of our church, paintings, and pictures in the Bible, as a young white man with long brown or blonde hair, never smiling, surrounded usually by twelve men or preaching to or teaching an amorphous mass of white people mainly women.

Although most people in my neighborhood claimed that they believed in Jesus and were followers of him, their lives were to a large extent circumscribed by the sheer hustle and bustle of living under a colonial hierarchical regime that pinnacled white people on top, a middle group of mixed race and the vast majority of blacks at the bottom. Important decisions regarding jobs, education, professional advancement, the legal system were often based on skin color. It was in reality a caste society. In spite of our difficulties, to laugh and to have a sense of humor was paramount. In certain aspects, it was easier for me to identify Jesus with the severe colonial administrators than it was to see him as even remotely connected to my everyday world of ordinary colonized people.

In some ways, Jesus seemed irrelevant. Miracles, the Virgin Birth, the resurrection, walking on the sea seemed implausible particularly in the light of the British promulgation, and often enforcement of the view that believing in anything that one could not experience with one's senses—empiricism— was superstition. Obeah was illegal. Education, particularly in the sciences and mathematics was of paramount importance. Indeed to succeed, education was imperative in the British culture. Most jobs required some training and certification—doctors, teachers, librarians, dentists, nurses, policemen. At the same time Jesus' proper English (though quaint at times with thee and thou)—"Follow me and I will make you fishers of men" and not "Cum ya, cum fallah me" served to support the view that proper English is the language of God and thus the colonial administrator is closer to God. I did not find the New Testament relevant in terms of solutions regarding the issue of skin color discrimination, white and light skin color privilege or the navigation of our culture which included the colonial norms, mores, rules and regulations.

It was often intimated in sermons that the Jews were more concerned about their spiritual salvation than their political salvation and, so we, colonized by the British, should be more concerned about our spiritual salvation than our political salvation. In reality, we were more fortunate than the Jews because the Jews were still waiting for the Messiah; they did not recognize that the Messiah is Jesus. We should follow Jesus' example. He did not rebel in any way against the Roman authorities but indeed admonished his followers to "render unto Caesar the things that are Caesar's and unto God the things that are God." The Good Samaritan was often postulated as a model particularly the fact that the Jews considered the Samaritans inferior people. We all were to be Good Samaritans especially with regard to our social betters.

The importance of our spiritual redemption was not only reinforced by prayers and the teaching of religion in schools but also what we were taught about slavery in terms of God's plan for our salvation. We, as African descendants living in the West, were very fortunate that our ancestors were enslaved for had it not been for slavery we would not have been Christianized and hence civilized. Thus slavery not only led to our civilization but also delivered us from the destiny of eternal damnation which is the fate of our ancestors and many Africans who continue to follow the primitive, heathen, savage, and pagan beliefs of their tribal religions.

It took me years to see that there were several flaws in terms of the argument that a perfect, omnipresent, omnipotent Being needed to use the barbaric and cruel system of slavery that lasted for three to four centuries to bring salvation not to all Africans but some Africans and their descendants. At least under the Egyptians who were not Christians, and the Romans who were not Christians, the Jews were able to retain their religion, their language, and to some extent, their culture. Stripped of our African heritage, we had no culture outside of the British culture in terms of language, religion, mores and norms. Most Jamaicans were subsumed under the lower class of the British society. Because of our skin color, we were an outside caste.

In spite of the emphasis in many sermons in the Anglican Church about Jesus' commendation of the meek, and the recommendation that we emulate the lifestyle of Jesus, one of poverty, humility, quiescence to the status quo, and passivity, what was clearly modeled in terms of colonial leadership were elitism, aloofness, and snobbery. Everything seemed to be "up there" and thus beyond our reach—the white ministers from England who preached from pulpits above us and who never socialized with us, the colonial administrators who were above us socially, economically, politically, England the "Mother Country" that was way north of us, and heaven which was up there in the sky somewhere.

The colonial administrators who imposed the Christian religion and saw to it that it was upheld by the support of churches, church administered schools, enforced prayers and the teaching of religion in schools, certainly did not live a life style that emulated the lifestyle of Jesus. The colonial administrators lived in huge opulent homes generally located in the hills overlooking the plains and drove—some were chauffeured—the most expensive cars, sent their children to elite schools, had several servants to attend to them, and the elite who attended St. Andrews Parish Church, the Anglican Church, had reserved pews. I would look at the elite, as they regally sat in their designated pews and wonder,—when they hear sermons based on the story of the rich young ruler, Jesus' directive to be meek, or Jesus' lifestyle of poverty and suffering which culminated in the cross—did they not worry that they were not meeting the criteria of a true Christian? Did they not see themselves as the Pharisees, the Sadducees—the hypocrites who Jesus so often denounced?

103

Apparently, the colonial administrators were not the least perturbed by my thoughts. Indeed, they would pompously walk up the aisle of St. Andrews Parish Church magnificently dressed in their suits and ties, in spite of the tropical heat. Although the minister did wipe the one gold chalice that was passed around after each person sipped the wine, the colonial administrators were usually summoned first for Holy Communion so they were less susceptible to the germs from the saliva of the rest of the congregation. Usually it was members of the elite who were privileged to walk in the aisle and direct the passing of the collection plate from pew to pew. The governor or top colonial officials would generally read the lesson, with of course perfect English diction, from a huge Bible placed on a stand erected about the middle of the church a few yards below the communion rail. The exceptions to the top echelons of the society reading the Bible were the children of the colonial administrators or those who attended elite schools; these young people would read the Bible on Youth Sundays. Because I attended Wolmer's High School for Girls, I therefore was privileged to read the Bible.

The passages I had to read were always handed to me before so I could review them. For my mother, this meant I had to rehearse before the family—siblings, cousins or anyone who was around. Our dining room, separated from the living room only by an arched narrow wall, about two feet in diameter, was the stage. My mother corrected pronunciations and phrasings so that I mimicked the enunciations and intonations of the British colonial administrators to the amusement of my siblings who would quietly giggle all through the rehearsals. My father would sit silently through these sessions hardly able to contain his pride. I also was reminded by my mother that I should walk up the aisle like British royalty, erect. To read the lesson was quite an accomplishment. I am pretty sure I was the first girl of my complexion, two toned brownish yellow, and hair type, straightened springy hair, African features—long rounded at the tip nose, slightly protruding mouth, small somewhat narrow eyes—to read the lesson in St. Andrew Parish Church also known as Half Way Tree Anglican Church.

For several Sundays, I read the lesson without a hitch. Alas, however, one Sunday after a flawless reading of the lesson, and having got to the end of the passage with perfect diction, I sought to close in the usual manner by pausing and stating, "Here endeth the lesson." Well I was utterly taken aback when what came out of my mouth was, "Here hendeth the lesson." I was totally embarrassed because dropping h's or placing them where they were not supposed to be was certainly a sign of illiterate and poorly educated people who would generally drop h's or add h's when they are in the presence of their social betters. I felt therefore as though my roots which at least two generations of my family had tried so hard to bury had suddenly been disclosed just as how often perspiration or rain would reveal the roots of my hair which I tried to conceal by straightening. I do not know how I made it back to the pew with my giggling siblings. For weeks, all I could hear around the house was "here hendeth the lesson." What I felt was acute embarrassment for many months. My *faux pas* would be one of the reasons I used as the justification for leaving the Anglican Church to join the Fundamentalists. Little did I know then that I would feel just as much an outsider among the fundamentalists—indeed even more so than as a member of the Anglican Church.

The Church, and for my family, the Anglican Church, was supposed to be the moral force in our lives. We should find God within the church. We were to love and obey God who was omnipotent, omnipresent, mysterious, perfect and holy. We should see Jesus, who was obedient to God, who lived a life of humility, and who preached love as our model; we should love our neighbors as ourselves.

Except for the few members who lived within our neighborhood or who were our parents' friends, my family had very little social interaction with the ministers, who were white Englishmen, and the members of the church. When I was about fifteen or sixteen, a couple of young men and a junior Jamaican minister in training did visit our home. The young minister in training came to try to convince me to remain in the Anglican Church when I threatened to leave to join the Fundamentalists. The other young men valued my leadership (my father had other ideas and kept a strict eye on me) in the Youth Group of the Anglican Church established to compete with the growing evangelistic groups. I never visited the homes of these young men who either by skin color or class moved within a different social circle. Apart from these young men, the members (outside of those we knew as neighbors or my parents' co-workers) and the ministers never visited our home even in times of illness and death, or we theirs although I knew for a fact that there was social intercourse amongst the elite and the ministers. We were solidly divided by class and skin color. I felt constantly the social barriers that separated the minister and most of the members of the church from my family.

From my observations growing up, nobody really followed the precepts of Jesus. It was often implied that the precepts were not humanly possible to follow. As Jesus himself was reputed to have said, "Narrow is the way that leads to eternal life."[273] But what was the way?, I often wondered, as I saw the many contradictions sometimes exhibited in the same individual. The

---

[273]*Matthew* 7: 14; *Luke* 13: 24 (KJV)

Good Samaritan on Monday could be very hard, cold, and mean on Wednesday. One person could be meek and mild mannered to some and to others egoistic, and snobbish. Christians were often reminded, however, that they should always strive to be perfect. The following of the "narrow way" and the unattainable goal of being perfect, it was often preached, are indications of Christianity's high standards and that is why Christianity is a superior religion. Our objective should be to try to meet the "elusive" goal and for this reason we should attend services and receive Holy Communion for we would inevitably fail.

In truth and in fact it was outside the church, for the most part, that I really observed moral values of goodness, altruism, selflessness, warmth, caring, and affection particularly amongst women. There were the helpers who worked everyday from sunrise to sunset with only occasionally a Sunday off. Without the work of the helper, many women like my mother would have been unable to participate in church activities—play for church services, or teach in Sunday school. These helpers were absolutely selfless in the giving of their time, energy for very little pay.

Most helpers worked every day with only occasionally a Sunday off. They had no leave—sick leave, vacation, personal day. Their employers, for the most part, were Christian middle class and upper class people. Maternity leave most definitely was out of the question and often knowledge of pregnancy by the employer meant immediate termination without the benefit of a day's notice, much less two weeks' pay. My mother was more liberal than many middle class Jamaican women when it came to penalizing helpers for breaking a glass or dish; she was very resolute about not deducting money from the meager wages of the helper for broken or damaged items. She also was totally against the wearing of cap and aprons and the helper living in. Yet, similar to what took place in many Christian middle and upper class Jamaican homes, the helper could not sit at the dining table with us and had to eat in the kitchen. The helper also could not use the same cups and plates although she prepared the food. While we sat and laughed at the large family dining table, and ate from our china set and drank from our matching glasses, the helper would sit all alone in the kitchen eating from an enamel plate and drinking from an enamel cup often without even the benefit of a table in the kitchen on which to place her plate and cup. The helpers rarely complained, and were only too happy to please.

Besides the helpers, who were often kind and generous—these attributes were for the most part unacknowledged—there were friends, neighbors, and extended family who would regularly visit, offering kind comments and words of encouragement to us as children. They would give unstintingly of their time and meager resources—offering solace, comfort or advice through difficulties, death, and helping us as children during our childhood illnesses. Miss Fanny, for example, because of her knowledge of Jamaican herbs and plants, was reputed to save the lives of many children. I was one of the many whose life was saved as a baby by Miss Fanny.

Elementary school teachers including my mother worked hard, never missing a day from work. Besides a heavy teaching load, generally a class of about a hundred children, elementary school teachers would supervise the cooking of lunches for students. Often these were the only solid meals some students had for the day. I can recall my mother and her co-workers walking miles in the hills in a rural area to visit parents or wading through swollen rivers to the school building after a flood would inevitably wash away the only access, the footbridge, to the school.

There were women who adopted children or took care of old people without any compensation from the government or recompense from anyone. There were the "higglers"—women who would get up early in the morning almost every day to catch the bus to Kingston in order to sell their wares in the markets. Some of these women would make tremendous sacrifices so that their children could receive a secondary education.

The relationships amongst extended family, friends, neighbors, and other people of the community including the helpers were very important in the growth and development of young people in Jamaica. To me, this network of relationships was essentially what was missing from the gospels where the focus is on the individual's relationship with God. Indeed disciples left their families and communities to follow Jesus. Slavery was actually used as an ideal in terms of the relationship with God. One should be a slave for God.[274] Deprived of family, lacking a community, the slave could be totally committed to God. I never could understand this imagery, and from my upbringing and experience I am convinced that emphasis on the individual's relationship with God particularly in terms of the imagery of slavery is anti-human.

For my mother, the extended family was very important. Jesus, as portrayed in the gospels, seemed entirely divorced from the life style of my day to day existence. Jesus had a close knit relationship with disciples—all men—and he did address multitudes, but for the most part he was a figure without family—he did not have a wife or children—without neighbors—he wandered from place to place—and without community. There was no model—certainly not in the New Testament—of the kinship and community to which I was exposed—grandparent, aunts, uncles, cousins, and the neighbors and how their feelings, activities, behavior, conflicts impact each

---

[274]Kahl, *The Misery of Christianity*, p. 28-29.

other.

It was therefore difficult for me to see Jesus as a model for he never displayed the sheer joy of being amongst family, neighbors, and community nor did he ever point out how these groups can contribute to one's growth. All that matter, it would seem, is the unilateral relationship with God which in my experience and observation often led to dysfunctional relationships with family, neighbors, and community.

Of great significance also is the fact that Jesus' precepts were not often applicable to conflicts which frequently developed amongst groups—family, neighbors, community. Even if the precepts were applicable, they were often ignored. Many times decisions had to be made that were contingent upon circumstances that had no clear guidelines in the gospels. Can you afford to send money to a mother whose requests seem insatiable when your resources are limited and you have a growing family to feed? What should you do about your neighbor's chickens which constantly scratch and unearth your newly planted garden? Do you surreptitiously have your child christened over her father's objections when you took a vow in the sight of God to obey your husband? Do you tell your father the truth that you broke a glass and risk being whipped severely or you blame the cat for the broken glass? Should you advise someone to remain in an abusive relationship and expose her children to bodily harm or leave her husband and thus risk financial hardships and difficulties raising children mainly boys as a single mother? What do you say to a child as a teacher when she discloses to you that she has been impregnated by her father?

Many women in my social circle rarely turned to the Bible for solace, comfort, guidance or inspiration in terms of making decisions. Women in particular tended to draw on their own experience and tradition. Indeed whenever women gathered, frequent topics of discussion were: marrying, men, and husbands. I was warned several times about men. I must put my "education first". I was not "even to look at a boy". I can distinctly remember a friend and I being warned at sixteen about the pitfalls of marriage with the words "some of the ring dem bun".[275] Sometimes the women's method of handling problems could be humorous. A wife tired of her husband's complaining, told him, "Complaint department closed." The only quote, I remember being widely used from the Bible was "spare the rod and spoil the child." Needless to say I detested that quotation.

---

[275] A literal translation—some of the rings burn—does not have the same connotation and meaning. "Some of the ring dem bun" means many women are anxious to get married but what those rings really entail for women are lots of difficulties and pain.

The Bible as a point of reference was hardly a recourse with regards to dealing with conflicts. The manner in which a lot of problems were handled in my family and amongst neighbors and friends was through the use of reason and argument which at times could develop into heated exchange of words. Sometimes women would take the stand of Jesus before Pilate that is not saying a word or they would convince themselves that they were "turning the other cheek". The result was often a sulky solemn silence towards the offender, a harboring of grievance for days, sometimes months, without the wrongdoer actually knowing what law, rule, or custom he or she had violated. Malice, a weapon often used to punish an offender could be heartless, mean, and cruel; it could have more psychological damage than physical aggression. Sometimes too the Christian would claim that she (usually it's a she) had forgiven the wrongdoer without fully addressing the issue and the impact of the behavior on others which often meant a repetition of the offence.

As a matter of fact I often thought that the whole issue of forgiveness seemed to be a license for people to break not so much the laws, for then there would be repercussions such as prison, fines, etc., but certain moral and ethical codes which were considered Christian. Often the consequences of the violation of these moral and ethical codes were given very little thought. Though you are married, for example, you can succumb to your impulses and father two, three children as a result of extra-marital relationships without thinking what impact these children would have on your wife, your children, and indeed the entire community, because there will be forgiveness.

Indeed it was my mother who inadvertently caused me to think about the issue of God's forgiveness and unethical behavior. She would often point out from time to time with a tinge of animosity (for she was privy to a number of these indiscretions from disconsolate wives) how confident she was that Mr. So and So after living a "profligate" life, having children as a result of extra-marital affairs, and spending money on drink could be found in his declining years seated in church every Sunday with his wife and their children, his arm lovingly extended around his wife—the epitome of a pious devoted husband and father. His sins that caused hurt, grief, pain, humiliation would all be forgiven despite the concrete evidence in the form of the existence of two or so children who though innocent of their parents' deeds would carry the stigma and the scourge of being "outside children", "illegitimate children", "bastard children", not talked about and kept hidden from view. Except in very rare cases these "outside" children would be subjected to the anger, and resentment of the wife and their half-siblings. Though Mr. So and So's sins have been forgiven, the resulting progeny would not be seated in church with his wife and their children.

I guess even before I had reached age sixteen, I had seen too much and heard too much of the pain and suffering particularly of women and children as a consequence of renegade living to feel nothing but skepticism, anger, resentment, and indeed despair regarding the Parable of the Prodigal Son. Transformation of the prodigal does not often eradicate years of suffering, pain, and hurt, as the result of years of lack of resources and unmet psychological needs because for the prodigal, drink, gambling, womanizing had precedence over the needs of family. Sometimes too I would witness feelings of supreme joy over what seemed a total reversal of behavior of the prodigal only to have the behavior repeated once forgiveness was expressed. If the point of the Parable was to teach about God's love, redemption, and salvation, it was entirely lost on me for I never could understand the concepts of God's love, redemption, and salvation. I could not help identifying with the feelings of the son who remained at home. I felt he was unfairly treated.

What the parable of the Prodigal Son epitomized for me was a moral universe in which there was no need to follow social rules and mores. There was no need for discipline and structure. This flew in the face of my reality particularly under a British colonial system that enforced often very rigid rules. If you wanted to be part of the middle class to which my parents' aspired, you had to abide by rules and regulations. In many ways, it seemed to me that Jesus' lifestyle did not synchronize with the culture of the British. Although I did not realize it then, by the time I was fourteen, I had imbibed the view that rules and discipline were very important and that behavior had consequences that often could not be eradicated by "forgiveness". Consequently, I frequently identified with the Sadducees and the Pharisees in terms of their questioning the lack of structure, rules, and discipline which appeared to be the lifestyle of Jesus and his disciples.

Indeed, many many years after I could not help but concur with Freud that "sin is pleasing to God"[276], a conclusion I had drawn, but not quite verbalized from my years of observation of the behavior of many Christians and the matter of God's forgiveness. "Sin is pleasing to God is simply based on the premise, the more man sins, the greater the opportunity for God to display mercy. Thus "sin is indispensable for the enjoyment of all the blessings of divine grace, so that, at bottom, sin is pleasing to God."[277]

One area I found most difficult to apply Jesus as a role model was the area where he was most often attested as the prototype of how to cope with

---

[276]Freud, *The Future of an Illusion,* p. 48.
[277]Ibid., p. 48.

the vicissitudes of life—pain and anguish, that is suffering. No matter what pain or loss you encountered, I was often told, it could not be compared with the suffering of Jesus. I was to see Jesus' "bearing the cross" as model of how I was to cope with suffering.

Somehow, I could never find comfort or solace in Jesus' suffering. It seemed to me that unlike human beings whose existence is one of struggle from birth to death, Jesus' suffering appeared to be centered on one event, an event that took place at the end of his life. One may argue that Jesus knew that he was going to die, and that caused suffering particularly since he was innocent, but is not living with the knowledge that you are going to die the lot of every human being? It was often stated that Jesus suffered as a result of the compassion he felt for human beings in distress. He was, however, able to transform any pain or difficulty whether it was turning water into wine, raising Lazarus from the dead, calming a storm, feeding five thousand, healing the sick, at a moment's notice.

What, it was frequently asserted, greater suffering could there be than dying on the cross? I resented Good Fridays. For what was highlighted by sermons and by the reading of the Bible was that there was no justification for Jesus' suffering. He was a good person, indeed perfect, who did no wrong and suffered for the sins of mankind. There are the implications then that (1) if one is good one should not suffer, and (2) suffering is punishment for sin which is indeed one of the fundamental doctrines of Christianity.

The views that suffering is punishment for sin, one should avoid suffering as much as possible, and one should be happy are highlighted by the recount of the Garden of Eden and the belief in heaven. Before the "fall" of human beings, Adam and Eve lived in paradise, a state of pure bliss, and the Christian after death will live in paradise—an eternal state of pure bliss. What made me even more anxious about suffering was the belief that whenever I faced difficulties I should try to solve them as rapidly as Jesus' miracles--turning water into wine or the storm being stilled or Lazarus being raised from the dead.[278] It took me a long time to realize that suffering, as Buddhism propounds, is an inevitable part of the human condition[279].

Somehow in the light of the daily suffering around me, I began to "quantify" Jesus' suffering and to compare it to the suffering of others. Was the crucifixion the ultimate in suffering as is often postulated? Being nailed to a cross was indeed a cruel death. Jesus' cry of "My God, my God why has thou forsaken me?" demonstrates anguish and pain. When I was a child

---

[278] *John* 2;*Mark* 4: 35-40; *John* 11, 12:1 (KJV).
[279] Narada, *The Buddha and His Teachings,* (Kuala Lumpur, Malaysia: Buddhist Missionary Society, 1988).

I somehow thought that the crucifixion was a unique form of punishment that was specially devised for Jesus as sacrifice for the sins of human beings. I thought that the crucifixion of the two thieves was part of the setting to enhance the innocence of Jesus. Thus, as a child, I really believed that Jesus and the two thieves were the only people who were ever crucified. It was not until I was an adult that I realized that the crucifixion was the inhumane system of punishment during Jesus' lifetime. Men were actually crucified for stealing as evidenced by the crucifixion of the two thieves. Shouldn't God have been more concerned about the barbaric rite of crucifying people than to use that as a method to save human beings? Jesus, while on earth, did not question or raise concerns about crucifixion as an inhumane system of punishment. Why then would he raise concerns about slavery?

In "quantifying" Jesus' suffering, I came to the conclusion that Jesus was not the only person who suffered at his crucifixion. My mother's reaction to "Woman, behold your son, and son behold your mother," every Good Friday when the minister would repeat those words made me think of Mary's suffering, for sitting beside my mother I would observe how her face would become filled with sadness whenever she heard those words; she would quietly repeat them with a shake of her head. I know how much anguish my mother suffered whenever my brother was whipped by my father. How much pain and anguish Mary must have felt as she watched her son cruelly nailed to a cross? Would "woman behold your son, son behold your mother" be really comforting or was it somewhat dismissive of her suffering?

What about Peter who "denied" Jesus as Jesus predicted would happen? Was not his mortification regarding his denial of Christ, suffering? Pontius Pilate also suffered as he agonized about sending an innocent person to be crucified. It must have been a morbid task for the Roman soldiers who flogged Jesus, nailed him to the cross, and slashed his side with a sword. Not to mention that it was reported in the synoptic gospels that the whole earth was filled with darkness for three hours[280] which would have adversely affected a lot of people. The person, however, who suffered the most regarding the event of the crucifixion, in my view, was Judas Iscariot. He hung himself,[281] a horrific and gruesome death. What could be more indicative of great pain and anguish? According to *Matthew's* gospel, Judas was remorseful about betraying Jesus and attempted to return the money he was given to identify Jesus.[282] One would think that since Judas repented,

---

[280]*Matthew* 27: 45-46; *Mark* 15: 33; *Luke* 23: 44-45 (KJV)
[281]*Matthew* 27: 5
[282]*Matthew* 27: 3-4.

and God is a God of love, that God would have interceded, and assured Judas of divine forgiveness. Judas not only committed suicide but he has been maligned in history as a "traitor" and associated with land called the "Field of Blood"[283] when his role as betrayer of Jesus was determined and was actually a fulfillment of prophecy.[284] The life of Judas Iscariot clearly invalidates the free will argument.

Jesus' suffering on the cross for the "sins of the world" did not take place in isolation. The crucifixion took place within a culture that engaged in a barbaric form of punishment and it involved a number of people who had to play roles in the drama of the crucifixion. The crucifixion therefore was not a supra human event outside of the realm of the period and culture in which Jesus lived. The symbol of the cross should include a community of people who suffered along with Jesus. In terms of Jesus' crucifixion as a model as to how to cope with suffering, there are a number of people who suffered as much, if not more that Jesus.

What I often found puzzling is the fact that it is postulated by the church that suffering is a result of sin. Jesus died for our sins. Why then is there so much human suffering? My mother's life, filled with suffering, displayed, to me, first hand the unbridgeable gap between the world of the Bible and the world in the Twentieth Century. Death riddled my mother's family. An older sister died at a young age soon after giving birth to a son. When my mother was about eighteen her father, the main breadwinner, suddenly took ill and died. My mother while recuperating in the hospital from a miscarriage—her fourth pregnancy—received the news that her beloved sister who was in another maternity ward died while giving birth to her first child. Dotty was my mother's favorite sister. My mother never fully recovered from the blow. Within two decades, my mother would lose her last remaining sister, and I would lose yet another aunt and the only maternal aunt who lived long enough to have some impact on my life. A Christian, who worked hard to raise her six children, five boys and a girl, someone who never smoked in all her life, died from lung cancer.

My father was no less unfortunate in terms of loss of family. Indeed, in a sense, his life was more tragic. His parents, like a number of Jamaicans, migrated to Panama in search of work as a result of the building of the Panama Canal. My father then was born in Panama. After some years my grandfather, concerned about his children acquiring an English education, or he may have had other motives, shipped his wife and children to Jamaica. My father could not speak a word of English when he arrived in Jamaica and

---

[283]*Matthew* 27: 3-10.
[284]*Matthew* 27: 9.

apparently underwent a lot of trauma as a result of being whipped by teachers to speak English, and not Spanish. At first it seemed that financial support was more than adequate. My father was placed in a special boarding school. He dreamt of becoming a medical doctor. My father's wish, however, to become a doctor would be blighted; his academic goals would be thwarted. My grandfather stopped sending regular income to his wife and children. Later, the death of my father's mother and two or three sisters would add to his financial woes. Except for an older step-sister, he was the only survivor of the family.

At one point, the only job that was open to my father was to work as a laborer on a sugar plantation. One day overcome by his oppressive working conditions, my father wrote a letter to the manager of the sugar plantations. Impressed by the letter, the manager sent my father to a tertiary institution to become a Sanitary Inspector with the fiat that he would repay the company by working for them. My father's accomplishments in the light of his very traumatic and difficult childhood were amazing.

However, my father's lack of a nuclear family would have an impact on our lives even to this day and this is one of the reasons why I strongly disagree with Christian theology that postulates that a relationship between God and the individual is of paramount importance. Human beings need to be part of a family and a community. The Christian viewpoint that what is of primary significance is the individual relationship with God is asynchronous with demands of human beings as social beings. As pointed out, individual relationship with God leads to atomization which is a major contributing factor to the perpetual unjust and oppressive status of blacks.

For many years I would struggle with the issue of suffering and the eschatological hope, passive acceptance, feelings of guilt that underscored the teachings of the Christian religion regarding suffering. In *Is God a White Racist?* William R. Jones raises the issue of "authentic and inauthentic responses with regard to human suffering. [285] Basing his arguments on *The Plague* as a "literary portrayal of authentic and inauthentic responses to human suffering in particular and the human situation in general", Jones claims that the "inauthentic responses, on the whole, are accounts of theodicy with a long history in the Judaeo-Christian tradition".[286] According to Jones, Camus concludes that the Judaeo-Christian religion "has unfortunately adopted an understanding of human suffering that supports oppression".[287] Indeed, the Christian religion "fosters a spirit of conformity

---

[285]Jones, *Is God a White Racist?* p. 42.
[286]Ibid., p. 42.
[287]Ibid., p. 42.

to human suffering that ought to be obliterated; it ultimately leads to quietism—if it is consistent".[288]

If one seriously thinks about it, one can easily see how using Jesus' crucifixion as the model as to how to cope with suffering, believing that evil and injustices will be redressed in the next life, and that there is a benevolent God that rules the universe can lead to inauthentic responses, that is, quietism and support of oppression.

The community of family, neighbors, friends, and people who worked for us played an important role in my development, but I did not appreciate them then. I did not see the women who often visited us and helped us in many ways as good, kind, caring, and supportive. For one thing, we saw these women's foibles which were often far more prominent to us than their goodness. They had children out of wedlock. Some women were considered too business like, too masculine, not feminine, too feisty. The helpers sometimes fell short of our expectations—the clothes were not ironed properly or the house was not adequately cleaned or some part of the meal was undercooked or overcooked. The helpers were also often illiterate, did not speak proper English and had several children out of wedlock for different men. The elementary teacher could whip or punish you. Then there were women like Miss Fanny who would take care of you when you were sick but who could be downright cranky and miserable at other times.

There was, however, another reason why I saw mainly the foibles of those around me. Most of the people around me were dark skinned. By the time I was about nine I had already internalized that there was a link between skin color and morality. The darker one is, the more likely one is to be bad, the paler one is the more likely one is to be good. It seemed to me that most men including my father married very pale yellow complexioned women and as a result a number of the children in my community were of pale complexion. One particular little tan complexioned girl with wavy black hair was a source of envy for me. Her family was very interesting because two cocoa complexioned brothers had married two beige-pink complexioned sisters. Sylvia was the only child of one couple while the other couple had about five children, most of whom were darker than Sylvia.

I envied Sylvia and I am sure my father would have been appalled, if he knew. He had reprimanded me some years before for playing in the brown wavy almost straight hair of Cherry, one of the numerous children of our neighbor, a very poor couple mainly of European descent. With raised voice and angry body movement he managed to convey to me, I must have been around seven or eight, that playing in Cherry's hair was an indication that I

---

[288]Ibid., p. 42.

felt her hair was "better" than my own. It had an impact for I never again touched anyone's hair outside of my immediate family whose hair certainly did not fall into the category of Cherry's. My father, yelling at me in the presence of Cherry, meant also to convey to Cherry and me that I was "better" than Cherry because she was poor.

My coffee complexioned father's attitude to skin color would in many ways bewilder me. On the one hand, he would seem almost "militant" particularly because of his overt attention to me as the darkest child. On the other hand, he married my mother who had a very pale yellow complexion. He was very critical of the "white" Thomas family. It seemed to me that my father accepted the fact that it was okay for blacks to be poor but he had no tolerance for European looking people who were very content, in his view, to live at the bottom of the society. As far as he was concerned Cherry's parents had no ambition. I liked Cherry and her family. They were very pleasant and were very respectful in their attitude towards my father but without the kind of deference if the shoe was on the other foot. Whereas dark skinned black children knew their place—they would never come to play with us unless invited, European looking people saw their skin color as a privilege which they could use to cross social barriers. I could never go to Cherry's house to play but Cherry had no inhibition regarding coming to my house to play with me. It seemed to me that the Thomas' family who lived in a hut with several children was far happier than my family and the peanut complexioned hoity-toity family who lived across the street from us and who my father admired.

We moved from that neighborhood to a more homogeneous middle class neighborhood. This time it was Cutie. Cutie was almost the complexion of my mother, a pale yellow, but with a little more bronze. She had slightly tightly curled brownish-yellowish hair. She would often come over and play with me. My parents could not figure out the composition of Cutie's family. The house seemed to be filled with extended family of aunts, uncles, and a grandmother. I was never invited to Cutie's house. When I started going to high school, I was no longer allowed to play with Cutie because she did not speak properly, she did not belong to a nuclear family, she was probably "illegitimate", and she did not attend a high school.

Years later I, would meet Cutie again. It was during the Christmas holidays and I was working as a store clerk in a Hanna store on King Street. I only obtained this position because my pale skinned mother, in order for me to be employed in the store, practically genuflected to the peach complexioned store manager! Cutie was a very confident young woman who worked as Cashier, a job, because of my dark skin color, in spite of my attending one of the most prestigious schools in Jamaica, I would never have. In the 1950's, dark skinned people were not supposed to handle money in the banks and in the stores of the main commercial street of Kingston, King Street. Back then most of the people who worked in the stores on King Street or in the banks had to be of pale complexion—peach or pink with straight or wavy hair. When I saw Cutie, I eagerly went to greet her. It was now my turn to be snubbed by her. She hardly acknowledged our acquaintance.

My father had contempt for whites who did not live up to the norms of the society but he was definitely pleased whenever we brought peach complexioned, European looking friends to the house. Indeed, we were free to bring anyone to our house as long as they filled the middle class norms. My parents then were totally unaware of my envy of Sylvia and this was not so much due to the fact that I really wanted to have her hair and complexion per se but the fact that I thought that having that type of hair and complexion would give me the freedom and love that she had. Sylvia was never whipped.

Sylvia's parents adored her. I envied the fact that Sylvia could stand on her verandah and sing, very loudly, without the slightest inhibition, popular songs on the radio. Before I was twelve, my siblings and I were whipped almost daily by our father with the injunctions that "our skin was getting rusty" and "Chicken merry, hawk de near". We must never relax and be happy, that is, being frivolous. We must always be watchful and prepared in order to avoid being subjected to some catastrophic event.

I was terrified of being whipped. Although my mother did not use the strap as often as my father did, she did whip my brother and me, particularly for fighting. What I envied peach complexioned, pink complexioned, pale complexioned children for was the fact that from my observation they enjoyed a certain amount of freedom without the fear or threat of being whipped that I did not have. It seemed to me that they were able to dance on their verandahs, visit friends, smile and laugh, "run up and down and play", and this freedom gave them a pleasant air and attitude.

It seemed to me that skin color was a major issue in terms of the degree of punishment to which one was subjected. In the elementary schools the darker one was, the more likely it would be that one was whipped. Indeed in the suburbs of Kingston, in the mid-Twentieth Century, very few pale skinned children attended primary schools where corporal punishment was the norm. There was also the factor of class. Most cocoa, chocolate, coffee complexioned people could not afford to send their children to "prep" schools where corporal punishment was banned. There was a positive correlation between dark skin and poverty.[289]

Skin color was a great issue in our culture, and still is. As a matter of fact, ascriptions of character and attributes were often based on skin color. Thus light skinned women were expected to be "soft" and "gentle". The darker one is, the more likely one is to be strict, severe, and "mean". I often heard pale complexioned women in my family describe pale skin men as "namby, pamby", that is, lacking drive, gumption, and to some degree, arrogance. Thus, in my family, pale skin men were not considered very good prospects for marriage. Quite often individuals were forced to live up to the expectation regarding their attributes based on skin color. My mother in keeping with her complexion often had to be "nice". Woe unto a dark skinned man if for some reason he could not live up to the attributes of being mean, and strict. If he was soft spoken and gentle, there would be talk and analysis as to "what is wrong with him".

Sometimes in interaction of adults with each other one could not help avoid hearing adults describe the same characteristic as being "bossy" and "nosey" when displayed by a dark skinned female, but "nice" and "caring" when displayed by a pale skinned person. Sometimes, however, the skin color issue though painful could be quite ludicrous. Like many issues in life, skin color could be relative. Thus one may be considered dark in one part of the country, and accordingly develop the accompanying characteristics only to be considered, if one moves to another area of the country, "light" and is totally shocked at the deferential treatment meted out to you. Similarly a pale skinned person who is almost considered white in one area may be derogatorily referred to as "redibu" or "mulatto" in another part.

Skin color was further complicated by another factor in terms of social status and standing and that is hair. Generally at any initial contact one's hair is scrutinized as to whether it falls into the category of good hair or bad hair. Your hair could be a determining factor in terms of your eligibility for marriage, friendship, a job. "Bad" hair had to be straightened. It has always been a mystery to me that there is this dividing line between good and bad hair. Like the equator it is invisible, but somehow everyone knows what the dividing line is and therefore what constitutes "good" hair and "bad" hair. Length of hair is also important. If your hair is bad and reaches your shoulder, that is somewhat acceptable, but woe unto you (to use a Biblical expression) if it is no longer than an inch which was the lot of some women, especially poor women.

Skin color was and is a major issue in our culture and it was a major in my family. My mother was the lightest in her family. She was often teased,

---

[289]Nettleford, *Mirror, Mirror.*

however, because her very pale yellow complexion was topped by a mass of thick very tightly curled reddish brownish shoulder length hair. There was therefore this odd combination of a pale yellow complexion and very tightly curled hair. She had what was considered "bad hair" which fell under the category of having to be straightened. As a child, I often heard my mother refer to herself in a very derogatory manner as "redibu." It was not until I met a Nigerian who was pursuing a Ph. D., at the same time that my husband was pursuing his, that I made a connection of red and Ibo. Uka, an Ibo, was a pale peanut complexion. I concluded then that "redibu" was a corruption of Red Ibo.

My mother felt that she was not particularly attractive. Her sister who was somewhat darker (a tan complexion) and had shiny wavy hair was considered a beauty. My mother developed a theory which was based on her experience and observation that the darkest child usually has the "prettiest" hair and is the best looking. I deduced from this theory that having the "prettiest" hair and being the best looking is God's compensation for being the darkest. For many years this theory dominated my thinking and it was easily validated because there were so many "rice and peas" families as we say in Jamaica, that is, children that had varying complexions and types of hair.

One day my mother met a distant cousin whose three daughters put a dent in my mother's theory for one daughter who was the lightest had waist length hair that did not need to be straightened. She could almost pass for European. My mother, however, was not daunted by this set back in her theory. We should note that the darker sister who had shoulder length "bad" hair was the brightest and the best looking. If you were not compensated by "prettiest" hair, then you were compensated by being the best looking and if that failed by being the brightest.

I think that the fact that nearly everyone who visited our house would point me out as the darkest but the best looking caused my mother to cling to her theory even more. My complexion was always a topic of conversation. I think that when I was born I must have been an utter shock to my father and mother. They must have thought, since my father was a dark coffee complexion and my mother a yellow buttery complexion, by the law of averages that I should be somewhere in between. But somehow my genes were either in a hurry or they had an artistic bent or they had a weird sense of humor. Instead of getting the blend right it seemed as though they stood from a distance and hurled my father's brown over my mother's yellow so that I landed up with a blotchy brownish yellowish complexion. In any event, I turned out to be much closer to my father's complexion than my mother's.

My mother told me that when I was a baby, one day, as she was lifting me in her arms on King Street, she was reprimanded by a man as to why was she "straining herself", that is, carrying another woman's child. I was so dark compared to my mother that he did not believe I was my mother's child! I could not help but note that the man was more concerned about my pale complexioned mother than he was about me, a dark complexioned baby. What if it were the reverse? Would he have made the same comment?

My brother's genes took greater effort in pasting the dark coffee and yellow more smoothly so that he is a little lighter and of a smoother complexion than I. It seemed, however, as if the brown genes were willing to be totally obliterated by the yellow ones in my sister's case. My sister is almost as light as my mother while I am almost as dark as my father. My sister and I are almost like day and night. Interestingly enough it was my complexion to which reference was always made. Children would ask me, not my sister, if I am sure my sister and I "have the same mother and father". One young man when he met my mother blurted out—you are the very opposite of your mother—she is short, you are tall, you are skinny, she is fat, she is fair, and you are dark. Calling my mother fat which was really a gross exaggeration did not endear him to her.

Even though I was always complimented as being the best looking, it did not escape me that the best looking was always preceded by the "but"— she is the darkest but the best looking. I therefore internalized the view that there was something fundamentally wrong about being dark. This was reinforced by the fact that unlike the American system of classification, Jamaicans were not classified strictly on "race" with the exception of the Chinese and Indians. Black was rarely used except as an insult and was often linked with the terms ugly and sin. Black and ugly or black as sin could be hurled at you if you were dark skinned. Dark was considered the euphemistic term for those who were dark complexioned with "springy" hair and broad features. Indeed, there were several categories in Jamaica for the several types of skin color and hair. There was half-Chinese, Indianish, redibu, mulatto, dark, black, sambo, fair skinned. White was liberally used. My uncles used to call my sister, "the white lady." In all of the categorization, however, the objective was to get away from Africa as far as possible. You could be half Chinese or half Indian. You were never half African.

The Miss Jamaica Beauty Pageant was a constant reminder to us every year that white is normative as far as beauty is concerned—African hair and phenotype mean ugly. "Miss Jamaica" would not only be projected and paraded as being "beautiful" but would be given numerous awards and treated by top administrators and media as though she had achieved some major accomplishment in terms of intellectual, scientific, or economic development. And if, as "Miss Jamaica" of mainly European descent did one year, 1963 to be exact, the "Miss Jamaica" should win the "Miss World", or even be a runner up, there would be great rejoicing amongst the elite in Jamaica. This would put Jamaica "on the map." This would "boost the tourist industry". Rex Nettleford's analysis of identity and race in Jamaica is a salient commentary of the issue of skin color in Jamaica.[290]

From a very young child, I internalized the view that there was something inherently wrong with my skin color, my hair and my features.[291] One day when I was about nine—I was reflecting on peanut complexioned black wavy haired Sylvia and how she seemed to have freedom that I lacked to dance and sing on her verandah and just be. I felt acutely that I was subjected to a lot of whips, insults and snobbery because of my dark skin color. I was outside in the yard sitting on a tricycle that I had far outgrown even though in those days, as there were no "kiddy" bikes with training wheels and since children rode tricycles up to seven years old, tricycles were larger than they are today. My mother was inside. I called to her and she pushed her head through the window. "Mamma", I asked, "Why am I dark?" She smiled as though somewhat embarrassed and introducing her comments with 'they say", which only verified in my mind that there was some shame to what she was about to tell me. My mother then told me the story of Noah and his three sons. Noah was drunk and Ham looked at his father Noah while he was naked. As a result Ham was cursed and dark people are the children of Ham.

My immediate reaction was to be angry with Noah. Noah had no right to be drunk. Drunkenness was something to be abhorred. Drunkenness brought a lot of pain to families. My mother could not stand it when my father was drunk. I pedaled off riding awkwardly on the tricycle. I had to keep my knees outward to avoid them bumping on the handle bars of the tricycle. I did not put the thoughts into words but I felt then that in the scheme of things my mother, since she was lighter than I, was less cursed than I and that God played a role in my skin being dark since dark skin was punishment for Ham's disrespect. I was fortunate, however, that I was raised in a Christian family. At least, I would make it into heaven although I was sure, barely.

The view that there is a relationship between skin color and morality was reinforced by the Christian Church. The priests of the Anglican Church were for the most part Englishmen or Jamaicans of peachy pink complexion.

---

[290]Nettleford, *Mirror, Mirror.*
[291]See Curtin, *Two Jamaicas*; Nettleford, *Mirror Mirror.*

Jesus, Mary, the disciples and the angels were depicted in the stained glass windows, and in pictures in the Bible as Europeans. The angels were not only Europeans—they were golden haired. It left little imagination then to think of the devil as mainly of African descent or black. Indeed, besides these pictures there was the imagery in the Bible. Throughout the Bible there is the dichotomy between goodness as white or light and evil as black or dark. The imagery of white, light and day as good and black, dark and night as bad is easily transferred to skin color as Frantz Fanon pointed out in his seminal work, *Black Skin White Mask.* Since the term dark was often used to describe me I was particularly sensitive to the word, dark, and still am. It is significant to note also that goodness was and is intrinsically linked to wealth, beauty, and whiteness.

We did not only learn from the Christian Church that goodness is white in terms of the imagery and personnel in the Church, but also from the schools particularly the high schools which were attached to the churches. The books we read as literature reinforced white/light as good and black/dark as evil in the imagery and characters of works by authors, such as, Shakespeare, the Bronte sisters, and Jane Austen. Happiness and wealth as the reward for beauty which is linked to goodness and being white are depicted in Jane Austen's novels particularly in her most popular work, *Pride and Prejudice.* Shakespeare's half human, half savage, Caliban, in *The Tempest* and the mad mulatto wife of Jane Eyre's lover are examples of the ignominious insults in English Literature to which we were subjected in the Caribbean. I therefore can attest to what Frantz Fanon points out in his *Black Skin White Masks* how the onslaught of imagery of white as good and black as evil in European media impacts the prevalent view of whites as morally and mentally superior and blacks as morally and mentally inferior.[292] In Jamaica, anti-African sentiment was daily exhibited in the classrooms, in newspapers, on the radio and in the laws enacted by the government. Poor people of African descent were constantly subjected to dehumanizing and unjust laws by a predominantly British colonial regime.

In truth and in fact, however, goodness as white and beautiful were really ideation that was not often concretized in reality as far as our contact with Europeans was concerned. We would often discuss how our English minister had the reputation of being an alcoholic and a womanizer. We viewed a number of our British teachers as cold, aloof and prejudiced. Paradoxically although white was normative as beautiful, I can remember as children how we would often laugh at the complexion and features of

---

[292]Franz Fanon, *Black Skin, White Masks,* translated by Charles Lam Markmann, (London: MacGibbon & Kee, 1968).

Europeans.

Having to rely on Europeans—quite often clergymen—for jobs, and indeed for survival meant, however, seeing the European as good. My mother told me that my grandfather's employment as headmaster of the primary school was contingent upon his preaching and playing the organ for church. My mother's success over competitors for teaching positions at Elementary School was mainly due to her playing at times for church and teaching Sunday school. The clergy played an important role in hiring personnel in high schools because most high schools were built by Christian denominations. The clergy also played a significant role in hiring elementary school teachers because the clergy was appointed by the government to be managers of the elementary schools. Thus in order to acquire a teaching position, particularly in the elementary school, one had to be a member of a church. Ministers also played a very important role in writing what was then termed a "testimonial" (recommendation) in order to procure a job.

Since many high schools were attached to churches, the church by preparing high school students for employment played an active role in the distribution of wealth. As most of the personnel were Europeans in the church and as most wealthy people were white, it seemed imputing that God who is the main distributor of wealth must be white was logical reasoning.

There are a number of other factors that even further reinforced for me the whiteness of God and one is the music of the Anglican Church. The pipe organ was considered the instrument of heaven on which classical European pieces could be played and hymns structured in Anglo-German rhythms. Some of these hymns I would learn later were actually based on European folk music. It would have been unthinkable then to play drums, or jazz or calypso or any piece of music in the style and rhythm of our folk songs in the church. The drum, the fife, the guitar, jazz, calypso (which pre-dated reggae) were devil instruments and music. Any type of music that had to do with Africa was of the devil; European music particularly classical music was heavenly and of God.

There was the issue of work. Living in the United States of America, I have always been baffled by the term "work ethic" being applied to whites. In Jamaica, it was the goal of a lot of hard working poor and even middle class Jamaicans to acquire the status of "bukra", the Jamaican word for white man and so live a life of leisure, and not have work. One did not associate white people with work. It was quite a shock for me when I first arrived in Toronto in the 1960's to see white people cleaning their houses, sweeping streets, and driving buses. For the most part, except for a few poor whites in St. Elizabeth, whites lived the lifestyle of leisure of the landed class of the

British aristocracy that was portrayed, for example, in Jane Austen's novels. Although black people were often termed lazy, it was black people who had to do the most menial work—as evidenced by over three hundred years of slavery in Jamaica. We did not associate white people with work and we did not associate the Divinity with work. Indeed in the Bible, work is associated with curse. Work was instituted by God as a result of Adam's sin. "In the sweat of thy face shalt thou eat bread, till thou return unto the ground." (*Genesis* 3:19,KJV). Black people were enslaved as a result of Ham being cursed. When one thinks of heaven, one thinks of a place of leisure—not of work. The issue of work for the survival of human beings is epiphenomenal to the Gospels and the "spiritual" aspect of human beings. Indeed a number of Jesus' disciples left their occupation to follow him. (*Mark* 10: 28; *Matthew* 4: 19-20, KJV).

Since heaven or that which is holy implies minimal work, while work was associated with curse, and since most whites in Jamaica lived a life of leisure, then one could only conclude that God must be white.

The other area that contributed to a perception of God as white was knowledge. God is all knowing. We had to rely totally on whites for knowledge in the schools and in the churches. The knowledge of blacks was marginalized and in some instances demonized. We were taught that Africans had no knowledge of anything—manufacturing, trade, governance, the universe, medicine, epistemology—before whites colonized Africa. One could only conclude that since in terms of knowledge, whites were much closer to God than blacks, then God must be white.

Finally the factor that reinforced the whiteness of God was language. When white ministers spoke from the pulpit about "Pa-uwulll" on his way to "Da—mas-cusss", the enunciation and diction were very different from that of the majority of Jamaicans. The Bible, hymns, and prayers were all in proper English. God spoke correct grammatical English and not only did he speak correct English but his accent was British.

Concomitant with this was the belief that God demanded the best and since the best was English, he could not be identified with the masses, but with whites who were the elite of the society. On Sundays we wore expensive hats, (required then) expensive clothes, and shoes which we bought from exclusive stores (in spite of the fact that we would never be employed in those stores). The building where God resides, in keeping with European architecture, had to be the best. Piety, purity, the sacred were characteristics that were more closely identified with the lifestyle of the British than with the often rambunctious and recalcitrant black masses.

There was nothing that anyone could say or do, that would erase the feelings deep inside of me that God who is white disapproved of my skin color, my hair, and my features. I was bad and evil, not because of Adam's sin, but because of my skin color and hair. In terms of the Christian religion, I felt I was a Dalit.. I carried a stigma as a result of being cursed. Like the Dalit, I was polluted. Like the Dalit, the "stigma, congenital according to one's caste lasts a lifetime and cannot be eliminated by rite or deed."[293]

Critique of my Dalit status within the Christian religion came from, as far as I was concerned, an unlikely sector of the society. During my teenage years, as I walked to and from St. Andrew Parish Church nearly every Sunday, I would encounter cocoa, chocolate, coffee, complexion Rastafarians with long matted dreads sitting on the wall that partially encircled St. Andrew Parish Church. These Rastafarians would taunt me as I walked past them to and from Church: "Why should a beautiful daughter like you straighten your hair and worship a white God? I would smile in response mainly to hide my fear; my upbringing also demanded that I be polite to everyone. Inwardly, however, I had nothing but contempt for the Rastafarians although I was flattered by the fact that they called me beautiful. I was often termed not bad looking or good looking, but I had never been termed beautiful.

I thought I had truly dismissed their comments about "worshipping the white God" as coming from poor, dark skinned, uneducated people. Those words, however, did have an impact and would resonate with me from time to time.

In the late 1980's, I read a paper on the Death of God theology written by Kamuyu-wa-Kang'ethe that would totally authenticate my view regarding God, whiteness, and black humanity.[294] According to Kang'ethe, Kenyans had a perception of God as white as a result of whites assuming the role of God in the lives of Africans. Kang'ethe's article added important dimensions to what was actually my experience and thinking by delineating how whites in their relationship with blacks become identified with the attributes of God.

Kang'ethe claims that the death of God was a long process in Europe beginning with Jesus' cry of "My God, My God, why hast thou forsaken me?" To fill that void European humanity, particularly in the Eighteenth and Nineteenth Centuries, the era of belief in the progress of man, became God. The Europeans' encounter with Africans gave the Europeans the premium opportunity to fulfill the void. According to Kang'ethe, at "the turn of the nineteenth century Africa was, therefore, confronted by this seemingly

---

[293]Mahar, *The Untouchables in Contemporary India*, p. xxx
[294]Kamuyu-wa-Kang'ethe, "The Death of God: An African Viewpoint".

Eternal Great Humanity Divine—the white humanity".[295] It is significant to note Kang'ethe's assertion that this "humanity came increasingly to think of itself as a Divine humanity. The behavior, utterances, and attitudes of this humanity became like those of God."[296] Kang'ethe concludes that "the white Westerner *had finally taken over the attributes of God*[297]

Kang'ethe then examines the purported attributes of God and shows how whites identified with the attributes of God as all powerful, all-knowing, perfect, mysterious, demanding total obedience, loving but vengeful in their relationship with the Africans.   Africans were encouraged to love Jesus. Africans loved Jesus so much that "we hated our so-called 'pagan' parents and kinsmen...reported activities of freedom fighters to white people...risked death...misery...and poverty..." However "it never dawned on us not even once that what we loved was God who is Jesus, the white man! And not Ngai who alone is Ngai.[298]

This paper caused a seminal shift in my thinking. It ploughed deeper than the Rastafarian's postulation that, as a Christian, I was in fact worshipping a white God. It really fully awakened and authenticated my feelings that I had never fully articulated and expressed—the worship of God is in truth and in fact the worship of whites. This article would utterly free me from years of guilt, and shame—years of being a Dalit within the Christian religion.   Before this awakening or enlightenment, however, I *had to* undergo Christian rites and rituals to atone for my intellectual curiosity and my African ancestry.

---

[295]Ibid., p. 13.
[296]Ibid., p. 13.
[297]Ibid., p. 13, italics mine.
[298]Ibid., p. 13-16

CHAPTER SIX

CONFIRMATION

Lord, wash me and I shall be whiter than snow
Whiter than snow, yes whiter than snow
Lord, wash me and I shall be whiter than snow
Lines from a hymn

Membership of a Christian body, however, remained central to self-esteem and to social status in the community[299]

Shirley Gordon

In the preceding chapter, I highlighted some of the factors that shaped my thinking, as I was growing up, regarding the cultural dissonance which I often felt in the light of what was taught as Christian precepts and beliefs, on the one hand, and the norms, and mores of my family and community, on the other. As far back as I can remember, I have always experienced disquietude about Christ, the tenets of Christianity, and the church which I felt were alien to the social milieu in which I was raised. When I reached the age of thirteen or fourteen, however, I found myself being very critical not just of the precepts and practices of Christianity but of Jesus himself—what he said and what he did. This was based to a large extent on impressions I had from listening to Scripture passages being read, and sermons. I rarely read the Bible. These thoughts bothered me a lot for my views of Jesus differed from how I was supposed to perceive him.

I do not know why Jesus became the focus of my thoughts, and why he was subjected to such scrutiny in terms of my culture and upbringing during my early teenage years. It could have been due to my three years of high school education in which critical analysis of figures in works, such as, *Lorna Doone, She Stoops to Conquer, A Christmas Carol, The Tempest, Twelfth Night, Pride and Prejudice* somehow resulted in sharpening critical reasoning skills which I transferred from the secular to the sacred. It could also be that there was a lot of talk by my aunt, godparent, and my mother's friends about my being confirmed. After confirmation, I would become a member of the Anglican Church. Thus, I would be able to partake of Holy Communion, that is the body and blood of Jesus Christ in order to eradicate my sins, and I would be assured of going to Heaven when I die. Maybe it is

---

[299]Gordon, *Our Cause for His Glory*, p. 122.

the centrality of Jesus and the Holy Communion in the Episcopalian Church why Jesus became the focus of critical analysis during these years. The thoughts I had about Jesus were very troubling because they led me to the conclusion that he was not perfect.

Most of my critical analysis regarding Jesus was through the lens of my culture and upbringing. However, there were a number of issues that I found particularly worrisome. Maybe to many people my thoughts on the matter are insignificant in terms of the goodness of Christ, or the thoughts may seem strange, "out there", or I am magnifying minor issues, but these were thoughts with which I wrestled.

In my early teenage years, a major source of discomfort for me, was Jesus' response to his mother's concern about his disappearance for days. How could Jesus have spoken to his mother in the manner in which he did? I often wondered. Could I have replied in that manner to my mother? What particularly led to my questioning of Jesus' response was my parents' reaction one day, about this period, when, I did not return home at the expected time. Inveigled by my beige complexioned, brown wavy hair friend, as we were out walking, to stop at her friend's house, we did. I spent a couple of hours, at this house, having a good time talking and laughing totally unaware of time and oblivious to the fact that my beige complexioned, brown wavy hair friend had far more latitude than I. I was shocked when I returned home to find an angry coffee face of my father and an equally angry pale pine face of my mother at the door. "Where were you? We were so worried. You told us you were going for a walk. We expected you back by a certain time. We were so worried." I was about thirteen or fourteen then. I could never have responded, "Don't you know....?" I could only look contrite and apologize profusely.

Preachers have engaged in all kinds of intellectual gymnastics to rationalize Jesus' behavior at twelve. Jesus was special. Was he therefore permitted, I would muse, to cause his mother anxiety, be indifferent about it, expect her to understand that he is special, and not apologize or show some concern for her feelings? The gender issue did not escape me. My brother was allowed far more freedom and laxity in terms of his comings and goings than I was, but even so (i) disappearance for more than a day would not be tolerated (ii) apology and submissiveness would have been expected (iii) there would have been punishment for the behavior. I have often thought that gender is a major issue regarding the defense of Jesus' behavior by ministers. Mary's feelings as a female and mother were often swept aside. To me, the manner in which Jesus spoke to his mother violated my social norms in terms of respect for one's parents, particularly for one's mother.

As a child during the forties and fifties, in my family and community one had to be what was termed extremely "mannerly" particularly with regards to one's parents and elders. Having good manners was even of more significance than learning or acquiring a skill. Having been brought up in a rural community in the hills of St. Andrew, where my mother saw how being polite, that is, greeting people as they passed by could literally save your life, she was very strict about observing the courtesies of Jamaican society. She would overlook any violation of her rules except this one. Whenever we visited our aunt in the country, we were warned several times regarding displaying "good manners" to everyone. Graciousness, that is, being polite and courteous, was normative.

The other aspect in terms of Jesus' response that I found deeply disturbing was the phrasing of his response. "Don't you know I had to be about my father's business?" In my culture a response framed in such a manner was regarded as an insult. Though graciousness and being polite were normative, at times, this propriety could be hidden under scathing comments and expressions. As children we lived in a world that could sometimes see the other side of adults, the angry side which could erupt at times at an unpredictable moment. How did many adults deal with their anger? We were often, as children, the recipient of physical blows as the primary outlet, but the other weapon which was far more insidious was to hurl an insult at us. I do not know which I dreaded more, the insult or the blows.

The insult could take the form of the most belittling comments regarding the person with whom you are angry—totally oblivious of how the recipient feels. It may be due to the fact that high quantity of melanin hid the blood rushing to the face of dark skinned people, why, from my experience, we as dark skinned people were even more subjected to insults. Although having good manners was the norm, growing up in the suburbs of Kingston, Jamaica, I would often rehearse responses to possible insults that would assail me in unpredictable encounters once my springy hair, cinnamon complexion body walked through the doors of my home to the outside world.

Of course your status had to do with giving insults or receiving insults. The lower down the social ladder you are, the more likely you are to be insulted. Women were more likely to be subjected to insults than men. Helpers were particularly vulnerable to this kind of psychological attack. It was not unusual for the mistress to confront her helper in a loud voice in the presence of whoever—family, friends, neighbors, children. "Adassa, whe yu common sense? You stupid or something, how long yu working for me and yu don't know you can't wash the colored shirt with white?"

Besides helpers, children were another popular target. Adults often took pride in constructing phrases and sentences to demean children. "Yu big and fool fool" was what I was, at times, derisively told when I was upset about something or I was acting silly. It was not only the insult but the scathing look that would accompany the insults. Often, as adults made their comments, if other adults were present, there would be the utmost attempt to impress their audience regarding their genius at creating belittling insults as if demeaning expressions are an index of one's brilliance and superiority. "Melissa, how old are you? Yu outside playing when yu should be studying yu lessons? Your ambition is as flat as yu nose".

Whereas in the elementary schools, corporal punishment was used to discipline children, it was forbidden in high schools for girls. The insult was often therefore used, as it was in the boys' high schools also, as a weapon to mortify and humiliate students particularly those who were dark complexion, who could not "blush", and were of the struggling middle class. Mistakes and foibles were the opportunity for teachers to mock and jeer students. "Algebra was not meant for you, you know girl"..."The time you spend straightening your hair, you could learn your geometry theorems."..."You should not be here"..."Wolmer's is not for you"..."I have got my B. A. ... you don't want to learn...that is your affair." Some of these comments could be stinging especially when they came from expatriates, white grim faced European teachers or very pale solemn faced beige complexioned Jamaicans. Students modeling teachers' behavior would often adapt the same manner in their responses to you particularly if they were lighter in complexion and/or they deduced that your parents were of a lower rank than theirs.

Some of the Jamaican teachers did use humor as a palliative. Once I wrote "la padre" for my Spanish teacher who was Jamaican. She called me up to her desk: "La padre!"she said, with a laugh. She put her arms akimbo: "I do not know if your father is feminine…"

I developed a hypersensitivity to insults and my mother contributed to this greatly. My mother detested any kind of sardonic, sarcastic or belittling comment. I can honestly say that she rarely used that format in her dealings with others. In my early teenage years, I would therefore invariably cringe as I read some of Jesus' replies to individuals. For example, when the Pharisees asked Jesus why the disciples did not wash their hands before they eat, which was to me a perfectly legitimate question, Jesus' reply was eight verses long beginning with "Why do ye also transgress the commandment of God by your tradition?" (Matt: 15; 1-11 KJV) The Pharisees were indeed "offended" by Jesus' reply. (Matt: 15: 12 KJV). When the disciples pointed out to Jesus that the Pharisees were upset, Jesus' response was: "Let them alone: they be blind leaders of the blind. And if the blind lead the blind, both shall fall into the ditch." (Matt:15:14 SJV). Apparently, the disciples did not understand Jesus' reply and asked for an explanation. Jesus turned to his disciples and asked: "Are ye also yet without understanding?" (Matt: 15: 16 KJV)). To me this was a belittling response.

In school, whenever we asked questions, and teachers responded not with a question that would further one's understanding, but with a question that questioned your ability, we considered it an insult. Many of us were quite upset as children when teachers made statements, such as, "From the beginning of the semester, we have been solving equations, and you still do not know how to do it" which intimated that you are taking far too long to learn the concept and thus your ability is questioned.

This may be very surprising but in my early teenage years, I often did not see what the intransigencies of the Pharisees were that entailed their subjection to Jesus' tirades and the calling of names, such as, 'hypocrites". With regard to the matter of washing hands, (Matt: 15; 3-11 KJV), as my father was a Sanitary Inspector and insisted that we wash our hands frequently particularly before we eat, I could not help but concur with the Pharisees.

Similarly in the light of my upbringing and culture, I was baffled by Jesus' response, "Who are my mother and brethren?" (Matthew: 12; 46-50 KJV), when people pointed out to him that his mother and his brethren were looking for him. Years later I would be indoctrinated to accept the view that one's family is secondary in terms of doing God's will, but in my early teenage years brought up in a setting where family relationship was paramount, I could not help but empathize with Jesus' family and saw Jesus' response as indifferent, cold, somewhat hostile, and indeed an insult.

Linked to this brusque manner of responding to some people was the way Jesus handled criticism. Most adults in my social circle when I was growing up were very sensitive to criticism although they expected their social inferiors, including us as children, to graciously accept whatever admonition the adult felt necessary. It was very rare for a child to receive praise or to be commended because it was commonly felt this would foster pride, conceit—"swell headedness", as it was often termed. When criticized we were not supposed to sulk nor were we to say anything. One should handle criticism graciously even greater would be the approval if one laughed at the most scathing insult.

As the gospels were read in church, and at school, I could not help but note that the way Jesus responded to criticism was similar to how many adults handled criticism which was diametrically opposed to how we were told as children we should deal with unfavorable comments. Jesus never laughed and said, "Is allright man. Oonu can tan dey wid oonu aristocratic self. Me happy wid de sinners." Jesus indulged in a lot of name calling terming those who were critical of his lifestyle and views "hypocrites", "generations of vipers", "wicked generation".

Another factor that I could not help questioning was what was often postulated as Jesus' attitude towards rules. It was frequently asserted by ministers that the Old Testament was based on rules and the law while the New Testament was based on love. Jesus' breaking of the rules was portrayed to us in Church, and in Sunday School as his concern more about people than about rules.

It is ironic that the Anglican Church should promulgate Jesus as a non conformist regarding rules when the polity of the Anglican Church was dominated by rules and regulations. In terms of structure and organization, the Anglican Church was certainly no iconoclastic institution. There were rules which governed the personnel of the church that resulted in a hierarchical structure of deacon, minister, canon, bishop, archbishop. There were rules which governed the rites and rituals of the church—christening, baptism, marriage, funeral rites, holy communion. Spontaneity had no role in the order of service which began at a specific time and ended at a specific time. Hymns and prayers were sung and said in a particular order. There were even rules and regulations regarding the attire of the clergymen and when to wear specific robes. The Church sanctified the rules—the laws, mores and norms of the society. The Church often determined what was holy and what was sacred and was the centrifugal force regarding the establishment of rules in the wider society.

It is amazing the numerous rules we as children had to navigate at the high schools established by churches. Indeed there were rules regarding who would be admitted to these high schools. At Wolmer's, the high school I attended, as at all the high schools in Jamaica, the rules as divinely sanctioned were underscored by the prayers we said every morning in school. Rules, rules, rules dominated our lives. You have to wear your beret, your uniform, brown shoes white socks, your badges—you cannot be late for school—if you are absent from school you have to have a written note from your parents—you have to do your home work—you must have your own textbook, notebooks, pen, pencils, geometry set, two notebooks for every subject--you have to have gym uniform, gym shoes—you must walk in a straight line to the Assembly Hall—you cannot talk during prayers—you cannot speak in the classroom unless you raise your hand—you must stand when the teacher enters the room—you must sit at your own desk—you cannot get out of your seat without the teacher's permission—you cannot "talk back" to a teacher—you cannot chew gum in school—you cannot wear make-up, nail polish, jewelry except a watch in school—you must speak proper English at all times, etc.

We often violated the rules of God as we frequently lied or cheated to avoid being punished by our teachers. Realizing on the bus that one forgot the note from the parent as to why one was absent from school, one would have a peer write and sign a note in a desperate attempt to avoid "having a detention" that is being detained after school and losing points for your house. Needless to say we were often caught. My parents, particularly my father, insisted that we obey the rules at school, and indeed as much as they could, my parents complied with the rules and regulations of the country.

Besides, they, my parents, for the most part, shared the view of the elite and the middle class that the suffering of the poor and oppressed was due mainly to their lack of discipline, that is, their unwillingness to follow rules and laws of the society. This was a constant theme reiterated ad nauseum by politicians, priests, teachers, civil servants etc. Evidence of the lack of discipline, that is, the lack of regimentation and structure in the lives of the poor which often was translated as a lack of morals and decency was often purported to support the "facts" of their lawlessness and hence their poverty. "Look at them having the children out of wedlock—spending their money in the bars, leaning on the broom stick and talking instead of working." The Peters, the Jameses and the Johns, who took Jesus' injunction seriously whether wittingly or unwittingly, in terms of not caring about the "morrow" and not putting family first, that is abandoning their family and being around "publicans and sinners" or being "publicans and sinners" were despised as lawless, lazy, crooks, dishonest, having Anancy mentality and that is why they are poor and of the "lower class."

When sections of the Bible were read about Jesus breaking rules or sermons preached about Jesus being more concerned about love than about rules, I could not help but reflect on the significance of rules in our culture. Although I did sometimes balk at the many rules at Wolmer's, I did somehow realize that regimentation gave my life structure. I could not help but note also how in the elementary school which was not as regimented as the high school, life could be chaotic and one could be subjected to arbitrary punishment. I much preferred the environment of having rules where I somehow could predict what would happen if I broke a rule than one where I was subjected to the whims of love and as a result was often subjected to arbitrary punishment.

I never trusted love because love was unpredictable. Today I could feel very secure basking in the warmth of love, and tomorrow I could be subjected to severe lashings—without any explanation, totally irrational. How would I know that it is wrong for me to "make a lot of noise" while playing outside, if there were no rules about not making noise as you played outside? God loves you, I was often told. Divine love, I often mused is fickle. My first conclusion regarding the irrationality of Divine love was when I was seven. My beloved aunt died—there was no warning—just an arbitrary decision on God's part to "take her home." My earliest recollections are at my aunt's house. What kind of love would take away an aunt who loved me?

In terms of Jesus' disappearance when he was twelve, ministers in sermons would rationalize this behavior as Jesus being special. I often perceived Jesus as not only special but privileged. I had a "thing about" the privileged. I resented and, at the same time, I was envious of the privileged. The privileged white and nearly white students at Wolmer's High School would often pull rank. "Do you know who I am?" was stated or indicated by bodies held erect and faces filled with pride. "I am Mr. So-and-So's daughter. In the eyes of teachers and students your status would move up several notches if you were related to an important person. There was a famous person with my surname and the teachers would always ask if I was related to that person. I longed to say I was to upgrade my status in the eyes of teachers and peers but when I went home and asked my father if we were related, he said we were not and I was never to tell the teachers that I am. I therefore was very envious of students who would boast about their father being the town clerk or a doctor or a politician or the owner of stores.

Not only did I not have a relative that I could boast about, but I was actually ashamed of my father's profession. He was a Sanitary Inspector. My father would not allow us to "dress him up and parade him" as any profession other than that of a Sanitary Inspector, which my father held in contempt because he wanted to be a doctor. In this matter, however, I defied him. I told my peers that my father was a Civil Servant, a rank above my father's status as Sanitary Inspector. As he worked for the Kingston and St. Andrew Corporation and his office—he actually had an office—was in the same building as Civil Servants and Kingston and St. Andrew Corporation was somehow linked to the Civil Service—I convinced myself that I had only garnished a lie.

However, for some reason whenever I heard a passage being read from the Bible in Church, at Sunday School or at school—we rarely read the Bible at home—where Jesus said, "Do you know who I am?' I could not help but compare that question to my peers', stated or implied, "Do you know who I am?" As far as I was concerned, Jesus was pulling rank, as my peers did.

Based on all these thoughts I came to the conclusion when I was around thirteen or fourteen that Jesus was not perfect. For days I mulled over my standpoint—Jesus is not perfect. Normally I tended to discuss issues that preyed on my mind with my mother. It was her custom to listen and very often soothe or allay my fears and doubts. No matter how painful, and some of what I divulged must have pained her like my feeling alienated by my peers at school, she would calmly listen and comfort me by showing me another viewpoint or advising me how to handle the situation. I do not know whether she had ascribed this attribute because of her pale complexion or it was due to her personality or whether it was fostered as a result of the teaching of the Anglican Church, but my mother rarely showed anger—even when she whipped me—it was with a calm deliberation.

In spite of my mother's good nature, I was somewhat apprehensive about divulging my thoughts about Jesus because I felt they were sinful thoughts. The thoughts weighed on my mind for sometime. I was confident that my mother would listen, and although I had some reservations, particularly since I knew my thoughts were somewhat sacrilegious, there was just a flicker of hope that they would be considered insightful reasoning. It was very rare, very rare indeed, but not totally unusual for there to be an admiring look whenever I did or said something "profound".

My mother and I were standing on the back porch of our home when I suddenly blurted out, "Mamma, I don't think Jesus is perfect." I expected her to say, at least, "Why do you say that?" and then I would launch into my reasons as outlined above. I never before saw my mother react the way she did. It was as though I had struck her. Surprise, fear, and anguish registered on her face. She moved away from me and calling me by my name, she said in a very firm voice, "Never say that again. That is blasphemy. You will go to hell." And without another word, she walked into the rest of the house.

This would be a major turning point in my life. As I was terrified of going to hell, I decided that I would make peace with Jesus—I would no longer question his divinity.

After sometime, I wanted to appease my mother—her manner was a cold withdrawal—typical of Christians I have found—for several weeks. It was my mother's response and my desire to appease her that led me to the decision that I would seek confirmation. Such a decision was imminent, anyway. So anxious was I to make amends, however, that I decided to preempt my mother by telling her I wanted to be confirmed. She was very pleased and the atmosphere lightened. I began to hope that confirmation would transform the bad thoughts I had about Jesus.

Many years later I realized that my mother's reaction was not only due to her genuine fear of my spending eternity in hell, but she was also fearful that my atheistic father had triumphed over her, the Christian mother. As far back as I can remember, both my mother and my father tried to root out any trait or characteristic, they saw in me, as his, such as my impulsiveness, "bad temper", and not completing huge projects which I randomly undertook. I, of course, had these personality traits because of all the siblings I resembled my father the most. I, like my father, was tall, and of extreme significance I was closest to his dark complexion. Every time I reacted with any anger or did anything impulsive (which were frequent) I would be told by my mother, mother's family, and helpers. "See. You are just like your father." It was often implied that if my father were a Christian, it would no doubt have some palliative effect on his personality—but alas my father refused to become a church member.

Indeed, when I was born he emphatically and resolutely told my mother that he was an atheist and that I should not be christened. Eventually when I was about a year, my mother and my aunt (her beloved sister who died in childbirth) surreptitiously took me to the church during a weekday and had me christened. How ashamed my mother was not to have her husband present—to have me christened like "illegitimate" babies, as they were stigmatized then, on a weekday instead of on a Sunday when all her family and friends could be present to witness my christening –as an infant, not a toddler=- as the product of a stalwart Anglican family?

Very upsetting was the fact that my father drank a lot with friends, and he used to say, my mother told me, terrible things about Jesus—either that Jesus had girlfriends or that Jesus was, and here her voice would often subside into a whisper, "you know—it was not until I was an adult that I knew such things existed between men." My mother was very pleased and frequently congratulated herself on her wisdom, courage, and tenaciousness, in defying my father and having me christened. Tribute was often paid to her sister who initiated the enterprise and actually was instrumental in arranging my christening. Can you imagine therefore how devastating it must have been for my mother to listen to my propounding an argument that was similar to my father's and that before I was fifteen? I was not fifteen because I was confirmed when I was fourteen and my thinking about Jesus' perfection took place before I was confirmed.

My mother was no Bible touting Christian, but she did want me to adhere to the doctrines of the Anglican Church particularly in terms of believing in the divinity and perfection of Jesus. Probably it can be asserted that my father's atheistic outlook contributed to my sacrilegious view of Jesus. My mother would have been aghast to know, however, that my father's criticism of Jesus as having girl friends or being gay had very little to do with my questioning Jesus' divinity; rather, it was my mother's mores and norms regarding how one should relate to others that influenced my critique of Jesus.

My father did make some changes over the years. He stopped drinking although my mother often commented that she did not know which was better—his being out with his friends drinking or being home and being "cumuging" (curmudgeon). My father did not object to my siblings being christened. At times, he would attend, not the morning services, but the evening service at the Anglican Church mainly at the instigation of my mother who saw the family attending church as a necessary conduit to her career as a teacher. I think, however, that my father realized that it was difficult to remain totally outside the Church and have some kind of respectability. However, he never became a member of the church.

I was confident that confirmation would bring about my radical transformation. I eagerly looked forward to the classes that I had to attend in preparation for confirmation. There was some disappointment, however. After the first session which the minister conducted, we would sit many evenings, and wait in vain for the minister to appear. Sometimes a deacon was apparently asked to be his substitute or we would be sent home. My mother was furious. Preparation is important. She smiled, however, as usual and said nothing to the minister, each time she saw him at church. At the first session, the minister told us to memorize what should be our responses in the Confirmation Section of the Prayer Book. So eager was I to have everything right, that I tried to comply. All I managed to commit to memory, however, was: "What is your name?" N or M. Who gave you that name?" At the only other session the minister conducted, he desperately and as far as I am concerned futilely tried to explain the Trinity, that is, how God was three persons, Father, Son, and Holy Ghost and yet these three persons were one God.

I was however undeterred by lack of preparation. I was confident that I would receive the Holy Spirit and I would be changed. My bad thoughts about Jesus not being perfect, my temper, my impulsiveness, my starting huge projects and not completing them, would all go away.

Girls solemnly dressed in white dresses—I cannot recall if there were boys—knelt at the communion rail. Girls had to wear white for white stands for purity. I waited with eager anticipation as the Bishop of Jamaica, Bishop Gibson, a Jamaican of peanut complexion with a prominent nose, a wide mouth, and bespectacled tiny eyes, moved around the communion rail and placed his hand on each of our heads. I expected, although I did not know exactly what, that I would feel something, and there would be immediate transformation. Except for the weight of the Bishop's hand, I felt nothing. Nothing happened. I was very, very, *very* disappointed.

My only other memory of the service was the Bishop preaching to us and asking us questions to which none of us responded and his bellowing at us, in an Anglo Saxon accent in the pulpit, from time to time, , "You don't know your "Byyyyyy-bleees-s-s-s, you don't know your Byyyyyy-bleees-s-s-s" . If his questions were a test of our preparation, clearly the minister had failed. Remembering my mother's anger, I looked at the minister. However he seemed not at all perturbed. He wore as usual his wide u shaped thin lipped grin. Many Jamaicans were proud of the Jamaican peanut complexioned Bishop Gibson. For some of us, however, his, what we termed, "Anglo Saxon" accent was very funny—the unquestionable British accent out of a Jamaican face which clearly denoted some African heritage.

I was so disappointed on the day of confirmation. I felt nothing. The temper, the impulsiveness, the thoughts about Jesus did not go away. I could, however, take Communion and so ask forgiveness of my sins. Even though I felt that I was a bad person, I need not worry. I had some confidence that I would make it into heaven.

Or so I thought.

CHAPTER SEVEN

BECOMING A FUNDAMENTALIST-I; WOLMER'S HIGH SCHOOL FOR GIRLS

"It was in religion that Europeans worked hardest to influence Negro culture in the nineteenth century..." [300]

Philip D. Curtin

Many of us as high school students in the 1950's were totally unaware of the existence of the Cold War between the Soviet Union, the Communist Bloc, on the one hand, and the West primarily England and America, the Capitalist Bloc, on the other. The Cold War in the eyes of capitalist countries was perceived mainly as a communist threat, that is, the attempt of the Soviet Union to spread communist ideology, often referred to as communist propaganda, worldwide. We were also unaware that there was a lot of concern therefore amongst leaders in Britain and America, the capitalist Bloc that colonies, and former colonies of the British Empire would fall prey to communist ideology and thus would be a loss to British and American, that is capitalist, sphere of influence and dominance. Christianity was perceived by a number of leaders as the antidote to the communist threat. As a result, there was a global attempt to evangelize territories that were considered vulnerable to communist influence. Jamaica was considered one such territory.

There were a number of ironies regarding the reasoning about evangelizing Jamaicans to counter the spread of communism. First and foremost, Jamaica was and is a Christian country. The history of Jamaica officially begins when the Spaniards captured the island from the peaceful native peoples, the Arawaks. One of the three main motives of Columbus' enterprise in 1492 was "the desire to spread the Christian faith to distant lands." [301] From 1494, when the Spaniards captured the island from the Arawaks, Christianity was instituted in the island under the Catholic Church. In the ruling of their vast empire in the Americas, the Spanish saw the Catholic Church as "necessary to the maintenance of Spanish domination as were the government officials." [302]

---

[300] Curtin, *Two Jamaicas,* p. 28.

[301] Clinton V. Black, *The Story of Jamaica from Prehistory to the Present,* (London, England: Collins, 1958), p. 24.

[302] R. Augier F, et. al., *The Making of the West Indies,* (Jamaica, WI: Longman Caribbean, 1960), p. 134.

Led by Admiral Penn and General Venables, Jamaica was captured from the Spanish by the British, in the 1660's (officially ceded in 1670), as part of Oliver Cromwell's Western Design. There were frequent disputes over religion between Catholic Spain and Protestant Britain and so part of the motives for the Western Design, that is, the attempt of the British to capture lands from Spain in the Americas, was religious.[303] In the Spanish colonies, the Catholic Church "was the only form of religion tolerated by their governments."[304] Jamaica, however, became overwhelmingly Protestant after the British captured the island.

Slavery was instituted by Europeans from the inception of the colonization of the Americas. Spain issued a special license called the *Asiento* to sell slaves in the Spanish Americas. This license was coveted by the Dutch, the French and the English and indeed since the *Asiento* limited the amount of slaves that could be brought to the Americas, the British, Dutch, and French merchants engaged in illegally selling slaves.[305] In other words, Christian Europe engaged in the selling of slaves in the Americas.

In the British colonies, although a number of planters resisted the slaves being taught Christianity based on the fear that Christianity would re-orient the views of the slaves regarding their humanity, every attempt was made to uproot the religions of the Africans which were considered pagan and barbaric.[306]

The religious revival at the end of the eighteenth century increased the number of missionaries in the British West Indies, and although the missionaries faced many obstacles, mainly opposition from the planters, they managed to convert a number of slaves to Christianity and to continue the movement of the suppression of any survival of African religions.[307] Not only did white missionaries—Anglicans, Baptists, Methodists, Presbyterians spread the gospel amongst slaves but blacks also worked to spread the gospel. The first Baptist Churches in Jamaica were actually established by African Americans.[308]

In the 1950's when there was an influx of evangelicals to Jamaica to stem the tide of communism, there was hardly anyone in Jamaica who was not a Christian, that is, who had not been baptized or christened in some church. Some may argue that in what were termed cults or sects such as

---

[303]Ibid.

[304]Ibid., p. 134.

[305]Ibid.

[306]Curtin, *Two Jamaicas*; Gordon, *Our Cause His Glory*.

[307]Gordon, *Our Cause for His Glory*.

[308]Augier, *The Making of the West Indies*; Gordon, *Our Cause for His Glory*.

Pocomania, there were remnants of African traditional religions. In the first place, "cults', such as Pocomania were marginally practiced amongst the poor and had little impact on the vast majority of Jamaicans. When one thinks of Christianity, one has to think of the religion as integral to the governance of the island from the inception of colonialism and slavery by the Europeans. The Christian religion dominates Jamaican culture in terms of its laws, norms and mores. Major social events, marriages, funerals, induction of government officials are officiated by Christian clergy. Sundays are holy days when shops and stores are closed. Indeed, the only religious holidays Jamaicans officially observe are Christian holidays—Christmas, Good Friday and Easter.

During all my years of growing up in Jamaica, I was never exposed to any other religion, or met anyone who tried to persuade me to become a member of another religion. It is true Rastafarians would reprimand me for going to the "white man's church" and "worshipping a white God" but I do not regard Rastafarianism as a worldview that is totally distinct from Christianity. In my view, Rastafarianism is more of a syncretism of Christianity, particularly in its espousal of redemption and salvation and reliance on the Bible, and African philosophy or thought and resistance to years of oppression of African peoples.[309] The Rastafarians' lack of clearly defined theological postulates, lack of an institutional structure and their reliance on the Bible, even if they had attempted to convert me, would not have been a religious alternative.

Growing up, there was vague talk of Arabs, Syrians and Jews. They owned major businesses and stores in Jamaica and were extremely wealthy. In my mind, however, there was no distinction among them; they all belonged to the same group. Although the daughters of some of these business people sat in the same classroom as I, they belonged to an entirely different world. My mother would often state that she could not believe that people whom members of her rural community would "laugh at", because they walked from house to house selling jewelry from a suitcase which they carried on their heads, were now the owners of stores and businesses and were incredibly wealthy.

I became aware of the existence of Jews, as a religious group, in Jamaica when I was an adult, and read that there were Jews in Jamaica and that a synagogue exists in Kingston which I do not recall seeing. I have also been told that there is a mosque in Spanish Town. Outside of the Christian religion, except for what we were taught about other religions, which was generally sketchy and which usually focused on their weaknesses, I had no

---

[309]Chevannes, *Rastafari;* Nettleford, *MirrorMirror*; Owens, *Dread.*

idea of the belief systems of other religions.

The British government regarded the Christian religion as a moralizing force for African peoples, and in every elementary school, prayer service was instituted at the start of the day and at the end of the day. Scripture was part of the curriculum for the First Year Jamaica Local, an examination taken by students of the elementary school. Most of the high schools were built by churches and thus prayers every morning was an integral part of learning. Besides prayers, which it was imperative for us to attend, Scripture was also taught in the high school as a subject. Jamaicans are well versed with regard to the Bible and as Gordon asserts, the "language and phraseology" are part of the "discourse" of Jamaicans "at many levels". Indeed, "three Prime Ministers...have been called Joshua, the deliverer, and the prophet..."[310]

Who then in the 1950's were the missionaries from England, United States of America, and Canada to convert since most Jamaicans were Christians? The "Christian religious life in whatever form" Gordon points out "was well rooted" in Jamaica "by the 1860's.[311]

How can you be converted from the religion in which you were born, Christianity, to Christianity?

Another irony was that white missionaries came from countries, particularly the United States where blatant racism was practiced, to preach to a majority black population about "salvation". During the 1950's, when white missionaries flocked Jamaica to convert Jamaicans mostly of African descent to Christianity, African peoples in the United States were subjected to some of the most brutal, oppressive, segregation laws in the country[312] that headquartered many Christian denominations and is a major supporter of missionary and evangelistic work. The existence of Black Churches and white Churches in America is empirical evidence of blatant overt racism and segregation.[313] Indeed, as already pointed out, comparisons were frequently made between the status of the Dalits in India, and blacks in the United States of America in terms of their social ostracism.

That high school students were the target of the missionizing zeal of missionaries from the United States, Canada, and Britain, was also ironical. Race is not as clearly defined nor racism as overtly practiced in Jamaica as it is in the United States, but racism exists in Jamaica. In Jamaica, you were not excluded from attending a high school based solely on race. However, because of the history of an elitist system of education based on class which

---

[310]Gordon, *Our Cause for His Glory*, p. 121-122.

[311]Ibid., p. 121.

[312]Franklin & Moss, Jr. *From Slavery to Freedom.*

[313]Lincoln and Mamiya, *The Black Church.*

was to a large extent determined by skin color, the majority of Jamaicans, most of whom were of African descent, was excluded from high schools. In Jamaica therefore, students of African descent who were part of a privileged few to attend high school were subjected to evangelical onslaught from individuals from a country that denied equal education opportunities to African Americans.

World wide organizations, the School Christian Movement, the Inter-Schools Christian Fellowship and the Inter-Varsity Christian Fellowship headquartered in Britain all established branches in the high schools and at the University and which deliberately excluded the primary schools in Jamaica. Thus the evangelical movement then perpetrated the class and elite system that was part of the educational system in Jamaica.

It was also ironical that while the evangelicals targeted the high school students, the content of the Christian message and the approach to evangelization were anti-intellectual. Anti-intellectualism and ignorance pervaded a movement that targeted the "brightest" in the island.

How did I fall prey to this movement that would stifle my intellectual, psychological, and social growth for more than fifteen years?

There were a number of factors that caused me to be labeled as not very bright from a child. I did not speak until I was three and when I did speak I was not as entertaining nor did I ask as many questions as my brother who was a little more that a year younger than I. Added to this, was the fact that from a toddler, I was much taller than the average infant. I was constantly mistaken as being older than I was. The result was that I was labeled "fool fool" for I was acting my age in an older child's body; it was often stated that I had "outgrown my senses". This was an expression that was frequently applied to tall children. It seemed as if adults thought that there was a fixed amount of grey matter at birth or some earlier point in your life and that your brain does not grow in conjunction with your height so that if you rapidly grow tall, your brain would remain far too small to adequately think and reason in accordance with your age.

It was not until my middle child was three years old that it dawned on me why I was labeled "big and fool fool" and that I had "outgrown my senses." At three, my daughter looked like five or six, and in many ways her behavior seemed strange particularly when she threw a tantrum which she often did. She had a playmate, Suzie, who was also three. One day Suzie threw a tantrum. She jumped up and down on her little feet the same way my daughter jumped up and down on her longer legs. After a while, I began to notice that my daughter's behavior, in many other aspects, was no different from Suzie's and other little girls her age. She was not strange; she was acting her age. It suddenly clicked. I was a tall child acting my age and so whatever I did appeared magnified and stupid; hence the label "big and fool fool". The inverse of "big and fool fool" or "growing out your senses" worked for children who are very petite. Whereas the tall child of five who looks like eight appears silly, the child of eight who looks like five seems to be very clever. The brain for many adults functions more effectively in a more compact sized body. For years, my greatest fear was to do or look any way foolish, and sometimes in an effort to avoid being foolish, I did stupid things.

Besides being tall, and not speaking until I was three, I could not compute as quickly or as accurately as my brother the columns of figures my father would leave us before he went to work. No matter how hard I tried, invariably my answers would be incorrect and my brother's correct. One day when I was about eight, I debated about doing a sum—one in which I had to subtract a bottom row of three digits from a top row of three digits (hundreds, tens, units) with a zero in the middle. I did the sum correctly borrowing from the hundreds, etc., and then I looked at my neighbor's answer. She was not only a couple years older than I, (my father had insisted on our going to school younger than required), but she was of mixed Chinese and African heritage. Even at that young age, I had internalized that she must be brighter than I, not so much because she was older but because she was lighter than I, part Chinese "to boot". I erased my answer and copied hers. My mother was the teacher. I still was very unsure and remained riveted in my seat. The next thing I knew I was standing before my mother, in front of the class, receiving several lashes on my legs. My mother was not only upset that I had got my sum wrong, but I had hidden my book under the desk and remained in my seat instead of walking up to her to get my sums corrected as the other children did. She did not take kindly to my trying to "hide". As the teacher's daughter, she had to make an example of me. I received more lashes than the other children.

Maybe I would have forgotten the incident, for it happened when I was about eight, except for the fact that the error I made plus hiding my book under the desk provided empirical evidence not only regarding my ability to do arithmetic but my feelings towards arithmetic. For years, it was a mantra around the house "you hate arithmetic...you hid your book under the desk". I would never live down that episode of "hiding your book under the desk", and how "hiding" my "book under the desk" came to be linked with the fact that "I hate arithmetic", I will never know.

Now arithmetic was the index of being bright and it became a real issue in my case because it festered divergent views my parents had about ability. My mother strongly believed in innate ability; my father did not and this is ironic because my mother was a teacher and my father was not. My mother as a primary school teacher was greatly influenced by the pedagogical theories at the time, which to a large extent, was dominated by phrenological views that the brain was "composed of discrete organs, rather than being a homogeneous whole."[314]

Varying parts of the brain determined certain moral behavior and mental ability. The reason for the range of behavior in human beings is due to the fact that individuals have different sized "bumps" on the brain with regards to mental and moral capability. To support their claim, phrenologists gathered skulls from several regions of the world including Africa, Asia and Latin America. It is not surprising therefore that phrenology was used to buttress class divisions and racism. Based on the pseudoscience of measuring skulls, skulls of peoples around the globe were ranked. The outcome was that the skulls of upper class Anglo Saxons, of course, were the most superior. According to orthodox phrenologists, ability is fixed from birth and there is very little that education can do to enhance mental powers.[315] Thus the term numbskull was a popular term for "dunce" when I was growing up.

My mother would discuss how elementary school teachers would take delight in looking at a child's head, usually a boy, and argue amongst themselves whether the child is "bright" or "good at arithmetic" based on the shape of his head. Phrenological theory that the brain is composed of discrete faculties which are fixed at birth still dominates the educational system in America and the West. The brain is not seen as an organ, a homogeneous whole that can be stimulated by learning.

I do not know what it is about arithmetic—not English, science, foreign language or native language, history, geography—why it is used as an index as to whether one is "bright" or not. When I was going to school, since you did not receive partial credit for incorrectly computed sums, (multiple choice was unheard of) you would easily fall into the category of "dunce" if you failed to obtain an almost perfect score every time you did arithmetic. Once you could not calculate quickly and accurately, you were permanently cast into the mould of being "dumb". There was the misconception, which indeed still exists, that you are either born with the ability to do arithmetic (or any branch of mathematics) or you are not. It was believed and still is that any kind of struggle or frustration is an indication that you are not possessed with the ability to do arithmetic; you are not "bright". To develop skills in doing

---

[314] Adrian Desmond & James Moore, *Darwin's Sacred Cause: How a Hatred of Slavery Shaped Darwin's Views on Human Evolution,* (New York, NY: Houghton Mifflin Harcourt, 2009), p. 31
[315] Ibid.

arithmetic, or to show or teach you how you could improve is violating what destiny had determined for you.

Over the years, my mother and I would argue back and forth about being naturally bright or having fixed innate ability to do certain subjects like arithmetic, music, and art. It was pointless my using the argument of a Chinese co-worker who pointed out to me how working in her parents' shop from she was about six, (she had to stand on a box to reach the counter) having to quickly calculate cost of items and change (there were no adding machines or computers then) enhanced her ability to do arithmetic. She actually recommended I read a book called *Fanshen* which highlighted how population and competition affect Chinese performance. My mother would point out to me case after case of students, usually boys, who at an early age displayed phenomenal talent in music or art or who learned quickly and were very bright. She told me of the renowned Jamaican sculptor (I think it was Alvin Marriot) who from a little boy would abscond from school and go to the river where he would spend hours whittling figures from sticks. I was sometimes included in the list of people born with a specific talent. In her estimation, I had a natural "gift" for music in the light of the fact that I enjoyed playing the piano—note reading and playing popular pieces by ear.

I have often thought of the discussions I had with my mother as well as with others who maintain that you are born with ability to do certain subjects, particularly mathematics. What I have come to realize only recently is that the renowned Jamaican sculptor could spend hours whittling figures from sticks, or an artist can spend hours painting or I could spend hours playing the piano, we would never be considered lacking in ability in these areas. One, however, should not spend hours whittling away at mathematics, or chemistry, or physics. To spend hours whittling away at these subjects is evidence of lack of ability. It took me years to overcome this view, and unfortunately a lot of blacks and women are low achievers in science and mathematics because of a prevailing view that "if these subjects are not easy for you, then you do not have the ability to pursue them." Like art, like drama, like music, like sculpturing, mathematics and science have to be "whittled at" for hours.

It was my father's wish that my mother subject us to the kind of rigor that many teachers (in spite of their belief in innate ability) inflicted on their own children. It was the norm for children, as young as six or seven, of primary school teachers to spend hours after school, on Saturdays, and during vacation doing academic work with their parents. The object of these sessions was to enable the child to compete for the very few coveted government scholarships to the top ranking high schools or at least pass the entrance examinations for the most prestigious schools. A strap over the shoulder of the parent to reinforce their authority just in case of defiant behavior like expressing the wish to go outside and play, or for making "stupid" mistakes particularly while doing "sums" was not atypical. As a result, many teachers' children won government scholarships and so it was felt by the community at large that children of teachers were naturally bright.

My mother did not believe that the home should be the place for the sort of regimentation that my father wanted. Indeed, my mother felt that teachers who subjected their children to that kind of rigor were giving their own children, who may or may not be naturally "bright", an unfair advantage since some of these teachers did not exhibit a modicum of the intense care and concern for the majority of children they teach. The upshot of it was that amongst my peers, I never for the most part fitted the stereotype of the "bright" teacher's child which I really wanted to be.

My mother may have also been influenced by another prevalent pedagogical view that play in a child's life is important. Hours of unsupervised, unstructured play were for my mother an integral part of our life. Indeed, we would often get in trouble with our father who in the midst of our romping outdoors would call us indoors and whip us for "making too much noise" and not heeding his frequently quoted injunction, "Chicken merry, hawk de near." In other words, one should be careful about being too happy because it is when one is most happy that one is most vulnerable to misfortunes. It took my sister and I with whom I often discuss the "chicken merry, hawk de near" precept, years to rid ourselves of the fear of being too happy. I related to her how I observed, in my adult years, that hawks would swoop on chickens whether they were merry or not.

My father need not have worried about play for it seemed the bump on my skull for play was negligible or non-existent. After about half an hour of unstructured play, I was usually bored. My siblings could not understand how gradually I would cease playing with them altogether as I found playing the piano or "having my nose" in a book much more rewarding. My thirst for knowledge and intellectual pursuits—this did not include playing the piano which was regarded as a separate faculty altogether with its own bump—was often interpreted as compensation for lack of ability. I was labeled a plodder which essentially means I had very little innate ability or I was dumb and had to work hard to learn anything in the category of the academic.

What I believe mainly influenced my mother's thinking, however, is that she grew up in a household where there was to a large extent a lack of strict regimentation. Her father was a teacher and something of a phenomenon. Part of my grandfather's duties as headmaster of Cavaliers Primary School was to preach and participate in Sunday worship at St. Christopher's

Anglican Church, Cavaliers. He bought a little organ and taught himself to play from a book called *Smallwood's* and after awhile accompanied church services. He attempted to teach his children to play the organ with the caveat that you may need the skill to acquire a job. My mother was the only one who heeded his warning, however; she dutifully sat by him at the organ and learnt to read the notes. Just as my grandfather predicted, my mother's ability to play hymns was a great advantage over other applicants for teaching positions. My grandfather seemed to have also been interested in being part of the landed gentry because he bought a lot of property in the rural area of St. Andrew.

He married my grandmother—no doubt her very pale complexion and long black hair were part of her appeal—who was a dressmaker, and was very resourceful in terms of other skills, such as basket weaving, embroidery, and making items from straw. She had, however, very little formal education. She was, in awe of her husband whom she called "teacher". My grandmother never made any attempt to correct her oldest child in terms of calling my grandmother Amatty, patterning the speech of her older cousin's "Amatty" (a corruption of Aunt Matty) who was living with my grandmother at that time. Consequently, to my mother's embarrassment at times, all her children and her grandchildren grew up calling my grandmother "Amatty". Supervision in terms of formal education then fell more to my grandfather than to my grandmother who seemed to have had her hands full rearing her six children, taking care of extended family, running a household, supervising farm hands, directing "maids", plus looking after goats and pigs.

My mother and her five siblings were never whipped. It may have been due to the lightness of their complexion as a number of dark skinned children of the community opined; in their view, my mother and her siblings were "spoilt". It may have been due, however, to two horrendous events, as a result of corporal punishment, that had an impact on my grandfather: his brother after receiving a severe whipping from his father as a boy ran away and no one ever heard from him again and a little girl in Cavaliers, after being flogged, crawled under a bed and died.

My father strongly believed in effort. Shipped at an early age to Jamaica by his father from Panama where my grandfather had migrated to work on the Canal, my father was sent, as was the norm then for parents who wanted their children to succeed, to board with a teacher. Teacher Turner was renowned for achieving success by applying discipline, mainly through the use of the rod or the strap on the back or the rump. There was zero tolerance for giving incorrect answers or doing incorrect assignments. My father apparently applied himself diligently to learning. He told us as children how once he missed getting a whipping. During a session called General Knowledge which was part of the curriculum in those days, Teacher Turner asked, "What is the meaning of B.A? My father was one of the first to raise his hand. Teacher Turner turned to my father and said, "Ricketts, I know you know the answer, and asked another boy. My father said he was utterly astonished when the boy replied Bachelor of Arts, for my father newly arrived to Jamaica and speaking very little English, would have responded "Big Ass" the popular disparaging meaning for the abbreviated B. A. He shuddered at the thought of what would have been the result had he told Teacher Turner, "Big Ass".

My father's mother, Rebecca Ricketts (nee Bryan) was very tall and extremely strict. She would whip my father on the slightest pretext. One day after whipping him he hid in a tree and remained there for many hours. He only came down after he heard her wailing as to how could she inform her husband (who was in Panama) about the disappearance of their only son.

The question of my ability in terms of my father's expectations hovered between my parents during my formative years. Sometimes in the middle of play, my parents would call me over to solve a problem. Usually it was a "trick" question. Invariably my answer would be incorrect. I remember once they asked me, "If one egg takes three minutes to boil, how long will three eggs take?" There must be a catch I thought, but what could be the catch? I deliberated for some minutes trying to figure out what the answer could be other than 9. There was a vague doubt, but surely I must be right this time. "9 minutes" I told them semi-confidently covering up my doubt and hoping against hope that I was right. They both shook their heads and called a neighbor's peanut complexion, brown wavy hair nephew, Duke, who had the reputation of being very bright. Duke thought for just about a second and answered 3 minutes. As I walked away I heard my father say, "If she spent more time in the kitchen cooking" (for Duke as an orphan was constantly doing chores in the kitchen and around his aunt's house) "she would know that all the eggs would take the same amount of time to boil". Apparently, my father was not entirely convinced about the lack of a mathematical bump in my brain.

By the age of ten, however, I was convinced that I was dunce, a numbskull. My father was not deterred in his view that effort would bring about achievement. On June 19, 1952 to be exact, he bought me a copy of *Arithmetic* by Loney and Grenville, which I still have up to this day. Some time after the egg problem, my father asked me what high school I wanted to attend. I was elated. I would become part of the uppermost echelon of the four-tiered stratified system of education imposed by Britain on her Caribbean colonies. The high school served as the conduit to the top stratum of the society.

High school was for the privileged few. As Gordon points out "as fees were required only a small proportion of the population" could afford "more than a primary education for their children." [316]   High school students were greatly respected. Some would often return to visit Half Way Tree Primary School, the school I attended when I was nine and ten, proudly dressed in their uniforms. These students would be treated like royalty. I wanted to go to a high school. When my father asked me what school I wanted to attend, I told him Wolmer's thinking that the uniform—the white blouse navy blue tunic encircled at the waist by white crocheted belt—that some of the students who visited Half Way Tree Primary wore, and which I really liked, was the uniform of Wolmer's. It was actually Alpha's uniform, a Catholic school. It turned out that my father was delighted with my choice; he would not have been pleased had I chosen Alpha.

Wolmer's was a prestigious school partly because it was one of the oldest high schools in Jamaica and partly because it was the most expensive high school in Kingston. Over several weeks, my mother raised issues and concerns. Her arguments generally were as follows: Why will we be making a huge financial sacrifice to send her to a secondary school? Why does she have to attend a high school? What's wrong with her going to primary school, and then Shortwood College and becoming a primary school teacher like me? If she does go to a high school, why can't it be Ardenne or Merle Grove where she will meet and socialize with students of her socio-economic class? Mrs. Brown who was her elementary teacher but who is going to teach at Ardenne is very fond of her; Mrs. Brown expressed the wish for her to attend Ardenne. My father remained silent—implacable with just a hint of a smile on his face; it was as though my mother had not spoken. I would sit the entrance for Wolmer's.

However, before I took the entrance for Wolmer's, my father insisted that I take the entrance examination for St. Andrew High School. He was secretly hoping that I would go to St. Andrew. In the 1950's, St. Andrew had the reputation for academic rigor and was considered by many to be the best high school in Jamaica. St. Andrew was the top ranking school, followed by Wolmer's and then St. Hugh's. My mother had no doubt of what the outcome would be. Though I was fearful of going to St. Andrew, I hoped that I would pass the entrance examination and shock them both.

My parents were not surprised when I failed the entrance for St.

---

[316]Shirley C. Gordon, *A Century of West Indian Education: A Source Book,* compiled with a commentary by Shirley C. Gordon, (London, England: Longman, 1963), p. 239.

Andrew. From the moment I told them, immediately after the examination, as we were driving home in our Austen 8 car, that as part of the examination I read a passage aloud to a white person, and when she asked me what melancholy meant I told her "happy" they knew that my fate to attend St. Andrew was sealed. I learnt the meaning of melancholy then from their response, "Happy is the very opposite of what melancholy means!" The fact that being tested orally was part of the examination did not escape my father's notice. He commented to my mother that it gave the teacher the opportunity to accept or reject a prospective student based on class and skin color: it was not surprising therefore that St. Andrew had the reputation of excluding dark skin children, particularly those from the lower socio-economic class.

What my father observed was not over stating the case. All the high schools discriminated. As already pointed out they were fee based and since "the monied group", as Gordon postulates, "was white and fair-skinned" the "question of colour has often been raised in connection with admission to secondary schools".[317] For the most part, during the 1950's only dark skin, "springy, wiry" haired children who were exceptionally bright, that is, who won government scholarships, usually the children of teachers, attended St. Andrew. Wolmer's did not give an oral examination.

My parents were extremely delighted when they received from Wolmer's a thick envelope which included a pattern and instructions for my uniform. That I was placed in the lowest stream, 3^3, did not matter. I had passed the Entrance Examination for Wolmer's. The third form was officially the first form of the high school. The first and second forms were really an extension of the Preparatory School. Wealthy parents then circumvented their children taking the entrance examination by sending them to Wolmer's Preparatory School where they automatically were promoted to the high school, the lowest form being designated Third Form.

WOLMER'S HIGH SCHOOL FOR GIRLS

The first day I walked through the gates and under, directly above the gates, the steel arch with the motto "Agae quod Aegis" inscribed in the school colors, maroon and gold, it was as though I entered a world entirely different than my home, family and community surroundings. I should not say that it was entirely different than my home, family and community. To be more accurate, it was the concretization of the world in which my home, family, and community were marginalized, for in every sphere of our lives,

---

[317]Ibid., p. 239.

the upper class Anglo Saxon culture of Great Britain was the norm. Wolmer's in many ways replicated the private schools in England for the privileged class.

I was eleven years old and was convinced that I was inferior. In many ways wittingly or unwittingly, Wolmer's would corroborate this view. Unlike the elementary school, most of the teachers were from Britain or Canada or they were beige to peanut complexioned Jamaicans with wavy hair. For the seven years that I attended Wolmer's, Wolmer's employed only a handful of teachers that were of brownish yellowish, cocoa, coffee complexion with springy hair which they straightened.[318] Whereas the whites and Jamaican whites were almost a permanent fixture of the staff of Wolmer's, some remaining on the staff long enough to teach the offspring of children they taught, the few cocoa brown, springy hair Jamaican teachers , except for one or two, were transient. I clearly recall two suddenly leaving after, it was rumored, a short intolerable stay.

I had to make several adaptations to my new surroundings: six periods of the day each ending and starting at a specific time announced by the ringing of bells instead of a long structureless day of the elementary school where change in subject was arbitrarily decided by the teacher; different teachers and teaching styles, each giving a flurry of directions or instructions, many of which in my first year at Wolmer's, completely baffled me; British or Canadian accent of the teachers instead of modulated accent of Jamaican teachers. At Wolmer's, I had my own desk. At Half Way Tree Elementary School, sometimes five or six of us would have to share a desk built for the most three.

To attend a high school in those days was very costly. Unlike the primary school, a cardinal rule was that you had to have your own supplies; you could not borrow even a pencil from another student. Besides school fees, my parents had to purchase a whole set of exercise books, thirteen in all—all these books were imported from England and had the *insignia* of Wolmer's stamped on them; we could use no other. Then there were also text books, pens, pencils, rulers, geometry sets, materials for uniform, berets (which had to be dry cleaned) school bag, tennis racquet, if you chose to play tennis which I did, and brown leather shoes. Besides regular staples of lunch money and bus fare, there were also incidental requests for money to

---

[318]See photograph of staff of Wolmer's High School for Girls, 1946—many of whom were present when I attended Wolmer's 1953-1959—and photograph of staff, 1956 in Maguerite Curtin et. al. *In the Light of the Sun: the Story of Wolmer's Girls' School, Kingston, Jamaica,* (Kingston, Ja: Wolmer's Girls' Alumnae, 2009), p. 82 & 87.

purchase a gift for a teacher or make a contribution to some organization, for example. My parents had to make a lot of sacrifices to meet the expense of my attending Wolmer's.

We were rarely given home work in the elementary school. At Wolmer's, I just needed a few detentions to remind me about the responsibility of not only doing home work, but submitting it on time. Homework was just one of the several items I had to remember to take to school. My mother saved me from numerous detentions. Every morning as I walked through the gate on my way to the bus stop, she would run behind me, "Do you have your home work? Do you have your gym clothes? Do you have your geometry set? Do you have your badges? Do you have your handkerchief?"

My father felt that Wolmer's would open up for me a world from which he was excluded. Although my father passed the Jamaica Local Examinations and entered a tertiary institution, the Sanitary Inspector School, he had sat the Jamaica Local Examinations under the auspices of the Elementary School. He had not set foot one day in a high school. This in many ways restricted his employment and opportunities for upward social mobility. In fact, someone who had been to a recognized high school (the high schools which some enterprising Jamaicans established in their living rooms and verandahs were not recognized, although some evolved and achieved "recognition") for one term and had not been successful in an examination would rank higher in status than my father who passed the Jamaica Local Examinations and graduated from the Sanitary Inspector School. Indeed someone who had attended a recognized high school would have access to certain jobs, such as working in the bank and other private firms, from which my father was barred in spite of his certificates. The educational system was basically four tiered: (i) lowest tier, primary school education only, (ii) post primary education, (iii) some high school education and (iv) the highest tier, graduate of a university.

As most of the high schools in Jamaica were built and financed, with some government aid, by a denomination of the Christian Church, the church played, and hence the Christian religion played a significant role in this four tiered educational system. According to Gordon, there was an "increase in the number of secondary schools in the twentieth century" as "religious bodies continued to establish new schools" which "by different arrangements and at varying times in the different territories" received "government grants".[319] The church, with the overt agreement of the Jamaican government played a major role in the stratification of the Jamaican society

---

[319]Gordon, *A Century of West Indian Education*, p. 266, italics mine.

by building just a few high schools which served an elite, privileged group while the vast majority of Jamaican people were denied the right to a high school education and thus assigned to the lower ranks of the society. The only means of access to the high school were the few scholarships that the government provided. "The increased number of secondary school pupils, *though still less than 1% of their age group,* meant increased competition for the coveted Island Scholarships."[320]

Thus the Church, and hence the Christian religion by excluding the vast majority of the population from high school education promoted elitism in Jamaica. The churches then played a significant role in the caste system where education was the right and privilege of whites (the Brahmins) and poor people of primarily African descent (the Dalits) were excluded.

My father thought that attending Wolmer's would open up for me immediate acceptance into the elite society of Jamaica. He thought that wearing the same uniform —white blouse, turquoise blue A line tunic, turquoise blue beret, white socks and brown shoes—would be the great social equalizer in terms of the status of students who attended Wolmer's and the same equitable treatment would be applied to all. He did not understand that class and skin color transcended uniforms.

From my very first week at Wolmer's I could not help but note that not only were the teachers white or very nearly so but that most of the girls who attended Wolmer's did not look at all like me. While skin color was a factor, the real divisive factor was the hair. So someone of my brownish yellowish complexion with long shiny hair would rank in higher status than a straw complexioned or pine complexioned girl with wiry or springy hair that had to be straightened. At all the elementary schools, "shiny" hair students stood out amongst the wiry or springy hair students. Here at Wolmers, as was the case in most of the high schools, wiry or springy hair students clearly formed the minority. Most of the minority, pine, peanut, cocoa brown complexion students came from the elementary school while the shiny or straight hair beige, peach, pink, cocoa complexion students came from preparatory or "prep" schools as they were termed. For my first five years at Wolmers, the Head Girl, the top ranking student in the school was either white or peanut complexioned with shiny hair.

Although most of the students were from the upper echelon of the society, there were a few whose parents were in the same social bracket as my parents. For a number of parents in my parents' socio-economic class realized, like my father, the importance of high school education. Indeed, it seemed that the year I entered Wolmer's, 1953, a number of parents from a

---

[320]Ibid., p. 266, italics mine.

burgeoning middle class were determined to infiltrate the elite class promulgated by exclusive schools, such as Wolmers. Wolmer's, however, would in many ways bring to awareness the great social divide amongst the classes. Wealthy, middle class, and struggling working class sat in the same classroom but there was very little social interaction.

Within my first term, I soon learnt that rank and status played a very important role in the teacher's perception of the student. If you were Mr. So and So's or Mrs. So-and So's daughter or you were related to So and So or if your mother happened to have attended Wolmer's, particularly if she was taught by the teacher who is now teaching you, you would be beamed on, and elevated several notches not only in the estimation of the teacher, but in the perception of the students. I wanted to be beamed at.

In my anxiety to be accepted, one day in my first year at Wolmer's, I ran to the table, in the classroom, of one of the only Jamaican teachers who taught us that year to let her know that I was the daughter of the sister of her brother's deceased wife. Indeed from my classroom 3^3, I could clearly see the house where my aunt use to live, before she died, across from what was then known as Race Course (now National Heroes Park), a Park that faced Wolmer's. Mrs. Smith regarded me coldly, and barely made some assent. I walked away feeling acutely embarrassed and with the impression that I must have been misinformed; she apparently had no idea who I was and what I was talking about.

It was not until sometime afterwards that I realized that I was not the only one disappointed by Mrs. Smith's attitude. Not only in terms of certification was she an elementary school teacher, but her cocoa brown complexion, her short somewhat stocky physique, her wide round face with features like ours of the minority, reminded us of our elementary school teachers who we could touch and hug. She very early made it known, however, that the relationship particularly with us the minority would be patterned after the high school: cold, severe, and definitely not tactile. Mrs. Smith was one of the only two Jamaican "straightened" hair teachers who taught us during my first year at Wolmer's. The other was Mrs. Hazel Lawson Street, a renowned Jamaican pianist, and our music teacher. Mrs. Street was pine complexioned with somewhat angular features. I greatly admired Mrs. Street, not only for her beautiful renditions on the piano, but because she was not at all deferential to the white students, and indeed she was the only teacher who beamed at me the first year. But then, Mrs. Street was "only" the music teacher who was outside of the "academic" sphere and so her smiles of approval had very little impact on my self-image.

Mrs. Smith was something of a maverick. She had broken a lot of barriers. It was said that she could not "turn a tune", but she managed to conduct one of the most outstanding choirs in Jamaica. She was a product of a Teacher's College, and therefore should be confined to teaching at an elementary school or at the most, one of the lesser luminary high schools at that time, during the 1950's, such as Ardenne or Merle Grove. Here she was teaching English and being the Form Mistress (though limited to the First Year) at one of the most prestigious high schools in Jamaica. The story was told that when she was teased about the "shortness" of her hair, she curtly responded, "It is not what is on the head, but what is in the head."   Mrs. Smith was regarded with admiration and wonder amongst her peers with not a little mix of jealousy; to some of her peers, she was somewhat aloof and feisty.

Although issues of race in Jamaica were not as overt as the United States of America, they undergirded and were pervasive throughout the Jamaican society and frequently erupted as skin color issues that were socially, economically, and politically divisive. As a child, these issues, however, were rarely discussed in my family or amongst my parents' friends. It was during my first year at Wolmer's that I was privy to an open discussion, for the first time, on the matter of race. In my mind, I did not verbalize it then, but I was truly amazed at the level of sophisticated analysis of my cocoa brown, tan, cinnamon complexioned springy, hair peers, and a few cinnamon, cocoa brown complexioned shiny hair peers—the minority. The minority—eleven to twelve years old—was upset that we in Form 3^3 were coerced by Mrs. Smith into voting for J.T. as form captain.

J. T. was white with short yellow somewhat fuzzy hair. It was claimed that she was the daughter of wealthy Americans. Her last name was blazoned on the side of many trucks in Jamaica. I guess today J.T. would be diagnosed as having a classic case of Attention Deficit Disorder. Maybe J.T.'s behavior was due to the fact that she was exceptionally tall—she was the tallest girl in the class. She could not sit still. J. T. constantly violated the rules.   She seemed to be always bobbing out of her seat—interrupting the teachers—talking when she should be quiet which the minority—all from elementary schools—found somewhat abhorrent. Though we the minority could scream, yell, and frolic outdoors once we were indoors, we could sit absolutely still for hours. In elementary school, the cane or the strap would instantly cure you of any Attention Deficit Disorder.

During the first weeks at Wolmer's, we the minority thought, as was our custom in elementary school that it was perfectly permissible to run, play, laugh, and romp outside. We did know "running on the grass" and "along the corridors" was "wild and uncivilized". It took just a few weeks admonitions--being termed "wild and uncivilized" with contemptuous looks—for us the minority to quickly adapt to the norms of Wolmer's--being "little ladies" inside and outside the classroom.

The minority regarded J. T. as obnoxious. She often failed to observe one of the most important mores and norms of Jamaican etiquette that is not butting into conversations. The minority also resented her pointedly chasing them, and not the white or beige complexion students, around the classroom. In many ways, by being playful, she was displaying the same kind of behavior that we exhibited just a couple months before except that our rambunctious behavior would take place outdoors, not indoors. We now internalized being playful and frivolous as contemptuous behavior which actually reinforced for me my father's oft repeated injunction: "Chicken merry, hawk de near." That J. T. was white further magnified the disdain and distrust of the minority particularly in her deliberate choice to co-opt us in her romping, in the light of the dominant white norm that termed such behavior, whenever it was displayed by the minority, "wild and uncivilized". I listened to the minority's views with awe and wonder. J. T.'s behavior did not bother me one bit. Actually I was quite flattered whenever J. T., a white girl, spoke to me or chased me around the room.

The white teachers did not hesitate to give J.T. detentions for her misbehavior; J.T., however, was totally indifferent to the mounting number of detentions. Mrs. Smith thought she had the solution to J.T.'s deviant behavior for actually the number of detentions J.T. acquired placed her at risk of being "kicked out" of Wolmer's. Mrs. Smith felt her plan would radically transform J. T.'s behavior. She reasoned with us that if we elected J.T. as form captain, then the responsibility of being form captain, that is, having to discipline and record names of students who misbehaved in the absence of the teacher, mainly between change of classes, would undoubtedly have a radical impact on J.T.'s behavior. She would have to abide by the rules.

We all complied, but the minority was furious. I listened with awe as they pointed how Mrs. Smith was bending backwards to accommodate J.T. and forcing us to deviate from the normal process of electing form captains because J. T. is white. They pointed out how a pine complexioned springy hair student was "kicked out" of Wolmer's for an allegedly minor infraction and if J. T. were not white, she would have been asked to leave Wolmer's. It was the first in my life that I was privy to any such discussion on matters of race.

J. T.'s reign as form captain was a disaster and therefore short lived. We were totally out of control between classes or if the teacher was delayed for some reason. J.T.'s role as form captain had no impact on her behavior. She seemed to be at a loss as to what to do with her power and authority. Lacking the normal channel of control, an authoritative and firm form captain, instead of remaining in their seats as they were supposed to do, girls walked across the room and talked to each other. During class time, J.T.'s behavior was far from the model behavior it should be as form captain. She violated the rules as before—frequently bobbed in and out of her seat— interrupted the teachers—talked when she was not supposed to. Within a week or so, Mrs. Smith had no recourse but to have us vote for a new form captain from one of our peers who competently saw us through the rest of the term.

Every week I had to write a long composition for Mrs. Smith who was our English teacher as well as our Form Mistress. This plus the snub did not endear me to her. The composition had to be about four pages long, and according to Mrs. Smith, it must have an introduction, a body, and a conclusion. Writing compositions on topics, such as, "How I Spent My Holidays" or "A Day by the Sea" were to use a hackneyed expression "sheer torture" for me. Frequently, I did not know what to write and during these times with not a little help from my mother, I would manage to fulfill the basic requirement of four pages. It seemed to me that my search for words and expressions was not a problem for my better off peers. They easily injected into communication, discussions, and conversations with teachers and with us, their peers, sophisticated words and expressions. "What a catastrophe!" one of my peers said to me one day. I had never heard the word "catastrophe" before and one day at home when I tossed my head and said, "What a catastrophe!" in response to some event around the house, my mother smiled with pleasure.

Though not clearly articulated in my mind, I had this underlying feeling that the whole purpose of writing a composition was to impress Mrs. Smith that I was not truly who I was—a two-toned brown yellow complexioned, springy, hair daughter of struggling middle class but one of my more wealthy classmates who was exposed to language and expressions that made written and oral communication almost effortless. I was flabbergasted, (another word I learnt from one of my peers) when at the end of the year Mrs. Smith pointed out that as the daughter of a teacher, my academic performance should have been better. Although she never acknowledged it, she actually knew who I was for the entire year!

I not only encountered difficulties in writing "compositions" but also in writing essays in other areas. I did not have a clue as to what to study or how to study and got bad grades until I learnt I had to memorize a lot of facts about Europe and Britain, and write more than a paragraph when an essay was given to me. I felt overwhelmed by it all—History, Geography, and English Literature, but particularly English Literature. I felt bored and alienated by *The Christmas Carol* and *Wind in the Willows*. It seems incongruous, "always having a nose in book" repeated so often about me and English Literature being my least favorite subject and indeed the subject where I would experience the most difficulty.

It is one thing to read a book for pleasure, entertainment, and even for information. It is another to write a critical analysis of a work that requires knowledge and background of the author, the period the work was written, the characters, the structure of the work, and the plot etc. The books we were required to read and analyze for English Literature had very little to do with Jamaican history, culture, and landscape; they placed a great strain on my imagination and thinking. I had never seen snow. I had never witnessed changing seasons. I had no idea of what the city of London looked like. I had never seen the English countryside. It was not only that these factors were alienating but I had to constantly visualize white characters, their interaction and relationships. To write effectively, I had to become white. During my years at Wolmer's, I was not exposed to Jamaican literature and geography—Claude McKay, Louise Bennett, Roger Mais, the parishes, geography and landscape of Jamaica were totally non-existent and invisible.

No matter how evil (usually associated with imagery of dark, and black) a white person was, there was always the good white person who was generally beautiful or handsome to counteract the evil in literary works. Usually the good white person was rewarded with wealth in the end.

I internalized the view that was so widely propagated in literature and history that I was a descendent of "backward", "savage", "primitive", "uncivilized", "pagan" Africans and that Africa contributed nothing to civilization. When countries in Africa like Egypt produced "works of wonder" these countries were carved out of Africa and the inhabitants co-opted as "white." In my second year at Wolmer's, I read in my history book that Ethiopians were white people darkened by the sun! There was nothing that a descendant of Africans could be proud of; there could only be shame. However, there was hope—hope based on the fact that I was Christianized and being educated at Wolmer's. Yes, my ancestors were "backward", "savage", "uncivilized", "pagan" but only progress awaited me. How fortunate I was to be receiving the education at Wolmer's that would put me on par with white people!

Some part of me, however, resisted overcoming the alienation and anxiety of trying to internalize and integrate subjects—English Literature, History and Geography—presented as civilizing tools. Spanish—(it did not include Spanish literature at this point)--maybe as a result of feeling some kind of cultural link due to the fact that it was my father's first language and indeed the first European language of Jamaicans, and Mathematics were the only two subjects that I felt motivated to learn.

From the first day, when Ms. MacPherson walked into the classroom and said a^{100} means a x a and we were to repeat this one hundred times, I fell in love with algebra. I was fascinated by my geometry set and the diagrams that I could draw with them. Freed from the fear of being whipped for wrong calculations, my performance in arithmetic tremendously improved. In other words, mathematics became my favorite subject.

In my second year at Wolmer's, I found myself in the lowest stream surrounded by girls who were for the most part a mixture of European ancestry and African ancestry, but mostly European ancestry. In many respects, they were in-between—in-between whites and darker skinned African Jamaicans. The teachers from England regarded these students of mixed race with their shiny wavy hair, their peanut, peach, beige complexion as beautiful. Indeed a student from Wolmer's (on the continuum, she was far more European than African) was Miss World in 1963. These "pretty" haired students, the mixed race students in the lowest stream were usually chirpy, with seemingly not a care in the world; they displayed very little concern about their academic future. A lot of time was spent not only talking about their high status relatives, but also their other than African pedigree.

Pained by the constant discussion of European ancestry in which I could not take part, I complained to my mother. Oh she said, "Tell them that your great grandfather is Scottish". Something warned me that my features and hair belie the authenticity of such ancestry and for weeks I resisted relating this information to my peers. Then one day, I found myself blurting out, "My great grandfather is Scottish." The faces of my tan complexioned wavy haired peers betrayed no emotion whatsoever. They continued their conversation as though I had not spoken--such was the breeding of my thirteen year old peers, the caste Hindus, regarding what should be the attitude and manner to social inferiors, the Dalits. Then I heard an outburst of laughter. It was cocoa brown springy hair Barbara. I had made no attempt to befriend her.

My tan complexioned wavy hair peers were generally mild mannered; insubordination was displayed by a lackadaisical attitude to learning which often took the form of frivolous comments, making minimum effort, or not doing assignments.

What was I doing in the lowest stream amongst these shiny wavy haired beauties who in many ways thought that they need only make minimum or no effort? Most of the students who looked like me were in the higher streams. Teachers often found the frivolity, the not doing assignments or the minimum effort of the shiny wavy hair students exasperating. At times, teachers responded by making minimum effort themselves in terms of teaching. Sometimes in desperation with regard to the lackadaisical attitude which seemed to be an integral part of lower stream behavior, the teacher would exclaim, "You can continue to waste time...I have already got my degree."

If the teacher who said that was married, the comment could have a sobering effect, but if she was not, which was more often the case, the comment would often be met with laughter. How the shiny wavy hair students laughed at the teachers who they predicted would die "old maids"! The ultimate goal of my shiny wavy haired peers in the lowest stream was to get married, to get the MRS degree, as they so often joked about. For them attending Wolmer's was a kind of finishing school. Being taught drama, and how to enunciate our speech in the proper English manner served to reinforce the notion of Wolmer's preparing young ladies to perform the social graces of the upper echelons of society. When Mrs. Lyons asked the class individually to repeat the passage:

My mother is in London
And until she returns
I am not in a position to say
What she thinks of the matter
However, I do know that she will
Be delighted to hear the orchestra
Rehearse for the concert

I had no idea that she would be listening for errors in my diction. I had always been complimented by adults in our social circle about my proper speech. I was astounded to learn that I had mispronounced a number of words including "mother" (muther is the correct pronunciation) and "London" (Lundun is the correct pronunciation). My "muther" was delighted when I sauntered around the house repeating the passage with my very British elitist diction. My parents' attitude to the Jamaican dialect was reinforced at Wolmer's. Speaking what was often termed contemptuously "the Jamaican patois" was absolutely taboo at Wolmer's.

I was somewhat daunted when in my third year at Wolmer's, I once again found myself in the lowest stream even though I had done better than some of my peers. I had not been kept back nor was I asked to leave. However, I was not at all pleased because if I continued this trend, the next year I would find myself in the lowest stream, called not Lower V^3 as it should be but..............Removed.

Removed, as the name of this form or class indicated, was the termination of a weeding out process, and the end of your academic career at Wolmer's. Once you are placed in Removed, it meant that at the end of that year, you would not be promoted to a higher grade—you would have to leave Wolmer's. In keeping with their rank, the lowest streams were physically the last classrooms at the farthest end of the set of classrooms. Removed was not only at the far end of the building which included classrooms and the library; it was the last classroom at the very back of the school. The physical location of Removed seemed to reinforce the idea of termination. In my third year, then, my classroom, Upper IV^3 as the last classroom of a set of classrooms was perpendicular to the set of buildings of which Removed was the lower end. Upper IV^3, then, with just a little gap between them stood right across from Removed. Both set of buildings faced a rectangular lawn across which we were not allowed to walk. Although we could not see into the classroom which the students of Removed occupied, we could hear bursts of laughter or the screeching of chairs which was a regular occurrence in Removed. Removed had a bad reputation.

Often teachers would be seen hurrying from the classroom of Removed after being in the class for only five or ten minutes. Raucous laughter would follow the receding back of the teacher. Then after some minutes we could, seated in our chairs, see the shapeless white ankles in white oversize pumps carrying a middle age medium weight medium height English body in a flowery print dress with a head crowned by an indeterminate color—reddish yellowish wavy permed hair. With purposeful strides the ankles in their oversize white pumps would move rapidly across the forbidden lawn. There would be cries of "Ske is coming! Ske is coming" referring to Mrs. Skempton, the headmistress. As she entered Removed, there would be a bustle of screeching chairs as the girls hastened to their seats and then…silence.

I did not want to go to Removed. It was not that the girls were really bad. They engaged in what was regarded then as frivolous behavior for several reasons. Some did not have to apply themselves; they had options. They could become a housewife and if not, there would be jobs. Just a year at a high school gave my peers in the lowest stream, the shiny wavy hair students access to jobs in banks, in private industry, and even in the government Civil Service to which my parents and their colleagues in spite of their Jamaica Local and Teachers College and other tertiary institution certificates did not have access. A number of girls in Removed, and indeed, the lowest streams, were caught in a tracking system as a result of an alienating educational system that did not motivate one to really learn, and even if we were motivated to learn, we were not given clear guidelines as to how we could improve our study habits. It took me three years of trial and error before I began to realize what I needed to do to improve. Then there was the matter of teachers' expectations.

Most of the teachers had no formal training and had become teachers because that was one of the few professional options available to women. The teachers, particularly the Jamaican teachers, had been very successful academically when one considers the fact that only a privileged few had access to high school and of these privileged few, only a handful, particularly girls in the light of gender discrimination, would graduate with advanced certificates from the high school and university. A small minority of women were graduates of the university or the high school .

As teachers then, these women, for the most part, expected us to know how to study, and if we did not, it was generally our fault. These white or very nearly white Jamaican teachers would not have experienced, I imagine, the struggles that many of us in the lowest streams had. They would not have seen learning as a part of a compartmentalized being or something that is totally outside their being. If they had to learn, for example, Wordsworth's poem: I wandered lonely as a cloud/That floats on high o'er vales and hills/When all at once I saw a crowd/A host of golden daffodils...Would these white or nearly white teachers as students have felt inauthentic, like some "other" repeating this poem; they had never seen a daffodil in their whole life or even if they had not seen a daffodil, could they, because of their pale skin color, not make a closer cultural link to Britain and to Wordsworth than I? Did they experience any struggle in terms of identifying with the poem? When these white or nearly white teachers took up a book or sat down to study as students, did they receive suspicious looks sometimes bordering on disapproval and would they be told at times that "too much learning doth make you mad?"

It was not the norm for cocoa brown, chocolate, cinnamon complexioned springy hair girls to have their nose constantly stuck in a book. I am pretty positive that white and nearly white teachers as students had support of family and community. Just as how orthodox Hindus believe that Brahmins have the right to intellectual pursuits and Dalits do not[321], so within the Western culture, whites feel that they have the right to pursue knowledge, and blacks are discouraged from doing so.

Teachers at Wolmer's were not subjected to the oversight of an often authoritarian principal and arrogant Inspectors of Schools, as teachers in the elementary schools were. High schools for the most part were relatively lax in terms of accountability of the teachers, and a few teachers sometimes did take advantage of this. Rather than face rambunctious kids, some teachers opted to remain in the staff room. Most of the teachers, however, were

---

[321]See, for example, Mahar, *The Untouchables in Contemporary India*; Rajshekar, *Dalit.*

devoted and committed—Ms. Baxter, Mrs Carberry, Mrs Duncan, Mrs Girvan, Mrs Smith, Mrs. Mullings, Ms MacPherson, Mrs. Street—some rarely missed a day. What I think was very unfortunate was the fact that there was little or no communication between parents and teachers and also the low expectations of parents especially low expectations of girls.

What was I doing in the lowest stream? It was ironic that students whose parents could most afford to have their daughters waste time and be frivolous were the ones who demanded a lot of effort from their children. The daughters who were chauffeur driven, whose fathers were eminent doctors, headmasters, university professors were the students, with a few exceptions, in the highest streams. I wanted to be a success academically. I wanted to win the Jamaican Scholarship and have my name written on the board in the Assembly Hall at Wolmer's. Deep in my heart, I knew that that would never happen so I had compromised this dream to at least passing Higher School Examination administered by the University of Cambridge, England which was a requirement for entry to the University of the West Indies. Heading for Removed would not do.

As I said earlier, the first day Ms. MacPherson walked into class in my first year at Wolmer's and introduced me to Algebra, I fell in love with Algebra. Gradually the other two branches of mathematics would become almost equally as fascinating. There may have been several reasons for mathematics becoming my favorite subject. Mathematics did not demand the emotional conflict that English Literature, History and Geography did. As I solved equations, proved theorems, found proportions, I did not have to think about the British people, culture, or countryside. I did not feel that I had to be some "other", absorbing facts that culturally I was not a part of and that often denigrated my whole culture and being. I did not have to be white. To a great degree, doing mathematics meant dealing logically with cold hard facts. In spite of my parents' views, somewhat to the contrary, they and the elementary school had given me a good foundation in terms of basic arithmetic facts. A very important factor was that in high school, I no longer had to fear being whipped for getting a sum "wrong". Above all, the phrenological view that one is born with ability to do mathematics and certain subjects was not very evident amongst teachers at Wolmer's. Teachers expected students to apply themselves to learning.

One day I ran home to show my mother the big red checks I had received for finding correctly the Greatest Common Factor and the Lowest Common Denominator now termed the Least Common Multiple in the hope that she would be convinced that I was doing better at arithmetic. Her response was, "But, you already did that in elementary school". It would be one of many futile attempts to convince my mother that my feelings, as she perceived them, regarding Arithmetic had changed. Sometimes she would respond with a little chuckle and a reminder that "you hate Arithmetic—you hid your book under the desk."

By the third year, I began to outperform my peers in the lowest stream in most subjects, particularly mathematics. In mathematics, I gave the teacher and assignments undivided attention so much so that I can clearly remember a lot of what I was taught and the problems I did as if it were yesterday. Gradually I gained the reputation amongst my peers of being very good at mathematics. A factor that bolstered my performance in mathematics was the assistance I received from my mother. My sister reminded me recently that whenever I had difficulties, I would often "run to my mother crying for help" and would not be satisfied until she sat down and went over the problems with me. My mother's assistance was invaluable particularly as she interpreted my diligence as lacking in ability; step by step, very patiently, she would have me think through the logical process whether we were doing Ratio, Proportion, Simple Interest or what was then termed Simultaneous Equations.

Though my performance improved tremendously in my third year, whenever I looked across at Removed, I would become very anxious that the Removed class would be my destiny. Somehow, it began to slowly dawn on me that when I studied and worked hard, my grades improved. I gave utmost attention to mathematics, but I studied the other subjects also. As my grades improved, I received more and more encouragement from my teachers. In many classes particularly in mathematics and Spanish, I became the teachers' "pet".

Apart from my anxiety of being placed in Removed, L1V[3] would be my happiest year at Wolmer's. I finally achieved teacher's recognition and was often beamed at for most of my classes. I integrated better with my peers (mainly because of my role as tutor). A major accomplishment was that I was given a part in what was a revolutionary production in terms of Wolmer's history of performing British plays in the yearly Schools Drama Festival at the Ward Theater. The play entitled "On These Shores" written by our drama teacher, Mrs. Lyons, was about historical events pertaining to Jamaica.

My role in the play, along with two other cinnamon complexioned girls, was that of a slave. I had to speak the forbidden dialect—"Lawd dis kitchen ya hat fe true"—from a script written by drama teacher who, not long before, had corrected my enunciation of "mother" and "London". We also actually had to perform a dance and ironically the only picture that appeared in the newspaper, *The Gleaner,* was the picture of three of us, "slaves" dancing in this production. [322] Changes had begun slowly to take place but we were not aware of them then. That the picture appeared in *The Gleaner* was really surprising because the focus of the play was the upper and middle classes.

White and pale complexioned wavy shiny haired students had major roles. We cinnamon complexioned, springy haired students had minor parts, for the slaves had minor parts, just as how in the literature and history books of the West Indies, the thoughts, feelings, opinions, history and culture of slaves and their springy hair progeny are marginalized and regarded as a minor part in the history and culture of Jamaica, this, in spite of over three hundred years - over three centuries - of slavery in Jamaica.

In terms of my performance at school, and wider participation in school activities, and being regarded as "bright" by my peers in the lowest stream, my self confidence should have been bolstered, but it was not. I saw my studying and working hard as a result of the phrenological notion that my brain was compartmentalized and fixed at birth and therefore I had to study very hard to learn anything at all. The fact that I spent more time on my mathematics home work than any other subject I interpreted as not as a result of finding enjoyment or fulfillment from doing mathematics but as a result of the phrenological belief that the "bump" in the compartmentalized part of the brain for mathematics was to a large extent non existent.

In spite of surpassing my peers in a number of subjects, particularly mathematics, in the final examination I was placed third in the form, the closest I had ever been of having my dream to do well in school fulfilled. One student whose father was a prominent doctor went on a trip abroad for months and when she returned she out-performed us in English, History, and English literature. Her communication skills were superb. Her essays were read out loud as a model to which we should aspire. As one teacher remarked, her first hand experience traveling abroad with her parents gave her tremendous advantage. When I relayed her impressive performance to my parents, to my surprise, my father commented that as a doctor's daughter the language she heard around her gave her confidence to write and speak. What was she doing in the lowest stream as a doctor's daughter was often hinted at amongst the students? I think she fell in the lowest stream maybe because she was absent from school for a long period, or she was one of the students for whom Wolmer's was mainly a finishing school.

At the end of each school year, it was the custom of the Headmistress to read, in the general assembly, the list of names in alphabetical order which forms, beginning with the lowest, the students would be entering the following year. Although pleasant for those who did well, it could be very

---

[322]See Curtin, *In the Light of the Sun*, p. 93.

nerve wracking for some, particularly as the entire school would be privy to one's performance. I became very anxious when the Headmistress began reading the list of names for Removed. Even though there was some kind of hope that I would not go to Removed, I would have felt better had I come first and not third in the form. When Mrs. Skempton got to the R's and my name, Ricketts, was not called, I was delighted. I had made it to Lower V^2. The names of the girls who came first and second were amongst the list of Lower V^2. But then, when she came to the Rs for Lower V^2, my name was not called. My anxiety returned in full force. Did she overlook my name when reading the list for Removed? The girls in my form looked at me with equally perplexed faces. The headmistress started the list for Lower V^1. She got to R. There was an audible gasp in the hall as Mrs. Skempton called my name. I had been skipped from the lowest stream to the highest. Although I was placed third, mainly on my performance in mathematics, my teachers had recommended that I be placed in the highest stream even above the girls who had come first and second. I was overjoyed.

I had hardly time to revel in my joy midst some anxiety when I heard a deep voice behind me say: "Whether she will be able to keep it up is another matter". It was springy hair chocolate complexion Delia. Delia was one of the darkest students in the school. She was very bright and had always been in the top stream. I was very angry; she had expressed my fears, but what right did she have to say what she did?

In Lower V^1, we would be thrown together—in many ways two outsiders. Delia was a fundamentalist who would have an impact on my religious beliefs and hence my academic career. Unfortunately, my parents had not prepared me to deal with and cope with Delia.

When I told my parents that I had been moved to the highest grade, they smiled, but hardly a word was said to me by either of them.

Christianity and Black Oppression: Duppy Know Who Fe Frighten

CHAPTER EIGHT

BECOMING A FUNDAMENTALIST II: ATOMIZATION

You need Jesus...you need to be saved...Is there one tonight...Raise your hand to be saved...let me see that hand...Thank you Jesus...Is there another?
Fundamentalist Preacher

Son, you may be my son, but you may never be my son-in-law.
White evangelist to black "born again" Christian

I did not have much exposure to fundamentalism before the age of fifteen. When I was around seven or eight, my mother did send me in response to a young neighbor's request to Vacation Bible School held at Olivet Gospel Hall on Waltham Park Road. My recollections of the Vacation Bible School were that the hall was packed with children, that it was noisy, we were asked a lot of questions about the Bible, and at the final session, I was given a crown with stars. After the Vacation Bible School, the young neighbor asked my mother if she would permit me to go with her to Sunday School on a regular basis. My mother firmly told her no pointing out to her that Vacation Bible School was good activity for the summer but we belonged to Half Way Tree Anglican Church and that is where we would attend Sunday School.

When I was older, maybe about fourteen, my father was invited to a Fundamentalist Church by an alternative medical practitioner who first my father and then other members of my family were his patients. Nobody knew exactly what his credentials were or where he got them; rumor had it that he obtained his medical expertise from the United States. This caused his title of doctor to be somewhat suspect because it was a widely accepted belief in Jamaica, as a British colony, that any credential obtained from the United States was inferior to the British. Dr. W., however, was excellent and my father, who was generally skeptical of any alternative medical practice, be they local or foreign, was very impressed with him. Using prescriptions that were all diet based, he effectively cured ailments in the family and if he could not heal the ailment, as in the case of my mother, he recommended a regular doctor. Thus, he actually saved my mother's life. The family was astounded, however, when my father who rarely went to church accepted Dr.

W.'s invitation to attend his church. We were even more surprised when we found ourselves as a family attending the church a couple more times.

The church was a small cramped building, a hall, about one-sixth the size of St. Andrew Parish Church/Half Way Tree Church which had at least three large spacious wings. It appeared, at this Fundamentalist Church, that every five seconds the entire congregation was kneeling on the floor while someone said a long prayer. Even though there were cushions, getting down on our knees on the green with a touch of white tiled floor for what seemed an interminable length of time was painful and uncomfortable. How unlike Half Way Tree Church that had a little rack covered in velvet at the foot of each pew that you could kneel on; you also had the option to sit and bend forward. No one forced you to kneel. Besides the prayers at Half Way Tree Church were set prayers that were short. Each time we attended the fundamental church, Dr. W. preached a sermon during which he would burst into tears which I found very strange and disconcerting. Men in our society did not cry, much less in public and in the pulpit.

I was very relieved when I overheard my father tell my mother that he would no longer be attending services at that church nor would he ever join that church. I was beginning to worry after our second visit that after years of resisting becoming a member of the Anglican Church, my father had fallen prey to what seemed to me a chaotic and unstructured type of service. Rumor had it, my father told my mother, that there was often a turn over of nurses who worked for the doctor because it was the general practice of the good "doctor" and minister who was married to have affairs with his nurses. No wonder the nurse who was presently working with the doctor looked so unhappy! His nurses all had the same "look"—tan complexioned with shiny wavy hair and narrow features. Didn't my mother observe how the current nurse played an active and prominent role in the church services and where was the doctor's wife? Apparently my father's decision to attend more than one service was not so much due to the appeal of the service, as to the fact that he wanted to satisfy his curiosity and verify the rumors he had heard by observing the behavior of Dr. W. and his nurse during the church service. Besides the stint at Olivet Gospel Hall, and our family, at the behest of our father, attending a fundamentalist church about three times, I had very little encounter with fundamentalists until I was fifteen years old when I escaped being in Removed and I was thrown into Delia's company.

Delia was right. Just as she had predicted it was difficult for me to keep up with students who from their first year at Wolmer's were in the highest stream. The majority of the students in LV[1] were the daughters of the professional upper middle class. The rest of us fell into almost two extremes. There were the few chauffeur driven wealthy whites—one was the daughter of one of the wealthiest, if not the wealthiest family in Jamaica. The whites mingled amongst themselves and for the most part ignored the rest of us even though we sat in the same classroom. Then there was just about four or five of us—daughters of the struggling middle class.

In many ways, the students in the Lower V[1] were radically different from those in the lowest stream. The focus was not so much on skin color or hair but on being bright. The rooms of the brightest streams, in terms of skin color, were several shades darker than the rooms of the lowest streams. Ebony, cocoa pine complexioned girls with straightened springy hair exuded a lot of confidence. In clustered groups on the parapet that ran along the front of classrooms, the issue of race would sometimes surface. Cinnamon, cocoa brown, springy hair students of Lower V[1] would sometimes deride the students of Middle Eastern heritage as basically "dumb" and any achievement on their part was due to their access to tutors and volumes of encyclopedias.

It was strange that although in many ways Wolmer's promoted black inferiority and white superiority culled from books to which we were exposed particularly in English literature and History, and by the fact that certain roles, such as Head Girl, were ascribed to white, tan, peanut complexioned, straight or shiny hair students with small or narrow facial features, yet the view so prevalent in the United States that black people are born with inferior intelligence was not one that pervaded Wolmer's and many sectors of the Caribbean.

On the contrary, amongst certain sectors of the Caribbean, it was felt that the darker the skin and the more wiry or springy the hair, the "brainier" the person would be. Maybe one of the reasons for this is that many of the white teachers were actually foreigners, some of whom were paid by missionary societies. To justify their stipends, they had to prove that people of African descent could learn as any European. In the Caribbean, then, in terms of access to educational opportunities, it was not so much a matter of race, it was more a matter of class although economic stratification was tied to skin color. Consequently, many cocoa brown, chocolate, ebony complexioned people were poor. However, the British system in Jamaica did allow a few dark skinned individuals to break through the economic barriers without being shackled by stereotypical beliefs regarding mental ability. Of course, as many students who had the opportunity to study in England would attest, in England itself the situation was quite different. Students of African descent were often subjected to the same kind of stigma as students of African descent in the United States of America.

The girls in Lower V[1] exuded a lot of self-confidence. Unlike the girls of the lowest stream who sat for the most part quietly and sedately, Lower V[1] girls seemed to be perpetually in motion as they tossed around intellectual ideas or discussed events, school or their families. They were very competitive. In some ways, they were no better behaved than the girls in Removed. Like the girls in Removed they laughed a lot, but their laughter was about matters that were more profound—criticism of ideas expressed in textbooks, and not simply clowning around and poking fun at teachers.

In Lower V[1], it was forcibly brought home to me that class made a difference. I had been accustomed to white or peanut complexioned students with shiny hair expressing their ideas without fear. What was new to me were students about my complexion, looks and hair—daughters or relatives of high ranking professionals—the upper middle class articulately defending their views in prolonged exchanges with teachers without fear of reprisals. Peanut complexioned Mrs. Girvan (formerly Ms. Segree) with straightened slightly curly hair was our English literature and language teacher. She was Jamaican and very popular with the students. Mrs. Girvan was considered "nice" for she always smiling, a smile made beautiful by a set of pearly white teeth that tapered as her smile widened. This smile was often directed admiringly at cocoa brown complexioned Celia with straightened springy hair as they both engaged in a lengthy banter about some aspect of a literary text, or writing. Celia's father was a doctor. There would be times during these exchanges when the entire class would burst out laughing and I would not have a clue what they were laughing about. I, like the other students of the struggling middle class, would not speak unless called upon. If I had to speak, my heart would race, my stomach would be tied in knots, and my response would be as brief as possible and hardly audible.

Since, except for the three or four white girls in the class, most of the girls in the highest stream were just about a little lighter or darker than I— pine yellow, brownish yellowish, cocoa brown and a number had springy hair which they straightened, I should have felt more at home than I did with the tan peanut complexioned straight or shiny hair girls in the lowest stream. Actually, I felt more out of place socially and intellectually in LV[1] and more lonely that I did amongst the students in the lowest streams.

Most of the students lived in what was then, I thought, a solid middle class community called Vineyard Town. I lived on the other side of Kingston, on a little Avenue off Hagley Park Road.

My mother sometimes bewailed the fact that we did not live in a neighborhood such as Richmond Park or Vineyard Town, not so much because they were more residential than where we lived but because it seemed to her that there was a greater sense of community. Where we lived betwixt Waltham Park Road at one end, and at the other, Half Way Tree Church was an area of a mixture of modest one storey four bedroom houses with neat little gardens, and as one progressed up Hagley Park Road, opulent two storey houses some made entirely of brick on acres of land with huge spacious gardens and lawns. It was not a community; it had no name. On the other side of Waltham Park Road was a smorgasbord of poor ramshackle homes, next to one or two elegant four bedroom houses, empty lots, callaloo gardens planted on "captured land" (long before occupy Wall Street), and a huge manufacturing plant that made boots. At the very bottom of Hagley Park was Cockburn Pen, a poor community of African Jamaicans and Indians. The bottom of Hagley Park Road then was in stark contrast to the top of Hagley Park Road where Half Way Tree Church was erected.

In terms of size I was not really ashamed of our four bedroom house—what I was ashamed of was the furniture. I did not want my peers in LV[1] to see the furnishings in my house. My father had often asserted that he had "no intention of keeping up with the Joneses" and besides, attending high schools was far more important than furniture. He refused to get rid of the set of mahogany chairs, which included a two seater and a rocking chair all of which had weaved yellow matting in the middle, and purchase a living room suite which had just come into vogue. He refused to replace the ice box with a refrigerator, and the coal pots with a range.

When we complained about our living room not looking like the typical living room of the middle class, my father would point out to us oddly enough, that the very wealthy upper class, whose homes he had access to as part of his Sanitary Inspector duties, took great pride in their mahogany chairs. We did not care about the wealthy—all our neighbors had "suites"—lush large chairs into which you sank when you sat and which took up half the living room plus all the "suites" included a center table to boot. Instead of a center table, we had against the front wall an interestingly designed narrow elongated side table, about a yard in length and two feet in width that bulged a little, in the middle at the longer sides, and rested on four bow legs that were about three feet high. On this table sat an old Philips radio which, besides the piano, was our chief source of entertainment.

My father eventually did replace the hanging press in their bedroom with a wardrobe, but not with one from a furniture store in Kingston. We had to endure months of embarrassment until the local cabinet maker, after several trips by my father to his shop, and several dashed hopes, finally built the wardrobe he promised about six months earlier (along with a dining table and cabinet—the cabinet is still in the family).

My mother would eventually circumvent my father regarding the matter of the stove. It was really too time consuming and difficult for the helpers to have to take the two feet high grayish black semi-conical shaped coal pots out in the yard, trying every which way to get the coal to light—sticks, newspaper, kerosene oil, fanning,--having to deal with the smoke from the coal, and once the coals did "catch" that is they started burning on their own accord bringing the coal pots inside in the kitchen.   A three or four burner oil stove was bought with a detached oven.   Although the oil burner oven was a vast improvement to the kerosene tin oven we used on the coal pot, it was difficult to replicate the treacle tarts and jam tarts that I learnt to bake at Wolmer's for sometimes two of the burners were not available.

We were one of the few residents in the area who supported the ice companies.   Every time the ice truck stopped to drop off ice, I would be embarrassed although I must admit that whenever my father took us to the ice company to buy ice for whatever reason, sometimes to make ice cream, I was always fascinated by the ice manufacturing plant.   Three or four thin men dressed in long black coats and long black boots, as though they were in the temperate zone, would sit huddled together on a bench in front of a huge rectangular building.   When the order was placed one of these men would reluctantly lift a trap like door and out would come grey swirling mists of very cold air amidst blocks of ice. He would then with very large tongs deftly retrieve a block of ice and quickly close the flap.   As so much of our literature talked about winter, and as we never experienced winter in the tropics, I imagined that what I glimpsed in the ice factory was something of what winter must be like.

By not inviting my peers to my house, I could navigate around social exposure to what I perceived would result in acute embarrassment.   I could not avoid my peers, however, seeing my father's black Austin 8 two-door car. I do not think that B3262 (after these many decades I still remember the license number) believed that it had completely made the transition from a horse drawn carriage to a car.   It seemed to think that somewhere inside its black Austen 8 body was a horse that frequently needed tactile attention. Many days, after dutifully pouring water in the radiator which we had to do every morning, B3262 refused to start. We all had to get out of the car and push it and then to the sound of the spluttering engine we would hurriedly and agilely scramble into one of its two doors pulling the front seat down and then up again for our mother while we hoped with bated breath that the now revved up engine would not die. Rarely could we plan any event that demanded regularly traveling in B3262. Sometimes B3262 would suddenly stop in the middle of the road for no apparent reason.   At times, we were fortunate. Willing hands belonging to men casually standing on the side of the road saw our stalled car as a challenge and would eagerly run to the Austin 8 to offer help with no thoughts of any kind of monetary reward.

Any planned trip that meant traveling some distance into rural areas was fraught with anxiety; invariably the little Austin 8 would be engaged in some drama that resulted in either failure to arrive at the destination or a delay of the time of arrival by several hours. One day on a trip to Morant Bay, B3262 just decided that it had enough and tossed one of its wheels into a ditch that separated the road from the Caribbean Sea. Maybe it was a good thing that the car had only two doors; my siblings and I could not jump out which could have resulted in serious injury. We were scared as the car rocked back and forth on the surviving three wheels, but we were only subjected to fright, as B3262 landed safely into the ditch not too far from the wayward wheel. Another time just as my father was feeling elated by his Austin 8's performance up the steep and winding Mt. Diablo and through the narrow meandering beautiful Fern Gully, shortly before we arrived at Roaring River where he planned to spend time with friends, B3262 decided it would go no further.

Every time I overheard my father discuss his frustrations with dealing with mechanics, I hoped that the Austin 8 would be traded in for either an Austin Cambridge or a Ford Consul that was popular with middle class professionals. The only outcome of my father's frustrations was often philosophizing as to whether one should patronize the small man or the big man. So my father and B3262 would often fluctuate between the "small" mechanic who single handedly, with maybe one apprentice, operate a mechanic shop in a yard outside his or someone else's house, "and who would not overcharge you for parts and labor" or the "big" man who owned an auto shop, had better equipment, more knowledge of the cars as a system and had several apprentices working under him but whose cost would be "astronomical".

I thought, however, that I would never recover from the embarrassment I felt when one day my father decided to drop me in front of the staff room just when the girls were on their way to prayers. I could hear the giggles of the students for not only was B3262 quaint but in the back of the car were make-shift seats, a temporary replacement of the seats which my father had removed so that he could have them reupholstered. He had no intention of buying a new car. When one day I told my parents how my history teacher, Mrs. Duncan, cranked up her Austin car (a little bigger than ours, an Austin 10, according to my father) to the amusement of the students, my father smiled with pleasure and made some comment to the effect that he was sure she could afford to buy a better car. If I thought that he would interpret the laughter of my peers as social pressure to conform to appearances, I was sadly mistaken. That Mrs. Duncan drove a car which was similar to his and had to be cranked up only fortified his somewhat bohemian beliefs. My father failed to understand, however, one important factor. Mrs. Duncan was white.

My father thought that Wolmer's would automatically be for me the conduit to the elite society, but he did not realize refrigerators, ranges, living room suite, cars were often topics of discussion as were other aspects of students' and their parents' lifestyle on which I could only be silent. I remember once in cooking class a student with whom I was working, referring to the refrigerator, asked me to get an item from the "cooler". I had no idea what part of the refrigerator she was talking about and became very flustered. My peer was very cross and angry as I wasted minutes trying to fake knowledge. I kept looking at the top section of the refrigerator. I felt very foolish when she walked over to the refrigerator and pulled out the bottom drawer.

This not being able to socialize with my peers would have a very negative impact on my learning. I withdrew into my shell and a world of make-belief in which though feeling very inferior, I tried to adopt the mannerisms, and airs of the upper class. My father's somewhat anti-middle class bohemian outlook in reality masked a kind of "wannabe upper class snooty" contempt of the middle class that did not help matters. We were not from the upper class particularly that sector of the gentry that could afford to be eccentric in terms of the observations of certain values and norms of the society.

My father did not realize that not having our roots firmly and solidly planted in terms of who we are could only lead to lack of self-worth, self-esteem, and self-confidence. I needed these psychological factors to be successful at Wolmer's. There were students, not many, but there were a few cinnamon, cocoa, chocolate complexioned students with springy hair, who lived in more impecunious circumstances than I, and yet were successful academically and socially at Wolmer's. What they exuded was quiet self- confidence.

It always comes as a surprise when adults who I meet from time to time tell me how much they enjoyed visiting my home when we were children. For them, my house was a center of love and warmth.

Delia was the only student in LV[1] who lived in the same vicinity as I did about a mile or two from me. Although for years, we took the same bus and we went to the same music teacher for piano lessons, we never had any kind of social interaction much less to become friends, before I moved to LV[1]. Delia had a smooth chocolate brown complexion with just a flick of yellow in her cheeks, a thin long narrow face with a short flat forehead, a bony narrow nose, small sparkling brown eyes and wide lips that were always quivering with laughter. Her thin narrow face was somewhat out of proportion to her medium size body with a well endowed rear. Her hair, somewhat crinkly was generally neatly braided in about three short braids. It just missed the category of being "pretty" by being a little too tightly curled, and very dark brown—it was not black and shiny enough.

Delia had always been in the brightest stream, and as I was usually awed by people who I considered to be much brighter than I, I felt intimidated by her. I found her behavior, however, somewhat troubling. She always seemed to be poking fun at somebody. You could always hear her voice, which was a rich contralto, either laughing, a kind of mirthless laughter, or talking above everybody else, as she sat sprawled in an aisle seat (she seem to always sit in an aisle seat) on the Cross Town bus. Delia had the reputation of being mischievous in school. She was generally with a band of girls, talking or laughing.

My dislike of Delia was not only that she behaved like a boy, that is, she was not ladylike or prim and proper but she seemed to take delight in making fun at other people's expense. In LV[1], I would sometimes become her target. She would often call me "Old Soldier" not only because of my rapid strides, but also because of my determined "soldier like" militant effort to do well in school. My comments were often met with quick barbs and slights from her.

Sally attended Wolmer's and lived much closer to me than Delia did. We both lived about two blocks from each other on avenues off Hagley Park Road. Hers was the first avenue below Hagley Park Road, and mine was the first avenue above Hagley Park Road. We both knew each other from elementary school and attended Half Way Tree Parish Church together. In the first year at Wolmer's, we were in the same form. Our friendship, however, was tenuous at most. She had the complexion so characteristic of a number of Jamaicans of mainly European heritage—tan, peanut complexion. It was her brown hair, however, that fell in unruly waves, waves that were about an inch apart that ended at nape of her neck that somehow prevented her from being placed in the category of white. There was not much that she could do with her hair. It was not long and it was not straight so that it could not be styled in the prevailing fashion of Hollywood nor was it "bad" to be straightened, and then styled in the prevailing fashion of Hollywood. Her only alternative "to babyish drop curls" was to let her hair loose and subject herself to criticisms from people like Delia who would laugh and say that her hair "looks like puss drop into coconut oil."

Although Sally never, unlike Delia, made comments that made me feel humiliated, I often felt that skin color was a barrier between us. She would often talk about her mother (who she and the entire family regarded with awe), and her older brother as being able to pass as white in the United States. I felt that Sally's implication that she could not pass as white must have been due to some "flaw" in her father's genes, which I assumed must be African, although in my view, he was just as "white" as her mother because, to me, they were about the same complexion. The hair on his balding head was not only straight, but lighter in color than her mother's. His features could all be labeled European.

Sally's attitude to complexion, however, was somewhat ambivalent. One day as we were walking home, she turned to me and said, "I do not like your complexion" and in response to my mortified look said, "it is too blotchy blotchy" (repeating words for emphasis is a Jamaican peculiarism). "I like people with dark c-c-c-ool complexion." In a couple days, however, Sally would dump me for her tan, peanut complexioned shiny hair upper class friends.

Although in some ways I was more successful academically than Sally, she lacked my inhibition. Sally therefore had what I often admired—a freedom to be. I began to note over the years how she was able to gain admittance to social circles based on her skin color. I was not included in that circle. Swimming, lying on the beach, and tanning were forms of activity in which I could not participate. My skin was too dark for tanning; my hair too "bad" for swimming.

It was bad enough not to being able to swim in terms of one's social status but not to be able to tan automatically excluded one from access to the upper class. You would never imagine the significance in terms of your social status of being able to cry out in pain, as a result of a scorched red burnt shoulder unseen under a white blouse, being accidentally touched. The peach and beige "able to tan" school mates would commiserate. They also spent the entire day, Sunday, at the beach. Your apology would be met with stiff coldness. To meet the qualification that is required to purchase tanning lotion advertised by smiling whites on oversize—blocking the Jamaican scenic landscape—billboards catapulted one to a sphere that classed chocolate, cinnamon, cocoa brown blacks as being totally deprived, lacking, and therefore unworthy of esteem. For the peach and beige "able to tan" could identify themselves with "tourists", a group of people to whom Jamaicans should pay utmost deference. It mattered not if the "tourist" was a working class white who had spent years saving to take a trip to Jamaica.

How it is possible to make you feel inferior by someone who has very little and wants more of something that you have in abundance is a mystery. Instead of feeling proud of the quantity of melanin we possessed since there was a high premium on tanning, we felt deprived, disadvantaged, and unworthy of respect and regard.

I never learned to swim as a child for my hair was never to be irony of ironies wet. While Sally and her friends could at the beach use the facilities for showering after swimming, and appear in public with their hair in their natural state, I could not. While Sally and her friends could lie on the beach with their hair in their natural state, I could not.

I rarely went to the beach and whenever I did, I could not enjoy frolicking in the water because of my hair. I had to wash my hair at home which was an activity that entailed having to bend over huge basins of water while my mother lathered and rinsed my hair, and then standing in the backyard where only my neighbors could see my "bad" matted hair being dried by the sun. Then I would have to endure the ordeal of having my mother comb and braid the thick matted hair. What was the outcome of all this?—reduce hair washing as much as possible. Hence going to the beach was a rare activity in my household. Actually, my hair is much more manageable and easy to comb when it is wet.

After my hair was straightened with hot combs, possibilities of physical enjoyment became more limited because it meant that I would have to go through the whole process of not only having my hair washed, but having it straightened. Sally and her peach complexioned "good" hair friends could enjoy going to the beach, running in the rain, playing sports without the constraints and worry of having "bad" hair displayed in public. One could not therefore blame Sally for choosing to be with friends with whom she could better relate in terms of skin color and hair. Many black women do not realize the contribution the Rastafarian locks and the Afro have made in terms of liberating black women from the crippling fear of wearing their hair natural in public. We still have a long way to go as evidenced by extensions, weaves, and relaxers that condition young people from the time they are very young to think that springy or wiry hair in its natural state is inferior.

After a few weeks in Lower V[1], I began to notice that Delia was making attempts to befriend me. I was partially flattered that someone wanted to be my friend, but at the same time I was somewhat embarrassed by her behavior. She laughed a little too loudly, talked a little too loudly, and made comments that I did not really find amusing.

Gradually my resistance wore down, and I found that I was more happy to have Delia's company than not. As we walked to school, I could not help but observe that Delia spoke often about her church. Delia's church was in a struggling working class neighborhood, one of these neighborhoods that was designated with the word Town—Jones Town, Allman Town, Denham Town. Sometimes I wanted to talk about problems I was having with home work, or just talk about my family as I did with Sally but the conversation would always turn to her church. Delia would relate to me almost daily about her minister, M.L., a white American missionary as being tall and very handsome. It was the practice of M. L. during his sermons to frequently refer to his wife, B., who always sat at the back of the church with their several children, as "beautiful". It appeared to me that Delia would take some kind of voyeuristic delight in the exhibition from the pulpit of deep admiration and love expressed by the tall "handsome" white American minister for his "beautiful" red headed wife with milky white complexion. Something seemed very odd about this chocolate brown complexioned young girl with full lips, narrow bony rounded at the tip nose, crinkly hair, and a high well endowed rear being enraptured by the overtly attentive relationship between the young white American minister and his white wife during church services. Did it not appear to Delia that M. L. was displaying contempt for the congregation, and promoting white superiority when he from the pulpit made romantic overtures to his wife, and termed his white "wife" beautiful in an all black church?

I could not escape it—the glorification and adulation of whiteness. Actually, for all the years—two, three years that we were thrown together, Delia revealed very little about her family. I knew more about M.L. and his family than I knew about Delia's family.

To be honest I found the constant talk about Delia's church, M.L., his wife, and their children uninteresting, and not at all stimulating. As young people in the Anglican Church, we never discussed the minister except to point out his weaknesses, and certainly our minister never, in any of his sermons, alluded to his wife. Often I wanted to discuss my school work but whenever I attempted to do so, Delia would make some belittling comment, particularly if mathematics was the topic. My efforts would be dismissed as pretentiousness on my part to being bright. She would then resume the conversation about her church. I soon discovered that Delia's intention was not only to relate to me about the minister and his wife but to attack my Christianity.

I need to be born again. I was shocked when Delia disclosed to me that she was a Christian, and instead of using the fact that I thought she was one of the worse behaved students in the school as my chief weapon of counterattack, I tried to defend myself by convincing Delia that I was a Christian. I pointed out to her to what lengths my mother went in order to have me christened in the Anglican Church, Half Way Tree Parish Church, and that I had been confirmed in that church. I might as well have not spoken. My eyes would be filled with tears of anger and frustration. It seemed to me that Delia not only treated my anger and frustration with contempt but it actually appeared to give her some pleasure. The more angry and flustered I became, the more she would often smile which made me more angry as she repeated with reasons that I could not fathom my need to be "born again", to be "saved" or to have "Jesus Christ as my personal Savior". My feelings may have betrayed some kind of weakness or vulnerability but what foiled Delia's attempt to "convert" me was my belief that being a member of Half Way Tree Church guaranteed my place in heaven, and Delia's deportment.

Besides living in the same vicinity, taking the same bus, and being in the same form, Delia and I had one other thing in common, we had the same music teacher. I had been studying the piano with cocoa brown complexioned middle aged Ms. K. since I was eight years old. In the six or so years that I was a student of Ms. K., I never associated her hair not being straightened as an index of her being a "Christian". I did find her springy hair groomed in its natural state as if she were living in the era prior to the invention of straightening combs somewhat odd, particularly as one day she disclosed that she had attended Wolmer's, but then the entire household was strange. The household except for a man, who was always whistling and was often seen walking in the area at odd times of the day (which caused my sister and I to wonder if he was employed) and a little boy, consisted mainly of women. Frugality and hard work seemed to be the dominant themes of the women in the household. There was always constant movement of women—they were always busy.

Piano lessons were conducted in a room with piano and chairs on one side of the room and on the other side a bed screened off by a curtain behind which Ms. K. would often appear when we came for music. When Ms. K. pulled back the curtain to walk towards the piano, we sometimes would see the bed covered with material because Ms. K. also sewed. She once showed me a skirt (one of the few exchanges we had outside of our relationship as teacher and pupil) that she sewed entirely by hand. Besides the lessons, to augment their income, there were always in a glass case, luring hungry piano students to buy, delicious red and pink, and brown grater cakes, and brown cut cakes made from coconut and lots of sugar which were also sold to the elementary school children who attended a school nearby.

One day Delia decided to discuss the need for me to be a born again Christian at music lesson. She had the ammunition she wanted in terms of the support of the entire household. The attack became on-going. All activity would cease. Pine to dark mahogany brown members of the household would suddenly appear at the entrance to the room. They would solemnly repeat, reeling off passages of Scripture that I had not heard or read why I had to be "born again." Tears of anger and frustration would well up as I had to listen to the arguments of Delia fortified by Ms. K. and members of her household. I was extremely annoyed that time from my lesson was being taken away to pursue what I considered pointless arguments.

I enjoyed and looked forward to piano lessons in spite of the silver or green knitting needle which the other wise soft spoken and gentle but firm

Ms. K. would apply sharply at times to my fingers whenever I used the wrong finger or played the wrong note. I could not believe that Ms K. who was usually very strict and punctilious about time (indeed both musically and in terms of the clock!) would placidly sit so enraptured by these discussions that she would lose track of time.

To my surprise I found myself confronting Delia in a very aggressive manner about bringing up the matter of my need to be "saved" at music. It was the first time that I angrily confronted Delia instead of trying to placate her as I was wont to do. I anticipated a quick barb and was totally astonished when Delia confessed with a mischievous smile that she did it because she did not like playing the piano and so she would purposely initiate the discussion to avoid having the piano lesson! It is a pity that I did not heed an important lesson from that confrontation with Delia. I could have put a stop to the badgering if I had firmly asserted myself. Duppy know who fe frighten.

I do not know why I never spoke to my mother about these discussions. Although I often felt angry and frustrated about the constant attack that I was not "saved", I was by no means convinced by the arguments. The nagging and the badgering were, however, bothering me. I hoped to find solace by complaining to Sally who like me was an Anglican, about Delia's persistent arguments regarding my having to be born again. I expected support from Sally as a member of the Anglican Church. To my utter surprise and dismay, Sally told me that I had to be born again. That shook my confidence a great deal but I still resisted Delia's attempts to "convert" me based on my being a member of the Anglican Church. I was somewhat disconcerted by Sally becoming a fundamentalist but I comforted myself with the thought that Sally was going through another of her "fickle" stages. Not this time. She would remain up to this day a fundamentalist. I did not realize that I was being slowly encircled. My defenses would be shattered the day my brother came home and told me that I *have* to be born again.

My brother was just little over a year younger than I. When he was close to fifteen, he suddenly shot up to almost six feet liberating my father from a lot of anxiety that I, the girl, had inherited his gene for height while his son had inherited his mother's gene and was going to be short. This was all that my brother needed to boost his self-confidence in terms of asserting his opinions and views which undoubtedly were enhanced by my father's penchant, often reflected in the look of admiration, for discussions and debates with my brother. They would frequently lock heads together ignoring or barely acknowledging my mother's and my faltering interjections.

From an early age, my brother displayed a gift and ability to question, analyze, and communicate his ideas. Towering over his sisters at close to age fifteen gave further clout to the gender stereotype that boys are cleverer than girls. Although fifteen months my junior, it had early been settled in the family that he was intellectually superior to me and since he was intellectually superior to me, I reasoned he had better judgment in all matters than I. Whenever there was competition or conflict between him and me, I would defer to him as invariably right.

Although my parents wittingly or unwittingly fostered the belief that my brother's ability was superior to mine, my sister and I could not often help being impressed by his boundless energy, his wit, and above all the capacity to outsmart our father. We were in mortal fear of our father so anyone who could sneak out of the house, go see a movie and return without our father knowing had to be extremely clever. Anyone who would not eat his vegetables but could deftly scrape them off the plate through the dining room window under the nose of our father had to be extremely clever. Anyone who would come up with a scheme of selling empty bottles to make money to go to the cinema because our father refused to give us money must be very clever. When my brother told me therefore that I "have to be saved", I questioned the matter no further.

Held at a house in a very upscale neighborhood on Old Hope Road near Cross Roads, the meetings my brother invited me to attend as a follow up to his directive that I "have to be saved" were totally unlike any gathering I had ever attended. The house was huge with a wide veranda that ran to the front and the side of the house and which faced a very spacious lawn. To the side a little away from the house there was a podium and chairs to seat fifty to a hundred people mostly teenagers.

There were a few older middle aged individuals who hovered generally in the background and unobtrusively guided the meetings. Not one of these older middle aged people looked anything like my father or for that matter like my mother. They were for the most part white or very tan complexioned with straight or shiny wavy hair. Most of the students were of similar complexion and physiognomy. They had all been garnered mainly from the prestigious high schools in Kingston—St. Andrew, Wolmer's, Queens, St Hugh's, Jamaica College, Calabar High School. I felt somewhat out of place because I was by far the darkest girl with straightened springy hair, and rounded nose but doubts about my acceptance were somewhat rationalized by the observation of my pine-cinnamon complexioned short springy haired brother being surrounded by peach and tan complexioned long hair or wavy hair girls with alluring smiles. Therefore they could not be prejudiced. Indeed, my brother received more adoring looks than any of the tan complexioned to cocoa complexioned straight and wavy hair young men that formed part of the entourage that always milled around him.

I soon discovered that there were actually two parts to these meetings. The first part was extremely jocular whilst the second half was as solemn as the first was jocular. The first part began with games which were meant to foster mingling, but as far as I was concerned, they did not meet the objective of getting acquainted with anyone. I was given a quantity of peas and if I answered no or yes to a question, I would forfeit a pea. I felt guilty regarding the waste of peas, for in my family wasting food was almost criminal, and I found it difficult to maintain a conversation while at the same time concentrating very hard not to say "yes" or "no". After a while I usually just stood at the sides and listened in some wonder at the talk and the constant chatter. It was not something to which I was accustomed. Getting together for us in Jamaica meant dancing and, if not dancing then sitting quietly listening to music and watching others dance. Talking was constantly derided at home and at the elementary school. The saying "Empty vessels make the most noise" was frequently hurled at us.

It was the first time, too, that I learnt about charades. How the tan and peanut complexioned girls with long, wavy and shiny hair would hoot and clap their hands with delight when they deciphered the meaning of contorted bodies in these charades! The games would be followed by everyone sitting down in chairs arranged for the service. The service would actual begin with the singing of songs of about four lines called choruses. The theme of these choruses was that once you accept Jesus Christ as your personal Savior, you would be happy and joyful all the time. I really enjoyed the singing of these choruses particularly the way some of the young people had the gift to harmonize ad lib without reading music, and of course the feelings of happiness and joy which these "choruses" evoked.

The feeling that one should be happy was in complete opposition to my father's often quoted precept "Chicken merry, hawk de near." It was somewhat of a relief then to find that if you have God/Jesus in your heart you could be happy all the time. After the singing of choruses, hymns would be sung and prayers would be said. The hymns were unlike the Anglican hymns. They were jolly accompanied by guitar and accordion and prayers, unlike the Anglican prayers, were spontaneous. This part of the service also included some sort of entertainment in the form of a soloist or group rendering a song or songs usually with the same theme of finding happiness and joy in Christ. An important item in this section of the service, which was never done in the Anglican Church and was very new to me, was the giving of a testimony which took the format of a before...and after I accepted Jesus Christ. Someone would state how bad and sinful they were before they met Christ, that is, accepted Christ as their own personal

Savior—they would drink, dance, smoke, go to the movies, wear make-up—
they were on their way to hell but now they found Christ, they were sure to
go to heaven, and how happy and free from sin they are.

The purposes of this first part of the service then was to establish that if
you want to be happy then you need to accept Christ and also to set the stage
for the preacher. Usually the preacher would start his sermon with a couple
of jokes and then the solemn part would begin. My father's precept "chicken
merry, hawk de near" was very relevant at this point. Preachers generally
focused on stirring guilt and shame centered on the reasoning that 1) because
of Adam and Eve you were born in sin. 2) God sent his son to die for your
sin. 3)You need to accept that son in your heart to cleanse you from sin. 4) If
you accept Jesus, you will go to a place called heaven when you die, if you
do not, you will go to hell. The sermon in and of itself was not what really
drove me to see the need to eventually "put up my hand to be saved".

What drove me "to put up my hand" were the tactics and strategies used
as to what would happen to you when you die, if you do not accept Christ. It
was no use your thinking that you are young and therefore death is not
imminent and consequently, it is something that you need not concern
yourself with just yet. Many stories were told about young people attending
a service "just as this, hearing the message, refusing Christ" and being hit by
a car on their way home or committing sin by going to the movies, and being
burnt in a theater. The service would end with the haunting, slow strains of
"Just as I am" during which the preacher would plead, "Is there one? Yes I
see that hand. Is there another?" and between the pleading and thanking God
for the hands raised there would be more preaching and more stories with the
objective of using guilt, shame, and fear to get you to raise your hand and
walk to the altar. Over the years I could not help but observe that the
evangelists use the same art and style that are used in commercials to
persuade one to buy products on television.

Of course being young, tall, good looking, and having a good command
of the English language were definitely attributes that contributed to the
success of the evangelist.

Tired of the harassment and also hoping that this would result in the
transformation that confirmation failed to accomplish I decided to become a
"Christian" at one of the meetings. I found myself raising my hand and
walking to the altar. Prior to my being badgered by fundamentalists, even
though I felt underlying guilt and shame regarding my thoughts about God, I
was not unduly worried about my relationship with God because the
Anglican Church assured me that once the rituals of the Anglican Church
had been carried out, that is, once I was christened and confirmed and took
Communion every Sunday or as often as possible, I was assured that I would

go to heaven when I die. That was really my chief concern although I would have liked to have had warm feelings about God and Jesus Christ.

The fundamentalists however, as a result of their constant preaching about being saved rekindled the feelings I had regarding God and Jesus. I was hoping that when I walked to the altar, that something wonderful would happen and there would be a radical change in me. With great anticipation I walked up the aisle, knelt at the altar and repeated the words the preacher said, something to the effect that I was a sinner, and I now accept Jesus as my Savior. Now unspeakable joy should flood my soul.

I did not feel anything. I did not feel any happiness or joy as preachers often stated would happen. I told myself, however, that I had gone through the process and therefore I am "saved". However, after a while, I could not remember the date when I first put up my hand to be saved. This created a serious problem particularly in giving one's testimony. There had to be a specific time like Saul Paul on his way to Damascus that I could say that there was conversion so that my testimony could be dramatic, and therefore be effective. Hearing that Billy Graham was to come to Jamaica, I decided that I would repeat the process. Surely Billy Graham would succeed where Bishop Gibson and less luminary preachers failed.

I was sixteen years old. My only recollection of Billy Graham's sermon was his assertion that the first question when he got to heaven would be to ask God or Jesus why he chose him to be a successful evangelist or something to that effect. If I was not convinced about God being white before, I was convinced about it then. In my mind's eye I saw Billy Graham ahead of everyone in heaven standing toe to toe with God. I was deeply disappointed about his sermon and did not at all feel "moved" to go the altar. Although I did not clearly articulate my feelings, I felt that he was pompous and arrogant—so unlike the British who felt that one should be subtle about boasting or showing off. However, I was desperate for assurance. I thought at least, if I go to the altar, something dramatic would happen and I could pinpoint this as a particular moment, so that when asked to give my testimony I could state definitely when I received Christ. "It was at the Billy Graham meeting". This time I would be confident about being saved.

Once again to the sad haunting strains of "Just as I am" in the background", feeling a little foolish, I walked up to the altar, knelt at the altar and repeated the affirmation that I accepted Christ as my Savior. I felt nothing. I was very disappointed. Yet, I decided to carry out the motions. I, like many others, was taken to a make-shift tent where I was counseled by a creamy complexioned very thin young man who appeared to be an American and who drew the analogy of living the Christian life with four legs of a chair: I should pray everyday, read my Bible everyday, be in fellowship with other Christians, and testify for Christ.

Alas, the Billy Graham meeting did not help this gnawing feeling that I was not saved. Indeed, it just got worse. I was frequently in a state of panic or torment particularly when I attended meetings. I continued to put my hand up or walk up to the aisle at every meeting for almost a year until one day my brother yelled at me, "If I ever see you put your hand up or walk up the aisle to be saved again, you see...." I think he went on to say that once you accept Christ you are saved. But I wasn't really listening. Neither his argument nor the argument of preachers ever convinced me that I was saved. I was terrified of saying that what I was looking for was concrete empirical evidence that Jesus had come into my heart.

After that remonstrance from my brother, I never walked up to the altar again. I, however, continued the practice of silently asking Jesus to come into my heart, over and over again, even after I became a minister's wife. Each time, I would tell myself, after carrying out the process, that I was saved, but my confidence generally never lasted for more than a couple weeks. An articulate and charismatic preacher would only have to, in his plea, preach about death as imminent, and the possibility of spending eternity in hell, and my confidence would dissipate.

Why I should have a great fear of going to hell in spite of complying with all the criteria needed to be saved, that is christening, baptism, confirmation, raising my hand, I can only attest to a deep feeling of unworthiness, alienation, and disconnect. While I felt that God could not truly love me because of my skin color and hair, I was not particularly desirous of that love because of what appeared to me to be a number of failings on God's part. Not only was he portrayed as cruel, vindictive, and petty in the Bible, but in the accounts of him in terms of the history of Western civilization, and in my encounters growing up, he displayed these characteristics besides being unjust, and fickle. Since he was all powerful, and perfect, however, I could not allow myself to feel superior to him, so I convinced myself that I was unworthy of being saved. I truly took no delight whatsoever in the thought of being in heaven. I, however, feared an eternity of constantly raging fire.

It was not until many years later when I read Bertrand Russell's *Why I am not a Christian* that I was liberated from the fear of going to hell and, indeed, the idea of immortality. According to Russell, belief in immortality springs from the fear of death and the wish to live forever. "If we were not afraid of death, I do not believe that the idea of immortality would ever have arisen." [323] After years of pain and suffering based on fear of going to hell, I

---

[323]Russell, *Why I am not a Christian*, p. 53

was overjoyed to read that there is no scientific evidence for the existence of a soul for the "soul must pervade all space."[324]   Though it is not at all flattering, I was convinced by Russell's arguments regarding the belief that "that when I die I shall rot, and nothing of my ego will survive".[325]

Once I realized that I did not have to fear going to hell, then I began to allow my critical faculties to engage in rigorous analysis of the religion. This would be many years after I initially became a "born again Christian." Just after I became a "born again" Christian, the more I attended services, the less resistant were my critical faculties particularly, ironically, when the fundamentalist preacher claimed university or seminary credentials and his sermon appeared to appeal to the intellect. This type of preacher would include scientific facts and names of prominent intellectuals particularly those who wrestled with atheism. C. S. Lewis was often paraded as an intellectual *par excellence* who had not only converted from being an atheist to being a Christian but wrote several books to support the argument for the existence of God. Voltaire was often cited as a non-believer who converted on his death bed. If highly educated men like C. S. Lewis and Voltaire were convinced about the need for God, who was I to question or doubt? Thinkers and philosophers, such as, Darwin, Freud, Feuerbach, and Bertrand Russell were never mentioned. Needless to say Karl Marx, his communist ideas, and his followers were branded as evil and there was always proof to support the fundamentalist's belief.

One summer a hurricane hit Cuba, missed Jamaica, turned around and hit Cuba a second time. The evangelicals were ecstatic. In sermons, the hurricane's activity corroborated the evangelical's argument that Cuba, a communist country, was evil and therefore God was punishing the Cubans. The preachers never discussed the vast amount of flooding in Jamaica that led to the loss of lives and property as a result of that same hurricane. Indeed, some politicians declared that in some ways the flooding was more disastrous for Jamaica for it was easier to apply for and receive international aid in terms of damage from hurricanes than it was from flooding.

C. S. Lewis' publisher was undoubtedly happy with all the purchases I made of that author's works as I sought to quell any doubt about my need to be a follower of Christ. To be otherwise, I was convinced, would not only result in my becoming a candidate for hell, but I also would be plummeted to the bottom of society.

---

[324]Ibid., p.53.
[325]Ibid., p. 54

CHAPTER NINE

FUNDAMENTALISM
AND
THE FOUR LEGS OF THE CHAIR

Nettie say somewhere in the bible it say Jesus' hair was like lamb's wool, I say.

Well, say Shug, if he came to any of these churches we talking bout he'd have to have it conked before anybody paid him any attention. The last thing niggers want to think about they God is that his hair kinky. (p. 177).

Alice Walker, *The Color Purple*

We were young filled with what appeared to be boundless energy, skills, and talents. The missionaries saw how they could capitalize these resources. My brother and a team of boys organized many Youth for Christ rallies and ISCF meetings; they preached, they sang, they testified; they attracted many young people, particularly girls. My brother tall, good looking, a high school student (first Jamaica College, and then Calabar, prestigious high schools in those days) and charismatic, was very popular. He was regarded as an effective preacher and organizer.

One area, at which I was never successful, although I tried very hard, was winning souls to Christ. I handed out leaflets; I talked to strangers, and friends, but to no avail. I quite despaired of having any stars in my crown. Giving a testimony at a meeting or at a church service which for some was a great source for winning souls to Christ, was for me sheer agony. It was not only that I did not want to speak in public but I did not feel at all authentic about being "saved" made worse by the fact that I could not recall an actual turning point in my life.

At one particular Youth for Christ rally, I stood on the podium, and tried desperately hard to make my testimony convincing by stating all the "bad" things I use to do before I "got saved". I remember distinctly fumbling through "dancing" and I cannot remember what else I highlighted. A pine with very faint pink complexioned young man with brownish reddish springy hair, seated almost at the back, burst out laughing. We were acquainted with each other because he was a member of Half Way Tree Anglican Church. I was so embarrassed by his laughter that I do not know what I said next, and rushed back to my seat. After the meeting, in a discussion, it was intimated to me by mutual acquaintances that he could not help laughing at my stating that I had done "bad things". That was absolutely ridiculous.

"What bad things had I done?"—we young people—the elite, students of prestigious high schools who American evangelists targeted, were extremely prim and proper and well behaved. During the 1950's there were many rules regarding deportment that we as students particularly as high school students had to observe. We were subjected to strict discipline both at school and at home. In high schools, caning boys for the slightest infraction such as being disrespectful, for example, "talking back and not using sir" in responding to a teacher was not unusual. In the eyes of quite a few Jamaicans, children of American missionaries often violated a number of social mores known in Jamaica as "good manners." Indeed a cream complexioned, dark wavy hair Jamaican clearly expressed her disgust at the behavior of the children of American evangelists. They did not possess the manners of Jamaican children. They certainly did not show deference to adults. Jamaican children would not dream of staring at adults or talking back to adults much less calling adults by their first names! She was also very upset about some of the games like "spin the bottle" that were played at Christian gatherings. Dancing she felt was far less sexually provocative and therefore less sinful than some of these games.

Indeed, my behavior, conduct, and deportment deteriorated after I "accepted Christ as my personal Savior". Inside of me was a constant turmoil of grey emotions as I relegated thoughtfulness, rationality, critical analysis to an inferior status, and at times regarded any kind of intellectual critical analysis as of the world and of the devil. God speaks through the Bible, through preachers, and through the Holy Spirit. Barring impious acts which the fundamentalists clearly outlined, such as, dancing, wearing jewelry, fornication, going to the movies, I would often react impulsively to people and events telling myself that I was being guided by the Holy Spirit. The belief that I now had a personal relationship with Christ as a result of being saved or born again deleteriously affected my conduct, my self-confidence, and my self-esteem.

Besides wrestling with doubts about being saved, were anxious thoughts about surrendering every moment to Christ. It was absolutely crazy. Here was I a female cinnamon brown, springy hair, rounded nose female asking a white male to take control of my body. Whatever I was doing, I was to think, would Jesus approve? I could not listen to certain songs, read certain books, associate with non-Christians because Jesus would not approve. My actions often resulted not from the discipline structured behavior that my parents and the school inculcated in me but from impulsive and chaotic thoughts. I was very often insecure.

Within the Anglican Church, there was some respect for certain values, such as, education and respect for parents and for family. Your becoming a

Christian is the responsibility of your parents. Of course, social climbers often used the Anglican Church's polity of having god parents to include high ranking members of the society in their social circle or place them ahead of lower status aunts and uncles. At least, however, godparents meant the support of parents.

As a "born again Christian", I now subscribed to the fundamentalist doctrine that accepting Christ as my personal Savior meant an individual relationship with Christ. Thus, I began the process of atomization. If having an individual relationship with God means disregarding your parents' and the community's mores and rules, well so be it. The most painful memory of my becoming a fundamentalist was the disrespect it fostered for my parents.

The attempt to "convert" us as high school children from our denominations was unethical to say the least. It was an attack on our parents, our parents' values, and our parents' way of life. What evangelical missionaries asserted was that the churches our parents belonged to and which played an integral part in our upbringing were not only inadequate but wrong and sinful. For us as high school students, all under the age of eighteen, we were told in sermon after sermon that in order to grow spiritually in Christ, once we make the decision for Christ, once we are born again, or have accepted Jesus as our personal Savior it is imperative for us to have fellowship with other Christians. Many of us were lured, therefore, to leave our denominations—the Anglican, the Catholic, the Methodist, the Presbyterian—to become members of evangelical churches.

No attempt was made by missionaries or evangelicals to reach our parents or consult with our parents about our leaving our denominations. It meant a loss of the supervision or input of our parents, families, and friends of our parents, during an important phase in our lives. Ironically my father was very upset. My mother was often distraught about my siblings and me leaving the Anglican Church.

My parents' views did not matter. They were not saved and it was our duty as born again Christians to bring them to Christ which often meant monitoring our parents' behavior. The different perspectives regarding Christianity resulted in many conflicts in the household. We became very upset with our mother, and lectured and scolded her, when one Christmas, she decided, as was her custom, to give a bottle of beer to the "bread man", who delivered our daily supply of bread. Our mother, we argued, "would be causing the 'bread man' to sin and go to hell". My mother retorted that she did not see how drinking a little beer would send anyone to hell—after all Jesus turned water into wine—her not giving the "bread man" beer does not mean that he would not obtain beer elsewhere, if he wanted to." The "bread man" got his beer.

When I first started playing Jamaican folk songs on the piano, my father was absolutely delighted. After that it became the custom for me to entertain the family, particularly on a Saturday evening, by playing Jamaican folk songs and popular foreign usually love songs on the piano. It was not uncommon for the family to dance to these tunes. My parents were aghast when I told them that I could no longer play popular songs or Jamaican folksongs on the piano because that would hinder my Christian witness. As a "born again Christian", I now had to dedicate my skills solely to the Lord. "What" asked my mother despairingly, more than once, "is wrong with playing "Carry me ackee to the Linstead Market" the song with which I would invariably start the medley of folk songs. "It is of the devil" would inevitably be my response. "My hands must be used only for the Lord."

It did not dawn on me that the "born again" Christians did not find singing American folk songs sinful. As a matter of fact when we went to Christian camps, retreats, and meetings we were given sheets which consisted of a compilation of folk songs that offered us a choice of several secular American songs which we would heartily sing. It has been many, many years; however, I sang some of these American folk songs so often that I am quoting this one from memory:

They strolled the lane together.
The sky was studded with stars
They reached the gate together
And he lifted for her the bars
She raised her brown eyes to him
There is nothing between them now
For he was just the hired hand
And she the Jersey cow.

Another one I remember singing was "The thinnest man...from Old Hoboken.

So what was wrong with "Carry me ackee?"—for one thing, it used Jamaican dialect which no doubt offended God's ears for God spoke only proper English in prayers, in sermons, in hymns, and of course the Bible. Consequently, there is the implication then that the Jamaican dialect was "of the world" and sinful. It was often interesting, and sometimes very amusing to hear semi-illiterate Jamaicans preach. Although some never traveled beyond the shores of the island, once these preachers stepped into the pulpit, I do not know how the transformation took place, but the insidious Jamaican dialect would be immediately dropped for the intonation and drawl of an American accent in total oblivion of the violation of grammatical rules. The Jamaican dialect was never spoken in church.

Besides the folk songs' use of dialect, there was the matter of rhythm. It is a well known fact that God does not approve of syncopated rhythm with a lot of dotted quavers (eighth notes) and (semi-quavers) sixteenth notes. He likes very steady rhythm preferably using minims (half notes) and sparingly crochets (quarter notes). Why is it okay to sing the two songs quoted above and sinful to sing ? :

Carry me ackee to the Linstead Market
Not a quattie worth sell
Carry me ackee to the Linstead Market
Not a quattie worth sell
Lawd what a nite what a nite
What a Saturday nite
Lawd what a nite what a nite
What a Saturday nite

The lady was lamenting not getting her ackees sold. As in the case of many folk songs, "Carry me Ackee to the Linstead Market" was a commentary in song of an event—in this case, ackee poisoning in Jamaica. The memory of depriving my parents of delight is still painful to me.

What was overlooked by the evangelists is that my piano lessons were a huge sacrifice on the part of my parents. God and the evangelists should have been extremely grateful to my parents and their wishes should have been respected. Besides, my lessons were classical piano based on The Royal School of Music Curriculum. It did not appear that God objected to the playing of scales and pieces for the Royal School of Music Examinations, but he was firmly opposed to the playing of Jamaican folk songs and popular pieces on the piano. Playing for evangelical services overtly or covertly contributed to the growth of the evangelical movement. God and the fundamentalists therefore benefitted from my parents' commitment to the development and growth of my musical skills.

It is true that in some ways playing for church services did enhance my skills, and some loss of inhibition regarding performing in public. At the same time, however, the pieces I was required to play for Christian services were not all that challenging and indeed may have in some ways hindered my growth by my being forbidden to listen to and play jazz and popular music particularly at a time when I was young, free from a lot of responsibilities, and had a number of opportunities to explore different genres of music.

There were many other areas that created conflicts in our home. In a very didactic manner we told our parents that the Bible must be taken literally. Our often arrogant, belligerent, and hostile manner affected our relationships with extended family and friends of our parents for whom the Bible was marginal in terms of their way of life. Not being able to dance, go to the movies, be involved in community activities outside of "born again Christian" activities also affected the relationship between our parents and ourselves and to a great extent, their control.

Some years later my sister and I would discuss how we noted on reflection that while the American missionaries tacitly encouraged us as children to disrespect and disobey our parents, which contributed unfortunately to our atomization, the children of the missionaries were constantly under the surveillance and supervision of their parents. At every function the missionaries were present in the background and even if they were not present, some one would be delegated to "keep on eye on their children."

In becoming fundamentalists, we had merely exchanged the British colonial master and culture for the American colonial master and culture. We did not see how Christian evangelization and proselytization of peoples is as p'Bitek points out in reference to Africa "double edged. The missionaries came to preach the gospel as well as to 'civilize' the Africans and in so doing they were an important vehicle of Western civilization, which readily lent to the churches its wealth, power, and influence."[326]

In Jamaica, the Anglican Church, in its rituals, prayers, hymns, services and sermons, was totally dominated by British culture in which we had to pay homage to the British monarchy and colonial administrators. African culture and history were non-existent in the rituals of the Anglican Church. Indeed, the Anglican Church catered to the elite. The Anglican Church was an integral part of the socialization process in which although it afforded us channels for upward social mobility by building schools and providing jobs, the Church served, in many ways, to remind us that our status was limited to a certain sphere. Pews were reserved for the upper class; schools were built for the elite; the church assiduously supported the norms, mores, and rules of the ruling class.

However, the Anglican Church never engaged in the arrogant individualism, and anti-intellectualism of the American evangelicals. How could it as an elitist institution? While the fundamentalists preached that the individual relationship with God is paramount, we did not see how the "personal salvation" resulted not only in oppressive atomization as a result of abandoning our family and community, but also in the control of our thoughts and behavior by the evangelicals. They completely controlled our

---

[326]p'Bitek, *African Religions in Western Scholarship,* p. 54.

thoughts and behavior with their long lists of rules regarding our activity and our relationships. If African culture and history were marginalized in the Anglican Church, they were actually demonized amongst the American evangelicals.

I cannot remember after which of the many times I "got saved" that I told Delia that I was "saved". I thought Delia would be delighted, that the barbs and the insults and calling me names such as "Old Soldier" would cease, and she would be actually nice to me; this was not to be. After about a year of walking together to and from school, even though I preferred her company to none, I was still not particularly fond of Delia and I cannot imagine why I wanted her approval. It was not Delia's fault. In many ways I was being insincere and inauthentic.

Delia did not appear to be thrilled about the idea of my becoming a Christian. She seemed somehow disappointed in me. I never got closer to her. Indeed, one day on my way home from the Church I now attended which was on her street, I saw her standing at the fence of one of the best kept houses on the street of a heterogeneous mixture of board houses and concrete houses. Delia's white concrete house with its neat lawn and garden stood out amidst the surrounding yards each composed of about two to three board houses on bare brown earth with no lawn or garden. Delia stood at the fence looking like a lost child of about seven years rather than her seventeen years. She totally ignored all my overt and covert attempts for her to invite me inside.

Now I became the fanatic fundamentalist telling Delia about the Youth for Christ rallies I attended. Delia never attended any of these rallies. She was, however, a member of the Inter School Christian Fellowship at Wolmer's, and regularly attended the meetings. As I talked about my involvement in Christian activities, and preached to her about the Christian path, Delia would be very quiet. After a while I noted that while I was speaking to her, she would from time to time glance at the top of my head. Then one day it came out. I was not really a Christian because I straightened my hair.

I was dumbfounded. My hair now became the source of conflict. I was totally unprepared for this. I had given up dancing, going to the movies, singing and playing Jamaican folksongs, wearing dresses without sleeves, wearing make-up, wearing nail polish, listening to music of the world.

I did not realize that the straightening of the hair would be an index of one's Christianity. To corroborate her argument, Delia told me that a white missionary at her church asserted the view that it was ridiculous for black people who have naturally curly hair to straighten their hair and then curl it up again. As Delia spoke, a visual image of my hair in its natural state sprung to mind and I thought hyperbole is an understatement of the missionary's description of my hair as curly—it coiled at the roots and then became very wiry and springy. There was one factor, however, about my hair which every one found peculiar and that is, after being washed, twisted in African knots and oiled, it would be straight almost as if it had been straightened with a straightening comb. Unfortunately, this property of my hair was not fully maximized because it was believed that my hair after being washed had to be completely dried by the sun, not towel dried, or I would "catch a cold". When it was dry, it was thick, extremely "matty" and difficult to comb. What then should have been a very easy process, that is, combing my hair when wet, turned into moments of torture and an ordeal to be resisted as much as possible.

Up to age fourteen, except for one futile attempt when I was twelve, I had never combed my hair. Every morning I had to march with a huge comb with teeth spread apart to my parents' bedroom where I would sit in a chair and my mother would go through the motion of combing my hair, one of the many duties she had to perform in the morning before leaving for her job as a teacher. The two braids at the back that barely reached the nape of my neck and the one in front made me look like seven years old instead of the fourteen years I was supposed to be. In fact, I was taller than my mother and looked more like sixteen / seventeen than fourteen. My peers with "good" hair or those with straightened "springy" hair could style their hair so that they looked more like a teenager. It was infradig to have to ask my mother at age fourteen to comb my hair. Why could I not have my hair straightened?

My father: he had instituted a rule that my hair was not to be straightened until I was sixteen. I had two more years to go. Now there was a group of women who kept clamoring to my mother that it was "time for" my "hair to be straightened." Enough said my mother one day, when I was fourteen, and did what she was wont to do when she determined on a course of action in opposition to my father, she called in a troop of women: Colette, Mrs. Lawrence, and my cousin Pearl.

Colette, my friend, about two to three years older than I, lived two houses down on the other side of the avenue from me. My parents adored Colette who they regarded as remarkably gifted. She could sew. I would sometimes watch in amazement as Colette would cut from a bit of material parts for a dress. In an hour or two, she, her hands working with quick dexterity at the sewing machine, without a pattern, and sometimes without even a tape measure, would complete the dress. At seventeen, she made dresses without a pattern for my sister and me which were greatly admired. She could play the piano; in keeping with her non-conformist or creative

196

personality, she did not like to read the notes. She fostered my playing by ear by showing me chords. Amongst her friends, she had the reputation of being very competent with regards to straightening and styling hair. My parents could not understand why Colette was not doing well in school. They did not realize that in the high school, in spite of talents and abilities, you had to apply yourself to study. Colette did not apply herself to study.

Besides Colette, there was Mrs. Lawrence, our beige-yellow complexioned tenant with golden brown wavy hair and matching eyes, who claimed she was a hair dresser. Mrs. Lawrence of mostly German ancestry was originally from St. Elizabeth. She was separated from her husband, a very short ebony complexioned man who always wore a hat that almost fulfilled what seemed to be Mr. Lawrence's objective—concealing his features. If that was the objective, the hat did not entirely accomplish it, however, for under the partially covered face, one could still see the prominent nose and lips. It was embarrassing the way Mr. Lawrence would stand outside, at the window of Mrs. Lawrence's room, for she would not allow him to enter the house, and plead and whine for Mrs. Lawrence to return to him.

No adult in my household, that is, the helpers, my mother, and anyone who came to visit in spite of direct and indirect prodding could ascertain from Mrs. Lawrence why she left Mr. Lawrence. Although they felt sorry for Mr. Lawrence particularly when they heard him whining, there were comments from time as to how "Mrs. Lawrence could have married Mr. Lawrence" meaning how someone of Mrs. Lawrence's beige yellow complexion and wavy golden brown hair could have married someone as dark and often imputed as "ugly" as Mr. Lawrence even though Mrs. Lawrence's dull beige yellow complexion, short somewhat flat nose and thick wavy hair denoted some African ancestry. The adults in my household and those who visited our house came to the conclusion that Mrs. Lawrence married Mr. Lawrence to escape poverty in St. Elizabeth, and now that she had moved to Kingston was ashamed of him. They had two daughters, the older of which had a light lemony complexion, a wide mouth and short springy reddish brown hair. She was about three years old and was not talking. The younger was over a year of peanut complexion with hair and features amazingly like her mother's.

My mother was often upset regarding the way Mrs. Lawrence unabashedly showed preference to the younger daughter and in many ways mistreated the older one punishing her for being active and doing what is natural to a toddler. She would often leave the older daughter alone and confined in the room for hours. It was imputed by my mother that Mrs. Lawrence showed preference for the younger daughter because her features were narrower, and her hair was "prettier", and discriminated against the older because she was darker and resembled her father. I could not help but note over the years how my mother would point out to me disparity particularly on the basis of skin color in the treatment of children. My mother never said a word to Mrs. Lawrence, however, about this issue.

I did not care for Mrs. Lawrence. Although her proper enunciated though grammatically incorrect speech—"they will comes to see me", for example—was often a source of amusement "behind her back" it was interesting to note the respect she commanded from everyone including my mother in her presence. Head held high, she would often traipse in her high heel shoes no matter what time of day with her supercilious smile. Since her foibles particularly her lack of formal education, and her attitude to her husband and older daughter were often discussed in her absence, I could not help but think that the deference ascribed to her in her presence was due to her beige yellow complexion, her golden brown hair, and the fact that she felt that deference was due to her because of these physical characteristics.

My older, by about ten years, bronze complexioned red headed freckled face cousin with somewhat short stubby nose and very small mouth that was ever ready to make a witty comment or to tease was the third person co-opted. Her job was to stand guard at the gate in order "to look out" for Mr. R.'s Austin 8 car. It was my father's policy never to let anyone know his itinerary so that they, the women, could not gauge what time he would be home. In this way, he could maintain strict regimentation of the household for the women not knowing when Mr. R is going to show up, would constantly observe his demands and expectations—the alternative would be subjection to his rage as a result of being found derelict in their duty.

As soon as my cousin spotted the car, at the end of the road she should rush to the back porch, where the illicit straightening was taking place, to warn everyone that Mr. R. was on his way. By the time Mr. R. was to drive the Austin 8 car to the gate, open the gate, and drive the car into the yard, it would give the women enough time to hide the equipment. One day it was decided to put the plan into effect.

Two pairs of hands one peanut complexioned pair, the other a beige yellow began the process. My mother skirted around me, gave suggestions, checked the coal, and tried to soothe me. The whole process seemed interminable—the sizzling sound of fried hair, the heat of the hot comb, the hot oil on my scalp. Tensions would heighten as my cousin bored with her sentry duty and wanting to be more involved in what was happening kept running to the back causing our hearts to race. "You see Mr. R." "No". "Then go back to the gate." From time to time, my mother would touch my shoulder and express sympathy. It is almost over, she would say, just a little more. Towards the end of the process, the anxiety of my father returning increased which was aggravated by the more frequent appearances of my cousin's freckled face. "Is Mr. R. coming?" "No a doan see de car." "Then go back to the gate."

When they were finally done, I burst into tears partially from the ordeal and partially from relief that my father did not appear. My mother and her cohorts could not have picked a better day. As fate would have had it, my father did not return until very much later than usual—he returned at night. For the first time I could comb my hair, even though I winced, when the comb touched parts of my scalp that were tender from the hot oil and hot comb. The hair miraculously lengthened to reach a little beyond my shoulders. How my hair had grown from three stubby little plaits that barely reached the nape of my neck to now extend a little below my shoulder, I did not know.

For over a year, my father said nothing. One day pointing to a tiny scar, he asked, "What is that?" Thinking that he was referring to my hair, I hastily said, "It is not straighten, I straighten it Papa, I just washed it" referring to the fact that my hair would seem as though it was straightened when washed. One morning about a year after that, and about two years after I first straightened my hair, I felt a stinging blow to my face with the words, "you think I do not know that you are straightening your hair." I was sixteen. The pretext for hitting me was because my mother had asked me to help prepare the breakfast and I pouted. I do not know who was more upset, my mother or I.

After that I no longer had to hide. Deception: in some ways deception had haunted my life from an infant. I was christened surreptitiously without my father knowing and my hair was straightened clandestinely.

At thirteen fourteen when I told my mother that I did not believe that Jesus was perfect, her response was that I should not say that again because I would go to hell. Would not Jesus Christ know, if he really exists, that the only reason why I am not going to repeat that he is not perfect is because I fear going to hell? Later I would make several attempts to deceive God when I became confirmed and then "saved". I was never convinced by the arguments of any of the preachers about why I should be saved. What led me to be "born again" was my fear of confronting my brother, my peers, and all those who constantly badgered me about being born again and of course my fear of going to hell. As a fundamentalist for years I would carry out this charade of pretending to believe something that I did not. This is the Christian stance and it is ironic because if God is omniscient, then he could see in my brain that I was deceiving him as a result of my fear of his power of sending me to hell. As a matter of fact, he would know my thoughts even before I thought them!

It seemed to me that fear and deception were the hall marks of my life as a fundamentalist Christian.

Delia was not the only one who applied pressure about the "straightening of the hair". It was a sin claimed a number of Christian men and Christian women. I was beginning to have serious conflicts about sin and straightening my hair. I had no recourse but to speak to my mother about the conflicts. I needed my mother as an ally. I had never combed my hair in its natural state and she had by supporting the straightening of my hair saved me from the disapproval of many Jamaicans.

Without even a minute's reflection, my mother responded to my concern. If God did not want women to straighten their hair, argued my mother, then he would not have given man the knowledge to invent the straightening comb.[327] She warned me about the danger of being a "long face Christian" and told me the story of a man on seeing a donkey remarked that the donkey must be a Christian because it had a long face. I was not entirely convinced by my mother's arguments, but I allowed by self to be swayed by them. I would deceive God by having him think that I did not believe straightening my hair was a sin. I hoped that he would not really notice or that he would not be extremely offended by it for I had no intention, no matter what, to stop straightening my hair.

Some months after Delia told me that I am not really a Christian because I straightened my hair, Delia appeared one day with her hair straightened. It was the happiest I had ever seen her particularly, as after a couple months, her hair which was shorter than mine in its natural state grew longer than mine when straightened.

Straightening the hair was not the only issue with which I would have to contend now that I was a Christian. A factor that dominated the fundamentalists' doctrine which was not to me as evident in the Anglican Church was the factor of "the world". For the first time in my life I found myself satiated with ideas and beliefs that the universe was dichotomized into a spiritual or holy realm and "worldly" or evil realm. Overseeing this "worldly" realm was a being called Satan or the Devil. As born again Christians we were to avoid the "things of this world" which could ensnare us, ruin our testimony, and cause us to lose our faith.

---

[327]It would appear that my mother did not know that it was actually a woman, Madame C. J. Walker, who is credited for inventing a special straightening comb for black women. However, there is much controversy surrounding whether Madame C. J Walker actually invented the straightening comb or merely popularized it.—www.yahoo.com

The figure, Satan, was now introduced into our lives in a manner that terrified us. It is not that I was totally unaware of Satan's existence but as an Anglican I was taught that Satan's role was peripheral, that is, relegated to causing original sin and being the guardian of Hell. He was, however, conquered by Christ's death and resurrection. As long as I partook of the sacraments particularly Holy Communion, I did not have to be at all concerned about Satan.

For the fundamentalists, however, Satan became a dominant figure with whom we had to struggle moment by moment as he completely controlled what is "the world". I should have no part therefore of "the world" which included a long list of forbidden activities, ways of dressing, and relationships. The observation of this list—not participating in certain activities, such as dancing, not speaking to certain people because they are not Christians, conforming to a style of dress that repressed creativity and sexuality led to increased atomization and oppression.

One of the things my sister, some of our female friends, and I could not help but note that in the matter of sin and appearance, there was clear gender discrimination. Most of the rules applied to women: no make-up, no dresses without sleeves, no short skirts or low cut blouses, no pants, shorts, jewelry—earrings, bangles, no straightening of the hair. Men could wear the latest fashion without being a bit concerned that they were committing sin, but women were constantly attacked and under surveillance about their appearance. Women were far more likely to commit sin than men and this view was frequently reinforced in sermons regarding sin and the origin of sin. It was Eve who tempted Adam. As one evangelist (laughing as he said it) opined, woman means "woe man".

If there was gender discrimination regarding women and sin, it was further complicated by race discrimination. Black women were more likely to sin because of their hair. Since straightening one's hair fell under the category of "things of the world" and therefore was sinful, amongst black women therefore, hair was an index of one's Christianity. Indeed, Delia told me that her brother was dating two women and could not decide which to marry. His indecision was based solely on hair: one straightened her hair and the other did not. "Good hair" women were not faced with the dilemma regarding the straightening the hair.

Since good hair women did not have to deal with this vexing issue, one could only assume that good hair was in better standing with God since God created human beings. One could only conclude that God is white and that black women are cursed.

It was not the case that born again Christians' postulation of not straightening the hair promoted positive and good feelings about black hair.

It was totally based on the view that straightening the hair is "something of the world". This placed a lot of burden, a feeling of being a Dalit, on black women. Black women are often filled with shame, fear, and guilt. As a matter of fact when wearing one's hair natural, that is, the Afro came into vogue during the 1960's and 1970's, black Christian women were chastised, and I have concrete evidence of this as one of those women, for wearing the Afro. Wearing the Afro became "a thing of this world". Christian women were then told that they should straighten their hair! Black women are still faced with this dilemma of hair as an index of one's Christianity. Wearing one's hair natural particularly wearing locks or dreads does not meet the approval of God and a number of Christians.

The fundamentalists targeted mainly the young at a period in our lives when dating and marriage occupied our thoughts. Indeed, ironically, the fundamentalists who were so other worldly in many ways focused a lot on romantic love. Reference was frequently made to romantic love in sermons, in testimonies, at gatherings and meetings. I have already alluded to the fact that Delia used to often talk about ML's romantic references to his wife from the pulpit. Public display of affection was the norm. Foreign white couples and Jamaican white couples would sit arm in arm at church services. Public display of affection was not the norm in Jamaica.

Married fundamentalists would often relate in their testimonies how God led them to their spouses. Young people, particularly women, were encouraged to pray for spouses with the constant caveat that they should accept God's will and should not marry someone from the world which could include men from mainline churches. It should be noted that chastity—a woman being a virgin (this was not as highly stressed for a man) was of supreme moral value. While the American and British missionaries spoke a lot about God's role in bringing couples together, we could not help but note, however, that as soon as there was any indication of romance brewing between the Afro-Jamaican youth and the daughter or son of the missionary, the daughter or son would be whisked off to the United States or England.

We could not help but observe also that shiny wavy hair girls were far more likely to be dated by Christian boys than springy hair girls. At the same time, there was a higher premium on shiny wavy hair boys than springy hair boys. This further blighted springy hair girls' already limited or negligible prospects for marriage.

Hair was a major issue amongst fundamentalists. Indeed, the response of a brilliant young woman (her parents were teachers) a few years older than I who I was trying to "win for Christ" left an indelible impression on me. She made no attempt to counter my arguments but with a laugh dismissed them by stating that as a student at St. Andrews High School for Girls, she attended a number of ISCF meetings held there. She observed that the "pretty hair boys" who were invited to lead these meetings would condemn hair straightening. "Don't straighten your hair" they would preach. The girls would obey, she continued, and then with a very melodious laugh she stated, "the boys then went ahead and married 'pretty hair' girls who did not have to straighten their hair !"

Little did she know how this exchange would have an impact on my thoughts about Christianity, hypocrisy, and the oppression of black women. Instead of "winning" her to Christ, her remarks actually mark a point in my liberation.

Interestingly, a number of young men outside the "Christian" fold believing that obedience and chastity were far more important than hair were therefore willing to marry springy hair Christian girls based on the view that obedience and chastity ranked high amongst Christian girls and therefore they would make very good wives. Alas, however, these girls were often dogged by Christian men who had no romantic interest in them but who would preach to them about "being unevenly yoked", that is, marrying men who are "of the world", men who were not "born again Christians". I speak from observation and experience.

Some springy hair young women would exhibit piety by working very hard within the church—teaching Sunday School, attending prayer meetings, singing in the Choir. Often the object of this piety was to obtain a "born again" husband. What actually happened often, however, is that the object of the piety, usually a minister or preacher would, guided by prayer, fall in love with a "beautiful angelic" shiny wavy hair girl who attended church haphazardly and did not lift her peach or tan complexioned finger to help in Church activities. Indeed Preacher John would lead hard working springy hair Mary to believe there is hope and may have even dated her a few times only to be told that he prayed about it and it was not the "Lord's will". "The Lord's will" broke the hearts of many pine, cocoa brown, chocolate complexion women with springy hair.

Appearance played a key role amongst women but it also played a key role amongst men. If you had the reputation of winning souls you can be sure that you are tall, lean, young and good-looking. Throngs to Christ were never led by short, balding, fat, not so good looking old men.

It would take years for me to be liberated from the oppressive weight of Christian fundamentalism. The dichotomization of the universe into good and evil and regarding things of the "world" as evil blocked my intellectual and social growth, increased my atomization, particularly as my social circle was restricted to "born again" Christians. Limiting social relations to "born again Christians" contributed to lack of development of social skills aggravated by restricting my experience and exposure to knowledge. Christian fundamentalists not only demonized knowledge; the fundamentalists also demonized people and even nature. In truth and in fact, I could not even enjoy the natural beauty of the beaches, plants, rivers, and mountains, of Jamaica, locked as I was in thinking about heaven as good and the world as evil and that Jesus would soon be returning to earth.

It is interesting to note that while Christian fundamentalists deplore the world they have no qualms in using items of the world, such as, motor cars, telephones, airplanes, microphones, movie projectors, electricity, skills, knowledge, and not to mention money. The fundamentalists also had no inhibitions to use ideas of the world, if they felt the ideas could advance their own agenda of oppression and mind control. They use science to "prove" that God exists; their preaching styles and skills are based on the persuasive methods and strategies of "people of the world."

It took me years to appreciate life as an integrated whole and that we are all connected. What a wonderful thing to be able to dance, my chief means of having fun, and not feel guilty that I am committing a sin! How gratifying it is to appreciate the beauty of my wiry hair, my two toned cinnamon brown complexion and my round tipped nose! What a great experience it is to open oneself to learning from a diversity of books and people! I no longer have to feel guilty or shun people of different philosophical or religious beliefs— atheists, Buddhists, Indigenous Peoples, Jews, Hindus, Muslims, Rastafarians and of course Christians. How wonderful it is to read Darwin, Marx, Freud, Malcolm X, Marcus Garvey, and Walter Rodney without feeling guilt and fear!

It would take many years to overcome the oppression of Christianity, particularly that of Christian fundamentalists, but little did the fundamentalists know, seeds of my liberation were being planted even while I was fanatically handing out tracts, preaching, testifying, and witnessing for Christ.

CHAPTER TEN

"THE WRETCHED OF THE EARTH"

It is becoming increasingly clear that the fortunes of the North Atlantic peoples are closely related to the misfortunes of Third World peoples, in many fundamental ways. [328]

George Beckford

In the midst of editing this chapter, my husband bounds up the stairs. "You will never believe it", he says. "The Bible is being translated into the Jamaican dialect". I am devastated. I follow him downstairs to watch a U Tube video of two well dressed black men in suit and ties being interviewed by an equally well dressed black male regarding the translation of the Bible into the Jamaican dialect. One interviewee is the President of the Bible Society of the West Indies and the other is an employee of the Wycliffe translators. Translating the Bible into the Jamaican dialect has been an ongoing project for some years, they say. The projected time for publication is 2012, in time for the fiftieth anniversary of Jamaica's Independence. A lot of thoughts swirl through my head. I think: this puts a dent into my theory that God identifies with the elite and not with the poor because he speaks perfect English in the Bible, and not the Jamaican dialect. Now in 2012, after all these years of speaking perfect English, God has decided to speak in the Jamaican dialect. And then I think, isn't this going to lead to a further divide between the middle class and the poor uneducated masses ?

The debates I heard in the 1960's and 1970's based on the proposition that the Jamaican dialect be an official language permeate my thoughts. The image of a television broadcast with Louise Bennett[329] as the main proponent of the Jamaican dialect as a language is in the fore of my mind. As I listen to the President of the Bible Society of the West Indies, and the Wycliffe Translators employee present their arguments for the translation of the Bible into the Jamaican dialect in impeccable English, I remember being struck by the fact that Louise Bennett on that television broadcast defended her points in well articulated English.

A few days later I call my sister who is living in Canada. She laughs

---

[328]George L. Beckford, *Persistent Poverty : Underdevelopment in Plantation Economies of the Third World,* (New York, NY: Oxford University Press, 1972), p. v

[329]Louise Bennett is a Jamaican poet who wrote poems and stories in the Jamaican dialect.

when I tell her that the Bible is being translated into the Jamaican dialect. "That is a joke" she says and continues by pointing out that the Jamaican dialect is an oral language. It is spoken, not read. I verified her response by telling her that I could not read some of the passages, on the screen, excerpted from the Bible, in dialect. It is difficult to read, she corroborates and asks rhetorically: Have you ever tried reading Louise Bennett's poems? She raises some of the arguments used by the opponents in the Jamaican dialect as a language debate. It is not standardized. There are almost as many versions of the language as there are people, she says. I point out to her that the promoters of the Bible in Jamaican dialect assert (in well spoken English) that at one stage the English language was a dialect just as how the Jamaican patois is a dialect. Tyndale's translation of the Bible from Latin to English, according to the President of the Bible Society of the West Indies, helped to promote the recognition of the dialect as a language. So the Bible being translated into Jamaican dialect will help raise the perception of the Jamaican dialect as a language of the lower classes. The translation of the Bible into dialect will bring respectability to the dialect.

We both agree that this is very faulty reasoning. The English language, even if it were at one stage a dialect was, to a large extent, clearly distinguishable from Latin. English, unlike the Romance languages, Spanish, Portuguese, and Italian is not as directly descended from Latin. Most of the people of England communicated in the English dialect. There was then a universality regarding the English dialect. This is not the case in terms of the Jamaican dialect. The middle class and upper class would have to learn the Jamaican dialect because generally in interactions amongst themselves they do not use the Jamaican dialect.

The Jamaican dialect has a very limited vocabulary and depends almost exclusively on English. It is one thing to express oneself orally using simple sentences and phrases; it is another to articulate one's views and ideas that call for extensive vocabulary. Can textbooks—medical, physics, mathematics, engineering and academic works by authors such as Braithwaite, DuBois, C. L. R. James, Fanon, Freud, Marx, Rex Nettleford, Nietzsche, Walter Rodney, Eric Williams be translated into the Jamaican dialect? What are the words, in the Jamaican dialect, for derivatives, calculus, stock exchange, shares, biomedical ethics, technology, surgery and commonly used words such as bed, table, chair, lamp, book, sofa, piano etc ? What about numbers ? Does the President of the Bible Society of the West Indies envisage Jamaica's colonization and enslavement of peoples as was done by the British in order to spread the growth and development of the Jamaican dialect ?

My sister is not very enthusiastic about my idea that time could have been better spent promoting Spanish, Chinese, Hindi, and Swahili as second languages in Jamaica than trying to raise the Jamaican dialect to the rank of a language by translating the Bible into the Jamaican dialect. She is an English as a Second Language teacher and argues that there are a number of difficulties involved in trying to teach students a second language when they have not mastered their first language. Trust me, she says, it is very, very difficult. I have deep reservations about the distribution of Bibles, I persist, but it would have been more productive had resources been used to distribute Bibles in Spanish, Chinese, Hindi and Swahili than to translate the Bible into the Jamaican dialect.

It would have been more beneficial, she countered, from her experience as a teacher of English as a Second Language, to use passages in the Bible to teach illiterate and semi-literate Jamaicans to speak Standard English. For example, "Jesus spoke to his disciples" could be used to ask: What is the subject of that sentence? What is the verb? What is the object of the sentence? She is not totally convinced by my arguments that it is in my Spanish classes that I learnt a lot of English grammar and how the structure of Swahili with the focus on nouns has brought greater awareness of English grammatical rules regarding nouns. Do you know how difficult it is, she maintains, for students who have not mastered the English language to read and understand word problems in mathematics?

We both agree that we are living in a competitive world and trying to promote the Jamaican dialect as a recognized language would only result in greater insularity, isolation, and, indeed, oppression of uneducated Jamaicans. She tells me how students from an Asian country complain about the hurdles they have to overcome since their official language was switched from English to their local language. As their language is spoken only by the inhabitants of this particular country, it has presented a lot of difficulties in terms of global communication, for many, particularly the poorer natives, of that country.

My sister does not entirely agree with my idea that Jamaica should become a multilingual society. I am not, however, advocating languages being taught the way I learnt Spanish in school, that is, as though it is a dead language so that I am able to read and write in Spanish, but I cannot speak it fluently. My objective is far more ambitious. Spanish (as well as other languages) should be recognized as second languages so that children will be able to communicate in both Spanish (and other languages) and English although English will be the primary language. We are part of the Caribbean where Spanish, French, Dutch are spoken besides English. Not only is Cuba our nearest neighbor but Spanish was the first European language of Jamaicans as a number of Spanish names of places, such as Ocho Rios,

Negril, Spanish Town, Oracabesa, Rio Cobre, Rio Grande, Mt. Diablo, indicate. Jamaica was colonized by the Spanish for over a century. In many ways we share the same heritage of Latin America, that is, slavery and colonization. Besides, a number of Jamaicans have migrated to areas of Latin America. My father was born in Panama and my grandfather migrated to Panama and then to Cuba where he died. I have several relatives in Costa Rica. Chinese and Indians were brought to Jamaica after Emancipation and yet the vast majority of Jamaicans know very little about Chinese and Indian languages and culture. Having been stripped of our African language, I think it is important to learn an African language as an integral part of reclaiming some aspects of our African culture.

Instituting Spanish (and other languages) as a second language[330] will not only contribute to Jamaicans communicating with our neighbors in the Caribbean and Latin America, but it will also enhance the ability of Jamaicans to participate in a global economy. Think of how this could boost the Jamaican economy in terms of requirements for teachers, translators, publishers, tourism, and trade. Learning other languages will focus on meaningful activity; enough of metaphysics. I am utterly amazed that linguists from the University of the West Indies, as stated in the interview above, could be engaged in what seems to me a pointless task of translating the Bible into the Jamaican dialect.

When I was growing up I was forbidden to speak the Jamaican dialect. Use of the Jamaican dialect was not only not permitted in my home and at the high school I attended, Wolmer's, but I had to pronounce my words in the manner of what was considered upper class British enunciation. This was very alienating. Although my family often attended performances including the annual Jamaican Pantomime where Louise Bennett and Ranny Williams would delight the audiences using the Jamaican dialect, reciting poems written by Louise Bennett was taboo. This was very unfortunate for Ms. Bennett's poems are actual brilliant commentaries on social and historical issues that would have enhanced my education not only regarding occurrences in Jamaica but also international events. Indeed, the Table of Contents of *Jamaica Labrish* is divided into City Life, War Time, Politics, and Jamaica—Now and Then.[331]

There is a lacuna in my education as a result of the segregation of the

---

[330] An attempt was made to institute Spanish as a second language in Jamaica in the 1970's by Hon. F. Glasspole which unfortunately, I think, was resisted.

[331] Louise Bennett, *Jamaica Labrish,* with notes and introduction by Rex Nettleford, (Kingston, Jamaica: Sangster Book Stores Ltd., 2003).

dialect and consequently the banning of works, such as, "Ms. Lou's" poems being taught in most of the high schools. My younger siblings, however, were not as subjected to the directive of not speaking the dialect as their older siblings were. In this outcome, we, the older siblings, played a role. We shielded our younger siblings from the taboo of not speaking the dialect for we realized that not to speak the dialect led to traumatization, alienation, and, indeed, ignorance. Today many of the Jamaican elite can lapse into the Jamaican dialect without any inhibition, guilt, or shame. Jamaica has certainly moved from the stand that was so prevalent regarding the Jamaican accent and the use of the dialect prior to Independence in 1962.

Besides, as with all languages and dialects, there are certain social issues that need to be addressed in terms of the elevation of the dialect to the status of a language. Although it is widely used amongst the masses, there is the overall consciousness that the standard language is English and so on occasions when Jamaicans who are not educated are required to communicate in Standard English, they find it difficult to do so. Let us face it, Jamaicans have had a long history of migrating to other areas of the world for employment and education. It will be unfortunate if Jamaicans find themselves unable to compete or have to take examinations and do courses, because English is their second language. The educated elite are able to express themselves in Standard English and the Jamaican dialect. We have to think of the uneducated poor who migrate to other countries and let us not forget that many of them provide financial help and assistance to relatives in Jamaica. Another important point in terms of the social issue is that even if we managed to standardize the dialect, there would be localized spin-offs of the standardized dialect.

I do not object to speaking the Jamaican dialect. Certainly speaking in dialect—"how yu do mi chile me no see yu dis long time"—can exude warmth, belonging, and acceptance that Standard English might not convey. I cannot romanticize the speaking of the dialect, however. The dialect used in brawls and conflicts is not a pretty sound. Yelling in any language is not at all pleasant to hear but often to me because the dialect is an oral language it allows for greater expressions of feelings and emotions and hence, very often, a greater loss of dignity—think of the swear words or profanity in the Jamaican dialect.

There is also the lack of development of thought regarding mores, norms, and etiquette regarding social relationships. Thus in many ways the dialect maintains traditional mores with regards to gender, inter-generational, employer-employee roles. Asserting oneself particularly if one is young, female or an employee can be interpreted as "rude and disrespectful" behavior. With regard to translation, as with any translation, the dialect has certain nuances, when spoken that cannot be conveyed when written. "Give we food fe nyam" not only has a different connotation from "Give us this day our daily bread" but it has certain implications regarding class. For "Give us this day our daily bread" conjures a middle class person or struggling poor person actually requesting God's care of him or her. On the other hand, "give we food fe nyam" implies a poor person who because nyam has the connotation of being greedy" is "lazy" and only concerned about his stomach. Will the translators of the Bible into dialect use duppy for ghost? I am sure many church people, particularly members of the Anglican Church, will object to ministers saying, "Fadaa, Son, and Holy Duppy". The dialect will only further highlight certain nuances with regard to the stratification of the society.

The masses who use the dialect exclusively are severely limited in terms of vocabulary. As already pointed out, the dialect relies heavily on English. Let us take, for example, some verses of Louise Bennett's poem entitled: Jamaica Patois.

Is wha Miss Liza she dah-form
Dah-gwan like foreigner!
Because her sister husband get
One job up a Mona!

You hear her cut Spanish, like
She jus come out from sea!
So till dem buoy start fe call her
De dry-lan-refugee!

Toder mornin me go ask her
Wat she tink bout de war
She gi out "Ah tink de war is
Muyee malo me amar

Wen him ask her how much me owe,
Missus it frighten me,
Fe hear Miss Liza bawl out
"Is shillin an quatty".

... ...

So Liza she cant form no more
Pon dis Senorita
For me know say she understand
We Jamaica Patois.[332]

Note how many English words are used in the poem by Louise Bennett quoted above. In the first three stanzas and the last two, and I am not including words that are obvious English words that have a slight deviation in spelling, for example, "husband" and "morning", English words are: is, like, she, foreigner, because, her, sister, get, one, job, up, a, Mona, you, want, hear, cut, Spanish, come, out, from, sea, call, dry, refugee, how, much, frighten, owe, so, ask, about, war, him, no, more, for, know, say, we, Jamaica. Incidentally, it is significant to note particularly in terms of the title, Jamaica Patois, "Miss Lou's"(as she was affectionately called in Jamaica) interweaving of Spanish phrases and words in this poem.

The translation of the Bible into the Jamaican dialect is only a perpetration of colonial hegemony.

In *The Wretched of the Earth*, Frantz Fanon discusses how the colonialist bourgeoisie allies with the intellectual elite of the colonies during decolonization so that the colonialist bourgeoisie can maintain "domination". "[D]uring the period of liberation, the colonialist bourgeoisie looks feverishly for contacts with the *elite,* and it is with these *elite* that the familiar dialogue concerning values is carried on."[333] Who is translating the Bible into the Jamaican dialect? It is not the poor—many of whom will not be able to read it. It is the middle classes. With whom is the middle class collaborating regarding the translation of the Bible for to translate the Bible must be very costly?

The whole enterprise of translating the Bible into Jamaican dialect makes me think of resources and how resources are used to maintain hegemony of Euro-American interests in Jamaica after fifty years of Independence. In other words, how resources are used to maintain the Racial Contract.

I look up the Bible Society for the West Indies on the Internet[334]. Under the heading, Bible Society of the West Indies and Sowing the Seed in the West Indies the following is written on the home page:

---

[332]Bennett, *Jamaica Labrish,* p. 87.

[333]Frantz Fanon, *The Wretched of the Earth,* translated from the French by Constance Farrington, (New York, NY: Grove Press, 1963), p. 35.

[334]www.forministry.com, Saturday December 31, 2011.

The Bible Society of the West Indies, like you, is extremely concerned about the poor quality of life demonstrated by the high incidences of crime, violence, savagery, brutality, etc. that seem to be the order of the day. In fact, we are alarmed that much of this kind of reprehensible behavior is targeted at the most vulnerable among us, particularly the young defenseless and impressionable. But instead of cursing the *darkness* (italics, mine) we need to light a candle. To that end we have a wonderful opportunity that we are hoping you will want to identify with.

In 2006, we would like to make available to children in particular violence-prone/poor communities a complete Bible in an easy-to-read contemporary translation. Our research has revealed that in many homes in these communities, when the violence flares and "all hell breaks loose" and persons are cowering in their homes, it is the audible reading of the Word of God (especially the Psalms) that helps them to cope and to keep their 'sanity'. [335]

I read this and I weep. Nothing has changed. Four hundred years of Christianity in the West Indies and it is still the same.

Did not the European Christian missionaries four hundred years ago in their first encounter with Africans, regard the Africans as savages, primitive beings, evil, and uncivilized? The European, however, possessed the ideological tool that would civilize the African. The ideological tool the European possessed was religion—the Christian religion. Christianity would transform the African from the wild savage beast to a cultivated human being, somewhat akin to the European. As p'Bitek points out, it was the goal of the missionaries to 'civilize' the Africans. [336]

In announcing the Negro Education Grant in 1834, the Imperial Government, that is, Britain stated, it is significant to note, that "[i]n the appropriation of those Funds the Minister of the Crown will be guided by the principle that *instruction in the doctrines and precepts of Christianity must form the basis and must be made the inseparable attendant of any such*

---

[335]The Bible Society of the West Indies. www. Forministry.com—home page.
[336]p'Bitek, *African Religions in Western Scholarship,* p. 54

system of Education. [337] (Italics mine)

In *Two Jamaicas,* Curtin corroborates the significant role of Christianity in terms of "civilizing" blacks after emancipation. According to Curtin, the "Jamaican government" violated its responsibility, in terms of "bringing the ex-slave within the framework of the European Jamaican. Instead, the job of speeding acculturation fell to the missionaries, the only group of Europeans in close and friendly contact with the Negroes". [338] It is significant to note that, to some extent, "as a result" of the "interest" in the "social struggles of the working class" the "growth of membership in the mission church was immediate and overwhelming. The Baptists jumped from about 10,000 in 1831 to 34,000 in 1845. Methodist membership in the same period almost doubled, and other missions had similar increases." [339]

Shirley Gordon's *Our Cause for His Glory: Christianisation and Emancipation in Jamaica* is a testament to Christianization of Jamaica in which Jamaicans were actively involved after Emancipation. [340]

Since Europeans have purported that Christianity is a civilizing force particularly for Africans and their descendants, how is it that after four hundred years of Christianity, the Bible Society of the West Indies states on its home page that they are "alarmed" and "extremely concerned about the poor quality of life demonstrated by the high incidences of crime, violence, savagery, brutality, etc. that seem to be the order of the day".

Let me clarify that the Bible Society of the West Indies is referring to the West Indies in the article on the home page as clearly indicated by the word "us" in the sentence: "In fact, we are alarmed that much of this kind of reprehensible behavior is targeted at the most vulnerable among *us*, (italics, mine) particularly the young defenseless and impressionable". [341] It would seem to me that the desire "to make available to children in particular violence-prone/poor communities a complete Bible in an easy-to-read contemporary translation" [342] is actually harking back to the time of slavery and post Emancipation when Europeans felt that Christianizing people of African descent was imperative as a moralizing force in the light of their economic, social, and political conditions.

Not only is Christianity being touted as a moralizing force, but it is an

---

[337] Gordon, *A Century of West Indian Education*, p. 20.
[338] Curtin, *Two Jamaicas*, p. 162.
[339] Ibid., p. 162.
[340] Gordon, *Our Cause for His Glory*, 1998.
[341] The Bible Society of the West Indies. www.Forministry—home page, Saturday December 31, 2011, italics mine
[342] The Bible Society of the West Indies—home page, December 31, 2011

ideology to better one's life and conditions. "Our research", the home page of the Bible Society of the West Indies states, "has revealed that in many homes in these communities, when the violence flares and 'all hell breaks loose' and persons are cowering in their homes, it is the audible reading of the Word of God (especially the Psalms) that helps them to cope and to keep their 'sanity'".[343] I can't help but wonder how does the "audible reading of the Word of God (especially the Psalms)" help individuals "to cope and to keep their 'sanity'"? Is it merely due to belief or does the actual reading of the Word of God have power to deflect the violence ? If the latter, shouldn't the reading of the Word of God eliminate violence altogether in these poor neighborhoods ? If the former, then the question still holds.

I think it is time for us as African descendants, to seriously analyze whether Christianity is really the moral force it is purported to be and whether if you do not believe in this religion particularly if you are African or you are African descended, you will have no morals, no scruples, no ethics, no principles. You will be uncivilized, barbaric, and savage. We have to put the issue of Christianity as a moralizing force or agent under a microscope, so to speak. It is not that Christianity is a moralizing force. It is that Christianity is, as should be very evident from this work, a "Europeanization" force and on which the Racial Contract is built.

I scroll to the bottom of the Home Page of the Bible Society of the West Indies and sure enough highlighted in blue small print is the American Bible Society. I go to their home page and amongst the sliding screens is one with black children used as an appeal, no doubt, for donations. Members of the rich predominantly white North American country sees distributing Bibles to poor black communities in the West Indies and elsewhere as the solution to the horrendous social, economic, and political conditions these communities face.

In analyzing whether the distribution of the Bible is the solution to the problems of the poor particularly those who live in violent societies, I cannot help but ask: Where are Bibles printed? Who benefits from the process of the printing, sales, and distribution of Bibles? Besides personnel: directors, managers, fund raisers, advertisers, computer technologists, cleaners, accountants, lawyers, doctors, nurses, there is the need for equipment and supplies in the printing of Bibles: printing press, paper, desks, chairs, pens, toilet paper, soap, electricity, telephones, computers. Needless to say buildings and the maintenance of buildings are involved in the process, not to mention firms that also have investments in the printing of and production of Bibles, such as banks, trucking firms, cargo planes, post offices, etc.

---

[343]Ibid.

Many firms directly or indirectly profit from the printing, sales, and distribution of Bibles. Many jobs are also created. Who is making a profit from distributing or selling Bibles?

The Bible is not printed in Jamaica. Undoubtedly, the Bible Society of the West Indies reaps some reward in terms of employment of West Indian workers. However, it is the companies in North America who are the main beneficiaries from the sales and distribution of Bibles in the West Indies. Thus companies in North America benefit from the "poverty, violence, and savagery " in the West Indies for the misery of people in the West Indies— "the high incidences of crime, violence, savagery brutality" provide a "wonderful opportunity" in terms of the distribution of Bibles. To North American companies go the power and the glory. In *Breaking the Spell,* Daniel Dennett discusses the high cost of religion. Churches, for example, are huge buildings that are closed for most of the week.[344] Every Bible bought in Jamaica is a depletion of the resources of Jamaica because Bibles are not printed in Jamaica. Every pipe organ, communion cup, piano, ministerial robe, parson's collar, hymn book, glass window, cross, ring is a depletion of the resources of Jamaica because these items are not produced in Jamaica.

The Bible Society of the West Indies hopes that by translating the Bible into the Jamaican dialect it will make the dialect more respectable. The rationale behind the project is to sanitize the dialect based on the view that when all Jamaicans read the "Scriptures" in dialect it will no longer be identified as lower class. At the same time, the Bible Society of the West Indies does not see how it segregates knowledge for the Bible is "Scripture" and thus sacred.

Consequently, there are several books regarding the history and culture of the West Indies that should be but will not be circulated or distributed by the Bible Society of the West Indies. Besides academicians, how many people in the West Indies read Frantz Fanon, for example, or have even heard of him? The segregation of knowledge is very important in terms of moral and ethical questions which I will address later.

The Bible Society of the West Indies although "extremely concerned" about the "high incidences of crime, violence, savagery, brutality, etc." will not distribute books which document how the West Indies was born in violence and violence has been the dominant theme perpetrated against, for the most part, non-white colonists during the four hundred year history of

---

[344]Daniel C. Dennett, *Breaking the Spell: Religion as a Natural Phenomenon,* (New York, NY: Penguin, 2006).

colonization and domination by Christianized Europeans.[345]

When the English captured Jamaica in 1655, there was not a single native Jamaican living on the island. According to the English, the Arawaks had all been wiped out by the Spaniards. The horrendous barbaric inhumane slave trade and slavery have been documented.[346] As Fanon states the colonists "first encounter" with colonial powers "was marked by violence and their existence together – that is to say the exploitation of the native by the settler – was carried on by dint of a great array of bayonets and cannon."[347] Fanon further asserts that the "colonial world is a world cut in two" and the "dividing line, the frontiers are shown by barracks and police stations".[348] Fanon's observation about the role of the police and the soldier is applicable to the West Indies in spite of Independence. We are subjected to the Racial Contract. "In the colonies it is the policeman and the soldier who are the official, instituted go-betweens, the spokesmen of the settler and his rule of oppression.[349]

In the *Wretched of the Earth,* Fanon discusses violence particularly in terms of the Algerian struggle from French domination. For Fanon, the issue of violence amongst the colonized Algerians was to a large extent the result of inhumane and unjust conditions of poor struggling Algerian communities. The *Wretched of the Earth* was a response to the view held by some French psychiatrists and Europeans that the violence that often erupted amongst Algerians was as a result of the Algerian being a "born criminal".[350] Fanon noted that "criminal tendencies of Algerians in France differed fundamentally from those of the Algerians who were submitted to exploitation which was directly colonial."[351] That Fanon was from the West Indies, and that he was a psychiatrist are very significant. The Algerians were demonized just as how communities of the West Indies are being demonized by the Bible Society of the West Indies as violence prone. "The Algerian's criminality, his impulsivity and the violence of his murders are

---

[345]See for example, Jose Bengoa, *Conquista y Barbarie: Ensayo Critico acerca de la Conquista de Chile,* (Santiago de Chile, Chile: Ediciones SUR, 1992); Augier, et. al. *The Making of the West Indies*; Black, *The Story of Jamaica.*

[346]See for example, Augier, et. al. *The Making of the West Indies*; Black, *The Story of Jamaica*; Franklin & Moss, Jr. *From Slavery to Freedom.*

[347]Fanon, *The Wretched of the Earth,* p. 30.

[348]Ibid., p. 30.

[349]Ibid., p. 31.

[350]Fanon, *The Wretched of the Earth,* p. 242.

[351]Ibid., p. 247

therefore" according to Fanon "not the consequence of the organisation of his nervous system nor of characterial originality, but the direct product of the colonial situation.[352]

Fanon further points out that Algerian "criminality takes place in practice inside a closed circle. The Algerians rob each other, cut each other up and kill each other. In Algeria, the Algerian rarely attacks Frenchmen, and avoids brawls with the French." The Algerian is

> exposed to temptations to commit murder—famine, eviction from his room because he has not paid the rent, the mother's dried up breasts, children like skeletons, the building-yard which has closed down, the unemployed that hang about the foreman like crows—the native comes to see his neighbour as a relentless enemy. If he strikes his bare foot against a big stone in the middle of the path, it is a native who has placed it there; and the few olives that he was going to pick, X...'s children have gone and eaten in the night.[353]

I would say that the West Indian is subjected to similar conditions as the Algerian. I can see similar reasons for the commitment of black on black crime in poor neighborhoods.

Many Jamaicans, like the Bible Society of the West Indies are concerned about the crime and violence in the West Indies. Indeed, it is imperative that we analyze the crime and violence in the West Indian society. I am asserting, however, that we have to (1) analyze the crime and the violence and (2) the Christian religion because the Christian religion has been postulated as the moralizing force or agency for the transformation of Africans and African descended peoples.

The Bible Society of the West Indies will not distribute *Persistent Poverty* in which George L. Beckford asks why "have plantation economies" in spite of "four hundred years of direct participation in the modern world economy...still find themselves underdeveloped countries with the bulk of their inhabitants living (rather, existing) in the most wretched conditions of poverty?[354] Beckford concludes by stating that "maybe there are factors inherent in the plantation system which serve to impede transformation from

---

[352]Ibid., p. 250
[353]Ibid., p. 249.
[354]Beckford, *Persistent Poverty*, p. xxiii-xxiv.

a state of underdevelopment.[355]

The factors that Beckford sought to address in 1972: "very low levels of income, malnutrition, disease, poor housing, sanitation, and medical services, and little or no education" as the "lot of the majority of the people" in the light of the "rich resources of the Third World"[356] are still relevant today. Indeed, I would say for many people in the Third World, conditions in the second decade of the twenty-first century are far worse than they were in the decade following the independence of a number of Third World countries, the 1970's.

According to Beckford, plantation economies, are not only countries that rely on the plantation system but include those economies that are very dependent on "metropolitan countries in different ways", such as, "mineral exploitation, banking, and financial intermediation, trade and the processing of raw materials, technological innovation, and even in policy formation."[357]

Unfortunately however, whenever black scholars analyze dependence on metropolitan countries, religion is generally not included. There is the need to heed the very important point that Beckford raises regarding the fact that underdevelopment is a "dynamic process." "Underdevelopment", Beckford asserts, is not normally considered to be a dynamic process in the same way as development is accepted as being. Instead the view is usually taken that an economy is in a state of underdevelopment and remains so until some stimulus initiates the development process.[358] For Beckford, "underdevelopment is itself a dynamic process" and actually "there are systematic forces which operate in the direction of keeping underdeveloped countries continuously underdeveloped, so much so that powerful development stimuli (such as trade) do not initiate a process of sustained development".[359]

There will be eyebrows raised, and ranting and raving by ministers if I state that the Christian religion is one of the "systematic forces" in the underdevelopment of people of African descent. The churches and steeples are seen as pristine moral agencies which transcend trade agreements, banking, policy making and all the institutions of the metropolitan countries on which people of African descent rely. The Christian religion is viewed as outside of the plantation economy although it is fundamental to the plantation economies in the West.

---

[355]Ibid., p. xxiii-xxiv.
[356]Ibid., p. xvii.
[357]Ibid., p. xviii
[358]Ibid., p. xxi.
[359]Ibid., p. xxi.

What is not addressed is how the pristine chapels, churches, and steeples that are more numerous in poor black communities than rich wealthy white communities are structures and symbols of wealth and metropolitan control. As I already pointed out, the depletion of resources in terms of Christian paraphernalia, such as Bibles, hymn books, organs, pianos, robes, cement blocks for buildings, paint, wine, grape juice, communion cups, iron railings, parson collars, bishop rings, collection plates, rosaries, metal crosses contribute to the wealth of metropolitan countries and the persistent poverty of countries, such as, Jamaica. The belief that the paraphernalia of the Church is for the spiritual benefit of people particularly African descended people overlooks how reliance on metropolitan countries for these items fosters the plantation economy.

Underdeveloped countries not only rely on metropolitan countries for religious goods and artifacts but also on services (pun not intended) and ideas usually in the form of doctrines. Belief in being born again, baptism, speaking in tongues, redemption, salvation, sin, immortality, christening, confirmation, the Sabbath are doctrines that are not indigenous to underdeveloped and developing countries. In addition, there are rites, rituals, and ceremonies, such as weddings, funerals, confirmation, baptism, christening which are dominated by metropolitan culture and which contribute to the depletion of resources of plantation economies.

Indeed, the issue of how wealth and poverty are intricately linked to morality needs to be addressed. Jesus is usually presented as being poor. He was born in a stable, and he is someone who identifies with the poor. Generally, therefore, Christianity is viewed as for the poor or on "the side of the poor"[360] when this is far from being the case.

Although it is often postulated that God identifies with the poor, wealth plays a significant role in the propagation of Christianity. Churches are very costly to build and maintain. Shirley Gordon points out the tremendous sacrifices Jamaicans made after slavery to build and maintain churches.[361] While it is often postulated that God identifies with the poor, at the same time it is asserted that he is perfect, omniscient, and omnipotent. These attributes demand the biggest, the best, and the most expensive for God. The finest buildings, artwork, music and other artifacts are dedicated to God. According to Gordon, being well-dressed for church was important for the ex-slaves. She also points out how church attendance was affected by economic difficulties during the post Emancipation period because many ex-slaves could not afford the kind of clothes that they thought church

---

[360]Cone, *God of the Oppressed.*
[361]Gordon, *Our Cause for His Glory.*

attendance demanded.[362] If God is omnipotent, then God must be wealthy. Wealth is intricately linked to the attributes of God.

In terms of Christian morality then, there is a bias in favor of the rich. In poor communities where churches are more abundant this is even more evident as many of these churches are maintained by the "better off" in the community or wealthy donors from rich communities. The Bible Society of the West Indies falls under the auspices of the wealthy American Bible Society. The churches in poor boarded up crime infested communities are usually majestic emblems of middle class and upper class wealth and tributes to European and American architecture. One thing I must say for the tradition of my African ancestors is that it did not require the outlay of wealth that Christianity does.

Another important issue that needs to be analyzed with regards to Christianity in terms of the plantation system, and indeed in terms of Christianity as a moralizing agent is the role the misery of "others" plays in the religion. As quoted from George Beckford at the head of this chapter, "the fortunes of the North Atlantic peoples are closely related to the misfortunes of Third World peoples in many fundamental ways".[363] The West Indies as a bedrock of misery is an opportunity for Christian charity. This is discriminatory. In this regard then, the condition of the West Indies should never really be ameliorated because it provides opportunity for wealthy Christians to donate to Christian organizations, such as, the Bible Society of the West Indies.

Linked to the misery of "others" is the perception of "others" as demons. Note that the Bible Society of the West Indies' assertion that the "poor quality of life demonstrated by the high incidences of crime, violence, savagery, brutality, etc. that seem to be the order of the day" negates the many hard working, honest, West Indians within these poor communities. Demonization of peoples by members of the Christian religion is nothing new. African, Asian, and Native Americans have been dehumanized as primitive, savage, pagan, heathens. In the light of what I have been postulating throughout this entire work that the perception of African peoples as morally inferior has not changed for four hundred years, Fanon's observation regarding the "native" and "ethics" is very apt. The "native" is "declared insensible to ethics" and of extreme significance is also the "negation of values", the "enemy of values" and "absolute evil." The native is the "corrosive element, disfiguring all that has to do with beauty or morality; he is the depository of maleficent powers, the unconscious and

---

[362]Ibid.

[363]Beckford, *Persistent Poverty*, p. v.

irretrievable instrument of blind forces."[364]

When a terrible earthquake shook Haiti January 2010, Pat Robertson declared on his Christian 700 Club Television Show that Haiti was "cursed" because Haiti made a "pact with the devil" when they drove the French out of Haiti. The Haitians are "desperately poor" and need to have a "great turning to God", Robertson said. [365] This is a classic example of Christian morality. The earthquake and poverty are punishment from God. God does not approve of black people fighting for their liberation from whites. Therefore, the Haitians are cursed. Thus God is on the side of the French. Apparently the devil approves of Black people fighting for their liberation while God does not.

Pat Robertson makes unfavorable comparisons of the Haitians with the people of the Dominican Republic. "The Dominican Republic is prosperous, healthy, full of resorts, etc."[366] God is on the side of whites. God is on the side of those who are prosperous. Poverty is a curse. While God does not approve of liberation struggles particularly of black liberation struggles he does not disapprove of white liberation struggles for God has not punished the descendants of the colonists who fought against England for their Independence. Indeed, God has blessed them for they are the richest and most powerful country on earth. Neither has God punished the Europeans who fought against German hegemony that led to the Second World War. We can only deduce, therefore, that God is white and God is racist.

The question of power is rarely addressed by adherents of the Christian religion. You *must* believe in God, they say. Most Christians believe that the individual who believes in God has a relationship with God and that is all that matters. That the poorest person can feel that he or she has a relationship with the most powerful being in the universe is empowering. As Bertrand Russell points out, "[i]f the world is controlled by God, and God can be moved by prayer, we acquire a share in his omnipotence".[367] She can control the mind of God by praying to him, and if he does not answer her prayer, then he knows best.

A colleague of mine and I would argue incessantly about Christianity. She was a devout Christian. On any given morning, before she started work, you could be sure you could see her sitting at her desk, her cocoa brown face bowed over an open Bible on the desk. She believed in tithing, she often

---

[364]Fanon, *The Wretched of the Earth,* p. 34.
[365]Pat Robertson, http://thinkprogress.org/politics
2010/01/13/77141/Robertson-Haiti.
[366]Ibid.
[367]Russell, *Why I am not a Christian,* p. 53.

told me, and she spent many hours in church. One morning as we were passing each other on the stairs, she stopped me and told me that her daughter was going to Jamaica as a missionary. I was so angry I could not speak for a few minutes and then I exploded. "Why would your daughter be going to Jamaica as a missionary? We do not need any more missionaries in Jamaica. We almost have as many churches as there are people. Jamaica should be sending missionaries to the United States, I maintained ignoring her response that her daughter planned to teach Jamaican people skills, but we cannot because while a citizen from the United States can fly to Jamaica without a problem, Jamaicans have to wait in a long line to file for a visa and often they are denied. She stood on the stair observing me with calm politeness—a hint of a smile lit up her dark brown eyes. Why doesn't your daughter go as a missionary to Scarsdale or Chappaqua (very wealthy communities in Westchester, New York). See, I said, God discriminates. She began walking away as she always does whenever I make the assertion that God discriminates. Sometime afterwards, we discuss the mounting layoffs. She is not perturbed. It is not in their hands, she says. I am very upset and feel an irretrievable loss when shortly after our discussion she tells me that she received a letter of termination.

The individual is empowered by his or her belief in God often denying the reality of the power of others in our lives—spouses, employers, policemen, politicians, teachers, doctors, lawyers, professors. Because Christianity focuses so much on the relationship between God and the individual, the aspect of belonging to a group, and how this empowers certain individuals is overlooked. The more resources you have, the more power you have, and the more power you have, the closer to God you are because God is omnipotent. Thus Pat Robertson is able to disseminate his views not only because he is wealthy (there are lots of wealthy people around the world) but because of other resources. He belongs to the white race, the privileged race, he is an American, a citizen of the most powerful country on earth, and he belongs to a group of Christians who have pooled their resources to spread their propaganda. Because of their wealth and their power, Pat Robertson and his cohorts know God's mind and they can speak for God.

My colleague would often walk away when I try to point out to her the reality of who God is, if she really believes there is a God. She often related to me how God has "opened doors" throughout her life. Stop, I often tell her. You are from the elite of your country. Don't you see, coming from the privileged class, how your education and social upbringing have opened up opportunities for you? What about the struggles of our ancestors including the struggles of African Americans? We must thank God for that she responds. My colleague in truth and in fact does not deviate too much from the reasoning of Christian thinkers like Pat Robertson who minimize the suffering and struggles of black people. Hasn't she noticed that all the doors of opportunity with regard to jobs that she has received are amongst black people? I have come to the conclusion, I tell her, that God does not operate outside of the racist structure. Why doesn't God, I facetiously ask, open up doors of opportunity for you in wealthy rich white areas like Chappaqua or Scarsdale? It is not God's will, she mumbles and anyway she is very busy now and she walks away.

Some scientists theorize that the need to worship God may be a part of human evolution.[368] Freud postulated that man has created God in response to a psychological need.[369] It would seem to me that there is also a need to be worshipped and to control others. As Fanon postulates the "white man acts in obedience to an authority complex, a leadership complex, while the Malagasy obeys a dependency complex."[370]

It is imperative then that we address whether the Bible and the Christian religion are sources of morality and antidotes to fear that is pervasive throughout violent prone communities or whether the Churches are really in league with the former colonial powers to maintain dominance in the West Indies. "The colonialist bourgeoisie, Fanon notes, "is helped in its work of calming down the natives by the inevitable religion. All those saints who have turned the other cheek, who have forgiven trespasses against them, and who have been spat on and insulted without shrinking are studied and held up as examples.[371]

I want to conclude this chapter by pointing out how the segregation of knowledge fosters persistent poverty within the plantation economy and the conditions of poor blacks as the "wretched of the earth". Pat Robertson displayed a lot of ignorance about Haiti's history, the social, political and economic conditions of Haiti and the Dominican Republic. He does not need to know. The Bible as sacred classifies works by C. L. R. James, Fanon, Garvey, Walter Rodney, Malcolm X as non sacred texts which is just a step away from being regarded as "of the devil". I can't help but observe although God is all powerful how insecure and easily threatened he is by knowledge. God is scared of Darwin's theory of evolution, was terrified

---

[368]See, for example, Dennett, *Breaking the Spell.*

[369]Sigmund Freud, *The Future of an Illusion*

[370]Frantz Fanon, *Black Skin, White Masks,* translated by Charles Lam Markman (London, England: MacGibbon & Kee, 1968), p. 99.

[371]Fanon, *The Wretched of the Earth,* p. 53.

when Galileo said that the earth moved around the sun, and is practically daunted by Marx and black revolutionaries.

I could not help but note how the two gentlemen, the President of the Bible Society of the West Indies and the translator from Wycliffe Translators in the interview on U Tube regarding the Bible being translated in the Jamaican dialect, kept valorizing and adulating Tyndale and Wycliffe. The two Bible Society gentlemen claimed that Tyndale and Wycliffe were subjected to persecution and martyrdom for translating the Bible into English. There is some resistance by Jamaicans to the Jamaican Bible being translated in dialect, they assert, just as how there was a lot of resistance regarding translating the Bible into English. I seriously questioned how such knowledge is relevant to the present West Indian situation. One would have imagined that reasons for resistance in Jamaica would have been discussed. It was not. The sum total of the argument is since the translation from Latin to the English dialect succeeded in England, then the translation from the English to the Jamaican dialect will succeed in Jamaica.

CHAPTER ELEVEN

DIVINE RACISM: TURNING BACK

> My heart was black with sin
> Until the Savior came in
> His precious blood I know
> Has made me white as snow
> And in the Book I am told
> I will walk the streets of gold
> Oh wonderful, wonderful day
> He washed my sins away.

The Blackness of Black people in this society has always represented the blemish, the uncleanliness, the barrier separating individual and society. Castration from blackness becomes the initiatory tunnel, the portal through which black people must pass if they are not to fall on their faces in the presence of society, fraternity, and hierarchy...Intellectual castration is a sign of suffering for the Larger Society's Love....[372]

How did I get to this point from a Bible believing fundamentalist to not only a disbeliever but one who is very critical of Christianity? I was very flattered when Mrs. J. came to see me as part of her duties as my Sunday School teacher at Grace Missionary Church. Attending Sunday School at sixteen was a strange phenomenon, for in the Anglican Church, Sunday School was regarded as a service for little children and therefore I had stopped attending Sunday School at about age eleven. Among the fundamentalists, however, Sunday School was very important in terms of reinforcing fundamentalist doctrine and was therefore an important arm of the church. Sunday School in the fundamentalist church is for everybody, young and old.

In all my years of attending St Andrew Parish Church (Half Way Tree Church) no member of the church personnel whether Sunday School teacher, deacon, or minister, except for a young seminarian, Rev. McNab, who had done so as a result of my mother's concern about my leaving the church, had ever visited me. Not only was Mrs. J. my art teacher at Wolmer's but she was also of Lebanese descent, which she repeated along with the fact that Lebanon was in the Bible, ad nauseum. Individuals of Middle Eastern origin rarely socialized with African-Jamaicans.

---

[372]Williams, *The Alchemy of Race and Rights,* p. 198.

As Mrs. J sat with me on the verandah, she asked me how much time I spent praying and reading the Bible. She then took out a bit of string and using a ratio of one inch to one hour, she marked off with her fingers how much time I spent praying and reading my Bible weekly in comparison with the hours in the week. The ratio of string held by her fingers to the length of string was minimal indeed. I was very dismayed at the amount of time I spent with God. Reading the Bible and praying were two of the four legs of the chair—the other two being having fellowship with other Christians and witnessing for Christ—that were fundamental to my Christian growth. I vowed then and there that I would spend at least one hour every morning reading my Bible and praying.

I decided to read the Bible from cover to cover. It was a daunting enterprise exacerbated by the fact that inerrancy of the Bible was basic fundamentalist doctrine. Long before becoming a fundamentalist Christian I had problems with the Bible, particularly the Old Testament, in terms of cruelty, violence, and partiality to one group of people termed the "chosen people" that pervaded the Bible.

I can recall as a child, I would squirm whenever I read about God having a chosen people which I interpreted to be a favorite people. Coming from a family where my brother was my mother's favorite, and I was supposed to be my father's, I saw where favoritism, perceived or otherwise, wreaked a lot of havoc among family members. Special treatment of the favored child by one parent did not only evoke intense anger, jealousy, and resentment amongst the siblings; it also evoked intense anger, jealousy, and resentment of the other parent.

It would seem that these hostile feelings that I sometimes had to endure would be a small price to pay for the privilege of being favored, that is, in my view, having some leverage to get away with behavior that my siblings could not. Alas, this was not the case. I was just as much whipped by my father as my siblings, except for my brother who received more lashes because he was a boy. Favoritism was shown to me by my father in the form of special gifts, looks, not being allowed to do menial tasks—housework— and often unspoken expectations in terms of behavior. I was placed on a pedestal. Indeed, I felt that I had to maintain my favored position which put a lot of pressure on me. I became a tattle teller as I tried anxiously to meet my father's approval which further aggravated the unhealthy relationships in the family. A major problem I faced was that I could not always predict or anticipate what was good behavior for my father, and I would be in sheer agony if I had the slightest intimation that I had not lived up to his expectations. I often hid from my father, and from myself, my true feelings, mostly feelings of inferiority, for eventually I interpreted the gifts, looks, being placed on a pedestal as compensation for my complexion genes' refusal to follow some mathematical formula and be an average between my mother's very pale complexion and his dark complexion. My father's compensatory acts, however, only resulted in making me feel very insecure.

I often felt sorry for the Jews who I thought had to please a God who was often as unpredictable as my father. The Jews were definitely placed on a pedestal, and given the Ten Commandments. They were, however, often subjected to arbitrary punishment by a God who could be intermittently angry at them or merciful to them, and who often demanded that they obey him unconditionally because he is a jealous God. Just as how favoritism led to dysfunction within my family, so I felt, it wreaked a lot of havoc within the human family. I was many times aghast, even as a child, not only at the discrimination perpetrated against people who were not favored by God, but at the violence that was often enacted against them. It seemed God could be vindictive, unjust, and arbitrary in his judgment and rulings. The story of Noah and the flood is an example of unbelievable inhumane suffering and cruelty. When interpreted from Noah's perspective, as is usually the case, the tremendous suffering of not only men and women but innocent children, babies, animals and the destruction of plants is ignored (Genesis 8: 20-21).

The New Testament, as the name implies was supposed to be transformative in terms of the relationship between God and the human family. The God of the New Testament was to bring hope, salvation, and love to the Gentiles, as we were termed, particularly in the person of Jesus. This was not much solace to me as several incidents and passages of Scripture in the New Testament were riddled with violence, and engendered guilt and fear particularly the passages that relate to the fate of everlasting damnation, if one does not believe. The very birth of Jesus as recorded in St. Luke's Gospel was plagued with the killing of infants. John the Baptist, the cousin of Jesus was beheaded. Stephen the first Christian martyr was stoned to death. I could never understand Revelations with its language of violence and earth shattering events that would precede the Second Coming of Jesus.

No one in the Anglican Church, however, had ever told me that I *have* to read the Bible everyday. As I now undertook to peruse the entire Bible, as a fundamentalist, I had to overcome a lot of resistance to keep reading Genesis. I told myself, however, that this is God's Word and "one leg of the chair" that must be included if I am to be a good "Christian" and therefore my critical faculties had to be repressed. I never got past Exodus, however. I was rescued, to some extent, from my torment by the discovery of a booklet, published by a fundamentalist group. This booklet had daily readings of selected passages from the Bible with commentaries. The passages chosen and the commentaries were geared to give hope, and even cruel and inhumane passages, such as turning Lot's wife into a pillar of salt, or flooding the entire earth during the time of Noah, were interpreted to highlight the goodness of God and the weakness of human beings.

My decision to leave Half Way Tree Parish Church for Grace Missionary Church was very disruptive in terms of the family. My parents viewed leaving St. Andrew Parish as falling several steps down the social ladder. On our way down we tumbled past the Methodist, the Presbyterian and the Baptist (English not American). In some ways I was influenced by the discussion of the young adults in the Anglican Church—who were in their twenties—that the Anglican Church was "dead" and lacked the vivacity of the growing fundamentalist churches.

The discussions were usually held outside the cold brick semi-dark Half Way Tree Church building which was surrounded by and built on tombstones. As the young people talked, they would make gestures and glances towards the fundamentalist church, Bethany Gospel Hall, which was just a few yards across from Half Way Tree Church. I could see in the well-lit building of Bethany Gospel Hall, the movement of shadowy figures in the golden light, and hear the distant sounds of hands clapping rhythmically to quick paced music all indicating the active participation of the members. What a contrast, it seemed, to the staid formal and very ritualistic services of the Anglican Church directed and led by a minister in which lay people including young people had very little input!

Enlisted by my mother, the young pine complexioned seminarian, John McNab, made two or three visits to my home in an effort to dissuade me regarding leaving the church; the visits proved futile. Perceiving that I was not at all convinced by his doctrinal and theological arguments, John McNab told me that I could still maintain my beliefs, but I should not leave the church. It would be a grave mistake, and one that I would regret, if I did. His predictions were correct. Later I would regret leaving the Anglican Church during my adolescent years.

I do not know why I felt that I would find greater social acceptance at Grace Missionary Church than at Half Way Tree when all the evidence in terms of fundamentalist social gatherings that I had attended, militated against it. I do not know why I continued to deceive myself that the feelings of isolation, alienation, and, indeed, increased atomization which I felt at "born again Christian" events, were not real. I gradually realized that the smiles and the hearty handshake, "Oh so good to see you, praise the Lord," were superficial. I was, for the most part, invisible.

Grace Missionary Church was built in a very upscale neighborhood in an area off the Constant Spring Road. The houses were palatial surrounded by well kept gardens. By building Grace Church in that area, it was evident that the church meant to "reach" the middle and upper classes. Indeed, the minister made it known that his missionary goal was to win the "mulattoes", a group he claimed had never really been targeted by missionaries for most missionary endeavors were aimed at black poor people. Now, mulattoes were generally wealthier and were more privileged in terms of social status than blacks.

Why I subjected myself to being snubbed, to ostracism and social isolation, is something that baffles me. I think it was mainly due to the fact that I did not identify with the black and the poor, but with the "mulattoes". Not only was the church located in one of the most opulent areas of Kingston and St. Andrew, the Corporate Area, but it was built in the latest L shaped architectural style of churches in the United States, that is a main section as the sanctuary for services and an annex for other activities.

The home owner opposite the church was very upset about the church's location in the neighborhood. I do not know how she accomplished this, but as soon as the service began, her dogs would begin to bark. The minister and the congregation were disturbed by the barking and decided to pray for her. I do not recall how the matter was finally resolved.

The church was funded by Christians in the United States. I am sure, however, that much of the money that flowed to Jamaica to pay for the building, upkeep, and maintenance of the Church returned to the United States for building supplies, the minister's car, gas, clothes for the family, Bibles, choir robes, hymn books, frequent trips by the minister and his family to the United States.

It took only a few weeks for me to be aware of my outsider status in the church. Although there were some young people who shared one or two of my physical characteristics in terms of complexion, features, and hair, I was the only one that had the combination of all three—cinnamon brown complexion, broad features, and straightened springy hair. I stood out. My tan complexioned sister and two distant cousins one light tan complexion and the other beige complexion with long golden brown hair blended right in and were cheerfully integrated into the group.

At Grace, I came across a world that was not visible to many cinnamon, coffee, cocoa, chocolate skinned Jamaicans. Although most of the young people were from the high schools, many of the older people were from the Jamaica white commercial class. Their entry into middle and upper class society was not based on education. It was based on skin color and money. At Grace Missionary Church, I was subjected for the first time in Jamaica, to outright American racism.

I faced discrimination at Wolmer's. Though not blatantly so, I sometimes felt skin color prejudice at Half Way Tree Parish Church. The sort of discrimination to which I was subjected at Grace Missionary Church was totally different from these other institutions. Although at Wolmer's and at St. Andrew Parish Church, inferiority of blacks and superiority of whites were pervasive in the doctrines, ideas, and beliefs that these institutions promulgated, yet I never felt totally boxed in or hemmed in by these beliefs. My teachers, for the most part, were supportive in my endeavor to succeed. At Half Way Tree Church, I was given opportunities for leadership and self expression within the boundaries of the religion.

What I felt at Grace were not mere sensations of inferiority which I at times felt at Wolmer's and at Half Way Tree Parish Church. What I felt at Grace were feelings of anguish, pain, and mortification because of my very obvious African ancestry. I was an outcaste, a Dalit, to be loathed and treated with contempt. Like the Dalit, I carried a stigma which is congenital and which I transmitted to others. It did not matter that I was attending Wolmer's. It did not matter that I could play the piano. It did not matter that I came from a family that upheld and instilled in us certain middle class values of propriety and ethics—speak properly, be honest in dealing with others, show respect to others, try to be circumspect in everything you do, education is very important, develop your talents and your skills, be gracious, polite and dignified at all times.

What was very significant about the racism and skin color prejudice at Grace Missionary Church was how discriminatory acts were conducted. It was imperative not only to socially isolate the recipient, but to ensure that the recipient be aware that he or she was being slighted. The way this was usually done was to greet those who are considered socially acceptable, in this case Jamaican whites or mulattoes, with lots of warmth, and friendliness usually in the presence of the socially ostracized who is pointedly and deliberately ignored. It is very important for the marginalized individual to learn that he or she is being socially isolated.

Such is American racism—a staged deliberate act of humiliation and mortification which is carried out in many Christian churches. The minister at Grace Missionary Church would stride past me, avoiding eye contact. He would then walk over to a Jamaican white or mulatto a few feet away and would warmly and enthusiastically greet and converse with him or her.

I often came to the conclusion that my presence ensured a greater bonding of the social circle of white and "mulattoes" in the church, just as how blacks in America foster greater social cohesion amongst whites. It was quite evident that the minister while he tolerated my brother and sister for they, particularly my brother, were like magnets, in terms of a following, to use a hackneyed expression did not welcome my presence at Grace Church. It was evident that he did not think that I belonged at Grace Missionary

Church.

My mother played a major role in my rapidly coming to the decision to leave Grace Missionary Church. She decided that since she could not persuade us to return to Half Way Tree Church, then she would attend Grace Church at times. Despite the insurmountable evidence of the lack of ethics, and principles on the part of fundamentalists, particularly in terms of the ostracism to which I was subjected, during the altar calls I would ardently pray for my mother to be saved. During these altar calls, while praying I would anxiously glance from time to time at my mother. My mother's hands always remained resolutely at her side while her pale pine colored face had a somewhat amused expression. She was as usual engaged in critical analysis of the service and the congregation which she would inevitably share with us at home after the service. This was usually in response to accosting her about "not putting up her hand".

Humor, a very important value in the Fisher family, my mother's family, would be interwoven into her analysis of what she termed fundamentalist hypocrisy. She made fun of the singing. We could not help but be overcome with laughter when she would, at home, mockingly hold a book and sway her body and the book to and fro as she mimicked the crooning of the choir at Grace. The singing of that choir was unfavorably compared to the illustrious and lofty renditions of the Half Way Tree Church Choir who held their bodies erectly and enunciated every syllable clearly. She made fun of the preaching at Grace. The sermons were lacking in structure, depth, and logic. Above all, there were grammatical errors which my mother considered more egregious than theological violations. As one Jamaican Anglican clergyman stated from the pulpit, whenever he is preparing his sermon, he is very conscious that there will be a number of teachers present in the congregation. He therefore is very careful to observe the rules of syntax for he knows that teachers will be following the subject to the predicate no matter how many words there are between.

It was my mother's humorous dramatization of the testimonies, however, that, no matter how much we resolved to be firm regarding so grave and serious an issue as her salvation, we would invariably find ourselves engaging in several minutes of uncontrollable laughter. "Yes, she would say, miming to a "t" the manner and words of the testifier, "I was on the broad road to hell….." She posited that singing the mournful hymn "Just as I am" was an important part of the strategy "for you to raise your hand".

With great amount of profundity, and I would say accuracy, she observed that the women in the church all looked very sad and she was sure that they were experiencing "man or husband problems" and that is the only reason why they are members of the church. She pointed out the big expensive cars that members of the congregation drove, and how "mean" they were not to offer us a ride home for we often had to take the bus.

What utterly astonished me, however, was her assertion that the minister and members of the church carried out blatant discrimination. This surprised me for it was very rare for my mother to perceive behavior as discriminatory. In social interactions, she would often chide my father as being "too sensitive", if he insinuated that he felt discriminated against because of his coffee brown complexion. My pale pine complexioned mother was just as much snubbed by the white minister and the Jamaican whites of the church as I was. This was something of a shock for my mother and me. Usually ministers, particularly ministers, for some reason reacted positively to my mother. "Hypocrites", she often hissed. "They are nothing but a bunch of hypocrites".

Although my mother used humor as a weapon in her critique of fundamentalist doctrine, she was often quite in despair about our membership of a fundamentalist denomination. It was a very painful period for her particularly in light of the fact that our attending church with her was a source of joy and comfort for her. Her humorous observations were not limited to the fundamentalists. I lost a lot of emotional support in terms of bonding with my mother, my extended family, and my mother's friends. What kind of ethics would foster the severance of the young from their families? Though I did experience some discomfort and anxiety, I felt that I was doing the right thing. In sermons, it was often preached, based on the words of Jesus, that we should "put him first above all things and everybody including family".

My mother sought solace and comfort from her family and friends. She did find a little bit of consolation in "Well...they are not really doing anything bad...it could be worse...they could be out partying all the time...pregnancy..." but not enough to overcome the isolation and loneliness she often felt. It was not just our refusal to attend the Anglican Church with her, and our frequent attendance at services which meant our being often absent from home, but the ideological split that often resulted in conflicts and censure of our mother. Little did my mother realize, however, that her critical analysis was not exactly futile. In less than five years, we would all sever ties with Grace Missionary Church and to a large extent the fundamentalists. My sister and I often, however, express regret about spending important years of our youth with a group that restricted our socialization and knowledge at a time when we should have expanded our relationships and world views. It made us insular and inhibited our social skills and growth.

One important outcome of the observations and discussions we had with our mother was the fostering of social awareness and consciousness of class divisions. She constantly derisively pointed out the luxurious and ostentatious lifestyle of the fundamentalists as evidenced particularly by their long cars. The fundamentalists viewed material wealth as blessing from God.

The denominations in many ways reflected the stratification of the society. The Anglican Church for the most part was comprised of the middle and upper classes mainly from the professional and landowning class. The fundamentalists were mainly drawn from the commercial class—business people, those engaged in trade.

While I was at Grace Church, Mrs. J. prevailed on her siblings to find work for my siblings and me for we were experiencing some difficult times financially. Somehow God in his infinite wisdom had given people from the Middle East the right to own major shops and stores, to be involved in trade, business, and industry while the vast majority of blacks were systematically excluded from owning or administering major businesses in Kingston. God in his infinite wisdom had assigned type of work to skin color. Blacks were to do menial tasks—laborers, gardener boys, domestic workers. They could be farmers as long as they did not own many acres of land. How did this differ from the caste system in India? God permitted a few blacks to break out of the mould of doing manual work to become teachers, policemen, sanitary inspectors, ministers, and a very, very tiny minority, doctors. (I knew of the existence of only one black—cocoa brown complexion doctor).

For some reason, however, a number of blacks were dissatisfied with the position assigned to them by God and sought ways and means to defy the caste system. For the four hundred to five hundred years of history in the West, black people have had to defy God and the status quo. I think, to a large extent, it is the defiance of God and the status quo why black people are perceived as immoral.

The job Mrs. J. found for us through her sibling, was to package numerous hair pins. Stooping in the living room, hair pins and paper wrappers on the floor, my siblings and I would systematically count a specific quantity of hair pins (I cannot recall—about two dozen) and neatly package them in the wrappers provided. It was very time consuming and tedious work for very little pay. Our mother constantly commented that what we were doing was really counterproductive in terms of hours of labor and amount we earned. She took the opportunity of what she considered to be outright exploitation to frequently observe how hypocritical and ruthless fundamentalists are.

After laboriously counting the number of pins, one day my brother asked: Do you think someone is going to really check the number of hair pins? After that, we simply estimated the quantity of hair pins to put in each package, but even then the amount of money that we received was not worth the effort. I was also given the job of painting flowers on sets of jugs and glasses. For this job, I had to travel by bus to the house of Mrs. J's sister who lived on the other side of Kingston in a decidedly middle class neighborhood off Windward Road. Though a nice neighborhood, it was not, however, as upscale and modern as Havendale; the houses and gardens were smaller. Mrs. J's sister briefly showed me how the painting should be done. I was dismayed at my results. My leaves and flowers were far from symmetrical and there were blobs where I had used too much paint. The leaves and the flowers did not look anything like Mrs. J's sister's sample. I was told I should not worry. Color made a great difference and I would improve over time. "Black people like bright and colorful things". The flowers and leaves on the sets of jugs and glasses made a huge difference in price and therefore in profit. I am sure there was no consideration as to whether the paint was toxic. I thought of the colored patterns on the sets that we had at home. Not only were they symmetrical, but they were clearly part of the manufacturing process—not added on later. Would the people purchasing these glasses not see that the paint was sloppy and could not possibly be done by the manufacturers?

I spent many hours painting flowers and leaves on jugs and glasses with very little improvement, I thought. A family friend who lived in that vicinity offered to provide lunch for me. After a day or two, however, I saw my reliance on her for lunch as an imposition. Apparently, when the promise was made she was either swept by feelings of the moment, or she was assuming some financial remuneration. The pay that I received was barely enough to cover transportation much less to cover the cost of lunch. I was very relieved when my mother pointed out the futility of my continuing to work for so little pay. I no longer had to sit isolated for hours doing something I thought I was incompetent to do, something that was insulting to poor African Jamaican people, and having lunch with a family who saw me as added expense. Mrs. J. was not at all pleased. She regarded my no longer working for her sister as ingratitude particularly as I just abruptly stopped working without giving any notice or indication that I would not return.

Shortly after that I left Grace Church. I did not return to Half Way Tree, however. Instead, at the invitation of Sally, I attended a fundamentalist Church, a different denomination from Grace. This church belonged to the Gospel Assemblies. I had no idea and still do not know in what ways they differed from Grace Missionary Church and what were their doctrinal beliefs. The piano was closed. The church had no pianist. I opened the piano and played. Oh my, they said. This is an answer to prayer. The pastor of the Church, part Arab, part Jamaican began to weep. The Lord could use me in the spread of the gospel and so I became a member of Bethel Gospel Assembly.

As most of the members except for the pastor, Mr. K, who was Arab-Jamaican, his cousin, Mr. A, and his cousin's wife, Mrs. A, who were Arabs, shared my physical characteristics, I thought that I would have complete and unconditional acceptance. Education and ironically, the African feature, my hair, would be alienating factors. There were only three of us as members of the church who were high school students. We were under constant surveillance and often were the target of mean looks and gossip. The fact that Ruth and I straightened our hair aggravated matters. Straightening one's hair was sinful, of the world, and un-Christian. Barbara the third high school student in the group was fortunate. God had given her "good" hair and so she was spared committing the sin of straightening her hair.

No matter what the three of us did, playing the piano, singing, (Ruth had a beautiful voice), teaching Sunday School, attending church services, we never met the approval, particularly Ruth and myself, of two of the senior female members (in terms of leadership not age) of the church. There was quite a hullabaloo when one of these senior sisters made a trip to the United States for some months and returned with her hair straightened. As a result of innuendos, contemptuous looks, and negative comments, after some months, Sister Mac, had to revert to not straightening her hair.

The pastor of a sister church of Bethel Gospel Assembly was not acclaimed for his dynamic preaching. He had gained some popularity based more on his willingness to preach than for the substance of his sermons which were usually rambling and lacking in structure and thought. Not being able to elicit spontaneous "Amen" and "Hallelujah" which were indicative of how moved the congregation is by the sermon this particular preacher had a habit of coercing the congregation to say Amen and Hallelujah every sentence or so. "Say Amen, say Hallelujah", he would often ejaculate during his sermon.

Now it is strange but we three high school students, Ruth, Barbara, and myself, had never discussed the issue of shouting Hallelujah and Amen during church services. Somehow, however, we had by implicit consensus agreed that shouting Hallelujah and Amen in church was "low class" undignified, and was not at all befitting of high school students. Particularly annoying was Pastor W's *demand* that we say Amen and Hallelujah. Well, this particular Sunday Pastor W. kept repeating "Say Amen" and as he did so he was observing the three of us closely for we were sitting right up front. Undoubtedly, he saw the look of derision on our faces. When we refused to comply he looked at us and said, "you do not want to say Amen—then using

1 Corinthians 1: 17-25, he lambasted us. "Not many wise will be saved because "the foolishness of God is wiser than men; and the weakness of God is stronger than men. The preaching of the Cross is to them that perish foolishness; but unto us who are saved it is the power of God." (1 Corinthians 1: 17-15 SJV)

I was shaken by these words which became etched on my brain because it would be used over and over particularly by Pastor W. and semi-illiterate preachers to compensate for their lack of education and their lack of knowledge. These preachers would delight, based on that passage, in asserting how *it is the Holy Spirit* and *not formal education* that is required for the effective preaching of the gospel. This would be repeated particularly when they observed our uncontrollable smirk or laughter at their bad grammar or faltering speech especially when imposed upon an ersatz American accent. It is significant to note, however, how the members of the church most of whom were semi-illiterate would react to preachers who had some formal education and could express themselves with some degree of eloquence and articulation. The "Amen" and "Hallelujah" would be spontaneous without pressure from the preacher. Even illiterate and semi-illiterate members were often able to differentiate between sermons delivered by preachers who had some degree of formal education and unstructured, rambling, sermons.

I Corinthians 1: 17-25 would be a source of conflict in my struggles with the Christian faith. I saw knowledge and education as a threat to God. What would follow would be "intellectual castration"[373] which would only reinforce in many ways my status as a Dalit. I was not shaken enough, however, by Pastor W's reprimand to shout Hallelujah and Amen in church service. The three of us, Ruth, Barbara, and I were as resolute as ever that shouting Hallelujah and Amen in church was definitely beneath the dignity of high school students. This demonstrates how Christianity does not often transcend prejudices.

I do not know why I allowed I Corinthians 1: 17-25 to cause me such anguish and despair with regards to knowledge and learning when there was so much overwhelming evidence that knowledge plays an integral role in the spreading of the gospel. That Paul should have made such a statement is ironical in the light of the fact that Paul because of his education and knowledge was far more effective in terms of his leadership role in the Christian faith than Peter who was less qualified intellectually. The use of airplanes, cars, microphones, printing presses, electricity, medicine, etc. by missionaries is evidence of the salient role of science and technology in the

---

[373]Williams, *Alchemy,* p. 198.

proselytization of Christianity.

It never struck us that while education was often minimized from the pulpit, it was the three of us, high school students, who in many ways gave dynamic leadership to the church. The Arab-Jamaican pastor, Mr. K, was quick to note that I was a far more effective Sunday School teacher than his semi-literate Sunday School teachers who were often extremely cross and impatient with children who displayed signs of boredom as a result of the teacher's inarticulate instruction. I was sometimes asked to teach the entire Sunday School, as a model of how it should be done, much to the chagrin of the older women and men.

I did not like to give my "testimony" but Ruth and Barbara had no inhibitions about doing so which they would in well-articulated English. Ruth had a beautiful voice and her singing was enhanced by her poise and grace as a high school student. Our education contributed a lot to the church. Mr. K was aware of this and as a result would transport us to and from church services and do whatever he could to foster our active participation in the church. Yet, I frequently minimized and devalued education, critical analysis, and thought for I saw knowledge as a threat to God in the light of I Corinthian 1: 17-25. I was convinced about the inerrancy of the Bible.

It would take many years to overcome the fear of subjecting Christianity to critical analysis. Underlying my subjection and subordination to the Christian principles and views was the issue of class. If it were not for the fact that the Christian Church was instituted by the upper class as evidenced in the Anglican Church and the fundamentalist by the rich commercial class, I would not have given Christianity the time of day.

The other factor that for me was troubling as a member of Bethel was the fact that the church, located as it was, in the midst of a struggling community had very little impact on the neighborhood. I have to give my mother credit for this observation. She often expressed concern about the poor. We would often tease her about her "social" work. The neighbors of the Bethel church would conduct their business in yards crowded by two to three small wooden homes. Laughing and talking, the inhabitants of these homes would wash their clothes over huge wash pans and cook outdoors on coal pots, totally oblivious of the blaring sounds of preaching and hymns declaring that they need to be saved. Sometimes, Mr. K, in order to reach more members would have "Revival" meetings or special gospel services that had little or no impact on the community. Very much influenced by my mother, I sometimes would ask Mr. K: Should we not give them something tangible in the way of food and clothes instead of just preaching to them? No, he said, if you give them something, it will develop a sense of dependency. I did not realize how angry I was that he was more concerned about the "souls" of black African peoples, than he was about their bodies including their minds. It never occurred to me then to point out that nowhere in the gospels did I read that Jesus warned against giving to the poor because it would create a sense of dependency.

It was strongly believed that once individuals hear the Word of God and become saved, then God will bless them, that is, satisfy their economic needs. It was intimated that the reason for the poor conditions in which most of the people lived on St. Joseph Road where Bethel Church was located was as a result of the individual's life of sin and their refusal to respond to the gospel.

That Mr. K owned furniture stores which he had inherited from his father and that he owned vast amounts of land did not at all factor in his Christian outlook. He did not question how being saved would alter the fact that Middle Easterners owned stores and other business on the main streets of Kingston. He did not question how being saved would alter the fact that Middle Easterners dominated the commercial sector and that African descended people were excluded from this sector. He did not question how being saved could alter the fact that African descended peoples could only find jobs, other than low status jobs, if they fulfilled the education requirements in fields, such as, teaching, nursing, civil service, policing.

How would being saved transform the lives of the poor? For the two or three years I was a member of Bethel, I saw no great transformation in terms of the members' social and economic conditions. One or two young men did find jobs in one of the pastor's stores but most of the families lived almost in abject poverty. A woman who attended church faithfully every Sunday with her two daughters lived in a hut on the edge of a ravine. Abandoned by her husband, she earned her living by selling in the market. Her conditions were a huge source of embarrassment for her two daughters. Mr. K did not see it fit to help them for to do so would not only create a sense of dependency, but would have many others banging on his doors.

Not only was there very little advancement socially, in terms of upward mobility but there was very little mingling amongst the members of the church. We were all Christians but the issue of skin color and class were salient in terms of social interaction whether it was the Anglican Church, the Missionary Church or the Gospel Assembly. For the many years that we were members of St. Andrew Parish Church, we were never invited to have tea with the Minister at the Rectory nor did he ever visit our home. Indeed once when my mother sent me to see the minister to make an appointment— we did not have a telephone then—I was received by the minister's wife at the back door and was not invited to enter. Besides the two neighbors who lived across from us or families we knew through my parents' professions, we never socially interacted with members of the church.

At Grace Missionary there was some social interaction amongst the in-group outside of church activities but this was still selective. In spite of my brother's dynamic leadership role in his church, the minister never visited our home or my brother, his. When I was a member of Grace, if I were early for church for some reason, usually because of the bus schedule, I could see through the windows of the minister's house, for the house was built not far from the church, the black maid dressed in uniform waiting at the table on the white family—the minister (a Jamaican who claimed he was white) his wife and their five children. I cannot recall ever seeing her in church.

One would think that there would be greater social interaction at Bethel Gospel Assembly located as it was in a poor struggling neighborhood. Mr. K, the Arab-Jamaican pastor, his Arab cousin, Mr. A and his Arab wife, Mrs. A would week after week attend the church and before and after the church services Mr. K and Mr. and Mrs. A would heartily shake hands and greet the members of the church. Never once, however, were we as African descendants ever invited to the homes, though we were all Christians, of the Arabs. Indeed, the Arabs did not live in our neighborhoods. They lived in the wealthy and opulent parts of Kingston. The Arabs, however, in terms of associating and attending church with blacks were regarded as very good people for this was outside the norm of Arab-black relationship. Never mind the adoration and literally worship they received as African descendant members of the church would eagerly shake their hands and line up to shake the hands of Mrs. A who would remain seated in her pew. (She never stood up or left her pew to greet the congregation. She was shy, her husband said). While the Arab couple sat lovingly in their pew—and the Arab wife did not have to sing, give her testimony or teach Sunday School—most of the black women sat husbandless in the church. Black women were made to feel that they should be active in the church. Black women were not allowed to be shy.

Besides the two high school students, I never befriended anyone in the church although I was a member for a number of years. Although the three of us were friends, we had very little social interaction outside of church. Besides, we all felt a deep sense of inadequacy which we desperately tried to cover up—illness, caring for several younger siblings, poverty. The Christian Churches in spite of the preaching of egalitarianism are often the repositories of snobbery, elitism and as a result, alienation. In terms of social stratification, Christianity shares a lot of commonalities with Hinduism. How can there be equality between a poor black woman and a rich white man who has money and resources to build churches and schools for the proselytization of the gospel?

Where did all the money go that was collected at services at Bethel? We all felt that it went to God who would return it to us, but how? Most of the money went out of the community for equipment, upkeep of the church, and to the pastors for it was not the policy to pay Sunday school teachers and pianists. Mr. K did, however, build a school close to one of the sister churches largely I flatter myself at my instigation. As teachers, we were constantly reminded that the main goal of the school was to win souls for Christ which was the objective of the school's daily Morning Prayer services. In spite of I Corinthians 1: 17-25, we all had to meet the educational requirements to teach on the staff.

I will conclude this chapter by talking about prayer, another leg of the analogy of the chair with regard to Christian growth. I was seriously convinced that prayer would dispel all the difficulties and anguish I was facing at this time of my life. My father was often plunged in despair. Just as how my grandfather had abandoned my father, so it seemed my father abandoned us when we were teenagers not so much physically but psychologically.

I was not doing as well at school as I hoped. The fundamentalists chose passages from the Bible that supported the view that all one needed is faith and any obstacle could be overcome. "Faith can move mountains", "Seek and ye shall find, ask and it shall be given to you" were often cited passages that kept me believing that I would escape from my difficulties and anxieties. "If you have faith as a mustard seed, you can move mountains". Why should I worry? "Look at the lilies of the field, they toil not, neither do they spin, and yet their heavenly Father takes care of them." Jesus could walk on water, turn water into wine, calm storms. Why was I constantly filled with anxiety and worry?

I thought prayer would overcome the difficulty I was experiencing with my school work. In the Sixth Form at Wolmer's, it seemed failure was constantly hovering over me. I prayed. I studied. I did not realize that I would have to do extensive reading of critical analysis of the works of Wordsworth, Shelley, Keats, Coleridge, Chaucer, Jane Austen, Shakespeare, Milton which I was required to pursue for Higher Schools so as to be able to write analytical essays that were now required of me.

I was not singular with regard to my academic performance. Part of the problem was that it was the first time in Wolmer's history that Wolmer's found itself with a majority of girls from the struggling middle class in the Sixth Form. We were for the most part alienated and extremely bored with English literature. What did *Samson Agonistes, The Tempest, Mansfield Park, The Pardoner's Tale* have to do with our lives in the Caribbean? Indeed we felt Caliban in *The Tempest* representing "natives" as half man and half beast was positively insulting. What was the point of the "Rime of the Ancient Mariner?" we frequently asked.

How did praying and reading the Bible, having fellowship with other Christians, testifying, help me through these difficult times? The more I felt alienated and overwhelmed by my school work, the more I plunged myself in Christian activities—I.S.C.F., Bible meetings, Youth for Christ, Church services, Sunday School, Quiet Times—the worse was my school performance.

What had been tradition at Wolmer's for many years—prefect as a rite of passage once you were in Sixth Form was not to be in 1958. We were certainly a deviation from the elite class. Although Curtin asserts that Wolmer's suffered less from the "manifestations" of "colour and class prejudice" that "reflected the Jamaican society" than "students in some other schools; suffer they did." [374]

And suffer we did. Was it because of our behavior? We were not really bad. Even Delia who had made it to the Sixth Form had calmed down tremendously in terms of making fun of others particularly I think after she straightened her hair. After every announcement of newly appointed prefects, our Sixth Form room would be filled with despair, gloom, dejection and anger as a result of dashed hopes particularly in the light of the fact that the entire school including the lower grades knew of our slight. We did not have the privilege or right to command the respect of the teachers, the respect of the students, and to be part of an inner circle of teachers, staff, and the headmistress. In the school system, we were truly Dalits.

I prayed. I fasted. I tried to assume the demeanor of those who had been made prefects. I stopped clowning around with my peers and gave them disapproving looks whenever they joked around and sang the popular songs on the radio. I became withdrawn justifying my behavior on the grounds that as a born again Christian I should not be associating with non-Christians and engaging in activities of the world. Indeed, Delia became quite concerned about me. Who is this person who had metamorphosed from a rational being to a fanatic "born again", "holier than thou" Christian? She would pull me aside sometimes. "Is there something wrong? Tell me." I threw myself in more Christian activities in spite of the constant feeling of mortification of not being a prefect that negated accolades regarding my leadership role in these activities outside of school. Every morning I would ask Jesus who in my mind's eye I saw as a white man with long brown hair to take over my entire body. I handed out tracts. I tried to "win some souls for Christ"—all in an effort to change God's mind about my becoming a

---

[374]Curtin, et. al. *In the Light of the Sun,* p. 88.

prefect. I was unable to bend the mind of God. It did not matter my input regarding my involvement in Church and Christian activities. I could not bend the mind of God. God could not work outside of the social structure and stratification of the Jamaican society.

I can't remember exactly a turning point in my life in terms of my becoming an apostate. A major contributor, however, was a conversation I was privy to at Moorlands Camp. Moorlands Camp was located on acres of land that included a huge cave in Manchester, Jamaica. It was owned and administered by fundamentalists. One day at this camp, three of us were sitting in a dorm E.C, the eldest daughter of the minister at Grace Missionary Church, Jenny a member of Grace, and I. Jenny and E. C. were very good friends. They called themselves twins and were always seen together. Jenny and E. C. were engaged in a conversation in which I was not included. I kept quiet observing the Jamaican etiquette that you do not participate into a conversation unless you are invited to do so, I remained quiet.

As the conversation was not particularly interesting, I allowed my mind to drift. I was startled by what seemed to be a vehement outburst from E. C. the daughter of the minister of Grace Missionary Church. "I have absolutely no black blood in me at all". Her father was Jamaican and her mother a white American. Then Jenny said, with her very infectious laugh, "and I am half Indian". The other half, her black mother, who I happen to know worked very hard for Jenny was totally eradicated and denied—made absent—castration of blackness. I was flabbergasted, although why I do not know after experiencing American anti-black racism amongst fundamentalists particularly at Grace Missionary Church.

I did not quite put it in these words but I felt: American anti-black racism is rude, disrespectful, showing a lack of proper upbringing, totally lacking in social skills and insecure.

Whenever I raise the issue of racism, anti-Black and anti-African beliefs, within the Christian religion, black Christians and white Christians tell me that there is a pure pristine Christian religion that "has nothing to do with Christianity as practiced by its adherents". Racism is of the devil, it is of the world, it is man's doing. It is not that blacks have not wrestled with the issue of the incongruity of racism and purported Christian beliefs, such as, God is love and Christians are brothers and sisters in Christ. You can rest assured, however, that whenever blacks attempt to pursue the issue of the perpetuation of racism within the Christian religion which really translates into divine racism there are black ministers, theologians who issue apologia regarding the Christian religion.

A case in point is the response of black theologians and ministers to the critique and analysis of racism during the Civil Rights movement. Instead of giving support in terms of their knowledge and experience by undertaking rigorous critical analysis of the Christian religion, a number of black ministers and theologians, based on illogical reasoning and superficial evidence, seek actually to negate the knowledge, experiences and views of blacks by purporting that Jesus is Black and Jesus identifies and supports Black revolution. A major proponent of Jesus is Black theology is James Cone. A critical analysis of Black theology in response to the assertion of divine racism is the topic of the next chapter.

Christianity and Black Oppression: Duppy Know Who Fe Frighten

CHAPTER TWELVE

"JESUS IS BLACK" THEOLOGY: CASTRATION FROM BLACKNESS

I'm putting it to my black brothers and sisters that the colour of our skins is the most fundamental thing about us. [375]

Walter Rodney

For some of us in 1972 to hear James Cone declare in the Mona Chapel of the University of the West Indies (UWI) that Jesus is black was just the palliative we needed to deal with the conflicts we faced as African descended people worshipping in reality, for many of us, a white God. That God is white was never really explicitly stated but it was implicit from the imagery in the Bible, glass stained windows, movies, illustrations in books. It was not unusual to see a framed picture of a white Christ adorn the living rooms of relatives and friends.

The attributes of God also underscored the whiteness of God. Since God is all-powerful, all knowing, perfect, and the great distributor of wealth, then, in the scheme of things whites are far closer to God in terms of his attributes than blacks, and since God is the Absolute, then God must be white. Every sphere of our lives was governed by whites. There was not one area of our lives in which we did not have to report to whites. It meant not only relying on whites for our economic needs, but whites as governor, ruler, supervisor, and administrator did not only enact laws, but also monitored our behavior. It was natural therefore to transfer whiteness to the supreme distributor of goods, supreme law giver, and supreme judge, that is, God.

It was the maldistribution, however, between blacks and whites in terms of suffering that often raised the question of the color of God. The magnitude of suffering of blacks, the slave trade, slavery, poverty, oppressive laws in comparison to the ease and comforts of whites in terms of wealth, power, and domination raised the question of divine discrimination. In the light of horrendous black suffering in comparison to white, God must be white.

The whiteness of God has been problematic for a number of Christians and indeed has been an underlying factor in the development of the

---

[375]Walter Rodney, *The Groundings With My Brothers* (Chicago IL: Research Associates School Times Publications, 1990, c1969) p. 16.

Rastafarian movement.[376] Some blacks sought to deal with the issue of God being white by claiming that they were the first Jews[377].

Amongst the evangelical Christians, however, during the 1960's serious thought was not given to the matter of the whiteness of God. Indeed, as fundamentalist Christians we never gave much thought to social, political and economic factors for we lived in an "other worldly" cocoon that negated any kind of profound critical analysis of social, economic, and political issues. During my years with the evangelicals from the late 1950's to the late 1960's, except to point out the evils of communism, there was hardly any reference to political matters. Events such as The Civil Rights Movement, colonial uprisings in Africa, Asia, and the West Indies including of course Jamaica swirled past us like distant grey clouds in a clear blue sky.

I cannot even say we were apolitical. No we were in fact supporters of the status quo for obedience should be the hallmark of the Christian. Rebellion was not an option.

There are several passages in Scripture that support deference to authority. "Render, therefore, unto Caesar the things which are Caesar's and unto God the things that are God's" is an injunction of Christ.[378] Children should obey their parents: "Children, obey your parents in the Lord; for this is right."[379] In *Ephesians* 6:5, servants are told that they should obey masters: "Servants, be obedient to them that are *your* masters according to the flesh, with fear and trembling, in singleness of your heart, as unto Christ."[380] The injunction is repeated in *Colossians* 3: 21 with very similar wording. In *Titus* 2:9 subservience to masters is equally explicit: *Exhort* servants to be obedient unto their masters, *and* to please *them* well in all *things* (italics KJV) and indeed Paul adds: *not answering again* (italics mine). Wives are told repeatedly that they should obey their husbands. They are to "*be* discreet, chaste, keepers at home, good, obedient to their own husbands, that the word of God be not blasphemed."[381] Christians are not only to obey "them that have the rule over you, and submit yourselves"[382] but they should "pray *for* kings and all that are in authority"[383]

---

[376]Barrett, Sr. *The Rastafarians;* Chevannes, *Rastafari.*

[377]See, for example, Albert Cleage, *The Black Messiah,* (New York, NY: Sheed & Ward, 1969); Frazier, *The Negro Church of America.*

[378] *Luke* 20:25 (KJV)

[379]*Ephesians* 6:1(KJV)

[380]*Ephesians* 6:5; *Colossians* 3: 22 (KJV)

[381]*Titus* 2:5

[382]*Hebrews* 13: 17.

[383]*I Timothy* 2: 1-2 SJV, Italics SJV

Apparently, it is prayer and not any kind of struggle or revolution that will "lead to a quiet and peaceable life in all godliness and honesty."[384] Indeed *Romans* 13:1-3 could not be more explicit in terms of what should be the attitude of the Christian toward government:

> Let every soul be subject unto the higher powers. For there is no power but of God; the powers that be are ordained of God.
>
> Whosoever, therefore, resisteth the power, resisteth the ordinance of God; and they that resist shall receive to themselves judgement.
>
> For rulers are not a terror to good works, but to the evil. Wilt thou, then, not be afraid of the power? Do that which is good, and thou shalt have praise of the same;[385]

This passage was often used in sermons to assert (1) God's sovereignty (2) governments and rulers are put in control by God (3)therefore struggle, resistance or revolutionary activity is disobeying God's will. Paul's decision to return Onesimus, after Onesimus was converted to Christianity, to Philemon, Onesimus' master, from whom Philemon had run away, concretized the importance of obedience and subservience to authority.[386] It is true as Christian apologists often point out that Paul added the fiat that Onesimus should be treated kindly, but not addressed are (a) why, in the first place, Onesimus should run away from a Christian master (b) Onesimus' feelings about returning to his master and (c) master servant relationship in terms of the oft-repeated assertion that Christianity is an egalitarian religion.

Added to obedience and subservience to and compliance with the status quo, is often the implication that economic hardship is due to a lack of faith. In sermons and testimonies, preachers would declare how God has blessed them as evidenced by their very smart and expensive suits and their long cars. Blessings come from God and all we have to do is to have faith. Norman Vincent Peale, a minister, who used Bible verses to support the power of positive thinking in obtaining wealth and overcoming obstacles, was very popular amongst fundamentalist Christians.

There were other doctrinal teachings which taught how to cope with social, political, and economic issues and indeed all obstacles. What can ever surpass "we know that all things work together for good to them that

---

[384]*I Timothy* 2:2
[385]*Romans* 13: 1-3.
[386] *Philemon* (KJV)

love God, to them who are the called according to *his* purpose"[387] in terms of giving consolation to the distraught and the distressed? What even gave greater hope and comfort is apocalyptic and eschatological doctrines: (a) evils would be redressed in the next life: "God shall wipe away all tears from their eyes"[388] (b) evil—wars, natural disasters, injustice were signs of the Apocalypse and Jesus' Second Coming:

> For nation shall rise against nation, and kingdom against kingdom; and there shall be earthquakes in various places, and there shall be famines and troubles: these *are* the beginnings of sorrows.[389]

(c) The greater the disaster and the greater human distress, the more these signified Jesus' imminent return:

> But in those days, after that tribulation, the sun shall be darkened, and the moon shall not give its light,
> And the stars of heaven shall fall, and the powers that are in the heavens shall be shaken.
> And then shall they see the Son of man coming from the clouds, with great glory and power.
> And then shall he send his angels, and shall gather together his elect from the four winds, from the uttermost part of the earth to the uttermost part of heaven.[390]

In sermon after sermon, sometimes implied sometimes it was explicitly stated that any kind of protest, rebellion, revolution, is bad, sinful, evil, disobeying God, and bound for hell and damnation. The University at Mona was regarded as an institution that bred radical, militant Marxist students that were bound for hell and damnation.

We, as fundamentalist Christians, left it to the students dubbed "Marxists", "radicals", "militants" to grapple with issues of human existence, suffering, and evil particularly in the light of racism, colonialism, oppression, injustice, and class inequities. The students dubbed "Marxists", "radicals", "militants" were informed by works of Fanon, Sartre, Marx, the cries of "Black is beautiful" and "Black power", the speeches and works of

---

[387] *Romans* 8: 28 (KJV; italics KJV)

[388] *Revelation* 7: 17 (KJV)

[389] *Mark* 8-9. (KJV)

[390] *Mark* 24-27 (KJV)

Martin Luther King, Marcus Garvey, James Baldwin and the banned books by the Jamaican government of Malcolm X and Stokely Carmichael.

The young people in the United States mainly of our racial make-up being arrested, beaten, bitten by dogs, fire hosed, imprisoned and murdered for basic human rights and the squalor in Jamaica examples of which were just a few miles from the campus, and which was often reflected in some of the plaintive sounds of ska and reggae were not what we discussed at our Inter Varsity Christian Fellowship (IVCF) meetings at the University of the West Indies, Mona Campus, during the time I was a member, 1963-1966. Our main concern was effective Christian living and witness based on the belief that as more people become Christians, their lives would be transformed and thus the transformation of the society depended on the aggregate of Christians. It was not therefore the uprisings, protests, and revolutionary movements that became central issues but the role of the Holy Spirit, speaking in tongues, and the subordination of women.

Focus on the role of the Holy Spirit was largely due to the infiltration of Pentecostals mainly from other parts of the Caribbean including Guyana. The Pentecostals' infiltration of the Inter-Varsity Movement fueled disputes in terms of their dogmatic belief that speaking in tongues and being led by the Holy Spirit were integral signs of being a Christian and that women should be unassertive—compliant, obedient, chaste, and demure.

The invitation to one of our meetings of an Indian evangelist who told us that God would provide us with answers to our examinations which were imminent was the kind of belief to which the Pentecostals wanted us to adhere. The Indian preacher's proof was his experience of sitting in examinations and feeling completely at a loss as to what to write. As he prayed, however, to God, the Holy Spirit dictated the answers which he wrote. This in actual fact was said to the most educated sector of the West Indies, the students of the University of the West Indies. In truth and in fact, the Indian preacher did not deviate from the view of the Pentecostals and members of the IVCF who felt that not only could one rely on the Holy Spirit for assistance, but one *should* rely on the Holy Spirit to direct one in all areas of life.

Besides, the "Marxists", "radicals" and "militants" however, there was another group, the Student Christian Movement (SCM), comprised mainly of members of mainline Churches, the Methodists, Presbyterians, Baptists (English not American), and Anglicans with whom we as fundamentalists often had to contend. For this group, members of the IVCF were fanatics and believers in an "other worldly" and "pie in the sky" religion. The SCM was more prone to discuss social issues and doing good works—visiting patients in hospitals etc.

It was through the instrumentality of one of the leaders of the SCM, that Dr. Martin Luther King was invited to speak at the Valedictorian Service at the University of the West Indies in 1965. Because of the large crowd, the service was held, not in the Mona Chapel but at the Assembly Hall at the University of the West Indies. I was fortunate to obtain a seat close to the front and in my mind's eye I can still see Martin Luther King seated on the platform. I am happy to have that memory but I am extremely saddened and pained that my memory of what he had to say was obscured by the fact that as a fundamentalist Christian, I felt a lot of disquiet about Martin Luther King's radical position as a Christian minister.

As a fundamentalist, I had integrated the warning of the guardians of the Christian faith—the priests from the pulpit, relatives, and friends—that I should not pursue the broad and wicked path of the black conscious radicals who were disrupting the society by thinking that they could hasten a revolution which God in his own time and infinite wisdom would surely bring to pass. I was therefore critical of Martin Luther King's protests and resistance regarding the appalling conditions of blacks.   Protests and resistance are un-Christian.

By 1972, my position would have shifted somewhat largely due to my living in Toronto, Canada for almost three years where I was confronted with racism although Canadians, for the most part, felt that there was no racism in Canada. Thus, Canadians were very upset about race riots at Sir George William University in Montreal during 1968 to 1969.

It was not as though many of us were not aware of skin color discrimination in Jamaica, for, indeed, that was part of the reason why some of us migrated to Canada in the late 1960's. We were disillusioned by what we considered the snail pace change, if any, of 1962 Jamaican Independence. Of reddish bronzed complexion and reddish-brownish springy straightened hair, a Wolmerian who had done extremely well at the University obtaining a degree with top honors in science told me one day on King Street with tears in her eyes how difficult it was for her to find a job in the private sector in Jamaica. Particularly humiliating was after long waits for interviews while tan complexioned wavy hair young female employees who probably had only a year or two in high school would traipse past her, she would be told that either the manager was busy, or he was out and she should return some other time. Frequently after finally obtaining an interview she would be invariably asked by the tan complexion shiny wavy hair manager: why does she not look for a teaching position? The daughter of teachers, she exclaimed, "I do not want to teach". Many of us had settled on teaching because we knew besides the Civil Service that as springy haired members of the society teaching was our only option.

It was to us as teachers, however, that the entrenched anti-black racism was very apparent. Poor springy hair chocolate skinned children were far more likely to be kicked out of the elite schools than tan colored wavy hair children. Tan complexioned wavy hair students were more likely to be made head boy or head girl than chocolate complexioned children with springy hair. White teachers and Jamaican white teachers were granted far more respect than cinnamon to chocolate complexion teachers with springy hair. In 1968 Jamaica declared Walter Rodney a brilliant University professor from Guyana persona non grata after he attended the Congress of Black Writers in Montreal.[391]

However, although often slighted in Jamaica because of dark skin color and springy hair, many of us as African descended peoples never saw ourselves as part of a group. I certainly did not identify with members of the poor who shared my physical characteristics. The reality in Jamaica was a denial of racial divisions and assertion of racial harmony in spite of underlying racial discrimination in Jamaica.[392]

It was a culture shock therefore to be faced with housing discrimination and job discrimination in Canada based totally on being a member of an outcast group, that is, being black. Most humiliating and shocking, however, was the discrimination we faced in churches. In Toronto, as West Indians moved into the churches, whites moved out of the churches.

In 1972, it was therefore with eagerness and great enthusiasm that I sat in the Mona Chapel to hear what James Cone had to say about Jesus being black. I thought of recent discussions at a Baptist Church about the imagery of White/good and Black/evil in a lot of our hymns.

I listened intently to what Cone had to say but after a few sentences I found that I was totally unable to follow his reasoning. Every time Cone declared "Jesus is black", there was enthusiastic response from the audience. At the first mention of "Jesus is black", Sally, my tan complexion brown wavy hair friend walked out of the chapel. James Cone came to the end of his talk and I did not follow his arguments or understand what he said, but I joined the audience in enthusiastic applause.

Springy hair, chocolate, cinnamon, and cocoa brown complexion women cornered tan complexion wavy haired Sally outside the chapel and engaged her in a heated debate regarding the skin color of Jesus in which everyone was talking and no one was listening. Some seminarians from the mainstream denominations of the United Theological College of the West

---

[391]Rodney, *The Groundings with My Brothers.*
[392] See for example, Nettleford, *Caribbean Cultural Identity;* Rodney, *Groundings.*

Indies stood by observing us silently. Afterwards, the seminarians told us that what James Cone was talking about was not the issue of skin color. We were perplexed. The seminarians tried to explain but it would take me years before I understood that what James Cone's Jesus is Black theology was addressing was the issue of black suffering and black liberation in the light of the sovereignty and goodness of God.

For a number of black theologians in the United States, the issue of black suffering was problematic in the light of God's omnipotence, God's sovereignty and the goodness of God. Suffering servant, hope, and working with God were theologies some black theologians used to counter the theodicy of the suffering of blacks as due to sin or a curse. [393] For James Cone, "Christianity is essentially a religion of liberation...and for the oppressed...their struggle for political, social, and economic justice is consistent with the gospel of Jesus Christ."[394] God wants to liberate the oppressed from their suffering. God identifies with the oppressed, and since the oppressed are black, then God identifies with black, and therefore Jesus is black.[395]

James Cone's theology has been the subject of a lot of critique particularly from the scholar, William R. Jones, who asserts that Cone's argument, as well as other black theologians in their efforts to address the theodicy as a result of black suffering raise the question: Is God a white racist? The black theologians, Jones claims, have not dealt with the multievidentiality of black suffering nor have the theologians shown any cataclysmic event that clearly demonstrates that God is on the side of blacks.[396]

It has been forty years since James Cone's Black Theology address at Mona and the question to ask is what impact has this theology made on Christians generally and Christianity in Jamaica in particular. The mere fact that James Cone speaks of a Black theology suggests that this is in response to a white theology or white theologies.[397] Cone's logical reasoning that God is concerned about the oppressed, and since blacks are oppressed, God is on the side of blacks and therefore God is black has, as Jones points out, several weaknesses.

In Jamaica, we had never seen Christianity as an ideology for social

---

[393]For arguments and analysis of Black theologians, See Jones, *Is God a White Racist?*
[394]Cone, *A Black Theology of Liberation,* p. 11
[395] Cone, *A Black Theology of Liberation;* Cone, *God of the Oppressed.*
[396]Jones, *Is God a White Racist?*
[397]Ibid.

revolution. Indeed, as colonized peoples, it had been drummed in our heads that Christianity was apolitical. However, there were other factors of James Cone's theology that caused disquiet besides the discomfort of dealing with the issue of race. Black theology seemed to run counter to what we had been taught to believe as Christians. We had been taught that we were brought to the island as slaves for our Christian redemption. We were very fortunate that God had redeemed us from paganism, heathenism, and barbarism of Africa. Those of us who had become Christians were saved from eternal damnation which would not have been the case had we remained in Africa.

As a matter of fact, many of us as the intelligentsia had bought into the notion that we were marching unto progress, a belief that I would assert is integral to the Racial Contract. Slavery was the nadir of our Christian experience. As graduates of the University of the West Indies, we had surpassed by leaps our ancestors including our parents. In several ways we who listened to James Cone at Mona were part of a privileged group. We were teachers, civil servants, doctors, lawyers, ministers who in many ways aped the lifestyle of the middle classes in America with our well furnished homes, our two or three cars, our well stocked shelves of food, our closet filled with clothes, our privilege to travel, and above all our maids, euphemistically called helpers, and our gardener boys to serve us. We simply thought based on attendance at recognized high schools and three or so years at the University we had the right to amass in one year what our parents had taken a whole generation to acquire.

Thrown out of the window were our parents' injunctions of not keeping up with the Jones and living within one's means. We had the right to the car, the latest furniture, the opulent house, current latest gadgets. There were suppliers particularly from the United States in tandem with wealthy merchants in Jamaica ready to feed our insatiable appetites. Even economists who had achieved degrees with high honors from the Mona Campus of the University of the West Indies and who had often rhetorically spoken of the "masses", "exploitation", the "bourgeoisie" and the "lumpen proletariat" were in the scramble for high class living. We were, as Freire asserts inoculate[d] individuals with the bourgeois appetite for personal success."[398]

And the rumblings of the masses the "Children of Sisyphus", as Orlando Patterson termed them, were often unheard by us. The masses were dubbed criminals to be gunned down and shot by police at sight. In 1974, the Gun Court Act was established:

---

[398]Paulo Freire, *Pedagogy of the Oppressed,* translated by Myra Bergman Ramos, (New York, NY: The Seabury Press, 1968), p. 147.

Under this act, if a person is found guilty of possessing an unlicensed firearm, or even a few bullets, he receives a mandatory sentence of "detention for life with hard labor." A gunman can be released from this sentence only when deemed fit to live a wholesome life in the community and that at the discretion of the governor general of Jamaica.[399]

Black poor people in Jamaica are inherently criminals and this was and, indeed, is the belief of most middle class and upper class Jamaicans who are black. Black middle class Jamaicans do not identify with poor blacks. Indeed underlying Jamaican culture is an anti-black, anti-African culture.[400] "Most of us who have studied at UWI" asserted Rodney, "are discernibly black, and yet we are undeniably part of the imperialist system."[401]

I sometimes lost sight of the irony of Civil Servants arriving at work well after 9:00 a.m., and after a break at 11:00 a.m., leaving for lunch at 1:00 and not returning until after 3:00 p.m., because they had to pick up their children, declaring how lazy the black and poor are. "Look at them sitting down doing nothing getting government money to clean up the place. Look at them leaning on their broom stick". We used pious phrases sometimes linked to rhetoric but we rarely ever carried out as we sat in our pristine churches real systematic analysis about the oppressive life of the poor: how, for example, helpers had to work from Sunday to Sunday without vacation, without maternity leave and to a large extent neglect of their children while they looked after ours.

It pains me to think how I internalized the world view of my colonial masters. Just as how I could only gain entry to the minister's rectory through the back door, so I, as a minister's wife, received the poor at the back door of the manse, and the well-to-do through the front. I cannot recall many of us, as ministers' wives, sitting with our "helpers" or the very poor in church. How pleased we were when renowned members of the community attended or joined our church! In the Jamaican context then, who is oppressed? On whose side is God?

Besides some of the fallacies in reasoning, which Jones[402] points out, in terms of Cone's Black theology, one issue that has been problematic for me

---

[399]Barrett, Sr. *The Rastafarians*, p. 14

[400]See for example, Barrett, *The Rastafarians,* Campbell, *Rasta and Resistance*; Nettleford, *Mirror, Mirror.*

[401]Rodney, *Groundings*, p. 32.

[402]Jones, *Is God a White Racist?*

is Cone's use of God's liberation of the Israelites from Egypt as an analogy for black liberation. As Jones asserts blacks have had no cataclysmic event, such as, the drowning of Pharaoh and his armies in the Red Sea and the deliverance of the Israelites from Egyptian slavery and oppression to demonstrate that God is on the sides of blacks.[403] In addition, what I think is clearly overlooked is the fact that the Egyptians and the Israelites did not share religious beliefs. The Israelites and the Egyptians did not worship the same God as the slave masters and the slaves. God therefore could clearly demonstrate he is on the side of the Israelites because he was not the God of the Egyptians. However, in terms of Black Christians and White Christians, and in terms of middle class Christians and poor Christians, the situation is entirely different. Black Christians, White Christians, middle class Christians and poor Christians all believe in the same God. Consequently, in my view black theologies purport a schismatic, dissonant and indeed schizophrenic Christianity as God is pulled in different directions with regard to taking sides.

In Cone's Black theology and, indeed, amongst theologians and apologists for Christianity, denominationalism is hardly addressed. It is as a minister's wife that I became aware of the divisiveness in Christianity amongst Christian ministers. One day a teacher, a co-worker, a self-acclaimed atheist, who I greatly admired but could not get better acquainted with because it would have tainted my reputation as a minister's wife, in one of her tirades against the Christian religion, named and counted thirty four churches in a three mile radius in a poor rural community of Trelawny. For many of the ministers of these churches, it was the only way to make a living. What she found upsetting is that the churches had very little social, economic and ethical impact on the community.

Sometimes it was nothing less than internecine warfare amongst the denominations. It was particularly painful to me to hear the Seventh Day Baptist—mark you—not the Seventh Day Adventist but the Seventh Day Baptist minister rile against my spouse over a loud speaker on a Saturday morning. My spouse, as a Baptist minister, the Seventh Day Baptist minister proclaimed for the entire village to hear was leading souls to damnation and hell.

One day we woke up to see a church being built very close to one of our Baptist Churches. It was being built by the Church of God denomination supported and funded by white Americans. Before the building was fully completed a tent was set up and revival meetings were held. To the dismay of a number of the older members of our Baptist Church, many of the Baptist

---

[403]Ibid.

young people flocked to the tent. A nurse in the district accurately predicted that she would be delivering a lot of babies in nine months.

Now it was an integral part of the Baptist teaching that there should be some months of preparation before one is baptized and becomes a member of the church. Not so said the Church of God pastor. He used passages of Scripture to support his claim that people who "accepted Christ" should be baptized the very next day. What is more baptism in the river is more authentic than baptism in the pool which was under the platform of the Baptist church. We watched helplessly as a number of our young people with whom my spouse had worked very hard follow the Church of God minister to the river.

Few black Christians agree with me that the imagery in the Bible in terms of black being negative and white positive is a fundamental issue with regard to the perception of black people as inherently evil and white people as inherently good. Some of my black Christian friends generally shrug their shoulders and say that the imagery has nothing to do with skin color. For Fanon, who was a psychiatrist, however, imagery is fundamental to the feelings of inferiority of blacks and superiority of whites. "Sin is Negro as virtue is white."[404] "In Europe," claims Fanon, *the black man is the symbol of Evil"* (italics his). He goes on to point out that the "torturer is a black man, Satan is black, one talks of shadows, when one is dirty one is black— whether one is thinking of physical dirtiness or of moral dirtiness." He continues by stating that it would be "astonishing" to "see the vast number of expressions that make the black man the equivalent of sin.

In Europe, whether concretely or symbolically, the black man stands for the black side of the character." The list includes "blackness, darkness, shadow, shades, night, the labyrinths of the earth, abysmal depths, blacken someone's reputation." On the other hand there is "the bright look of innocence, the white dove of peace, magical, heavenly light." Whereas we speak of the "magnificent blond child" that conjures up "hope", "joy", "peace" there "is no comparison with a magnificent black child." He repeats the fact that "in Europe, that is, to say in every civilized and civilizing country the Negro is the symbol of sin. The archetype of the lowest values is represented by the Negro."[405]

Note how the Bible Society of the West Indies in the passage on the home page uses darkness in a pejorative sense: "but instead of cursing the

---

[404]Fanon, *Black Skin, White Masks* p. 139
[405]Ibid., p. 188-89.

darkness we need to light a candle". [406]   Most black Christians do not see the association of black and darkness with evil and Satan and white and light with goodness, purity, holiness, and God as very significant in terms of skin color, race, and how blacks are stereotyped as evil.   They are living in a state of denial.

James Cone's Jesus is Black theology does not address the question of imagery which I maintain plays a significant role in the stigmatization of blacks as morally and mentally inferior.

In the first encounters between blacks and whites, the Christian religion played a significant role in corroborating the negative imagery of dark/black and the positive imagery of light/white in the Christian religion. Indeed Winthrop D. Jordan points out that in "England perhaps more than in southern Europe, the concept of blackness was loaded with intense meaning" and "embedded in" this "concept was its direct opposite—whiteness." [407] Thus "[w]hite" connoted "purity", "virginity", "virtue", "beauty", "beneficence", and "God"   and "black connoted", "filthiness", "sin", "baseness", "ugliness", "evil" and "the devil". [408]

The first encounters of Africans with Europeans established the superiority of Europeans and the inferiority of Africans in the world view of Christianity.   Let us recall that the Europeans were armed with the superior Christian religion while the religions of blacks were labeled "pagan", "heathen", "savage", "uncivilized", "of the devil", "backward". [409]   What is often overlooked is, the unquestioned and unchallenged view that Christianity brought to the "natives" a pure pristine religion that was separate apart (not even transcended) but totally set apart from European culture.   This view that Christianity is set apart from European culture obfuscates the reality that Christianity is intertwined with European culture. Bengoa propounds in terms of the role the Catholic Church played in the conquest of the Americas that religion was the entire culture—"era toda la cultura". [410]

The Judaic-Christian religion is an historical religion that was revealed to a particular people, at a particular time, at a particular place in history. Christianity is rooted, grounded, and developed in Europe.   When Africans

---

[406]The Bible Society of the West Indies. www. Forministry.com—home page

[407]Jordan, *White over Black,* p 7.

[408]Ibid., p. 7

[409]Jordan, *White over Black*; p'Bitek, *African Religions in Western Scholarship*; Kang'ethe, "The Death of God."

[410]Bengoa, *Conquista y Barbarie* p. 20.

were brought into the religion by Europeans, their status was an inferior one and that has not changed in spite of four hundred and in some cases five hundred years of Christianity. The main reason for this is the continued dominance of European culture in the religion which is evident in the doctrines, the rituals, the services, the structure of the buildings, the theologies, the music, the instruments, and the hymns.

Jesus is Black theology does not address the fact that Christianity is a European religion. We need to take Russell's observation seriously. "Christianity arose in the Roman Empire among populations, wholly destitute of political power whose national states had been destroyed and merged in a vast impersonal aggregate."[411] Christianity is an imperialistic religion. Russell continued to make the very salient point that for "the first three centuries", Christians "could not alter the social or political institutions under which Christians live although they were profoundly convinced of their badness."[412] To circumvent this problem, what the Christian did therefore is to focus on individual salvation. An "individual may be perfect in an imperfect world and the good life has nothing to do with this world."[413] Stating that Jesus Christ is black does not address the issue that the Christian religion focuses on individual salvation. Since blacks are viewed as a collective within this religion, then the religion contributes to the perpetuation of black oppression.

Except peripherally, in terms of the style of worship and singing, black history and culture have had no impact on Christian theology or doctrines. Indeed, black history and culture are not only marginalized; they are often demonized. Let us not forget that Christianity was the tool that was used to rid the African of his/her worldview. As pointed out several times in this work, Christianity has absorbed the ideas of European philosophers, and European historical events have had an impact on Christian theology. Black thought and events are totally outside the realm of Christianity. It is easy to fall into the trap of regarding the religion as pure, holy, pristine, and not see how it is intricately linked to the European culture.

Incidentally I noted some years ago, as a cataloger that in the religious volumes of the *Library of Congress Schedules*, a primary classification scheme of human knowledge and intellectual endeavor, entire sections were devoted to white theologians. In the area of theology, the intellectual output of black theologians is infinitesimal to that of whites. What does this mean? It means that black ministers and white ministers can graduate from

---

[411]Russell, *Why I am not a Christian*, p. 72.
[412]Ibid., p. 72.
[413]Ibid., p. 73

seminaries without any in depth study of black history and culture. It means that whites are main topics of intellectual studies, theses, and dissertations. I am sure you will find far more theses and dissertations on John and Charles Wesley than you will find on Richard Allen. The heroes, gods, and goddesses of the Brahmins are superior while those of the Dalits are inferior.

Just as how the Brahmans are the chief priests in the Hindu religion, so whites are the leaders of Christianity.

Linked to the dominance of white culture and resources in the Christian religion and the positive imagery of whites and negative imagery of blacks is the perception though denied of God as white based on attributes, such as, powerful, all-knowing, mysterious, supreme ruler, supreme judge.

It does not matter how much we may "blacken" Jesus whether in terms of skin color or theoretically, Christianity will remain a white European religion. Christianity is a white European religion as a result of two thousand years of European dominance as I have already stated regarding its buildings, doctrines, rituals, services in which African worldview, history and culture are not only marginalized, but often demonized.

Thus Christianity fosters black oppression.

Christianity and Black Oppression: Duppy Know Who Fe Frighten

CHAPTER THIRTEEN

DOES GOD EXIST? A CULTURAL PERSPECTIVE

The history of Christianity is the best school for atheism[414]
But the less a man knows about the past and the present the more
insecure must prove to be his judgement of the future[415]
Sigmund Freud

Throughout this work, I have tried to show how Christianity is fundamental to the oppression of blacks. It is not merely that blacks as a group are oppressed. It is the nature of the oppression. Blacks are stigmatized as inherently mentally and morally inferior. This stigmatization of blacks is genetic and can be transmitted. One drop of black blood pollutes.

Before the 1960's a number of writers made comparisons and parallels between the ostracism of the Dalits formerly Untouchables of India and the ostracism of blacks in America. In both societies, the ostracism of Dalits in India and the ostracism of blacks in the United States are based on a stigma and a curse which are congenital. Since the 1980's when conditions improved in both societies the comparisons have lessened although studies still unearth parallels. The Dalits have a party which they call the Panther Party.[416] The term Dalit is "derived from the root, *dal*, which means to crack, open, split."[417] According to Massey, the "use of the term Dalit" dates from the "nineteenth century" when the "revolutionary Mahatma Jotirao Phule used it to describe the outcastes and untouchables as the oppressed and broken victims of our caste-ridden society."[418] It is interesting to note that Frazier describes the slaves as "lost", "isolated", and "broken" men.[419] In 2001, at the World Conference Against Racism held in South Africa, Dalits claimed that caste as a basis for the segregation of peoples in terms of their descent and occupation is a form of apartheid and a distinct form of racism.

Social ostracism of any group is painful. However, untouchability has

---

[414] Overbeck, *Christentum und Kultur,* p. 265 quoted in Joachim Kahl, *The Misery of Christianity*, p. 71.

[415] Freud, *The Future of an Illusion,* p. [5]

[416] James Massey, *Roots: A Concise History of Dalits,* (Bangalore, India; Delhi, India : CISRS, ISPCK, 1991).

[417] Massey, *Roots,* p. [9]

[418] Ibid., p. [9]

[419] Frazier, *The Negro Church,* p. 16.

to be one of the most if not the most dehumanizing means of social ostracism in any society. Based on the belief that the Dalit is able to pollute by touch, the Dalit is subjected to laws that restrict contact with the pure caste Hindus. Pollution is not only transmitted; it is also genetic. What philosophy, ideology, worldview or thought could construct a belief system that would subject a whole group of people to dehumanized status? The justification for the outcaste status of the Dalits is based many Hindus and Christians claim on passages of Scripture within the Hindu religion which purports the classification of human beings into castes. Doctrines of purity and pollution and dharma and karma play a major role in the hierarchical stratification of castes and the outcaste status of the Dalit.[420] "The idea of pollution-contagion", states Pauline Kallenda "is universal in Hindu India." It is significant to note that "[a]nything touched by a polluted person spreads the pollution to others who touch it. Consequently, "there are rules about giving food and water, and touching persons and their belongings." An "orthodox Brahman will not take boiled food or water from anyone of lower caste rank."[421]

Christians and Hindus have been very critical of the Hindu religion in terms of the caste system particularly the outcaste status of the Dalits.[422] The Hindu religion some Christians and Hindus maintain fosters the caste system and is a fundamental factor to the outcaste status of the Dalit.[423]

While hierarchical stratification is seen as built into the Hindu religion, the Christian religion is postulated as an egalitarian religion.[424] This view that the Christian religion is egalitarian has not been subjected to profound critical analysis by the proponents of Christianity as an egalitarian religion. As pointed out several comparative studies particularly before the 1960's have been made regarding the social ostracism of Dalits in India and the social ostracism of Blacks in the United States. Dalits are not only outside of the Hindu caste system and blacks outside of the class system of

---

[420]Human Rights Watch, *Broken People: Caste Violence Against India's "Untouchables"*, (New York, NY: Human Rights Watch, 1999); Ambedkar, *The Untouchables*.

[421]Pauline Kolenda, "Purity and Pollution" in *Religion in India,* edited by T. N. Madden, (New Delhi, India: Oxford University Press, 1991).

[422]See, for example, Massey, *Roots*; A. M. Abraham Ayrookuzhiel, *Swami Anand Thirth: Untouchability: Ghandian Solution on Trial* (Delhi, India : ISPCK and Bangalore, India: CISRS, 1987)

[423]Ambedkar, *The Untouchables*; Behera, *Ethnicity and Christianity;* Massey, *Roots*.

[424]Behera, *Ethnicity and Christianity.*

the United States of America but these two groups carry a stigma that is genetic and can be transmitted. Repeatedly one of the major differences highlighted regarding the social ostracism of these two groups is the factor of religion. Whereas, it is often asserted, that caste Hindu finds justification for the stigmatization of the Dalits in the hierarchical Hindu religion, the Christian will find no such justification for racism in the egalitarian Christian religion. Slavery, the slave trade and racism are totally in violation of Christian precepts and the root of these evils is to be found in human beings and or the devil.

As Ambedkar points out, however, every society has some kind of belief about defilement, the sacred, the pure, and as a result, there is segregation based on these beliefs.[425] I want to point out that Christianity is no exception. "Purity", "purify" and "pure" are certainly words to be found in the Bible and though they may not have the connotation as the Hindu religion, they certainly indicate the possibility of defilement, and hence segregation. Indeed, Christians are told:

> Wherefore, come out from among them, and be ye separate, saith the Lord, and touch not the unclean *thing;* and I will receive you,
> And will be a Father unto you, and ye shall be my sons and daughters, saith the Lord Almighty.
> Having, therefore, these promises, dearly beloved, let us cleanse ourselves from all filthiness of the flesh and spirit, perfecting holiness in the fear of the Lord. [426]

Christianity is also no exception with regard to segregation that is an in-group and out-group based on terms, such as, purity, pure, holy, clean, chosen which are to be found in the Bible. The existence of numerous Christian denominations all based on Scripture is evidence of a non-egalitarian religion. The Jehovah Witness will tell you that only Jehovah Witnesses will be going to heaven and you may receive similar assertions from the Catholic, the Brethren, the Pentecostal, the Church of God, the Seventh Day Baptist, the Seventh Day Adventist, and so on.

The dichotomy between the sacred and the profane in Christianity has led to deep segregation within the Christian church and outside of the Christian Church as to what is sacred and what is profane. What is sacred and profane have contributed to the proliferation of denominations. What is

---

[425] Ambedkar, *The Untouchables.*
[426] 2 *Corinthians* 6: 17-7:1

of extreme significance is that a number of Dalits to escape their oppressive status within the Hindu religion converted to Christianity based to a large extent on the claims of Christians that Christianity is an egalitarian religion. What these Dalit Christians found, however, is that somehow the caste system seeped into the Christian religion creating stratification based on caste within the egalitarian Christian religion.

It should be noted, however, that Christians (and even some non-Christians) are quick to come to the defense of the Christian religion and to assert that it is *not* the Christian religion that is to be blamed for the violation of what is claimed to be a fundamental precept of egalitarianism. The fault *entirely* lies with the Hindu religion and customs which tainted the egalitarian Christian religion with hierarchical beliefs.

Behera claims that while the "Hindu social philosophy and Hindu ideology alone endorse the rigid status organisation in the caste system...there is no such theological notion in the Bible which supports social division and hierarchy among Christians." Indeed, Behera asserts that a "number of verses from the Bible emphasise the brotherhood of Christians and reject altogether all ideas of ethnic and class distinctions." According to Behera, "every student of society knows", however, "that there is a gap between what is ideal and what is real" and so the "Indian caste ethos which pervades every aspect of Indian life, engulfed Christianity too."[427]

In paragraph after paragraph Behera repeats how the egalitarian Christian religion has been influenced by the stratified Hindu religion. His summation should be perused carefully.

> As a result, untouchability which was condemned by the missionaries as a social curse continues in one form or the other among Indian Christians. The social bar of the caste system tends to foster group conversion to Christianity, though even after conversion, the social stigma does not vanish completely. It is beyond doubt that the untouchables, in accepting conversion, were often responding to the appeal of an egalitarian religion, but in fact their social situation is not improved either in the Hindu milieu or even, we shall see, in Christian milieu. Even after conversion, the 'Harijans' are treated as untouchables by the upper caste Christians. They continue to suffer the same humiliation and discrimination also in Christianity. *In a nutshell, Christianity in India has not*

---

[427]Behera, *Ethnicity and Christianity,* p. 10-11.

produced an egalitarian society. Rather it has added some
more exclusive groups. The converts from various groups
eventually transformed into something like new castes.[428]

Behera then reviews literature that demonstrates the survival of the caste system amongst Christians.

Let us grant that the hierarchical caste system is so entrenched in Hindu society that it is impossible for egalitarian Christianity to transcend it. The hierarchical Hindu caste system is solely responsible for the stratification of Christian churches. I do not think that we can blame the Hindu religion for the stratification of the American society as a result of slavery and the slave trade. Slavery and the slave trade came out of Christian Europe and were transported to Christian United States of America. I do not think we can blame the Hindu religion for outcast status of blacks within Christian America. The poorest ill-educated white person may feel superior, and have access to more privileges than the wealthiest black.

Racism is built within the Christian society of Europe and America. We cannot say that one of the cruelest systems of stratification, the apartheid system is due to the Hindu religion. Apartheid was established in South Africa by Christians. Christianity has never been able to transcend social and cultural divisions whether in Europe, America, Africa, or India. As Joachim Kahl has pointed out Christianity and the Bible have been used to justify slavery, the persecution of pagans, the persecution of the Jews, the persecution of Christian 'heretics', and the defamation of sexuality and of women.[429]

It is true that some denominations, like the Mormons, the Mennonites, are able to use the Christian religion to accrue wealth and to raise the status of its white members. There is no cultural dissonance regarding Christianity and being white. It is not unusual to see huge massive churches in black neighborhoods amidst boarded up buildings. In spite of the investment of money, time, and energy in black churches, many blacks are poor and unemployed.

The banning of the Dalits from caste Hindu temples is fundamental to the political, economic, and social ostracism and hence oppression of the Dalit. Banning Dalits from temples means that Dalits are not only excluded from the economic and political resources that are linked to caste temples but perpetration of oppression of the Dalit is sanctified. The temple sanctifies

---

[428]Ibid., p. 12, italics, mine
[429]Kahl, *The Misery of Christianity.*

caste Hindus privileges and practices particularly those of the Brahmin.[430] Brahmins are the priests and leaders in the Hindu religion and it is significant to note that Brahmins regard access to knowledge, a very important factor in maintaining their resources and privilege, as their right.

We do not see that 11'0 clock as the most segregated hour in the United States perpetrates the inferior status of blacks and the superior status of whites. The segregation of churches does not only have an impact on the American society. The segregation of the churches in America has a global impact Segregated white churches sanctify the privileges and practices of whites. Segregated white churches are fundamental to the Racial Contract. While for many centuries whites denied blacks access to quality education, whites regard access to knowledge as their right. Many universities, colleges, and schools are linked to white churches.

Just as how the Brahmins are the leaders of Hindu faith and theology in which Dalits are ascribed inferior and outcaste roles so whites are leaders in terms of Christian doctrine and theology in which blacks play inferior roles as students of mainly white established and administered seminaries and perusers of white dominated theology in which black theology has had little or no impact.

One point I hope the reader has grasped is the fact that religion is fundamental to the outcast status of Dalits and it is fundamental to the outcast status of Blacks. The social ostracism of Dalits is pivoted on their social ostracism in Hindu temples. The social ostracism of blacks is posited on the segregation of black churches and white churches. That the stigmatization of the Dalit is genetic and can be transmitted is rooted in Hindu religion so the stigmatization of blacks as genetic and can be transmitted is rooted in the Christian religion.

There are two other factors that contribute to the inferior status of blacks (a) the atomization of blacks, and (b) the anti-black, anti-African, intellectual castration, and castration from blackness that pervade Christianity. As I have pointed out the oppression of Dalits in India is very painful, but I think that there is one advantage that Dalits have over blacks. They are part of a family, a group, a community. The focus on individual salvation amongst blacks has contributed to social isolation where the mantra is "I am blessed" with very little regard for the suffering of poor blacks.

We have to ask: does God exist? We ask this question in the light of the conditions of blacks, particularly, of poor blacks who have invested time, effort, money, and energy into Christianity for more than four hundred and in some cases more than five hundred years. In the light of the belief

---

[430]Ayrookuzhiel, *Swami Anand Thirth*

propounded by Christianity that God is the sovereign ruler, and that he intervenes in history on behalf of human beings, in terms of the overwhelming suffering of blacks we have to ask if blacks are subjected to divine racism. How can God exist in the light of the persistent suffering of blacks?

A number of white scholars have critiqued the Christian religion based on philosophical and scientific reasons.[431] These books were of tremendous value in reorienting my view about God. No one can fathom the joy I felt when I first read Russell's work, *Why I am Not a Christian*. That book was the first book that I read about atheism. I could not believe that someone actually, and a brilliant philosopher at that, addressed a lot of my doubts and fears about Christianity. I could not believe that Russell's book on atheism included not only a critical analysis of Jesus but some of my own crtitique as a young adolescent. Russell's analysis regarding the "Defects of Jesus' teaching", "Salvation: Individual and Social", "How the Churches Have Retarded Progress", "The Existence of God", "Sources of Intolerance"[432] served to free me from a lot of guilt and fear that were the only basis for my being a "Christian".

Before I even avidly read and re-read Kahl's work several times for its edifying content, I found the title *The Misery of Christianity,* therapeutic because it expressed my feelings about Christianity. Kahl, a former minister, discussed in this work many of the atrocities conducted by Christians throughout the two thousand year span of Christianity. He also pointed out Christianity's unethical behavior towards Jews, Pagans, Women, and Heretics. Freud's radical critique in the *Future of an Illusion* as the culmination of Feuerbach's anthropological interpretation of the religious experience allowed me to do my own introspection of my religious worldview. The nature of Freud's critique affected not only my religiosity in the most profound way, but allowed me to re-examine social structures, political institutions, and even closer home, familial relationships.

The encounter with these seminal thinkers has not only allowed me to come up with a negative answer to the existence of the Christian God but has in a positive and much more wholesome way put my life on a new trajectory.

In search for new alternatives, it would be fruitful to reach back in our past, not only in terms of antiquity, but certainly one of the most horrific experiences of all of human history, chattel slavery and draw strength and instructive lessons as we search for alternatives to build our communities

---

[431]See for example, Russell, *Why I am not a Christian* ; Kahl, *The Misery of Christianity*; Dawkins, *The God Delusion.*
[432]Russell, *Why I am not a Christian,*

and explore our common destinies as peoples of the world. We need institutions that will promote knowledge of and the ethos and ethics that undergird black liberation struggles.

CHAPTER FOURTEEN

POSTSCRIPT

HUMANITAS:
TOWARDS A BLACK NARRATIVE
FOR
BLACK LIBERATION

Those who profess to favor freedom,
and yet deprecate agitation,
Are men who want crops without
plowing up the ground.
They want rain without thunder and lightning.
They want the ocean without the
awful roar of its waters.
This struggle may be a moral one;
Or it may be a physical one;
Or it may be both moral and physical;
but it must be a struggle.
Power concedes nothing without a demand.
It never did, and it never will.

Frederick Douglass
Aug 4, 1857
-Excerpt from a speech on West India Emancipation delivered at Canandaigua (In Quarles, 1969, p. 354).

Rev. Dr. Theophilus Wright sat across from Rev. Dr. Thomas Freeman at the long oblong table in the Rev. Dr. Freeman's office where generally leaders of the denomination meet to discuss matters pertaining to the denomination. At the suggestion of Rev. Dr. Felicity Springs that a round table would be more communal, the Rev. Dr. Thomas Freeman had at one time thought of replacing the oblong table with a round table, but had to abandon the idea because of the shape and size of the room. It was not a very large room to begin with, but it seemed to the Rev. Dr. Theophilus Wright that it got increasingly smaller every time he entered it. He came to the conclusion that this was mainly due to the fact that the Rev. Dr. Thomas Freeman, the highest ranking official of the denomination, was constantly adding books to his already overcrowded shelves. There were books everywhere—on shelves, on top of cabinets, on the long oblong table, on two end tables next to a brown sofa with several colorful cushions, and on the floor. Those on the floor were piled in neat little towers around the room close to the book shelves and one tower Theophilus Wright noted, for it was not there the last time he was here, was more than half way up the side of a small desk. Usually the secretary a somewhat plumb nutmeg complexion older woman with graying short dreadlocks sat at the desk, on which there were a flat screen monitor, a key board, and a lap top, to take minutes.

Today the chief leaders of the denomination were meeting because of the impending crisis in the denomination. It is all these books thought Theophilus Wright since Dr. Freeman's predecessor, who did not have a Ph. D., had only one shelf of books in his office. Now, under the present incumbent, the Rev. Dr. Thomas Freeman, every inch of wall was covered with shelves stacked with books piled up to the ceiling. Theophilus felt a little guilty and ashamed of the thought that he could be blaming knowledge for the crisis in the denomination, for after all he had a Ph.D., and he himself had a lot of books, not in his office at the church where someone could "permanently borrow" them, but in his den at the rectory, for he prized his books very much. Theophilus thought about the books he had on his shelf mostly theological and philosophical works on or about philosophers and theologians, such as, Bultmann, Tillich, Buber, Moltmann, Brunner, Schleiermacher, Calvin, Luther, Kant, Kierkegaard, Locke, Mills, the Niebuhr brothers, and several commentaries on the Bible. His collection did include books by or about Marx, Nietzsche, Camus, Sartre, James Cone, and a handful of books on the history and culture of the West Indies some of which were textbooks from high school, others were required reading at the United Theological Seminary of the West Indies, and some noteworthy ones he had acquired over the years.

Somehow today Dr. Freeman's collection struck Theophilus Wright forcibly. He knew the collection was integral to the thrust and direction a number of prominent leaders of the denomination wanted the denomination to go. Besides the clutter, it was somewhat untoward and unsettling that the top ranking official of the denomination should have not one but multiple copies of books by or about Marcus Garvey, Malcolm X, C. L. R. James, W. E. B. DuBois, Frederick Douglass, Walter Rodney, Claude McKay, James Baldwin, Louise Bennett, the Maroons, slavery, the Civil Rights Movement, Africana philosophy, the history and culture of Africa.

It was somewhat disturbing because the Rev. Dr. Thomas Freeman's collection was subject to the piqued interest or the prying eyes of all who had access to his office—church members, ministers, and people from the community. Rev. Dr. Theophilus Wright was particularly embarrassed at the thought of members and clergy of other denominations seeing the collection.

He realized that this sort of collection was not peculiar to Rev. Dr. Freeman and indeed led by Rev. Don Daring a number of churches had installed shelves, that were filled with books, on the walls inside the church building and what is more had framed pictures of Marcus Garvey, Walter Rodney, Malcolm X, Paul Bogle, Martin Luther King, Jr., Nanny of the Maroons, and other freedom fighters also on the walls inside the church. It was being said that the interior of the churches of the young radical clergy did not look like churches anymore. Although he had heard that "good things were happening", he had no doubt that this was embellished by Don Daring and others in their effort to radicalize the denomination.

The denomination was rapidly developing a reputation of having clergy who were dubbed "militants", "radicals", "Afrocentric", "way out" by the other mainstream denominations, and "ungodly", "of the devil" and "on their way to hell" by the fundamentalists.

No wonder the denomination is in crisis, thought Theophilus Wright, repressing any guilt or shame he felt that the crisis had to do with Rev. Dr. Thomas Freeman's Afrocentric collection of books. It seemed to Theophilus Wright that there were only two options regarding the future of the denomination (i) to have the entire denomination break away and form a new denomination except it could not be called a denomination in terms of the ludicrous radicalism that was pervading the denomination (ii) throw the radicals out in spite of the inevitable struggle and difficulties that would ensue as a result of depleted members of the clergy and resources particularly in the light of the fact that the radicals were clearly in the majority and had the support of the Rev. Thomas Freeman and other high powered officials in the church, and for him there was a third option to (iii)leave the denomination and join some other denomination. Theophilus Wright thought that (ii) or (iii) would be his options if Thomas Freeman allowed the radicals to pursue their objective although he preferred (ii) to (iii).

At times the disputes had got so heated that they almost came to blows had it not been for the calm, deliberate, rational interventions of the Rev. Dr. Hugh Moore who Theophilus Wright asking for the Lord's forgiveness secretly detested. Hugh Moore was always laughing and poking fun at everything and everyone in the church which Theophilus Wright thought often bordered on the sacrilegious. He also found some of Hugh Moore's innuendos wearisome. For example, Hugh Moore once interrupted a very important meeting to ask his fellow clergymen whether they had seriously pondered the theological implications of the rapid changes in technology. He seriously wondered whether the never changing God could keep abreast of e-mails, passwords, GPS, internet, blogs, etc. Then as usual he laughed almost hysterically showing a strong set of white teeth in a chocolate complexion, and what was considered a good looking face particularly because of his narrow somewhat pointed nose. Theophilus Wright, however, grudgingly admitted that when they, the top ranking officials of the denomination were embroiled in conflict, which was so often lately the case, the Rev. Dr. Hugh Moore's sense of humor was very effective in producing some calm, peace, and rationality to the proceedings. As a result he had been asked to chair this meeting.

Now they were seated in battle formation with the proponents Rev. Dr. Thomas Freeman, Dr. Don Daring, Rev. Dr. Felicity Springs, Rev. Dr. Seymour Hope, Rev. Dr. Stan Wood, and the Rev. Dr. Hugh Moore seated on one side of the table and he as de facto leader of the opposition was seated directly opposite Dr Thomas Freeman with the Rev. Dr. Pius Ray on his left, Rev. Dr. Faith Haven on his right and beside Dr. Faith Haven sat Rev. Dr. Kwame Obengo. Rev. Wright tried to suppress some annoyance he felt towards Rev. Dr. Kwame Obengo who had as usual greeted Rev. Wright with a hearty handshake a cheerful smile and "how are you doing today my brother" in his inimitable New Jersey, North American accent.

Dr. Kwame Obengo was an enigma to Rev. Dr. Theophilus Wright. He could not understand why the Rev. Dr. Kwame Obengo, who was some shades lighter than himself, a yellowish pine complexion, should insist on not merely identifying as black, but as African. And so Kwame Obengo had changed his name from Ronald Jackson to Kwame Obengo. Dr. Obengo was very popular among his parishioners, no doubt aided, Dr. Wright thought with some bitterness, by his yellowish pine complexion, his brownish reddish wavy hair, his grey green eyes, and in keeping with his slightly rotund body, a round face, always pleasant, with a little narrow flattish nose, the only feature that clearly betrayed African ancestry, on which, somewhat awry, a pair of spectacles now rested, and his American accent. Rev. Dr. Obengo was not without his critics, however.

Although quite a number of his parishioners and members of the community were pleased that his wife was of cocoa brown complexion, some of the tan complexion, cocoa brown and chocolate complexion springy hair women were not at all too happy with his choice of Joy Springs. Joy Springs did not only wear her hair in dreadlocks which she often tied with an African style head wrap, but was very outspoken, frequently using the Jamaican dialect, and was indifferent to the gossip that she socialized with the poor and downtrodden in the community.

Dr. Obengo, his critics observed, somehow could not internalize even after three years of living in Jamaica, that he was a "brown skin" man and should behave accordingly. He not only failed to rein in the behavior of his wife, but also the behavior of his children, one of whom was adopted. The children were constantly seen playing with Rasta and other poor children and on the lawn of the rectory at that! His association with the Rastas and his general life style of working with the poor and the oppressed led to rumors and gossip regarding his motives—was he working as an undercover agent for the United States?—was the helper his mistress? The helper, a nutmeg complexioned young woman who the Obengos had rescued from poverty and paramour abuse accompanied the family almost everywhere, and sat with his wife and children in the same pew at church. Obengo refused to have his helper ride in the back of the car when his wife was not present, and the helper sat at the dining room table and had meals with the family whether his wife was present or not.

Rev. Dr. Theophilus Wright knew that the rumors that Obengo was an undercover United States agent and the helper was his mistress were totally unfounded. Rev. Dr. Obengo did not understand the dynamics of working in a very rural area in Jamaica and the risks involved in associating with the "lower class." Several times Theophilus pulled Obengo aside to try to warn him about the gossip and rumors, but Obengo would smile, shrug his shoulders and point out how Jesus was often accused of being with publicans and sinners. Theophilus Wright sighed and tried to squash the memory of Rev. Hugh Moore, his shoulders shaking with laughter, alluding to Kwame Obengo as having a "Savior complex due to his light skin complexion." Theophilus Wright knew that Rev. Kwame Obengo was very committed and serious about his social gospel ministry.

Theophilus Wright was aware that, unlike Rev. Obengo, many of his parishioners thought him "hoity-toity" particularly as his wife was tan complexioned with long wavy shiny hair. Well they could call him "hoity-toity" all they want. He had to be extra careful because of his chocolate brown complexion, somewhat wide though not very flat nose and full lips. He knew what it was like to be poor—it was not at all romantic. Warmth, love, enthusiasm, exuberance could suddenly, because of harsh living conditions, and struggle for survival, without any warning, turn into meanness, cruelty, suspicion, and distrust. He asked the Lord to forgive him but he had no intention of pursuing a "go slumming" gospel. The membership in Obengo's church had increased, but Theophilus Wright did not believe that the output was anywhere near Dr. Obengo's extraordinary input in terms of time and energy. He was positive that Dr. Obengo would "burn out" very soon. That was not the path for him, Theophilus. He liked the security, stability, and to a large extent the predictability of his middle class church.

Rev. Dr Kwame Obengo's introduction of drums and dance in the church was also cause for some concern. Though this undoubtedly increased the membership, particularly of young people, indeed, one or two of the Rastas had joined the Church, a number of his parishioners had left Obengo's church and had become members of Rev. Pius Ray's church, the adjoining church, where they felt more inspired and soothed by the staid organ music, the singing of traditional hymns, and the performance of the traditional rituals. Even Dr. Obengo's popularity could not persuade the members of his parish to remove the painted glass windows of the white Jesus and replace it with painted windows of a Jesus, who looked a lot like Bob Marley, that hung over Obengo's desk in his office. The top officials of his congregation would not hear of it, not even the radical ones. They refused to admit a discomfort about a painted black Jesus with locks even if he did look like Bob Marley installed in the windows of the church. They used the prohibitive cost of painted glass windows and "it is definitely something that they should consider for the future" to obstruct Dr. Obengo's proposal.

Dr. Obengo who was not given to the Jamaican characteristic of feeling easily slighted was somewhat peeved when the Rev. Dr. Felicity Springs sister to his wife, Joy Springs, said that she noted that the black Jesus' above his desk was of tan complexion and she had no doubt that at the root of his locks was "pretty" hair. As a matter of fact she had observed that in all the paintings and pictures she had seen so far of a black Jesus, he had tan complexion and "pretty" hair; none looked like Marcus Garvey.

The Rev. Dr. Theophilus Wright was somewhat annoyed with himself for being so critical of the Rev. Dr. Kwame Obengo for Obengo's views and ideas were not nearly anywhere as preposterous as those of the clergy seated on the opposite side of the table—Rev. Dr. Freeman, Rev. Dr. Seymour Hope, Rev. Dr. Don Daring, Rev. Dr. Felicity Springs, Rev. Dr. Stan Wood and Rev. Dr. Hugh Moore. Dr. Obengo still believed in the centrality of the gospel with regards to black people especially the black and the poor. Dr. Obengo greatly believed that Jesus was concerned about the poor and the oppressed and was on their side for liberation.

Rev. Dr. Thomas Freeman, the highest official ranking clergy of the denomination, was being led by the young idealist and dreamer Rev. Dr. Don Daring who in a few minutes would be addressing his fellow clergymen. Theophilus Wright was bitterly disappointed in Rev. Dr. Thomas Freeman. They had known each other from high school and had developed somewhat of a fraternal bond for except for the fact that Freeman was from the middle class, whereas Wright was poor, and Freeman's face and features were more angular, and his round, they were about the same age, now in their early fifties, the same chocolate brown complexion, the same height, tall, and attended United Theological Seminary of the University of the West Indies (UTC) at the same time.

He could not believe the transformation that had overcome Freeman. When often plagued with doubts at UTC, after listening to thought provoking lectures and reading works particularly by Sartre and Camus who questioned God's existence in the light of human suffering, it was Freeman who had frequently encouraged Theophilus to take Kierkegaard's "leap of faith". He could not believe that Thomas was now being led by the young Don Daring who had actually instituted for about four months a radical shift in his church. Black people and Black narratives would be the center and focus of his ministry.

Theophilus resolved to give the utmost attention to Don Daring who was about to speak although he felt very positive that he could predict what Daring, who began his presentation by distributing to each clergyman a set of some six or seven books that were lying on the table, was going to say. Black history, literature, and culture are marginalized in the Christian religion. Leaning a tall very slender body forward, his cocoa brown narrow face with wide somewhat high bridged nose, dark eyes, and full lips filled with passion, Daring asked his fellow clergymen and clergywomen to reflect on the required reading for their theology and philosophy graduate courses: How many books authored by an African or an African descendant person were on the list of required readings?

As well educated clergymen they are all aware that Christianity has incorporated Western philosophy from its inception. To know the Christian canon, you have to be familiar with Plato, Descartes, Kant, Sartre, Feuerbach, Kierkegaard Nietzsche, Marx, Schleiermacher and who are the major theologians?—Barth, Tillich, Moltmann, Luther, Buber, Calvin, Bonhoeffer, Brunner, the Niebuhr brothers—all white males. Obengo murmured James Cone. Ah, James Cone, said Daring, riveting for a while his gaze on Obengo, as you all know Cone contributed to the splintering of Christian theology into Liberation theology, Minjung theology, Feminist theology, Womanist theology, Native American theology, etc., all these theologies, including James Cone's Black theology, attempt to address glaring social issues within the Church. However, these theologies remain marginalized and have had very little impact on Western theology in general. He, Daring, wants to emphasize that Western theologians are influenced by the ideas and events that took place in Europe, such as, the First World War, existentialism, and the studies of anthropologists. Indeed, Cone in *A Black Theology of Liberation,* pages 166-167 states:

Modern theology, following Schleiermacher's unhappy clue to the relationship of theology and anthropology, forgot about Luther's emphasis on the depravity of man and proceeded once again to make appeals to man's goodness. The nineteenth century is known for its confidence in rational man, who not only knew what was right but was capable of responding to it....

World War I did much to shatter this ungodly view of man. Rudolf Bultmann with his existential, form-critical approach, Paul Tillich with his ontology, Emil Brunner with his own brand of neo-orthodoxy, and Reinhold Niebuhr with his ethical orientation made such an impact on liberalism that we are likely never to see it again the way it used to be.[433]

As they all are aware, Daring stated, Cone himself was very much influenced by white theologians, such as Tillich, Bultmann, and Moltmann. Thus, for example, in his *A Black Theology of Liberation* Cone asserts that he "takes seriously Paul Tillich's description of the symbolic nature of all theological speech"(, p. 27), that a "place to begin for this new eschatological significance is the theology of Rudolf Bultmann" (p. 242), and "Moltmann's analysis is compatible with Black Theology's concern" (p.245).

Daring then asked were there not feelings of alienation during their years of seminary and pursuit of the Ph.D. as a result of the marginalization, indeed, non existence of Black history and culture? He questioned whether they had successfully rid themselves of these feelings now that they are clergymen. If they have not rid themselves of the alienation, how can they effectively function within a theology in which they feel alienated? He referred them to Charles Mills *Blackness Invisible,* p. 84: "Though the Christian church has a long, culpable history of anti-Semitism, the mainstream Western religious tradition is still *Judeo*-Christian tradition, not an *Afro*-Christian tradition".[434] It needs to be emphasized, stated Daring, that Christianity is still "Judeo-Christian"; it is "not an Afro-Christian tradition".

From his, Daring's standpoint, black history and culture are not only marginalized in the Christian religion; black history and culture are not only absent within the Christian religion; black history and culture are often demonized within the Christian religion. If we are honest, we must admit that reference to freedom fighters, Marcus Garvey, Malcolm X, Harriet Tubman, W. E. B. DuBois, Nanny of the Maroons, Walter Rodney, Bob Marley in church on a Sunday morning would be regarded as sacrilegious,

---

[433]Cone, *A Black Theology of Liberation*, p. 166-167.
[434]Mills, *Blackness Visible,* italics his.

sinful, and the epitome of impiety.

He wanted to remind the clergy that the birth and development of denominations, particularly the Protestant denominations resulted from struggles within the European and American society and therefore in their structure and organization, are dominated by white culture, mores, norms, history, and tradition. No where is it more evident that the church is greatly influenced by white norms, culture, mores, history and tradition than in the rites and rituals of the Church. If we take the marriage rite for example, the entire wedding ceremony—the wearing of a white dress (which was not always the case), the veil, having a bridegroom, giving away the bride, the bouquet, the throwing of the bouquet, the ring, the cake, the speeches developed within the European tradition. There is nothing African about the marriage ceremony including what generally precedes the ritual—a European invention—the idea that romantic love is the sole criterion for a successful marriage.

The clergy should seriously consider how the marginalization and, indeed, often demonization of Black culture and history within the Christian religion contributes to white supremacy and the perception of blacks as mentally and morally inferior, and to the oppression of blacks.

Were it not for the firm intervention of Rev. Hugh Moore, cinnamon complexioned gentle Pius Ray would not have been heard above the clamor that erupted as a result of Daring's speech. When he could finally speak, wiping beads of perspiration from his brow no doubt from the heat of the room and the clerical collar which Pius Ray constantly wore, Ray admitted that black history and black culture were marginalized but they were overlooking a number of issues (i) intertwined within black culture is the Christian religion. Slaves often found the religion a source of comfort and throughout the history of African descended people in the West, Black men and women—Martin Luther King, Jr., Sam Sharpe, Nat Turner, Sojourner Truth, Paul Bogle—were inspired by Christianity to fight oppression. (ii) Central to the gospel is the matter of soteriology. Christ did not die to save only black people. He came to save all people. One of the appeals about Christianity is its universality. As Ray said this, Theophilus Wright could not fail to observe pine complexion slightly wavy hair Rev. Dr. Faith Haven lean forward to give Rev. Dr. Pius Ray, accompanied by several nods, a huge smile that showed a set of white teeth that tapered towards the corners of her mouth.

When we say we are focusing on black people and black narratives, continued Pius Ray, besides the fact that it is un-Christian, how will some of my congregation feel? I have members of every hue and race in my church, browns, blacks, whites, Afro Indians, Afro Chinese. Everyone is encouraged to participate in activities of the church irrespective of race or complexion. (iii) I am willing to incorporate some of the history and culture of black people in my sermons and I do, but I do not think it is the role of the church to teach black people their history and culture. That should be left to the schools. Let us not forget as Christians, the role of the church is to participate in God's salvation of all human beings.

Hugh Moore gave the nod to Rev. Dr. Felicity Spring to speak. Theophilus Wright tried to stifle his feelings of impatience and intolerance which he knew would be dubbed patriarchal by Felicity Springs had she been aware of them. It was not that he strongly objected to women being priests; it is just that he felt some discomfort about the matter. He was not too sure if he could support the idea of a female priest being the top ranking leader of the denomination. He did not mind Rev. Dr. Faith Haven. She was the first female priest in the denomination, and was quite satisfied, he thought, to be minister of a very small church. At least Faith Haven was demure, but Felicity Springs was just the kind of woman Theophilus had little tolerance for—outspoken, some would say assertive, he would say aggressive.

While Pius was speaking she was busy making notes. One could hear the scratch of an old fashion pen on the paper. Except for the fact that Felicity was just a shade or two lighter a kind of brownish yellowish cinnamon color, than her sister Joy, she resembled her sister to the "t": they had the same small dark somewhat sloe shaped eyes, not too wide a nose and a slight protruding mouth (Theophilus felt the slight protruding mouth was so in keeping with their somewhat rambunctious character). It was well known that Felicity Springs was one of the chief architects behind the Daring movement.

Felicity claimed that relying on the schools to teach black history and culture would be a grave mistake. Even in Jamaica, black history and culture are marginalized because black history and culture are still being taught as a segment of European history. Written mostly by whites, accounts of slavery, the slave trade, emancipation, and the post-Emancipation period are written from the perspective of whites. These important events regarding black history are usually condensed to a couple of chapters in textbooks which inadequately deal with the profundities of these topics and the view, feelings, and worldview of the slaves are marginalized. She also wanted to make the important point that not only is the worldview of blacks marginalized in the history and studies about blacks, but they are written from the perspective of blacks marching on to progress and so blacks are encouraged to distance themselves from a very important period in their history, that is, slavery. This view of blacks marching on to progress places a badge of stigma and shame on generations of blacks who were enslaved and minimizes the realities of European enslavement of African peoples and the traumatic experiences of the slaves. Distancing ourselves from slavery discounts the adverse impact of slavery for generations while at the same time it belittles the industry, creativity, discipline, courage of people who struggled to overcome overwhelming odds in the form of tyranny, brutality and oppression.

Unlike our ostracized brothers and sisters in the United States of America who have produced a phenomenal body of works about the oppressive state of blacks in America, Jamaican blacks have produced minimal studies on the appalling plight of blacks. Most Jamaicans have very little in-depth knowledge of slavery, the apprenticeship period, post-Emancipation, the Maroons, the modern era. As for Marcus Garvey whose name I guarantee you, you will find in every history book or study in the United States regarding blacks in the early twentieth century, he is given only nominal attention in Jamaica in spite of Garvey's phenomenal contribution not only to the Civil Rights Movement, but to blacks all over the world. We dust him off and parade him along with other national heroes every now and again but he is still very much marginalized, indeed ostracized, in the Jamaican society. We need institutions, whether we call them spiritual, religious, or ethical, which promote the knowledge, history, and culture of black people as endemic to our liberation and survival.

Confining the teaching of black history and culture to the schools has several disadvantages. Blacks would not necessarily have control over content, method of instruction, teachers, and textbooks. There is not enough time in the schools to adequately teach black history and culture. One has to think also that history has to compete with other areas of discipline. Besides, it would mean setting an age limit regarding formal exposure to knowledge of Black history for generally children graduate from high school at age eighteen.

If the Church made black history and culture the central focus of its mission, individuals at whatever age would not only be exposed to black history and culture but would be involved in transmitting this integral tradition to the young. In the United States, many of the older generation are in despair that the young are growing up unaware of the struggles of blacks particularly the Civil Rights Movement. But, where are they to learn about the struggles of their ancestors? In many societies, it is the function and role of religion to pass on the mores, culture, history, and tradition of the society. We need such a religion. How can we continue to subscribe to a belief system that regards our history and culture as sinful or demonic and one from which we should distance ourselves? It has been a struggle, but a successful one, to lead her congregation into thinking that it is not sinful or sacrilegious to not only read but to discuss the works and lives of Marcus Garvey, Malcolm X, Frederick Douglass, Walter Rodney, Louise Bennett, Sam Sharpe, Paul Bogle, George William Gordon, or to read about the Maroons, Rastafarians, slavery and resistance to colonialism in the church. She has seen tremendous growth in her church, intellectually, psychologically, socially, and economically.

She thinks that Carter Woodson is still relevant when he says in *The Mis-Education of the Negro,* p. xix:

> No systematic effort toward change has been possible, for, taught the same economics, history, philosophy, literature and religion which have established the present code of morals, the Negro's mind has been brought under the control of his oppressor. The problem of holding the Negro down, therefore is easily solved. When you control a man's thinking you do not have to worry about his actions. You do not have to tell him not to stand here or go yonder. He will find his "proper place" and will stay in it. You do not need to send him to the back door. He will go without being told. In fact, if there is no back door, he will cut one for his special benefit. His education makes it necessary.[435]

As clergy we have to seriously think in terms of the status of blacks particularly the outcast status of the black and the poor. We have to consider whether we as leaders of the clergy are not guilty of propagating a belief system, Christianity, the chief moralizing agent for blacks, which is Eurocentric, and which promotes white supremacy by controlling the thinking of blacks. We must not forget that racism is grounded in Eurocentric ideology; racism is the norm and not a deviation of white ethos as Charles Mills' postulates in *The Racial Contract.* She would like to point out that a significant component of the racist belief is to eradicate the African worldview because the African worldview is evil, pagan, etc. Christianity is the chief weapon used to rid blacks of their world view. Thus Christianity is anti-African and anti-Black. As far as she is concerned the eradication of African history, tradition, mores, culture, laws, customs and religion was the most brutal aspect of slavery. Slaves were forced to learn a

---

[435]Carter G. Woodson, *The Mis-Education of the Negro,* (Chicago, IL: Images, 2000, c.1933), p. xix

different worldview which included terms and concepts that were alien to the African culture, such as, sin, salvation, redemption, heaven, hell—as p'Bitek asserts in *African Religions in Western Scholarship,* Africans had to subscribe to a metaphysical worldview that blacks did not understand.

Rev. Dr. Faith Haven immediately responded. She was a middle-aged woman but she looked far younger because as Jamaicans say she " is very fine" meaning very thin. She was, indeed, so very petite that she seemed to be totally enveloped by the regular sized chair in which she was seated at the table. She was one of those Jamaicans who you could not clearly tell what is her racial make-up—mixture of every race she would sometimes say—pale pine complexion with slightly wavy hair, slightly graying, which she cut short which definitely highlighted her narrow face, narrow nose, small slightly slanted eyes and small mouth.

Faith Haven claimed that nobody had responded so far to the fact of the universality of the gospel. She can understand that a lot of clergy were angry having been exposed to the segregation of churches in America. This, however, is Jamaica. We do not have the systemic racism that exists in America. We have no white churches and black churches in Jamaica. It is true that historically in Jamaica whites and coloreds had greater access to education and well paying jobs, but a lot of that has changed. Focus on black history and culture apart from being irrelevant to Jamaica seems to spring from a lot of anger which is so out of keeping with the spirit of the gospel. Jesus said that we should love everybody and to focus on blacks is to exclude a number of people. She is aware that there is still a lot of poverty in Jamaica. She would say that it is due not so much to a race issue as a class issue. The church should try its utmost, as indeed Rev. Ray, Rev. Wright, and Rev. Obengo and she have been doing, to reach out to the poor in the community by instituting programs which help the poor in the provision of food, clothes, and basic education. The church cannot overlook the fact, however, that their chief function is the salvation of souls.

Rev Stan Wood a middle-aged man, somewhat short and stocky, with a kind of reddish bronze complexion, a long face with freckles, a huge high bridge nose, very dark brown somewhat beady eyes, short reddish brown springy hair then spoke. Although he had seen a number of changes in his own lifetime, to say that race and skin color are not major issues in Jamaica is living in a state of denial. We have a long way to go to eradicate the pernicious skin color discrimination that still pervades the Jamaican society. He is sometimes shocked when he sees a difference in response from little children regarding skin color—rejection of dark skin and acceptance of light skin. These children have internalized the worldview of adults. Many blacks still live in the most appalling conditions. When one thinks of poverty, one thinks of blacks. When one thinks of crime, one thinks of blacks. We know that a lot of this view stems from white racism.

The sad and painful thing is that we as blacks have internalized the stereotypical racist view of whites. As Walter Rodney says in *The Groundings With My Brothers,* p. 34 it "is as though no black man can see another black except by looking through a white person". In order for blacks to be empowered in the "West Indies and everywhere else" we "must begin with a revaluation of ourselves as blacks and with a redefinition of the world from our standpoint."[436] If we are waiting for white people to fix the problem, that is to sanitize our history, it will never happen. To state that a focus on black history and culture in Jamaica is irrelevant is denial of the facts.

Wood is aware that the postulation of Christianity's universalism, that is, Christianity is open to anybody has tremendous appeal but he has often questioned when this assertion is concretized whether this is truly the case. In truth and in fact the universalism of the gospel is countered by the fact that Christianity was revealed to a particular people, at a particular time, in a particular place. Most people who lived prior to the Third Century would not have known of Christianity. It was not until Native Americans, Asians, and Africans, except perhaps Ethiopians, came into contact with Europeans through the violent and brutal institutions of slavery and colonialism that they learned of Christianity.

Every one has to admit that Christian universalism meant the disruption of peoples, their history and their culture. Because Christianity was revealed to a particular people, at a particular time at a particular place some people were labeled pagan, heathen, barbarian, savage. Missionary activity and proselytization of the gospel are predicated on superior and inferior peoples. The missionary before he or she even sets foot on the territory of the missionized is, by bringing the gospel to the missionized, superior.

There have been numerous articles and books published by Africans showing how missionary activity was integral to the success of the colonization of African peoples. He would also like to refer them to an article written by Kamuyu-wa-Kang'ethe called "The Death of God: an African Viewpoint" which postulates how the European identified with the attributes of God in their relationship with Africans and how the Africans integrated the perception of Europeans as having the attributes of God. We have failed to come to grips with God as white and Satan as black as adversely affecting our perception of blacks and each other. He would also like to focus on the dichotomy between what is holy and sacred and what is

---

[436]Rodney, *The Groundings,* p. 34.

profane and this has had a devastating effect on black culture. For example playing classical music is sacred, playing the drums, dancing, singing folk songs is profane.

Who are the people etched in our memory as major contributors to our emancipation from slavery?—Wilberforce, Clarkson, Knibb, Phillippo. There are schools and universities named in honor of these men. Although Moses Baker and George Liele were missionaries to Jamaica and were responsible for the establishment of the Baptist Church, there is nothing except a few sentences in history books to commemorate their memory. Where is the headquarters of the World Council of Churches? Where is the headquarters of the Roman Catholic Church? How can God be on the side of blacks when the Christian religion is firmly ensconced within white European tradition in which black humanity is often negated? Declaring that Jesus is black cannot eradicate two thousand years of Christianity as a white European dominated religion in which blacks hold inferior status. We need to face the fact that the Christian religion is a Judeo-Christian and not African-Christian.

The Christian religion from its transformation from a Jewish sect has been firmly aligned to empire beginning with the Greco-Roman worldview to its current hegemonic expressions in Europe and America. These expressions include economic, political, educational, and many other social institutions.

Another major concern is the emphasis particularly in the Protestant tradition on individual salvation. This focus on individual salvation has done unaccountable damage to social relations in Jamaica particular to the family. The view of individual salvation which is a basic tenet of Christianity undergirded slavery for almost four hundred years. It did not matter how unjust, or barbaric the condition of the slave. It did not matter that the slave was completely in the control of his or her master or mistress; the slave did not need to have a family; the slave could be comforted by the knowledge of individual relationship with God. The denominationalism that exists among the churches has not helped matters. What unity can there be in a family when one member is Baptist, another is Methodist, and a third is Seventh Day Adventist?

Kwame Obengo responded by saying that it would appear from what has been said by some of the worthy members of the clergy that the Christian religion should be eradicated from the Jamaican culture. He sincerely hopes that this is not the case. Jamaican people are very religious and the Christian religion is deeply rooted and intertwined in the culture. The Christian religion means for a lot of people, hope and faith.

He is very much aware of the suffering of the poor especially of blacks.

He is particularly concerned about the women who are single mothers and the children who are abandoned by their fathers. He is also deeply perturbed about the women and children who are subjected to abuse and violence. When he visits black homes and families he finds that for a lot of people the Bible is very comforting in times of need and distress. He has never visited a home where there is not a Bible and he knows that every morning in these homes the Bible is read and prayers are said particularly by the women. If the adults in the household are illiterate, they will ask one of the children to read some passage from the Bible to them. Jamaicans find solace from passages such as "All things work together for good", "Wait upon the Lord and he shall renew your strength", "If you have faith as a mustard seed, nothing will be impossible". They love the Psalms particularly Psalm 23 which begins with the words "The Lord is my Shepherd, I shall not want". What can be more consoling to a dying person than "even in the shadow of death", God will be with him? Many times when he is feeling in despair, many Jamaicans quoting passages from Scripture will encourage him by telling him to "have faith, God will not give you more than you can bear, the harder the cross, the sweeter the crown" and will support these postulates by giving account of instances where their faith has helped them to survive.

What disturbs him about a number of the presentations he has heard so far is that as Christian clergymen the role and, indeed, the centrality of the gospel have not been mentioned. He believes that the only hope for those who are suffering is the gospel. He has seen some changes in the lives of a number of families.

As a Christian, he believes in the efficacy of prayer. One woman a regular attendee of his church told him recently that after praying for over twenty years, her "husband" has decided that he would stop drinking, they would marry and, so they could become members of the church. As a Christian clergyman, he believes that God is concerned about the poor and the oppressed and that Jesus came to save and redeem everyone including those who are shackled by the miseries of this life. That is the wonderful thing about the Christian gospel. God does not discriminate in terms of salvation. The church, he admits, can do much more to help the poor and the oppressed. As Christian clergymen we have to display a greater commitment to impart to those who are suffering because of an inequitable and unjust system that God is on their side. The Christian gospel is the gospel of liberation.

He agrees that the gospel should be relevant to the people. For this reason he has included African drumming and the steel band as part of his services. Initially, he received a lot of resistance particularly from the older members regarding allowing young people to have dance performances in the church but he is receiving greater positive responses in terms of these performances.

Undoubtedly, there should be greater focus on the history and culture of blacks. He suggests that the clergy considers planning a calendar of events around black history and culture which would take place once a month. However, for him, as a Christian, any plan, or policy, that excludes God, Jesus, and the Bible is in his view atheistic with which he cannot comply. The eradication of the Christian religion would lead to anarchy and nihilism. People need some kind of spirituality particularly to face the storms and vicissitudes of life, and for him it is the Christian religion. What is more, the Christian religion is the moral underpinning of the society. It is from the Christian religion that we obtain our principles and values—equality of all peoples, family values, the golden rule, peace, joy, hope, justice, and above all love.

Rev. Seymour Hope removing his glasses from an artistically designed triangular shaped curvy nose, a striking part along with two deep set dark brown eyes that were part of a chocolate brown somewhat angular face wanted to make it clear that his fellow clergy who take the stand that black history and culture should be the focus of their ministry and mission had no intention of eradicating Christianity. It is not we who are actually guilty of attempting to uproot Christianity. If we are to be honest it is Christianity during its encounter with African world views, and belief systems that has sought and still seeks to eradicate black history and culture as profane, pagan, savage, barbaric, heathen, and immoral. Christianity has never incorporated black history and culture into the religion. That dancing, drumming, and steel bands are now sanitized, as a matter of exigency for the church's survival, after five hundred years of being regarded as satanic is a case in point regarding the anti-African and anti-black beliefs of Christianity. It is patronizing and condescending to select, as acceptable, parts of our culture that now pose no threat to Christianity, as they once did, while the bulk of our thought history, and culture cannot enter the sanctuary of the church.

Christianity is a European phenomenon. Christianity was born within the Roman Empire. Christian theologies have been influenced by events, culture and philosophies of Europe. The buildings, structure, dogma, music, and the organization of the Christian Church are all deeply embedded and intertwined in European events, history, culture and philosophy. If Plato, Kant, Heidegger, Freud, Marx, Sartre, the German peasant revolts, existentialism, the World Wars can be points of departure for white theologians, why can't the works by or about Marcus Garvey, Malcolm X, W. E. B. DuBois, Frederick Douglass, Harriet Tubman, Claude McKay and events such as slavery, the Maroon uprisings, Civil Rights Movement, resistant struggles to colonialism be incorporated into the dogma, service, and rites of Christianity? If our history and culture cannot be the focus of our moral principles and beliefs, then we are in fact subscribing to the oft repeated assertion of whites, and indeed some blacks, that blacks are inherently inferior and can only find moral principles within an institution that was created in Europe, Christianity.

The point is that black history and culture have been systematically excluded from Christian theologies for if they are included, this would really shake the foundation of Christianity. The question of divine racism would be inevitable. Maldistribution of suffering, that is, surplus suffering of blacks, has been the lot of blacks from slavery to the present day. Currently, there are high percentages of black men and women who are incarcerated. In many cases, the conditions of these black men and women in prison are worse than it was under slavery. The suffering of blacks which is often justified on the grounds that blacks are inherently immoral is particularly consequential in the light of the religiosity of blacks and the fact that blacks were promised that Christianity would transform their lives from savage, pagan, heathen to righteous human beings. The reality for many blacks, however, within the Christian religion is suffering and oppression.

We have to address the issues of black oppression, that is, persistent and pernicious suffering, not only in view of the fact of the religiosity of blacks but also in the light of what as William R. Jones postulates, the attributes of God as benevolent and all-powerful and the inevitable criterion therefore that God is the sum of his acts. On page 14 of his work, *Is God a White Racist?: A Preamble to Black Theology,* Jones states:

> It is easy now to see how the principle of man as the sum of his acts enlarges the contours of the concept of divine racism. When one makes conclusions about *Who God is* on the basis of *what He has done* for black people, when one accents what is central to the black past—oppression and slavery—as the primary materials for reaching conclusions about the divine attributes, if we do not come to the analysis of the divine nature with the presupposition of His intrinsic goodness for all of mankind but let this conclusion emerge, if at all, on the basis of His actual benevolent acts in [sic] behalf of all, it is not difficult to see the category of divine racism surfacing. And when we are forced to make conclusions about God's nature and motives in the light of our subsequent

discussion of black suffering as a variety of ethnic suffering, the question, Is God a white racist, becomes an even more promising point of departure for black theology.[437]

Hope also wanted to point out that the role of the Christian religion particularly regarding its emphasis on universalism obfuscates the reality of the debased and oppressed status of blacks by denying blacks the right to focus on their history and culture and offering blacks sanctification and fulfillment of eschatological hopes through Jesus Christ. In terms of universalism then, Christianity has to erase skin color. We are all one in Jesus Christ and to be one and to be unified, you have to be white. There is no black—no color—in heaven. The less you think about skin color, the more virtuous and Christian you are. Whites do not have to think about the issue of skin color. Blacks do.

Hope claimed that the segregation of the churches in America, that is the existence of black churches and white churches reinforces his point of the exclusion of black history and culture in churches that term themselves black. Black churches exist, not because of a split in theology. Black churches exist because white people do not want to worship and socialize with blacks. Whatever impact blacks have had on Christian doctrine and theology is more style than substance. Probably with the exception of the length of service, the preaching style, and the singing, black churches in terms of their buildings, their dogma, their hymns, the structure and organization of services are carbon copies (pun not intended) of white churches. Let us not forget that most black ministers are trained by whites in white seminaries. Even Black established denominations, such as, the African Episcopalian Methodist Church, and the African Episcopal Methodist Zion Church base their doctrines, structure, and organization on those of white denominations.

We may not have the problem of black churches and white churches in Jamaica (though skin color is an issue within the churches); we cannot, however, say this matter is irrelevant to us for many white churches which ostracize blacks in their home countries have missionaries working amongst Jamaicans ruining families, and homes with divisive doctrines and deforesting our landscape with huge buildings that not only shut out the sun but Jamaican history and culture. If whites cannot transcend racism in America, what makes us think that they can transcend racism in Jamaica? Jamaica is open access to missionary activity without any question of

---

[437]Jones, *Is God a White Racist?* p. 14, italics, his.

accountability. The result is that we have almost every denomination in the Christian religion represented in Jamaica, and yet we are perceived by a number of whites and Christian organization such as the Bible Society of the West Indies as an impoverished and crime ridden country. Five hundred years of missionary activity has resulted in the empowerment and glorification of whites and the impoverishment and persistent oppression of blacks.

We cannot ignore the struggles of blacks in the United States as irrelevant to the struggles of blacks in Jamaica. We are bound by our common heritage of roots in Africa, slavery, the slave trade, and racism. We need to further foster the inter-cultural exchange that has had an impact on our music, our ideas, thinking, and life style. We have a lot to offer in terms of our Caribbean experience and it is important that for our own growth and development that we tap into the huge resource of analysis of the status of blacks by blacks.

How are blacks to be liberated from the oppression to which they have been subjected for some five hundred years? Blacks are often told that God is working with them towards their liberation. Does not God working on the side of blacks raise issues of helplessness, and powerlessness? For how is God going to fight oppression? For if blacks are in the struggle with God, whatever weapon God uses to liberate blacks, whether guns, education, knowledge, wealth, he will have to rely on whites. The plight of Blacks within the Christian religion is similar to the status of the Dalits who are outcasts within the Hindu religion. The Gods, priests, history, culture and being of the Dalits are inferior within the Hindu religion.

Black history and culture must become the center of whatever term we want to use—spirituality, religion or ethics.

Hope wanted to share with his colleagues some of the results of the concrete measures he had taken to implement the centralization of black history and culture in his church. There is greater participation by the congregation, for "sermons", now more appropriately termed lectures, were followed by animated discussions. For the first time in their history, members of his congregation are at liberty to critically analyze the Bible. The missionaries termed African religious beliefs superstitious. A study ought to be made of "Christianity as superstition" amongst blacks. For many blacks, their Christian beliefs are totally irrational, based on fear, and have very little to do with their day to day existence. They do believe that they will ward off evil by reading a Psalm for example. They pick and choose, as we all do, certain passages of Scripture which they think will help them survive, and block out entirely questions they have about the irrationality or implausibility of sections of the Bible and the fact that the Bible does not really address Black history and culture.

Now, whenever questions and conflicts arise regarding the Bible instead of engaging in the subterfuges as he would do in the past, he encourages his congregation to read books that he read in seminary and to reflect on their experience, history and culture in terms of the text. Ancient Jewish culture is no longer the norm; Black history and black culture is the norm from which they operate. He has also learnt as Walter Rodney asserts that it is important to listen to the people; one will learn a lot from listening to the people.

He openly discusses the efficacy of prayer. Undoubtedly, some members of the congregation particularly women claim that God "hears" their prayers because it is very comforting for them to believe that they can bend the mind of the most powerful being in the universe. He no longer repeats vague platitudes to those who feel their prayers are not answered. He encourages his members to express their anger and frustration regarding persistent prayers that for many years are unanswered or when unexpected tragic events take place in their lives. What do you say to an ardent Christian believer about unexpected death of loved ones? Why should someone have to wait for over twenty years to have the desired outcome of her prayers when in the Bible there are instances of God answering prayers immediately? What impact does the implacability of God have on your psyche? You feel that something is inherently wrong with you.

We work with people as to what they can do to fulfill their hopes and dreams and help them cope with tragedies in their lives. One significant outcome of this is the development of a communal spirit as individuals see that often in order to attain their dreams or to cope with difficulties they have to support each other. We find in events such as slavery, colonialism, the Jim Crow era and the lives of activists, such as, Marcus Garvey, Nanny of the Maroons, Malcolm X, Harriet Tubman, Walter Rodney, Sam Sharpe, Sojourner Truth, W. E. B. DuBois, and Martin Luther King Jr., important lessons as to how to cope with difficulties and tragedies—repression, violence, greed, torture, dishonesty, arrest, injustice, death, lynching—in our lives, and the significance of community spirit and organization.

The focus on black history and culture has had a remarkable impact on the young. It has not only led to inter-generational bonding, but young people are forced to read a number of books with multi-syllabic words particularly as we encourage the young to actively participate in discussions. Not only have the reading skills of young and old vastly improved, but focus on the history and culture have led to greater awareness of Jamaican geography and landscape which has resulted in immense development and growth in mathematics and science. Because there are numerous positive pictures and images of blacks, allusions to blacks as "ugly", "full of sin", "the devil" or very dark skin children as "burnt toast" have tremendously decreased. Amongst the adults, there is greater respect for each other because they now see within each adult not the badge of shame of slavery but the beauty of the fortitude, courage, discipline, wisdom, and humor that have survived years of brutality, terrorism, and oppression.

What has been remarkable also is the growth in employment, and industry. You know that Jamaicans and blacks in general are very creative. We have created reggae, rap, calypso, jerk food, jazz, revolutionized sports, etc. Jamaica is the only country that has produced an alternative religion to Christianity that has worldwide following—Rastafarianism. True to form the Rastas amongst a number of our very poor have become very active in our endeavor. They build book shelves, paint, make t-shirts, dolls, create items form straw, and some are even in the process of writing plays, stories, composing music, and producing films. We hold conferences which are often attended by blacks from the United States and other places of the world. Besides, blacks and whites as tourists find our focus on black history and culture a point of interest. This has brought a lot of revenue to the area. Just as how the Christian Church has been a source of revenue and income for whites particularly in terms of their buildings, and equipment—organs, pianos, Bibles, hymnals, prayer books, communion cups, gowns, surplices, collection plates, clerical collars, crosses, and doctrinal requirements—seminaries, colleges, theologies, professors so we have found that focus on black history and culture are sources of revenue for blacks. Let us not forget Max Weber's theory regarding the Protestant Church and the rise of capitalism. Every church building makes a significant contribution to white prosperity. Incidentally every Sunday to foster social bonding and communal spirit we have a full Jamaican meal as part of our ritual. Thus we support local farmers and provide Jamaican women and men who love to cook opportunities to show off their skills.

It has been implied that we cannot use our history and culture to derive moral principles and give hope and indeed faith to our people. There are important issues in terms of ethics, and morality that we have unearthed as a result of the study of our history and culture. When you peruse the history and culture of blacks—slavery, colonialism, the Civil Rights Movement, you will find (i) the values of persistence, courage, will to struggle, creativity, industry, honesty, discipline, wisdom, respect, community spirit, organization and humor. Indeed often these values have been in conflict with the purported plastic Christian values: love, joy, and peace. (ii) The study of black history and culture also raises the question of our human weaknesses and failings. We use the lives of our ancestors and freedom fighters to deal with our human failings—jealousy, greed, ill-will insecurity—which sometimes lead to conflict.

The tendency within our Christian religion is to condemn our freedom fighters and not see them as models because of some flaw. Our attitude to Jesus, Paul, Peter, Moses, David, Solomon, Abraham, is entirely different, except maybe Martin Luther King Jr., from our attitude to Marcus Garvey, Malcolm X, Sojourner Truth, W. E. B. Dubois, Walter Rodney, Paul Bogle, Sam Sharpe, William Gordon. (iii) For the first time, we can fully analyze events such as slavery, the colonial period and see how the laws, mores, and norms of white hegemony affect our relationships, family structure, attitude to each other, and why violence and crime pervade our society.

We were brandished as savage, pagan, heathen, barbaric, by Christians who saw no contradiction in Christianizing slaves and ostracizing them. White Christians saw no contradiction in brutal repressions when blacks made attempt to resist oppression. As you all know while a dozen or so whites were killed during the Morant Bay Riot, according to Horace Campbell in Rasta and Resistance p. 38, "[t]housands of dwellings were burnt to the ground, and more than one thousand blacks were rounded up and hanged. 400 were flogged. Paul Bogle was hanged...".[438] This is typical of white Christians' response to any kind of agitation, (there should be no cause for agitation in the first place) on the part of black Christians for within the Christian religion in spite of the precepts of love, peace, equality, the status of blacks is one of subordination.

The subjugation and inferior status of blacks is considered good moral conduct. Christianity has played a significant role in the perpetuation of this morality. Thus Shirley C. Gordon in *Our Cause His Glory* (p. 11) states:

> The missionaries for their part readily accepted the task not only of converting the population to the Christian faith, but as a corollary urging them to the acceptance of a laboring life as sugar workers in an acquiescent colonial peasantry. Missionaries who had over the years cited their own rights as British citizens now undertook the project of inducting over 300,000 new British citizens in Jamaica into the social values and work ethic of Victorian, nonconformist, class conscious Britain.[439]

Hope pointed out that in terms of class consciousness, which we must admit as Jamaicans is pervasive in our society and culture, some of the white

---

[438]Campbell, *Rasta and Resistance*, p. 38.
[439]Gordon, *Our Cause for His Glory* p. 11.

members of our congregation have suggested that we read books by Dickens, Trollope, Jane Austen, the Bronte sisters to see not only the snobbery and class consciousness that existed in Britain, which we regard as good behavior but also the cruelty, and barbarity that pervaded British society particularly with regard to the lower classes. We read the books recommended (or we may watch the movies) for we do not exclude any people or culture. Black history and culture is inclusive.

We are not without our critics. We have been called all kinds of names. Fundamentalists blare from microphones that we are on our way to hell. Mainstream churches see us as not quite respectable. "We no respectable, man". That has been our problem—the quest for respectability— respectability that has been determined, to a large extent, by Christianity. However, as Walter Rodney states on p. 68 of *The Groundings With My Brothers* ":

> Now not only have we survived as a people but the Black Brothers in Kingston, Jamaica in particular, these are brothers who, up to now, are every day performing a miracle. It is a miracle how these fellows live. They live and they are physically fit, they have a vitality of mind, they have a tremendous sense of humour, they have depth. How do they do that in the midst of the existing conditions? And they create, they are always saying things. You know that some of the best painters and writers are coming out of the Rastafari environment. The black people in the West Indies have produced all the culture that we have, whether it be steelband or folk music. Black bourgeoisie and white people in the West Indies have produced nothing! Black people who have suffered all these years create. That is amazing.[440]

When Seymour Hope read about "tremendous sense of humour" Theophilus could not help but glance at Hugh Moore, but Hugh Moore seemed to be in deep concentration. "I see a new day for us, concluded the Rev. Dr. Seymour Hope "as we seek to create our own "spiritual", "ethical", and "religious" narratives within institutions that will foster black history and culture as normative.

In spite of Theophilus Wright's stream of consciousness—the collection plate, job security, material well-being, rights, privileges, power and status

---

[440]Rodney, *The Groundings*, p. 68

of being a clergyman, his love of the rites and rituals of the church—and therefore his determination to pursue what he perceived as his Christian mission, Theophilus Wright found himself rising to his feet as he joined in the thunderous applause.

Duppy know who fe frighten.

Christianity and Black Oppression: Duppy Know Who Fe Frighten

BIBLIOGRAPHY

Ambedkar, B. R., *What Congress and Gandhi Have Done to the Untouchables,* Bombay, India: Thacker, 1946, c. 1945.

Ambedkar, B.R., *Who were the Shudras? How They came to be the Fourth Varna in the Indo-Aryan Society,* Bombay, India: Thacker, 1947.

Ambedkar, B.R., *Why Go For Conversion?* Bangalore, India: Dalit Sahitya Academy, 1981.

Ambedkar, B. R., *The Untouchables: Who Were They? and Why They Became Untouchables,* New Delhi, India: Amrit Book Co., 1948.

Arenson, Karen W., "Princeton Honors Ex-Judge Once Turned Away For Race", *The New York Times,* Thursday June 05, 2001.

Asante, Molefi Keti, *The Afrocentric Idea,* Philadelphia, PA: Temple University Press, 1987.

Asante, Molefi Keti, *Kemet, Afrocentricity and Knowledge,* Trenton, NJ: Africa World Press, 1992, c. 1990.

Augier, R. F, et. al., *The Making of the West Indies,* Jamaica, WI: Longman Caribbean, 1960.

Ayrookuzhiel, A. M. Abraham, *Swami Anand Thirth Untouchability: Gandhian Solution on Trial,* Bangalore, India: CISRS; Delhi, India: ISPCK, 1987.

Baldwin, James, *Go Tell it on The Mountain,* New York, NY: Dell, 1953, c.1952.

Barker, Dan, *Godless: How an Evangelical Preacher Became One of America's Leading Atheists,* Berkeley, CA: Ulysses Press, 2008.

Barth, Karl, *The Humanity of God,* Louisville, KY: John Knox Press, 1960.

Barrett, Leonard E., Sr., *The Rastafarians: Sounds of Cultural Dissonance,* revised and updated edition, Boston, MA: Beacon Press, 1988, c. 1977.

Beals, Melba Patillo, *White is a State of Mind: a Memoir,* New York, NY: Putnam, 1999.

Beckford, George L., *Persistent Poverty: Underdevelopment in Plantation Economies of The Third World,* New York, NY: Oxford University Press, 1972.

Behera, Deepak Kumar, *Ethnicity and Christianity: Christians Divided by Caste and Tribe in Western Orissa,* Bangalore, India: The Christian Institute for the Study of Religion & Society; Delhi, India: I.S. P. C. K., 1989.

Bell, Derrick, *And We Are Not Saved : The Elusive Quest for Racial Justice,* New York, NY: Basic Books, 1987.

Bell, Derrick, *Faces at the Bottom of the Well: The Permanence of Racism,* New York, NY: Basic Books, 1992.

Bengoa, Jose, *Conquista y Barbarie: Ensayo Critico acerca de la Conquista de Chile,* Santiago de Chile, Chile: Ediciones SUR, 1992.

Bennett, Louise, *Jamaica Labrish,* with notes and introduction by Rex Nettleford, Kingston, Jamaica: Sangster Book Stores Ltd., 2003.

Berreman, Gerald D., "Caste in India and the United States" in *American Journal of Sociology,* vol. 66, 1960.

The Bible Society of the West Indies, www.forministry, Home Page, Saturday December 31, 2011.

Billingsley, Andrew, *Like a Mighty River: The Black Church and Social Reform,* New York, NY: Oxford University Press, 1999.

Black, Clinton V., *The Story of Jamaica from Prehistory to the Present,* London, England: Collins, 1958.

Bonhoeffer, Dietrich, *The Cost of Discipleship,* Beaverton, OR: Touchstone Press, 1948.

Bultmann, Rudolf Karl, *Keryma and Myth,* New York, NY: Harper Collins, 2000.

Campbell, Horace, *Rasta and Resistance: from Marcus Garvey to Walter Rodney* Trenton, NJ: Africa Press, 1990, c.1987.

Carroll, Chas., *The Negro a Beast or In the Image of God",* [n. s.], 1900.

Cesaire, Aime, *Discourse on Colonialism,* translated by Joan Pinkham, New York, NY: Monthly Review Press, 1972, c. 1955.

Chandrasekhar, S., "Foreword—Personal Perspectives on Untouchability in *The Untouchables in Contemporary India,* J. Michael Mahar, editor, Tuscan, Arizona: The University of Arizona Press, 1972.

Chevannes, Barry, *Rastafari: Roots and Ideology,* Syracuse, New York: Syracuse University Press, 1994.

Cleage, Albert, *The Black Messiah,* New York, NY: Sheed & Ward, 1969.

Cone, James H., *A Black Theology of Liberation,* New York, NY: J. B. Lippincott Company, c. 1970.

Cone, James H., *God of the Oppressed,* rev. ed., Maryknoll, NY: Orbis Books, 1997, c. 1975.

Cose, Ellis, *The Rage of a Privileged Class: Why Are Middle-Class Blacks Angry?: Why Should America Care?,* New York, NY: Harper Perennial, 1995.

Curtin, Maguerite et. al., *In the Light of the Sun: The Story of Wolmer's Girls' School, Kingston, Jamaica,* Kingston, Ja: Wolmer's Girls' Alumnae, 2009.

Curtin, Philip D., *Two Jamaicas: The Role of Ideas in a Tropical Colony, 1830-1865,* Cambridge, MA: Harvard University Press, 1955.

Davis, Angela, *Women, Race and Class,* St. Paul, MN: The Woman's Press, 1982.

Dawkins, Richard, *The God Delusion,* New York, NY: Houghton Mifflin, 2006.

Dennett, Daniel C., *Breaking the Spell: Religion as a Natural Phenomenon,* New York, NY: Penguin Books, 2006.

Desmond, Adrian & Moore, James, *Darwin's Sacred Cause: How a Hatred of Slavery Shaped Darwin's Views on Human Evolution,* New York, NY: Houghton Mifflin Harcourt, 2009.

Diop, Cheik Anta, *Civilization or Barbarism: An Authentic Anthropology,* translated from the French by Yaa-Lengi Meena Ngemi, edited by Harold J. Salemson and Marjolijn de Jager, Chicago, IL: Lawrence Hill Books, 1991, c. 1981.

Dollard, John, *Caste and Class in a Southern Town,* Madison, WI: University of Wisconsin Press, 1988, c. 1937.

Douglass, Frederick, *Narrative of the Life of Frederick Douglass an American Slave,* New York, NY: Signet Books, 1968 [1854].

DuBois, J. A., *Hindu Manners, Customs, and Ceremonies,* Oxford, England: Clarendon Press, 1899.

DuBois, W. E. B., *The Autobiography of W. E. B. Dubois: A Soliloquy on Viewing My Life from the Last Decade of Its First Century,* [n.d.]: International Publishers, c. 1968.

DuBois, W. E. B., *Souls of Black Folk,* New York, NY: Penguin Books, Signet Classic, 1969.

Ellison, Ralph, *The Invisible Man,* New York, NY: Vintage Books, 1972, c. 1947.

Fanon, Franz, *Black Skin, White Masks,* translated by Charles Lam Markmann, London, England: MacGibbon & Kee, 1968.

Fanon, Frantz, *The Wretched of the Earth,* translated from the French by Constance Farrington, New York, NY: Grove Press, 1963.

Feuerbach, Ludwig, *The Essence of Christianity,* translated from the German by George Eliot, New York, NY: Harper, 1957.

Foreman, James, *The Making of Black Revolutionaries: A Personal Account,* New York, NY: MacMillan, c. 1972.

Franklin, John Hope, & Moss Jr., Alfred A., *From Slavery to Freedom: A History of African Americans,* 8th ed., New York, NY: Alfred A. Knopf, 2001, c.1947.

Frazier, E. Franklin, *The Negro Church in America*, bound with C. Eric Lincoln, *The Black Church since Frazier,* New York, NY: Schocken Books, c.1974, c. 1963.

Freire, Paulo, *Pedagogy of the Oppressed,* translated by Myra Bergman Ramos, New York, NY: Seabury Press, 1968.

Freud, Sigmund, *Civilization and Its Discontents,* translated and edited by James Strachey with a biographical introduction by Peter Gay, New York, NY: W. W. Norton, c. 1961.

Freud, Sigmund, *The Ego and the Id,* translated by Joan Riviere, revised and edited by James Strachey with a biographical introduction by Peter Gay, New York, NY: W. W. Norton, c. 1960.

Freud, Sigmund, *The Future of an Illusion,* translated and edited by James Strachey with a biographical introduction by Peter Gay, New York, NY: W. W. Norton, 1961.

Garvey, Marcus, *The Philosophies and Opinions of Marcus Garvey or Africa for the Africans,* vols. I & II, compiled by Amy Jacques Garvey, new preface by Tony Martin, *The New Marcus Garvey Library,* no. 9, Dover, Mass: The Majority Press, 1986, c. 1923.

Gordon, Shirley C., compiler, *A Century of West Indian Education: A Source Book,* compiled with a commentary by Shirley C. Gordon, London, England: Longman, 1963.

Gordon, Shirley C., *Our Cause For His Glory: Christianisation and Emancipation in Jamaica,* Jamaica, WI: The Press of the West Indies, 1998.

Green, J. Everet, "Is the Afrocentric Movement a Threat to Western Civilization?" in *Philosophy Born of Struggle,* edited by Leonard Harris, Iowa: Kendall/Hunt Publishing, 2000.

Hazari, *Untouchable: The Autobiography of an Indian Outcaste,* New York, NY: Praeger, c. 1951.

Hughes, C. Everett, "E. Franklin Frazier: A Memoir" in Frazier, E. Franklin, *The Negro Church in America,* bound with C. Eric Lincoln, *The Black Church since Frazier,* New York, NY: Schocken Books, c.1974, c. 1963.

Human Rights Watch, *Broken People: Caste Violence Against India's "Untouchables",* New York, NY: Human Rights Watch, 1999.

Jacobs, Bruce A., *Race Manners: Navigating the Minefield Between Black and White Americans,* New York, NY: Arcade Publishing, 1999.

Jones, William R., *Is God a White Racist? : A Preamble to Black Theology,* Boston, MA: Beacon Press, 1998, c1973.

Jordan, Winthrop D., *White over Black: American Attitudes Towards the Negro, 1550-1812,* New York, NY: W. W. Norton & Co., 1977, c. 1968.

Kahl, Joachim, *The Misery of Christianity: A Plea for Humanity Without God,* Harmondsworth, England: Penguin, 1971.

Kang'ethe, Kamuyu-wa, "The Death of God: An African Viewpoint" in *Caribbean Journal of Religious Studies,* Vol. 6, No. 2, September, 1985, p. 1-23.

King, Martin Luther, Jr., *The Autobiography of Martin Luther King, Jr.,* edited by Clayborne Carson, New York, NY: Intellectual Properties Management in Association with Warner Books, 1998.

King, Martin Luther, Jr., "Letter from Birmingham Jail" in *The Essential Writings and Speeches of Martin Luther King, Jr.,* edited by James M. Washington, New York, NY: Harper SanFrancisco, c. 1986.

King, Martin Luther, Jr., *Strength to Love* in *The Essential Writings and Speeches of Martin Luther King, Jr.* edited by James M. Washington, New York, NY: HarperSanFrancisco, c. 1986.

King Martin Luther, Jr., *Why We Can't Wait,* New York, NY: Mentor, 1964.

Kolenda, Pauline, "Purity and Pollution" in *Religion in India,* edited by T. N. Madden, New Delhi, India: Oxford University Press, 1991.

Kunjufu, Jawanza, *Critical Issues in Educating African American Youth (A Talk With Jawanza),* 1st ed., Chicago, IL: African American Images, 1989.

Lewis, Matthew Gregory, *Journal of West India Proprietor, Kept During a Residence in the Island of Jamaica,* New York: Negro Universities Press, 1969; Originally published London: John Murray, 1834.

Lincoln, C. Eric, and Mamiya, Lawrence H., *The Black Church in the African American Experience,* Durham, NC : Duke University Press, 1990.

Loftus, John W., *Why I Became an Atheist: A Former Preacher Rejects Christianity,* New York, NY: Prometheus Books, 2008.

McClendon, John H., III, "On the Nature of Whiteness and the Ontology of Race: Toward a Dialectical Materialist Analysis" in *What White Looks Like: African American Philosophers on the Whiteness Question,* George Yancy, editor, New York, NY: Routledge, 2004.

Mahar, J. Michael, "Agents of Dharma in a North Indian Village" in *The Untouchables in Contemporary India,* edited by J. Michael Mahar, Tuscan, Arizona: The University of Arizona Press, 1972.

Mahar, J. Michael, editor, *The Untouchables in Contemporary India,* Mahar, Tuscan, Arizona: The University of Arizona Press, 1972.

Martin, Michael, & Monnier, Ricki, *The Impossibility of God*, New York, NY: Prometheus Books, 2003.

Massey, James, *Roots: A Concise History of Dalits,* Bangalore, India: CISRS; Delhi, India : ISPCK, 1991.

Mathews, Marcia M., *Richard Allen,* Baltimore-Dublin: Helicon, 1963.

Meeks, M. Douglass, *Origins of the Theology of Hope,* Philadelphia, PA: Fortress Press, 1974.

Mills, Charles W., *Blackness Visible: Essays on Philosophy and Race,* Ithaca, NY: Cornell University Press, 1998.

Mills, Charles W., *The Racial Contract,* Ithaca, NY: Cornell University Press, 1997.

Moltman, Jurgen, *Theology of Hope,* London, England: SCM Press, 1967.

Morrison, Roy D., II, "Black Enlightenment: The Issues of Pluralism Priorities and Empirical Correlation," in *Journal of the American Academy of Religion,* Vol. XLVI, Issue 2, p 217-240.

Myrdal, Gunnar, *An American Dilemma: The Negro Problem and Modern Democracy,* New York, NY: Harper & Brothers, 1944.

Narada, *The Buddha and His Teachings,* Kuala Lumpur, Malaysia: Buddhist Missionary Society, 1988.

Naylor, Wilson S., *Daybreak in the Dark Continent,* New York, NY: Young People's Missionary Movement, 1904.

Niebuhr, H. Richard, *The Kingdom of God in America,* New York, NY: Harper and Row, 1959.

Neibuhr, Reinhold, *Christianity and Power Politics,* New York, NY: Charles Scribner's Sons, 1940.

Neibuhr, Reinhold, *Moral Man and Immoral Society: A Study of Ethics and Politics,* New York, NY: Charles Scribner's Sons, 1932.

Nettleford, Rex M., *Caribbean Cultural Identity: the Case of Jamaica: an Essay in Cultural Dynamics,* Kingston, Jamaica: Institute of Jamaica, 1978.

Nettleford, Rex M., *Mirror Mirror: Identity, Race and Protest in Jamaica,* Great Britain: William Collins and Sangster (Jamaica), 1970.

Ogbu, John U. ,"Low school performance as an adaptation: the Case of Blacks in Stockton, California" in Gibson, Margaret A. and Ogbu, John U. eds., *Minority Status and Schooling,* New York, NY: Garland Publishing, 1991.

Okwuosa, V. E. Akubueze, *In The Name of Christianity: The Missionaries in Africa,* Philadelphia, PA: Dorrance and Co., 1977.

Owens, Joseph, *Dread: The Rastafarians of Jamaica,* Kingston, Ja.: Sangster, 1976.

Patterson, Orlando, *Slavery and Social Death: A Comparative Study,* Cambridge, MA: Harvard University Press, 1982.

p'Bitek, Okot, *African Religions in European Scholarship,* Kampala, Uganda: Uganda Literature Bureau, 1980.

Phillippo, James M., *Jamaica Its Past and Present State,* Westport, CT: Negro Universities Press, 1970, c. 1945.

Raboteau, Albert J., *Slave Religion: "The Invisible Institution in The AnteBellum South"*, New York, NY: Oxford University Press, 1978.

Rai, Lajpat, *Unhappy India*, Calcutta, India: Banna Publishing, 1928.

Rajshekar, V. T., *Dalit: The Black Untouchables of India,* 3rd ed., Atlanta, GA: Clarity Press, 1995, c. 1987.

Roberts, Dorothy, *Killing the Black Body: Race, Reproduction, and the Meaning of Liberty,* New York, NY: Pantheon Books, 1997.

Robertson,Pat.,http://thinkprogress.org/politics 2010/01/13/77141/Robertson-Haiti.

Rodney, Walter, *The Groundings With My Brothers,* Chicago, IL: School Times Publication, 1990, c. 1969. See also London, UK: Bogle-L'Ouverture, c1975, c. 1969.

Rodney, Walter, *How Europe Underdeveloped Africa,* rev. ed., Washington, DC: Howard University Press, 1981, c. 1972.

Russell, Bertrand, *Why I am not a Christian and other Essays on Religion and Related Subjects,* New York, NY: Simon and Schuster, 1957.

Sack, Kevin, and Elder, Janet, "Poll Finds Optimistic Outlook but Enduring Racial Division", *New York Times,* Tuesday, July 11, 2000.

Schleiermacher, Friedrich, *On Religion: Speeches to its Cultural Despisers,* Cambridge, England: Cambridge University Press, 1996, c. 1799.

Sen, K. M., *Hinduism,* New York, NY: Penguin, 1967.

Shourie, Arun, *Hinduism: Essence and Consequence: A Study of the Upanishads, the Gita and the Brahma-Sutras,* Ghaziabad, U.P. India: Vikas Publishing House PVT, 1979.

Stewart, John J., *Mormonism and the Negro,* Utah: Bookmark, 1960.

Sullivan, Shannon, and Tuana, Nancy, editors, *Race and Epistemologies of Ignorance,* Albany, NY: State University of New York, 2007.

Thomas, Alexander, and Sillen, Samuel, *Racism and Psychiatry,* New York, NY: Carol Publishing Group, 1991, c. 1972.

Tillich, Paul, *Biblical Religions and the Search for the Ultimate,* Chicago, IL: University of Chicago Press, 1955.

Tillich, Paul, *The Courage to Be,* New Haven, CT: Yale University Press, 1952.

Tillich, Paul, *The Shaking of the Foundations,* New York, NY: Charles Scribner's Sons, 1948.

Twain, Mark, "Bible Reading and Religious Practice" in *The Complete Essays of Mark Twain,* edited with an introduction by Charles Neider, Garden City, NY: Doubleday, 1963.

Walker, Alice, *The Color Purple,* New York, NY: Pocket Books, 1983.

Weber, Max, *The Protestant Ethic and the Spirit of Capitalism,* translated by Talcott Parsons, introduction by Anthony Giddens, New York, NY: Charles Scribner's Sons, c. 1958.

West, Cornel, *Race Matters,* Boston, MA: Beacon Press, 1993.

Williams, Eric, *Capitalism and Slavery,* introduction by D. W. Brogan, London, England: Andre Deutsch, 1964.

Williams, John A., *The King God Didn't Save : Reflections on the Life and Death of Martin Luther King,* New York, NY: Coward-McCann, 1970.

Williams, Patricia J., *The Alchemy of Race and Rights,* Boston, MA: Harvard University Press, 1991.

Woodson, Carter G., *The History of the Negro Church* 2nd ed., Washington, D.C.: The Associated Press, 1945, c. 1921.

Woodson, Carter G., *The Mis-Education of the Negro,* Chicago, IL: Images, 2000, c.1933.

Wright, Bruce, *Black Robes, White Justice,* Secaucus, NJ: Lyle Stuart, 1987.

Wright, Richard, *Black Boy (American Hunger: A Record of Childhood and Youth),* New York, NY: HarperPerennial, 1993, c. 1944.

X, Malcolm, *Malcolm X Speaks:* Selected Speeches and Statements edited with prefatory notes by George Breitman, New York, NY: Grove Press, 1965.

Yearbook of American & Canadian Churches, 1993, Kenneth Bedell, editor, Nashville, TN: Abingdon Press, 1994.

Zelliot, Eleanor, " Gandhi and Ambedkar—A Study in Leadership" in *The Untouchables in Contemporary India,* edited by J. Michael Mahar, Tuscan, Arizona: The University of Arizona Press, 1972.

ALPHABETICAL INDEX

Made in the USA
Charleston, SC
20 August 2016